Prosody is generally studied at a separate linguistic level from syntax and semantics. It analyses phonetic properties of utterances such as pitch and prominence, and orders them into phonological categories such as pitch accent, boundary tone and metrical grid. The goal is to define distinctive formal differentiators of meanings in utterances. But what these meanings are is either excluded or a secondary concern. This book takes the opposite approach, asking what are the basic categories of meaning that speakers want to transmit to listeners? And what formal means do they use to achieve it? It places linguistic form in functions of speech communication, and takes into account all the formal exponents – sounds, words, syntax, prosodies – for specific functional coding. Basic communicative functions such as 'questioning' may be universally assumed, but their coding by linguistic bundles varies between languages. A comparison of function-form systems in English, German and Mandarin Chinese shows this formal diversity for universal functions.

KLAUS J. KOHLER is Emeritus Professor at the University of Kiel, Germany and Honorary Professor at Nanjing Normal University, China. He was editor of *Phonetica*, the International Journal of Phonetic Science, for thirty-five years.

In this series

COMMUNICATIVE FUNCTIONS AND LINGUISTIC FORMS IN SPEECH INTERACTION

KLAUS J. KOHLER

University of Kiel, Germany

CAMBRIDGE
UNIVERSITY PRESS

CAMBRIDGE
UNIVERSITY PRESS

Shaftesbury Road, Cambridge CB2 8EA, United Kingdom

One Liberty Plaza, 20th Floor, New York, NY 10006, USA

477 Williamstown Road, Port Melbourne, VIC 3207, Australia

314–321, 3rd Floor, Plot 3, Splendor Forum, Jasola District Centre, New Delhi – 110025, India

103 Penang Road, #05–06/07, Visioncrest Commercial, Singapore 238467

Cambridge University Press is part of Cambridge University Press & Assessment,
a department of the University of Cambridge.

We share the University's mission to contribute to society through the pursuit of
education, learning and research at the highest international levels of excellence.

www.cambridge.org
Information on this title: www.cambridge.org/9781316621790

DOI: 10.1017/9781316756782

First published 2018
First paperback edition 2022

A catalogue record for this publication is available from the British Library

Library of Congress Cataloging-in-Publication data
Names: Kohler, Klaus J., author.
Title: Communicative functions and linguistic forms in speech interaction /
Klaus J. Kohler, University of Kiel, Germany.
Description: New York : Cambridge University Press, 2017. | Includes
bibliographical references and index.
Identifiers: LCCN 2017023080 | ISBN 9781107170728 (alk. paper)
Subjects: LCSH: Versification. | Functional discourse grammar.
Classification: LCC P311.K65   2017 | DDC 415.01/83 – dc23
LC record available at https://lccn.loc.gov/2017023080

ISBN   978-1-107-17072-8   Hardback
ISBN   978-1-316-62179-0   Paperback

Additional resources for this publication at www.cambridge.org./9781316621790

I wish to dedicate this book to my grandson Alexander, who, around the age of 15 months, started using the syllable sequence [ʔaʔa] with down-stepping pitch, accompanied by index-finger pointing, to direct his mummy's attention to something he spotted in his action field: an example of a pointing call on an elementary articulation carrier without words, which shows up the fundamental role of communicative functions besides phonemes, words and sentences in language acquisition and use.

Contents

Preface

Sixty Years in Phonetics and Prosody

In 1948, Edinburgh University started a Linguistic Survey of Scottish Dialects. It was anchored in the Faculty of Arts in two ways, by creating a Chair in English Language and General Linguistics, which was filled by Angus McIntosh, and by setting up a Department of Phonetics, headed by David Abercrombie, a member of the London School of Phonetics. In the Phonetics Department at UCL, teaching and research focused on the sounds and prosodies of individual languages in a language-learning scenario, aiming at perfection in producing and recognising the spoken medium. This 'mouth and ear' approach to the sound of an individual language, immensely useful for acquiring proficiency in oral-aural communication, was not a sufficient basis for the analysis of sound systems in a survey of dialects. It had to be put on a general phonetic level of categorising the sound of human language. To this end, Abercrombie instituted an intensive one-year Ordinary Course of Phonetics, followed by a one-year postgraduate Diploma Course, and established a research environment in General Phonetics. Besides training linguists in the techniques of fieldwork and auditory-descriptive analysis, it included research into speech acoustics with the help of Walter Lawrence's speech synthesiser, the Parametric Artificial Talker (PAT), and into speech physiology in Peter Ladefoged's investigation of air-flow control for syllable and stress production, in cooperation with the Department of Physiology.

Having followed the thorough teaching in English language by the Anglicist Hermann Martin Flasdieck at Heidelberg University, who might be called the last Neo-Grammarian, and having been fascinated by his introduction of General Phonetics into the explanation of historical sound change, it was only natural for me to select Edinburgh for a year's stay in an English-speaking country as part of my degree course at home. I attended the Ordinary Course in Phonetics in the academic year 1957–8, and, after graduating from Heidelberg University, continued with the Diploma Course in 1960–1. Those were

formative years. Courses of ear training and performance of the sound repertoire of *homo loquens*, integrated with lectures on phonetic theory, laid the
foundation for the analytical assessment and description of spoken language.
These classes provided the core skills for any further phonetic analysis. They
were flanked by classes introducing experimental analysis, on the one hand,
and phonological categorisation, on the other. Thus, Elizabeth Uldall gave an
introduction to doing perceptual experiments with the Semantic Differential
Technique, using English intonation patterns that were systematically varied
with PAT, and Michael Halliday presented his system of English intonation
within his systemic grammar.

David Abercrombie's scientific thinking was strongly influenced by
Ogden, Richards, Malinowski and 'The Meaning of Meaning', as well as
by Ogden's translation of Vaihinger's *Philosopy of 'As If'* (see Vaihinger
1920), and, last but not least, by J. R. Firth's *Prosodic Analysis* and *Modes
of Meaning*, and his famous phrase 'Surely, it is part of the meaning of an
American to sound like one.' He saw General Phonetics as a unitary science of converging levels of analysis to describe and explain the transmission of meaning in human interaction. Nowhere were there dichotomies
of the subjects evoked, such as phonetics versus phonology, nor questions
asked of the type 'IS this phenomenon phonetic or phonemic?' I took this
conception of the subject with me when I left the Edinburgh Phonetics
Department in 1966, after another five years on the teaching staff, to take
up a research position at the Institute of Phonetics and Communication
Research (later Communication Research and Phonetics) at the University
of Bonn.

On the surface, this was quite a different world, where phonetic research
had been shaped by the psychologist Paul Menzerath, the physicist Werner
Meyer-Eppler and finally by the communications engineer Gerold Ungeheuer.
But I learned acoustics and grasped its algorithms for speech analysis, and I
expanded the interdisciplinary horizon of scientific pursuits contributing to the
questions raised in General Phonetics. The anchoring of General Phonetics in
Communication Research created the same kind of intellectual environment as
David Abercrombie's Edinburgh Department: the physical aspects of speech
analysis are subsumed under the functions of speech communication, and the
measurement of carrier signals must be related to the meanings carried. In
this interdisciplinary set-up I was introduced to Karl Bühler's *Sprachtheorie*
and his *Organon Model* and to Eberhard Zwirner's *Grundfragen der Phonometrie* (1936), where the schism between phonetics and phonology as subjects
in the sciences and the humanities, respectively, was overcome by relating

measurement statistically to language categories determined by meaning and communicative function.

When, in 1971, I accepted the offer of the chair in a newly founded Institute of Phonetics at Kiel University my aim was to make my interdisciplinary training, gained in Edinburgh and Bonn, the basis for building up a research platform of speech communication in a modern laboratory, combined with a fully fledged, four-year MA degree course in General Phonetics. To reach this goal I was able to rely on a competent and dedicated staff. The engineer Werner Thon was in charge of the lab with its two technicians, Heinz Janßen and Herbert Fuchs. He saw to obtaining the necessary analysis hardware in many speech production and perception projects, and also moved the Institute through the various stages of the computer age. The physicist Kurt Schäfer-Vincent looked after the computer analysis software and developed an analysis package that contained a powerful F0 analyser (Schäfer-Vincent 1982, 1983). This work was then continued by the physicist Michel Scheffers, the physics graduate Tobias Rettstadt and the phonetics graduate Matthias Pätzold from the Bonn Institute. The result was a labelling and analysing tool, which became the basis for setting up the database of the *Kiel Corpus of Read and Spontaneous Speech.*

This General Phonetics laboratory provided the environment for a broad range of investigations into segmentals and prosodies in speech production and perception in a variety of languages, within the theoretical frame of speech communication that I had imported. Research centred on two main topics: (1) articulatory reduction and its perception in connected speech and spontaneous interaction, focusing on German, but including other languages, and looking for universal regularities in human speech with reference to historical sound change, and (2) the development of KIM, the Kiel Intonation Model, for German. Here I was again fortunate to work with a congenial team who stayed for many years doing research for their PhDs or for their 'Habilitation' doctorates, first and foremost Bill Barry, who later got the Chair of Phonetics at Saarbrücken University, and then Andy Butcher, Hermann Künzel, Wim van Dommelen and Adrian Simpson, who moved to chairs in phonetics at universities in Adelaide, Marburg, Trondheim and Jena, respectively.

Beyond the thriving Kiel-based activities in General Phonetics, there was close cooperation with Björn Granström and Rolf Carlson at KTH in Stockholm in connection with the development of the German module in the multilingual Infovox TTS system. By introducing sets of reduction and intonation rules on the basis of the Kiel research results, the synthetic output of continuous read speech was greatly improved, and at the same time this TTS modelling provided a powerful test in the development of KIM. The Kiel Institute also had continual exchanges on phonetic issues, especially in its two core research areas, with colleagues in speech science institutes around the world, with Eli Fischer-Jørgensen, Jørgen Rischel and Nina Grønnum at Copenhagen, Björn Lindblom at Stockholm/Austin, Eva Gårding, Gösta Bruce and David House at Lund, Sarah Hawkins and Francis Nolan at Cambridge, Antonie Cohen and Sieb Nooteboom at IPO/Utrecht, Louis Pols at Amsterdam, Vincen van Heuven at Leiden, René Carré, Shinji Maeda and Jacqueline Vaissière in Paris, Albert di Cristo, Daniel Hirst, Alain Marchal and Mario Rossi at Aix-en-Provence, Pier Marco Bertinetto at Pisa, Daniel Recasens at Barcelona, Arthur Abramson, Leigh Lisker and Michael Studdert Kennedy at Haskins, Ken Stevens and Joe Perkell at MIT, John Ohala at Berkeley, Randy Diehl at Austin, Osamu Fujimura at AT&T Murray Hill, Hiroya Fujisaki at Tokyo/ATR Kyoto, Eric Zee at Hong Kong, Yi Xu at Haskins/UCL and Wentao Gu at Nanjing.

After my retirement in 2000, the scientific climate at the Kiel Institute changed completely. Measurement moved centre-stage with a vengeance, relegating communicative function to a *post hoc* adjunct. Worldwide, phonetics has been transformed from a holistic approach in speech communication to a diversification of labs attached to a great variety of superordinate academic subjects, getting ever so much closer to the intellectual framework Peter Ladefoged depicted for the International Phonetic Association in the *Journal of Phonetics* (1990, p. 338f): '[It behaves] somewhat like the Church of England – a body whose doctrine is so diffuse that one can hold almost any kind of religious belief and still claim to be a member of it.' Such an *ex cathedra* definition of a scientific discipline and of a professional body of practitioners undermines its recognition by the wider scientific community and by the general public, and may become fatal: the three Institutes of General Phonetics I have been attached to in my academic career, Edinburgh, Bonn and Kiel, have been closed. If a torso continues, primarily for teaching in linguistics courses, as in Edinburgh and Kiel, it is neatly divided into phonetics and phonology.

Nowhere is this deplorable development in our *universitas* more detrimental to gaining insight into speech communication than in the field of prosody. This monograph is to show the speech community what a unitary approach in General Phonetics can achieve. It summarises sixty years of thinking about speech, with contributions from a large number of teachers, colleagues, staff and students, to whom I am most grateful for having guided or accompanied me on this journey.

Introduction

The Study of Prosody and Intonation

The study of prosody in general, and of tonal aspects in particular, has occupied the human mind for centuries in the attempt to elucidate their contributions to meaning over and above that conveyed by lexical fields and syntactic structures. Systematic analysis of intonation has been carried out with increasing breadth and depth over the past century. In the London School of Phonetics, the auditory description of contrastive tonal patterns formed part of detailed overall phonetic accounts of languages, first and foremost of English, but also of other European and non-European languages, with practical application to foreign language teaching (Cruttenden 1986 (2nd edn 1997), Crystal 1969a, O'Connor and Arnold 1961). This descriptive framework was also applied to the study of hitherto unwritten languages within the British Empire, going back to the late nineteenth century. To establish the formal prosodic carriers of meaning was the primary concern in this approach, only followed, in a second step, by an analysis of the meanings carried. The descriptions were largely given in relation to syntactic structure, and *ad hoc* pragmatic minutiae were provided without a systematic semantic theory behind them. The same methodology applies to Pike's analysis of American English intonation (Pike 1945).

The division of speech science into phonetics and phonology eventually also shaped the study of prosody, resulting in the systemic and structural phonological accounts of intonation by Halliday in Britain and by Liberman, Pierrehumbert and others in Autosegmental Metrical (AM) Phonology in North America. The latter approach set a pattern for research in Europe and around the world, now moving over from auditory description to experimental and instrumental, mainly acoustic, analysis. The phonological perspective, more particularly in the frame of Laboratory Phonology, became all-pervasive in Robert Ladd's textbook (1996 (2nd edn 2008)). In a phonological paradigm, phonetic substantiation takes second place to underlying phonological form in the linguistic modelling of a language. To arrive at this form it is necessary to send speech signals through a linguistic filter that eliminates the exponents of the speaker's expressiveness and the attitudes to the listener, restricting the speech signal to a representational core. But, as was pointed out by Bolinger (1986), this deprives intonation of a substantial part of its specific signalling power in everyday speech communication, and reduces it to the status of the maid of syntactic structure.

As a logical corollary, meaning is subordinated to form in the resulting prosodic systems. The question is not 'What are the communicative functions in a network of human interactions, and how are they manifested by formal means – lexical, syntactic, prosodic, including gesture and facial expression – in speech acts in the languages of the world?' Rather, meaning is grafted onto formal linguistic structures, which Ladd (1996 (2nd edn 2008)) termed 'The Linguist's Theory of Intonational Meaning', focusing on the representational meaning of linguistic structures. Affect and attitude are brought in again *post hoc* by introducing 'intonological' choices, such as more or different pitch accents, as an overlay to linguistic intonational meaning.

Such form-oriented descriptive accounts of the prosodic phonology of a language are very useful as the first step of analysis, particularly when nothing or very little is known about the contrastive patterns in a language. But they do not give us enough insight into how speech communication works in all its facets of meaning transmission. Speech scientists should now prepare to take the second step and move from function to form in those languages that have been thoroughly investigated formally: the Germanic, Romance and Slavonic languages (especially Dutch, English, German, Danish, Swedish, French, Spanish, Italian, Russian and Czech), but also Hindi, Arabic, Japanese and Chinese, and develop an interlanguage network of communicative functions with their language-specific prosodic and linguistic formal exponents.

To make this successful, the prevalent paradigm of dealing with phonology in general and with prosody in particular will need adjusting. In recent decades, there has been an increased focus of structural linguistics on form through the introduction of speech signal analysis, especially in Laboratory Phonology, with its insistence on signal measures to substantiate phonological form. This may be subsumed under what the *gestalt* psychologist Karl Bühler termed *Stoffentgleisung*, i.e. 'the material fallacy' (Bühler 1934, p. 46), with pointed reference to Skinner-type behaviourist psychology, and to pre-phonology experimental phonetics of the early twentieth century (Panconcelli-Calzia 1948; Rousselot 1892, 1897–1901; Scripture 1902, 1935). The phonetics-in-phonology research paradigm of Laboratory Phonology (Ladd 2011; cf. Kohler 2013a) can even leave out the initial auditory observation stage and go straight into experimental testing.

The detachment from auditory observation and understanding of speech events has also removed the need for the analyst to be proficient in the language to be analysed; analysis software like Praat is supposed to do the work, and statistics provides the significance test. However, taking subjects to the laboratory and putting them in various experimental stylisations may not be the appropriate method for investigating exponents of communicative functions in natural speech. Therefore, rethinking the place of speech signal analysis in a function-form framework of language theory is becoming a pressing need.

A Change of Perspective

This monograph aims to develop 'A Speech Scientist's Theory of Intonational Meaning', in place of 'The Linguist's Theory of Intonational Meaning', by putting a network of communicative functions first and then relating formal exponents to them. Although the main focus will be on prosody, lexical and syntactic forms need to be taken into account as well, whenever they are part of the formal manifestations of particular functions. Therefore, the title refers to the wider *Linguistic Forms* rather than the narrower *Prosodic Forms*. The functional approach allows us to replace the linguistic and phonological filtering of speech by an allocation of signals in individual communicative acts to types of interrelated functions in human interaction. These speech act signals are, in turn, reduced to significantly distinctive property categories in relation to the system of communicative functions. This is 'phonology coming out of phonetics', rather than 'phonetics going into phonology'. The principal goal in writing this monograph is theoretical, to present a (partial) network of communicative functions in human language and to relate intra- and interlanguage speech forms to these functions. Prosodic form will be taken in a very broad sense, including the phenomena of *elaboration* in functional highlighting, as well as of *reduction* in functional attenuation, which both involve segmentals alongside prosodies in the narrow sense.

In developing a functional framework, the monograph takes its point of departure from Karl Bühler's *Sprachtheorie* (1934), and from an evaluative review of the relevant phonetic, phonological and linguistic literature against such a functional background. It includes a discussion on a methodology of data acquisition that is based on contextualisation adapted to the function-form paradigm. The presentation of a network of communicative functions is built around a comparison of formal exponents in German and English, with extensions across a wider array of European languages, including the more distant Romance family, especially French, a prosodically unique language within Europe. The theoretical framework is proposed as a powerful tool in comparative prosodic research into the world's languages. The potential of this approach is shown by the analysis of data from a tone language, Mandarin Chinese, which were collected in functionally contextualised scenarios, and are compared with functionally corresponding data from German and English.

The function-form paradigm is based on the axiomatic postulate that a core network of communicative functions is inherent in human speech interaction, irrespective of any particular language. For example, to signal authority and dominance, or subordination and compliance, to highlight or attenuate messages, or to stimulate dialogue partners into action through questions, commands or requests can, among others, be assumed to belong to such a communicative core in human interaction. However, the association of form at various levels of description from lexicon and syntax to prosody varies between languages. Yet there are also very clear cases of universally used forms for specific communicative functions, e.g. high pitch in certain types of question, or phonation features in negative intensification, or low- versus high-pitch register for the expression of authority versus subordination. In other cases, languages form typological groups, genetically related or not, using the same forms for particular functions, and, finally, formal features may be individual-language specific. Thus, the formal mapping of communicative functions across the world's languages becomes an exciting field of research in language comparison and typology.

Principles of a Communicative Phonetic Science

Doing phonetic analysis in a function-form framework follows general scientific principles. In all sciences dealing with experience of the world and of actions within it, scientific questions start with individual observations *hic et nunc*: this may be the legendary apple falling on Newton in physics, or the sound of an utterance impinging on the eardrum, and being understood by the brain, of a phonetician, who picks it up, e.g. during a bus ride on a particular day in a particular area. Both the physicist and the phonetician then start asking how they can explain these events beyond the *hic et nunc*. They have an idea that generalises to other occurrences of such events observable on other occasions. They then formulate first principled statements which they incorporate into the theory they already have of the universe they are working on, the physical world or the communication between speakers and listeners. On the basis of these principled statements incorporated into the theory, the physicist and the phonetician derive hypotheses 'If A holds, then B must be true.' They then take these hypotheses into the laboratory for experimental validation or rejection, representing the results in numbers.

Although there is in general perfect parallelism between the physicist's and the phonetician's investigation, a fundamental difference needs to be recognised between the 'events' the two deal with. The physicist simply observes events out there in the world; the phonetician observes and *understands* events in relation to a system of linguistic signs in linguistic structures used in action fields. This means that the phonetician must be able to understand the signals received for analysis, i.e. must have a sufficient proficiency in the language under investigation, or acquire it in the course of fieldwork. It also means that physical analysis of speech signals can never give the whole answer about the events the phonetician has observed. Contrary to quite common belief, the phonetician's analysis is not a discovery procedure for communicative functions and forms, either. It is a validation of hypotheses derived from a theory of *Communicative Phonetic Science*, which provides a scientific construct for analysing speech interaction in socio-cultural language settings by auditory evaluation and experimental measurement. Thus *Communicative Phonetic Science*, as conceived of here, combines principles of the natural sciences with the phenomenology of the humanities.

I see five essentials for this validation process in *Communicative Phonetic Science*:

(1) Phonetic science is built on a theory of speech communication in human interaction based on a small number of axioms.

(2) Specific research questions, raised by the phonetician, in observing *ad hoc* speech events, or in evaluating the state-of-the-art in the particular research field, are anchored in this theory.

(3) Hypotheses are derived for the validation of the specific questions within the theory, thus continually deepening the theoretical foundations.

(4) Appropriate methodologies are developed for the collection of communicatively valid data for the specific questions.

(5) In data analysis, auditory evaluation precedes measurement.

Here is an example to illustrate the progression from observation to scientific analysis. On a local bus in Kiel, I was sitting in a window seat beside a button for signalling to the driver that one wants to get off at the next stop. Diagonally opposite and facing me was a young woman who was playing with her smartphone. When the bus was approaching the stop where she wanted to get off, she put her smartphone in her handbag, looked at me, stretched out her arm and, with her index finger pointing to the button, said, 'Drücken Sie bitte' [Press (the button) please]. 'Drücken Sie' was high level, then there was a small step of about two semitones down to another level tone. In this communicative speech-and-gesture action, the woman presupposed shared 'world' knowledge between us for me to interpret her deixis appeal correctly in the way she intended it. I had this common communicative ground and understood her utterance to mean 'I cannot reach the button, please press it for me because I want to get off.' It was a pure stimulant to act on her behalf, without any command or exuberant request appeal. And I was quite happy to comply. Afterwards it occurred to me that if she had used a falling pitch on 'Drücken', ending in low pitch on 'Sie bitte', I would have received it as an impolite command. I have since extrapolated this to other instances of stepping patterns I have collected, and I have studied the relevant literature on the subject. A clear picture is beginning to emerge, which I have formulated as a principled statement in the function-form framework of speech communication in 4.1, preparing the ground for further testing.

Experimental testing of such interactive speech production becomes a problem because the data are so context-dependent and require such a great deal of empathy on the part of informants that it requires a lot of ingenuity to devise situational dialogue interactions between subjects. Therefore, research into phonetic exponents of specific speech functions needs to draw on two data sources. The *first data source*, comprising corpus data of various forms of spontaneous speech, collected in a variety of scenarios, provides a rich documentation of segmental and prosodic variability in words and utterances. The *Call Home* corpus of American English telephone conversations is one form of a spontaneous speech corpus, which allows the *Communicative Phonetic Science* analysis of an array of interactional phenomena, especially in a Conversation Analysis framework (Local and Walker 2005; Ogden 2012), of course only within the frequency and signal/noise ratio limitations of telephone speech.

Many other corpora that are called spontaneous are not spontaneous in the defined sense of natural communicative interaction. They are unscripted at best, generated in a metalinguistically designed scenario in a recording studio, such as the appointment-making scenario of the *Kiel corpus of spontaneous speech*; (IPDS 1995–7). These dialogues should be called semi-spontaneous. Generally, they have the sound of pairs of speakers playing games according to instructions, but there are some where the listener gets the impression that the speakers are interacting in a natural communicative setting of arranging mutually suitable days and times to meet. These dialogues contain typical non-lexical interactive sounds such as laughing. The *Video Task* scenario (Peters 2001) creates a communicative situation in the studio that moves one step further towards natural interaction. Similar but non-identical video clips from the well-known German television series *Lindenstrasse* are presented to two subjects sitting in separate rooms. After the presentation, the subjects discuss differences and similarities in what they have seen and heard.

The (semi-)spontaneous corpora lack the systematicity of experimental speech designs, but they allow the formulation of tentative hypotheses for further systematic data collection. These hypotheses can then be tested with a *second data source* which is constructed in the laboratory, taking care to achieve the greatest possible naturalness with data collection scenarios and data types that are communicatively plausible and meaningful. This rules out data samples of the type 'Die Nonne und der Lehrer wollen der Lola in Murnau eine Warnung geben, und die Hanne will im November ein Lama malen' [The nun and the teacher want to give a warning to Lola from Murnau, and Hanna wants to paint a lama in November], which are detached from communicative functions and serve a metalinguistic principle, i.e. to generate continuous stretches of voicing for F0 analysis (Truckenbrodt 2002).

The lab analysis of communicative functions, e.g. of focus, increases the insight into these functions when meaningful sentences are contextualised in plausible interaction scenarios. But question–answer paradigms of the type

Prompt:	Target:
Who may know your niece?	<u>Lee</u> may know my niece.
What may Lee do to your niece?	Lee may <u>lure</u> my niece.
Who may Lee know?	Lee may know my <u>niece</u>.
What did you say?	Lee may know my niece.

(Xu and Xu 2005), frequently used in the study of contrastive focus, do not meet this criterion. Quite apart from the questions being communicatively odd, their nominal and verbal elements would not all be repeated in natural dialogue answers, which would rather be given as 'Lee may', 'He may lure her', '(He may know) my niece.' The reason all elements are to be repeated by the informants again derives from a metalinguistic principle, this time to provide a homogeneous frame for comparing narrow focus realisation phrase-initially, -medially and -finally in relation to the broad focus of the fourth target. The analysis of such data sets can only make statements about focus exponents in this metalinguistic data generation and should not be generalised to focus in speech communication. We must not take subjects to the laboratory and put them through highly stylised procedures only to obtain numerical data under controlled conditions. The recordings may be substantially removed from natural talk in interaction and greatly limited in what they can tell us about the exponents of communicative functions.

Contextualisation requires a great deal of refinement to meet the requirements of *Communicative Phonetic Science*. To tease apart representational, attitudinal and expressive meanings, scenarios need to be devised in which competent speakers (whose proficiency in the use of their language is tested beforehand) enact communicative functions that are the goal of the analysis. Kohler and Niebuhr (2007) and Niebuhr (2010) use such a methodology of data acquisition for negative or positive intensification. But even the most sophisticated contextualisation procedures in the laboratory cannot guarantee natural interaction, crucial in spontaneous communication. For certain phenomena of spontaneous speech interaction, for example the use of pitch stepping, it is exceedingly difficult to obtain recordings of talk in interaction. In such cases, the speech scientist needs to accept the trained native language expert's auditory and visual observation of ongoing speech communication as a valid *third data source* beside the systematic analysis of recorded (semi-)spontaneous and lab-generated corpora.

This is Bertrand Russell's 'Knowledge by Acquaintance' versus 'Knowledge by Description', i.e. *ad hoc* native expert observation, and competent reproduction, of talk in interaction unfolding *in situ* as against extra-communicative formal and numerical analysis of recorded linguistic objects. This kind of *ad hoc* observation of meaning transmission through speech is even further removed from systematicity than phenomena in collected speech corpora, but it constitutes an essential and continually necessary step in the acquisition of knowledge about speech and language, and reinstates the very successful methodology of the traditional 'ear phonetician' in the London School of Phonetics. It may be extremely difficult to evaluate sensory observation of communicative action by subsequent measurement of its physical parameters because eliciting and recording communicatively relevant data is problematic. In such cases, numerical validation can be obtained through suitably devised speech perception and understanding experiments.

Methodologies of data acquisition in speech perception and understanding have already been practised for some considerable time, but they, too, need further refinement. When function-form structures have been clarified in speech production, listening tests can be developed that systematically present natural speech stimuli for judgement, either varied in natural production by a competent native speaker, or in systematic parameter manipulation (e.g. F0) of one or more natural base stimuli in such analysis tools as Praat. Judgement paradigms may be the Semantic Differential (Ambrazaitis 2005; Dombrowski 2003, 2013; Dombrowski and Niebuhr 2010; Kohler 2005, 2011b; Osgood, Suci and Tannenbaum 1957; Uldall 1960, 1964) or context matching of test stimuli (Kleber 2006; Kohler 1987b; Niebuhr 2007a, b; Niebuhr and Kohler 2004). The former are more powerful if the test stimuli are contextually embedded (Kohler 2011b). In the cited papers, semantic scales were constructed for the particular questions in hand. The strength of the Semantic Differential Technique in phonetic research will be increased in future when it is developed into a methodology of standardised sets of scales.

In any form of context matching, to be of use in a function-form framework, context and test stimuli should represent a natural communicative sequence, either in the same voice within a dialogue turn, or across two successive turns with a change of voices, preferably of gender as well. The test stimulus always follows the context setting to trigger an immediate response to it in its contextual embedding, which is not possible if the order of context and test stimulus is reversed. The context can either be given generally in the introduction to the whole listening test (Kohler 2011b) or, if it can be captured in a short enough phrasing within or across dialogue turns, it may be appended before each test stimulus (Kohler 1987b; Niebuhr 2007b; Niebuhr and Kohler 2004). The proper matching paradigm tests whether listeners do or do not apprehend the test stimulus as fitting into the preceding context, and the experimenter then interprets these responses as referring to the categories under investigation.

Content and Readership

This monograph develops a prosodic model within a function-form framework of human speech communication and then looks at prosodic, beside syntactic and lexical, manifestations of selected speech functions. The discussion starts with a focus on German and English. The variety of German is the Northern Standard, the variety of English the Southern British Standard, with occasional references to other varieties of English around the world, especially in North America. To keep function and form categories clearly distinct, the former are symbolised in small capitals, the latter in italics.

Chapter 1 **Speech Communication in Human Interaction** sets the theme by taking, as the point of departure, two central concepts of Karl Bühler's *Sprachtheorie* (Bühler 1934): (1) the *Organon Model*, which relates the linguistic sign to the Speaker, the Listener and the world of Objects and Factual

Relations in the three basic communicative functions of EXPRESSION, APPEAL and REPRESENTATION; (2) the two fundamentally different fields of speech communication, the *pointing* or *deictic* and the *naming* or *symbolic*. The chapter looks at the ways deictic communication is structured with reference to four pointing dimensions, the sender, the receiver, objects away from the sender and the receiver, and far-away objects. Illustrations are given from German and English.

The English translation of Bühler's *Sprachtheorie, Theory of Language* by Donald Fraser Goodwin, in collaboration with the sematologist Achim Eschbach, was first published by John Benjamins in 1990, and then in a new edition in 2011 (see Bühler 1934). It is a welcome production, with the Editor's (Achim Eschbach) *Introduction – Karl Bühler: Sematologist*, the translator's *Preface*, a modern-style bibliography of the works cited by Bühler and a glossary. The new edition also contains a *Postscript Twenty-Five Years after…* by Eschbach, and a paper by Abraham (2011). The pagination of the German book was inserted in the text of the English translation, so I will give page references to the German text, except in English quotations, where both page references are provided. The translation is on the whole good and in fluent English style, which is quite remarkable, considering the very complex academic diction of the original. However, a couple of key terms of Bühler's theory do not seem to me to be quite adequate:

- Bühler's 'Gegenstände und Sachverhalte' was translated as 'Objects and States of Affairs'. 'State of affairs' is 'Zustände', referring to something static and passive. 'Sachverhalte' is linked to the verb 'verhalten', and thus refers to the active relations that objects enter into. I therefore replace 'state of affairs' by 'factual relations'.
- Bühler's verb 'zuordnen' and noun 'Zuordnung' were rendered by 'coordinate' and 'coordination'. In walking and running the movements of the legs are coordinated, but what Bühler refers to is something different: the mapping of sound signs to objects and factual relations 'in terms of modern mathematics' (Bühler 1934, p. 29). I use the translation 'map'.
- Bühler distinguishes two types of deixis: (1) direct pointing in the actual situation in which the interaction between sender and receiver takes place, (2) mediated pointing in a situation constructed mentally in talk and displaced from the one of actual interaction. The second deictic situation is created 'im Bereich der ausgewachsenen *Erinnerungen* und der konstruktiven *Phantasie*' (Bühler 1934, p. 123),

which is translated as 'in the realm of ... fully fledged *memories* and constructive *phantasy*'. German 'Phantasie' is neutral or positive in meaning, English 'phantasy' has a negative connotation of a dream world; 'er hat Phantasie' means 'he shows mental capacities', 'he has ideas', which cannot be translated by 'he has phantasy'. Bühler calls (2) *Deixis am Phantasma* [phantasma deixis] (Bühler, 1934, pp. 121ff). This was translated as 'imagination-oriented deixis'. But 'Erinnerungen' [memories] are not treated by the sender as something imagined, but as real, yet displaced, and 'konstruktive Phantasie' is a constructive mental creation, for example in fairy tales. These two different components are not properly captured by 'imagination'. Moreover, direct pointing may also be imagination-oriented, for example when someone points to a cloud formation in the sky and says, 'Oh, look there, an old man with a long beard is looking down on us.' Garvin (1994) interpreted Bühler's concept in a different way, calling it 'fictitious deictic field', inasmuch as it is removed from the actual situation (p. 60). It is in the right direction but may get a negative connotation; more neutral, and covering exactly what Bühler means, is the term 'virtual deictic field', borrowed from computer science. This is the translation I use.

Bühler's functional approach is adopted in this monograph in comparison with other paradigms of modern linguistics. Since prosody occupies a central place among the formal means in a functional model of speech communication, a comparative survey of descriptive prosody modelling in other linguistic paradigms is also provided in preparation for Chapter 2.

Chapter 2 **Prosody in a Functional Framework: The Kiel Intonation Model (KIM)** builds on the survey of other models in Chapter 1, leading to the goal of the monograph: to place prosodic form in human interaction and thus to reverse its relationship to communicative function. The *Kiel Intonation Model (KIM)*, together with its labelling system *PROlAB*, is presented as an example of such a function-form perspective in prosody. Its categories are developed with reference to data from perception experiments in functional contextualisation. The model has been expanded by Dombrowski (2013) to include a system of stepping patterns, beside continuous ones, as elements of melody formation. They are outlined as the formal complement to the receiver-oriented function in the deictic field in Chapter 4.1. KIM and PROLAB are the basis for the discussion of experimental and descriptive auditory data in the other chapters.

Chapter 3 **The REPRESENTATION Function** picks up Bühler's notion of the two-dimensional symbolic field of linguistic signs in linguistic contexts for the REPRESENTATION of Objects and Factual Relations. The symbolic field provides the functional frame for the STATEMENT, which is structured, on the one hand, by morphology and syntax, and on the other hand by prosodic phrasing. The chapter examines the syntagmatic organisation of STATEMENTS by *syntactic structure* and *prosodic pattern*. It also introduces the functional scale of INFORMATION SELECTION AND WEIGHTING, from backgrounding to foregrounding, and links it to the formal scales of accentuation and of articulatory space-time trajectories from *reduced* to *elaborated* in sequences of opening-closing gestures. Following the discussion of INFORMATION SELECTION AND WEIGHTING and their formal manifestations, a distinction is developed between INFORMATION STRUCTURE and ARGUMENTATION. The former refers to the factual world, the latter is the result of the speaker's view of objects and relations under the categories of FINALITY, OPENNESS, CONTRAST and UNEXPECTEDNESS. The syntagmatic grammatical organisation of speech by syntactic and prosodic patterns is supplemented by a description of patterns of principally independent rhythmic organisation as an important guide function in meaning transmission to a listener. All the symbolic field structures are illustrated with examples from German and English.

Chapter 4 **The APPEAL Function** distinguishes three types of listener-directed APPEAL. The most elementary one is the pointing function to get listeners' attention and to control interaction, introduced as *ISTIC* DEIXIS in Chapter 1. The concept is further developed here and related to a formal system of stepping pitch patterns (set out in Chapter 2) found in many languages. Ample illustrations of deictic subcategories are taken from German and English.

The second type is the QUESTION APPEAL, by which a speaker solicits a *communicative response* (usually *verbal* but may be *gestural*, e.g. nod, shrug) from a listener to an unknown. The unknown may be a semantic constituent, such as PLACE, TIME, MANNER or the truth value of the queried STATEMENT. The former is an INFORMATION QUESTION, the latter a POLARITY QUESTION. A further QUESTION variable is whether the speaker inserts an unknown into a STATEMENT already made and asks for confirmation of a constituent or of the truth value: this is the CONFIRMATION QUESTION. There is further subcategorisation, depending on the addition of various kinds of EXPRESSION, such as surprise, friendly concern or indignation. These different functional categories are put in a systematic network and are linked to syntax and prosodic patterns, with particular reference to German and English. This is the core section in the monograph. It demonstrates the progression from functional categories to formal exponents for an insightful assessment of QUESTION versus STATEMENT. They are communicative functions, differentiated from *interrogative* versus *declarative syntax*.

The third type of APPEAL comprises COMMANDS and REQUESTS, by which a speaker stimulates actions of body and mind in a receiver in either a dominant or a considerate way. This differs from routine interaction control in the *ISTIC* DEIXIS APPEAL, with continuous, rather than stepping, pitch patterns. Illustrations from German and English demonstrate that this function must again be separated from its syntactic form, with *interrogatives* and *declaratives* occurring beside *imperatives*.

Chapter 5 **The EXPRESSION Function** deals with expressive sender symptoms of the linguistic sign, and proposes an elaboration of the *Organon Model* by developing the concept of EXPRESSIVE EVALUATION of communicative action along a scale from LOW KEY TO HIGH KEY. An example like 'I do not know' may be graded from the highly reduced mumbled aside to the insisting proposition with an accent on each word. The LOW KEY end is the expression of the speaker's detachment from the communicative situation, the HIGH KEY end is the expressive reinforcement of points of ARGUMENTATION. This is the ARGUMENTATIVE HIGH KEY. IT differs from a POSITIVE or NEGATIVE EMOTIVE HIGH KEY, for example when 'I do not know' expresses exasperation over a communication partner's persistent asking. The manifestation of EXPRESSIVE EVALUATION along the functional LOW-TO-HIGH KEY scale includes bundles of prosodic features – pitch, energy, phonation – but also segmental ones changing along an articulatory precision scale from *reduced* to *elaborated*, already introduced in Chapter 3, but now extended at both ends through LOW- and HIGH-KEY EXPRESSIVE EVALUATION. Prosodic and segmental manifestations of the functional LOW-TO-HIGH KEY scales are examined as overlays of the REPRESENTATION and APPEAL functions, as well as in the EXPRESSION function itself in the case of EXCLAMATIONS. Although the data are from German and English, some vocal features of EXPRESSIVE HIGH KEY may be assumed to be wide-spread, possibly universal in human speech.

Chapter 6 **Linguistic Form of Communicative Functions in Language Comparison** demonstrates the application of the function-form framework, developed around European languages in the preceding chapters, as a powerful tool of comparative prosodic research in the world's languages. It is achieved by creating functionally comparable scenarios and collecting data within them to investigate formal congruence and divergence for equivalent functions. This approach makes it mandatory to change the methodology of experimental data acquisition to one of contextualisation and situational plausibility. This procedure is demonstrated with data collection and analysis of the STATEMENT and QUESTION functions in Mandarin Chinese, in comparison with German and English. The discussion then leads to the question of a universal *Frequency Code* in speech communication.

Following the tradition of the London School of Phonetics, the statements made about prosody are firmly rooted in auditory assessment by trained observation. They are then complemented by acoustic analysis and by experimental methods in speech production and perception. Graphic displays of acoustic speech signals and of experimental results are provided whenever necessary for a good understanding of the written text. To make it possible for readers to listen to the sounds and prosodies of examples discussed in the monograph and to allow them to make their own analyses of the data, they are made available as wav-files at www.cambridge.org/9781107170728. A READ-ME is deposited there that links the sound files with the figures and sections in the text.

The proposed function-form paradigm of 'The Speech Scientist's Theory of Intonational Meaning' will complement the linguistic perspective in the existing canonical literature. The monograph may thus be of interest not only to linguists, phoneticians and modern language philologists, e.g. in departments of English or German language, and communications engineers in Automatic Speech Generation and Automatic Speech Understanding, but, more importantly, is also expected to attract attention in the social sciences: psychology, sociology, communication science and media studies.

List of PROLAB Symbols Used for Prosodic Annotation in KIM

To allow readers to refer quickly to the definitions of prosodic annotation symbols at any point in the monograph they are listed here in relation to the various prosodic categories they represent. Prosodic symbols are inserted in orthographic text or in segmental phonetic transcription as bold characters, preceded by the prefix **&**.

(1)   **Sentence accent** (see 2.2, 2.3)
At the centre of prosodic annotation is the marking of words according to their relative weight in utterances by sentence accent at four levels. Each word is prefixed by one of four accent labels, without a space; **&0** may be left unmarked.

Label	**Prosodic category**
&0	*unaccented (defocused)*
&1	*(partially) deaccented (partially foregrounded)*
&2	*default accent*
&3	*reinforced accent*

Examples
&2Anna &0came &0with &2Manny. &1Anna &0came &0with &2Manny.
&0Anna &0came &0with &3Manny. &3Anna &0came &0with &1/&0Manny.

(2)   **Downstep and upstep** (see 2.4)

Successive **&2** accents within a prosodic phrase are by default downstepped, i.e. lowered in pitch. This default downstep is not marked. Downstep may be broken at any point for information structuring within the prosodic phrase by stepping a **&2** accent up to, or above, the level of the preceding **&2** accent. This upstep is marked by putting I before the number.

Example
&2Anna &0came &0with &I2Manny.

(3)   **Lexical stress** (see 2.5, 2.6)

English and German have lexical stress which marks a place in the syllable chain of a word where a sentence accent docks when the word receives one.

Label (put before syllable nucleus)	**Prosodic category**
'	*stressed-primary*
''	*stressed-secondary*
(unmarked)	*unstressed*

Examples
'increase (noun), incr'ease (verb); b'uttercup (flower), b'utterc''up (butter dish); f'ourt'een, j'ust fourt'een, f'ourteen p'ounds

(4)   **Intonation** (see 2.7, 2.8)

Sentence accents receive intonation markings for (rise-)falls (peak patterns) or rises (valley patterns) or (rise-)fall-rises (peak-valley patterns) or level pitch. The markings have two components, the direction of pitch movement and the synchronisation of peak maxima (in peak and peak-valley patterns) and of valley minima with the timing of supra-glottal articulation in the stressed syllables of accented words. There are three levels of peak descent: to the speaker's low pitch range, or to a middle pitch range or levelling out at high pitch. Valleys and peak-valleys are either low or high rising.

Label	Prosodic category
&2./1./0.	*peak*
&,/&?	*valley*: *low* or *high rising*
&./&.?	*peak-valley*: *low* or *high rising*
&- &0.	*level*

The direction marker is put before the next accent or before a **PhrasinG-**marker **&PG**, always with spaces before and after.

Peak(-valley) maximum synchronisation has three location ranges: before accented-vowel onset, shortly after onset or late in the accented syllable. Valley minimum synchronisation has two location ranges: before or after accented-vowel onset. There is, of course, no difference in level synchronisation. The synchronisation labels are put after the number in the accent labels.

Label	Prosodic category		
Peak(-valley)			
&3)/&2)/&1)	*early*	(fall begins at or before accented-vowel onset)	
&3^/&2^/&1^	*medial*	(central rise-fall in the accented vowel)	
&3(/&2(/&1(	*late*	(late fall in the accented vowel, or in a following syllable, depending on timing constraints, preceded by extensive rise)	
&3^-(/&2^-(/&1^-(	*medial-to-late*	intermediate position between *medial* and *late*	
Valley			
&3]/&2]/&1]	*early*	(rise begins at or before accented-vowel onset)	
&3[/&2[/&1[	*late*	(rise begins in the accented vowel)	
Level			
&3-/&2-/&1-	accent strength is signalled by other properties (duration, energy)		

Examples

&2) Yes **&2. &PG**   **&2)**Yes **&1. &PG**   **&2^**Yes **&2. &PG**   **&2(**Yes **&2. &PG**

&2^Yes **&2., &PG**   **&2]**Yes **&2, &PG**   **&2[**Yes **&2, &PG**   **&2]**Yes **&2? &PG**

&3-Yes **&0. &PG**

(5)   **Concatenation of pitch patterns** (see 2.9)

The different accent-intonation patterns can be freely concatenated to code communicative functions. A special concatenation is the sequencing of peak patterns without a dip in between. The results are *hat patterns* with **&0.** at the first peak maximum. Since the characteristic feature of the *early peak* is its high-low descent into the accented syllable, it cannot occur in first position in a *hat pattern*. Similarly, since the characteristic feature of the *late peak* is its low rise before the late fall, it cannot occur in second position.

When a *hat pattern* is folded around a central frequency line in a time-frequency display we get a *tub pattern*. Tub patterns may be analysed as a concatenation of two *low valleys* without a high point between them. The direction feature of the first valley is labelled **&0**, analogous to **&0.** in the *hat pattern*.

Examples
&2(Anna came with **&0. &2**)Manny **&2. &PG**
&2[Anna came with **&0, &2**[Manny **&, &PG**

(6)   **Prehead and register** (see 2.11)
Unaccented words before the first accent in a prosodic phrase form its prehead, which may be either high or low pitch. High prehead is marked by **&HP** prehead initially.

A speaker may change to a higher or a lower register from a default middle one, for example to signal asides, or to expressively foreground long stretches of talk in interaction. These departures from a neutral register are labelled **&HR** and **&LR**, and put at the beginning of the prosodic phrase in which the change occurs.

(7)   **Prosodic phrasing** (see 2.12)
Information structure is coded by prosodic phrasing with different bundlings of F0 direction, duration, energy and phonation at the junctures between phrases. Four separation ranges, from weak to strong, are distinguished: **&PG1–4**.

1 *Speech Communication in Human Interaction*

1.1 Human Interaction and the *Organon Model*

Humans interact for a variety of reasons:

- for survival and procreation, and for play, which they share with the animal world
- for creating habitats and social bonds, which they basically share with many animals
- for making tools and using them in their daily activities
- for selling and buying, and for business transactions in general
- for establishing, enforcing and observing social and legal codes
- for social contact, phatic communion and entertainment
- for reporting events and issuing warnings
- for instructing and learning
- for asking, and finding answers to, questions of religious belief, of philosophical understanding, of scientific explanation, of historical facts and developments
- for artistic pursuits for eye, ear and mind.

Central to all these human interactions is speech communication, i.e. communication via an articulatory–acoustic–auditory channel (AAA) between a sender and a receiver, supplemented by a gestural–optical–visual channel (GOV). Speech communication is based on cognitive constructs that order the world and human action in space and time. These constructs are manifested in the AAA channel as words with their paradigmatic and phonotactic sound structures, and as syntagmatic organisations of words in utterances. The words and phrase structures are linked to articulatory processes in speech production by a speaker and to auditory patterns in speech perception and understanding by a listener. Speech communication on the basis of such cognitive constructs, of their formal representation, and articulatory and perceptual substantiation,

18

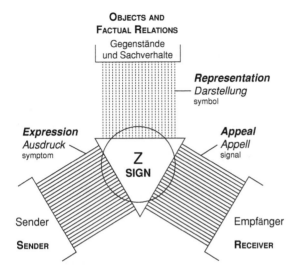

Figure 1.1. The *Organon Model* according to Bühler (1934, p. 28), with the original German labels, and their added English translations, of the three relationships, functions and aspects of the linguistic SIGN Z(eichen).

shared by speakers and listeners, performs three basic functions in sender–receiver interaction:

(a) the transmission of *symptoms* relating to the sender's feelings and attitudes in the communicative act

(b) the emission of *signals* by a sender to a receiver to stimulate behaviour

(c) the transmission of *symbols* mapped to objects and factual relations in space and time, constructing the world in communicative acts.

This is Karl Bühler's *Organon Model* (from Classical Greek ὄργανον, 'instrument, tool, organ', after Aristotle's works on logic: Bühler 1934, pp. 24–33; see Figure 1.1), which relates the linguistic sign to the speaker, the listener, and the world of objects and factual relations, in the communicative functions of EXPRESSION (a), APPEAL (b) and REPRESENTATION (c). The objects in the symbolic mapping of (c) are not just concrete things, e.g. 'table', 'mountain', but also include abstract entities, e.g. 'love', 'death', and attributes, e.g. 'redness', 'beauty'. The symbolic mapping to objects and factual relations constitutes *language structure [Sprachgebilde]* based on social convention binding individual speakers in their *speech actions [Sprechhandlungen]*. This is, in Bühler's terms (1934, pp. 48ff), de Saussure's *langue* versus *parole* (de

Saussure 1922). For the REPRESENTATION function, the human mind devised systems to capture linguistic signs graphically on durable material in order to overcome the time and space binding of fleeting signals through AAA and GOV channels. These writing systems are either logographic, with reference to the symbolic values of linguistic signs, or phonographic, with reference to their sound properties, either syllabic or segmental. The latter, alphabetic writing, was only invented once in the Semitic language family. It conquered the world and became the basis of linguistic study, which has, for many centuries, focused on the REPRESENTATION function in written texts, or on speech reduced to alphabetic writing.

The three aspects of the linguistic sign – sender *symptom*, receiver-directed *signal*, *symbol-to-world* mapping – are semasiological categories, with primary manifestation through the AAA channel, but accompanied in varying degrees by the GOV channel, more particularly for the functions (a) and (b). Bühler made it quite clear that he regarded the three functions of his *Organon Model* as being operative in any speech action at any given moment, but with varying strengths of each, depending on the communicative situation. In rational discourse, REPRESENTATION with *symbol-to-world* mapping dominates; in highly emotional communication, it is the *symptoms* of the EXPRESSION function; in commands on the drill ground, the *signals* of the APPEAL function; a balance of *signals* and *symptoms* occurs in words of endearment or abuse. An aggressive act may be totally devoid of symbolic meaning, as in the reported case of a Bonn student silencing the most powerful market crier in the Bonn fruit and vegetable market, eventually having her in tears, by simply reciting the Greek and Hebrew alphabets loudly with pressed phonation: 'Sie Alpha! Sie Beta! …' (Bühler 1934, p. 32).

The linguistic sign is at the centre of the model and has a direct iconic symptom or signal relationship to the sender or the receiver in EXPRESSION and APPEAL, respectively, and an indirect symbolic relationship to objects and factual relations in REPRESENTATION. The direct or indirect relationships are indicated by plain or dotted connection lines in Figure 1.1. The linguistic sign is encapsulated in a circle encircling all three functions. Superimposed on, and cutting across, this circle is a triangle connecting with the sign's three functions and covering a smaller area of the circle, as well as going beyond the area of the circle with its three edges. The triangle represents Bühler's principle of *abstractive relevance* applied to the phonetic manifestation of the linguistic sign, which is captured by the circle. The triangle contains only the communicatively relevant features of the total of phonetic properties, and at the same time it adds functional aspects in relation to the three communicative functions that are absent from the phonetic substance.

Abstractive relevance is also the basis for Bühler's concept of phonology versus phonetics, which he expounded in his seminal article of 1931 (Bühler 1931), and which Trubetzkoy took over in his *Grundzüge* of 1939. Abstractive relevance means that the total phonetic substance of the instantiation of a linguistic sign is reduced to its functionally relevant phonetic features by an abstractive scaling, not by abstract representation. Thus, phonology comes out of phonetics, phonetics does not go into phonology, contrary to Ladd (2011), who interpreted Prague phonology as an abstraction from phonetics that stopped short of its logical conclusion (cf. Kohler 2013a). The mistake Prague phonology made was not incomplete phonological abstraction from concrete phonetics but the postulation of two disciplines, phonology and phonetics, of which the former was furthermore linked with the humanities, the latter with the natural sciences. The reason this happened lies in the methodology of early experimental phonetics at the turn of the twentieth century, where linguistic concepts disintegrated and objective truth was sought in speech curves of various, mainly articulatory, origins and in the numbers derived from them (Scripture 1935, p. 135). This imbalance was put right again by the Prague linguists, who reintroduced the functional aspect into phonetics, which had always been present in the several thousand years of descriptive studies of speech sounds in languages since the invention of alphabetic writing. Bühler's concept of abstractive relevance shows how this dichotomy can be overcome: there is only one science of the sound of speech in human language – it determines the functionally relevant features in speech communication in the languages of the world from the broad array of sound in individual speech acts.

Bühler developed the concept of abstractive relevance in connection with the symbolic mapping of sound markers of the linguistic sign to Objects and Factual Relations in the REPRESENTATION function, especially the sound markers of names (words) assigned to objects. The entire sound impressions of words are not relevant for the differential name-object mappings; only a small number of systematically ordered distinctive sound features are. This is the principal aspect of Prague segmental word phonology incorporated into Bühler's theory of language. Apart from lexical tone and stress, this framework says nothing about prosodic phonology at the level of mapping formal phrasal structures and factual relations in the world. Bühler left a gap in his theory of language, which needs filling in two respects:

- He considers 'musical modulation' at the utterance level in the Indo-European languages to be irrelevant for REPRESENTATION, and therefore free to be varied diacritically in the other two functions, for example, adding an urgent APPEAL to the German phrase 'es regnet' [it is raining] in order to remind a forgetful person to take an umbrella (Bühler 1934, p. 46). Global unstructured utterance prosodies are seen as EXPRESSION or APPEAL overlays on structured phonematic lexical sound markers in REPRESENTATION. This is incomplete in two respects: prosody can and does map symbolic relations in REPRESENTATION, and it is highly structured in all three functions. In Bühler's time, prosodic research was still in its infancy, so he was not able to draw on as rich a data analysis as we can today.

- The function-form perspective is to map the functions of the *Organon Model*, as well as subfunctions in each, and their formal systems and structures at all linguistic levels, from phonetics/phonology through the lexicon and morphology to syntax. For example, the investigation into QUESTION versus STATEMENT needs to consider word-order syntax, question particles and prosody. In this way, prosody as the acoustic exponent in symbolic phrase-level mapping is treated on a par with other formal means, lexical and structural, and is thus fully integrated into the theory of language and of language comparison.

Bühler saw the gap in his theory and set a goal for further development:

> Let me stress the point once again: these are only phenomena of dominance, in which one of the three fundamental relationships of the language sounds is in the foreground. The decisive scientific verification of our constitutional formula, the Organon Model of language, has been given if it turns out that each of the three relationships, each of the three semantic functions of language signs discloses and identifies a specific realm of linguistic phenomena and facts. That is indeed the case. 'Expression in language' and 'appeal in language' are partial objects for all of language research, and thus display their own specific structures in comparison with representation in language ... This is the thesis of the three functions of language in simplest terms. It will be verified as a whole when all three books that the Organon Model requires have been written. (Bühler 1934, p. 31f [2011, p. 39])

He himself concentrated on the REPRESENTATION function, which he indicated in the subtitle of the book. It resulted from an extensive study of the extant literature of Indo-European historical linguistics, with its focus on such topics as the Indo-European case system, deixis and pronouns, anaphora, word and sentence, compound, ellipsis and metaphor, generally dealing with REPRESENTATION, written texts and historical comparison. He was also thoroughly familiar with the Greek philosophers, with modern logic and with the philosophy of language. He especially discussed Husserl's *Logische Untersuchungen* and *Cartesianische Meditationen* in some detail in connection with the concept of

Sprechakte [*speech acts*], in which a speaker confers specific discourse-driven meanings to words of a language, and which are distinguished from *Sprech-handlungen* [*speech actions*], the unique *hic et nunc* utterances by individuals. He also took de Saussure (1922), and especially Gardiner (1932) and Wege-ner (1885), into account, who added the linguistic expert perspective to what Bühler contributed as a psychologist working with language. The study of lan-guage is a study of creative actions, not of a static linguistic object, because language users interact through speech actions in communicative speech acts by means of a *Sprachgebilde* [*language structure*] to create *Sprachwerke* [*lan-guage works*]. This naturally led to the *Organon Model* and to looking beyond REPRESENTATION.

1.2   Deictic and Symbolic Fields in Speech Communication

In addition to the *Organon Model*, Bühler proposed a two-field theory of speech communication: the pointing or *deictic* field and the naming or *symbolic* field. The deictic field is one-dimensional, with systems of deictic elements that receive their ordering in contexts of situation. In a pointing field, a speaker sets the sender *origo* of *hic-nunc-ego* coordinates, which position the speaker in space and time for the communicative action. Within the set coordinates, the sender transmits gestural and/or acoustic signals to a proximate or distant receiver. These signals point to the sender, or to the receiver, or to the world of objects away, or far away, from (the positions of) the sender and the receiver. Receivers relate the received sender-, receiver- or world-related signals to their own *hic-nunc-ego* coordinates to interpret them. The understanding of their intended meanings relies on material signal properties that guide the receiver through four different pointing dimensions: *here* or *hic* deixis; *where-you-are* or *istic* deixis; *there or illic* deixis; and *yonder* deixis.

On the other hand, the symbolic field in its most developed *synsemantic* form is a field where linguistic signs do not occur primarily in situational but in linguistic contexts. It is two-dimensional, comprising systems of signs for objects and factual relations, a lexicon, and structures, a syntax, into which the systemic units are ordered. Another symbolic field is the one-dimensional *sympractical* field, which contains systems of signs that are situation-related in an action field, rather than being anchored in linguistic context.

1.2.1   Deictic Field Structures

In deictic communication, the sender creates a situational field in space and time by using optical and acoustic signals in relation to the sender's *hic-nunc-ego* coordinates, and the receiver decodes these signals with reference to the receiver's position in the created communal space-time situation. If the signals are optical, they are gestures, including index finger or head pointing, and eye contact. If they are acoustic, they include linguistic signs, deictic particles, demonstrative and personal pronouns, which function as attention signals. These signals structure the deitic field with reference to the four pointing dimensions. For each dimension, the relation may be *at, to* or *from* the reference, as in the Latin deictic signs 'hic', at the sender, 'huc', to the sender, 'hinc', from the sender; 'istic', at the receiver, 'istuc', to the receiver, 'istinc', from the receiver; 'illic', at a third-person place, 'illuc', to that place, 'illinc', from that place. Yet pointing in a situational field is always meant for a receiver, even if there are no specific receiver-deictic signals. The linguistic signs receive their referential meaning through the situational dimensions. 'here', 'I', 'yours', 'that one over there' are semantically unspecified outside the *hic-nunc-ego* coordinates of the deictic field. Languages differ a great deal in the way they structure the deictic field with deictic linguistic signs. Latin provides a particularly systematic place-structure deixis. Linguistic deixis signs are not only accompanied by gestures, but also by acoustic signals pointing to the sender or the receiver.

1.2.1.1   *here* or *hic* Deixis

Hic deixis signalling points to the sender in two ways, giving (1) the position and (2) the personal identification of the sender.

(1) Position of the Sender   When speaker B answers 'Here' from a removed place after speaker A has called out, 'Anna, where are you?', the deictic 'here' is defined within sender B's coordinates but remains unspecified for receiver A unless the acoustics of the uttered word contain properties pointing to the sender's position in space, or, in the case of potential visual contact between sender and receiver, are accompanied by a gestural signal of a raised hand or index finger. The acoustic properties of signal energy and signal directionality give A a fair idea of the distance and the direction of B's position in relation to A's coordinates, indicating whether the sender is nearby, e.g. in the same room or somewhere close in the open, but outside A's visual field, or whether B is in an adjoining room, or on another floor or outside the house. From their daily experience with speech interaction, both speaker and listener are familiar with the generation and understanding of these sender-related pointing signals.

A different variety of this *hic* deixis occurs in response to hearing one's name in a roll call, which depends on visual contact for verification. Raising arm and index finger and/or calling out 'Here'/'Yes' transmits the sender's position and personal (see (2) below) coordinates.

(2) Personal Identification of the Sender   A speaker B, waiting outside the door or gate to be let in, may answer 'It's me' in response to a speaker A asking 'Who is there?' over the intercom. This *hic* deixis is only understandable if A has a mental trace of B's individual voice characteristics. Their presence in a pointing signal allows the correct interpretation of an otherwise unspecified 'me'. Again, speakers and listeners are familiar with these material properties of individualisation in speech interaction.

1.2.1.2   *where-you-are* or *istic* Deixis

ISTIC DEIXIS signalling points to the receiver. Bühler thought that, contrary to the other types of deixis, there are no specific systematic pointing signals for ISTIC DEIXIS, although he lists a few subsidiary devices on an articulated sound basis, such as 'pst', 'hey', 'hello', or the reference to the receiver by 'you', or by the personal name, accompanied by index finger pointing and/or head turning to the person to establish eye contact.

However, an examination of the various occurrences of ISTIC DEIXIS, and of the pitch patterns associated with them in English and German, shows up a specific melodic device that is characteristic of utterances pointing to the receiver, and that differs from pitch patterns used in other types of deixis and in the synsemantic symbolic field of speech communication. It is level pitch stepping up or down, or staying level, as against continuous movement (see 2.14). Continuous pitch patterns form a system of distinctive differences for coding REPRESENTATION, APPEAL and EXPRESSION functions in speech communication in a particular language. They fill speech communication with sender-receiver-world content. On the other hand, stepping patterns function as pointing signals to the receiver to control sender-receiver interaction; they do not primarily fill it with expression of the speaker, attitudes towards the listener and representation of the world. The referential content is predictable from the discourse context, and the sender shares an established and mutually acknowledged routine convention with the receiver. These acoustic patterns of ISTIC DEIXIS may occur interspersed in speech communication at any moment to initiate, sustain and close speaker–listener interaction, with two different functions, either to control connection with a receiver or to induce specific action in a receiver. In all the varieties of ISTIC DEIXIS found in English and

German, which will be discussed as subcategories of an APPEAL function in 4.1, stepping pitch patterns operate as such receiver-directed control signals. When they are replaced by continuous contours in the same verbal contexts they lose the simple pointing control characteristic and become commands, expressive pronouncements and informative statements in acts of speech communication.

1.2.1.3   Proximate and Distant Pointing: *there* or *illic* Deixis and *yonder* Deixis

In order to point away from sender and receiver to objects in a proximate or a distant pointing field, arm and finger gestures are used as the standard signal. Demonstrative pronouns and position adverbs, such as 'that' – 'yon', 'there' – 'yonder'/'over there' in English, or 'der' – 'jener', 'da' – 'dort', 'dort' – 'dort drüben'/'jenseits' in German are linguistic signs used for pointing in sympractical usage, accompanied by gesture, but they also operate anaphorically in a synsemantic field. The distinction between proximate and distant positions in a speaker's pointing field coordinates is less clearly defined than the one between the positions of sender and receiver. Languages do not always have a stable, formally marked system of proximate and distant position adverbs and demonstrative pronouns. Even English 'yon' and 'yonder' are literary and archaic outside dialectal, especially Scottish, usage, and German 'da' versus 'dort' are unstable in their position references. Speakers use phrase constructions instead to define different field positions, for example 'over there' in English and 'dort drüben' in German, or they define distant positions in relation to landmarks. As regards signalling proximate and distant positions by gesture, stretching out arm and index finger in the direction of an object may be used for the former, an upward-downward arm–index finger movement for the latter.

Signalling in a pointing field may combine a deixis gesture to objects with a deixis gesture to the receiver. I recently observed an instance of this. I had just got some cash out of an ATM but was still close to the machine when another customer approached to use it. He turned his head towards me and, with his far-away arm and index finger, pointed to the machine, asking 'Fertig?' [Finished?] (with high-level pitch). He identified the object he wanted to use after me and, by looking at me, identified me as the receiver of his object pointing and his enquiry, which he spoke with the acoustic stylisation of ISTIC DEIXIS, a high-level pitch signalling 'May I use this machine?' This is a DEIXIS APPEAL, different from the QUESTION APPEAL 'Is it true that you are finished with the machine?' (see 4.1, 4.2). The response may be 'Ja, bitte' or just 'Bitte' [(Yes,) go ahead], which is impossible in the QUESTION context.

Now let's visit a Scottish pub to illustrate the whole gamut of communicative interaction that is possible with ordering beer, from a synsemantic description to mere gesture. One may give the order 'A pint of Caledonian 80/- please', with continuous pitch. In this situation, it is quite clear that it means 'I want to buy a pint of heavy draught beer sold under the Caledonian Company's trademark', but nobody would use this synsemantic description. The order may be shortened to 'A pint of Caley 80, please', again with continuous pitch. Or one may just point to the label on a draught pump and say 'Pint, please', with a high-level pitch pattern, to induce the receiver to act. This is accompanied by turning one's head towards the barman, to establish gestural contact. Or the customer may point towards the pump with one hand and hold up the other hand with fingers raised according to the number of pints wanted. In a pub near the Tynecastle Hearts football stadium in Edinburgh, called 'The Diggers', because it used to be frequented by gravediggers from a nearby cemetery, this gesturing can be further reduced to mere finger raising, because the barmen know that regulars drink one of their fourteen types of heavy, of course by the pint, and they also know who drinks Caley 80.

The speech versions of this pub order are self-sufficient sympractical signs in their own right, not ellipses of a synsemantic structure 'Sell me a pint of Caledonian 80/- heavy draught beer, please.' In such a sympractical communication field the transmission of symbolic meaning through speech is reduced to the minimum considered necessary by the communicators; the action field and the situation supply the referential meaning, and the EXPRESSION and APPEAL functions are of secondary relevance. They may come in when speakers do not get what they want. Interaction still works when gestures take over altogether. In this case, the question of an ellipsis simply does not arise, which also casts doubt on any attempt to derive the linguistically reduced forms from fully elaborated ones.

1.2.2   *From Sympractical Deixis in Situations to Synsemantic Symbols in Contexts*

A sender communicating with a receiver may establish a *hic-nunc-ego origo* in a deictic field relating to their actual situation. In its simplest form, communication is just by gesture or by gesture accompanying *sympractical* speech, or only by *sympractical* speech pointing to the situation that both sender and receiver are connected with (e.g. 'mind the gap'/'mind your step' announcements on the London Underground/at Schiphol Aiport, see 4.1.3(2)). The pointing in this *sympractical* speech may be done by deictic particles and pronouns with or without finger gesture, as in 'The flowers over there.' Direct pointing by gesture and/or deictic words may be removed in *synsemantic* place description in relation to the *origo*, as in 'The flowers are on the table at the window in the back room upstairs.' But there is still some pointing in relation to the position of the sender's *origo* in such utterances, because they are only intelligible with reference to the situation both sender and receiver are related to, and they presuppose the receiver's awareness of, and familiarity with, the locality.

In developing talk, a speaker may move the *hic-nunc-ego origo* from the *actual* sender-receiver situation to a place and time in memories and imagination, and relate symbols to this new *origo* position, thus creating a virtual deictic field, which Bühler calls *Deixis am Phantasma* [*Phantasma Deixis*] (Bühler 1934, pp. 121ff). In Indo-European languages the same deictic signs are used as for pointing in actual situations ('this (one)', 'that (one)', 'here', 'there'; German 'dieser', 'jener', 'der(jenige)'), supplemented by position and time adverbs and conjunctions. This pointing in displaced virtual situations is found in narrating fairy tales:

> *Es war einmal* ein kleines süßes Mädchen ... *Eines Tages* sprach seine Mutter zu ihm: ... *bring das der Großmutter hinaus...*

> *Once upon a time* there was a dear little girl ... *One day* her mother said to her: ... *take this to your grandmother...*

or in storytelling of past or future events:

> *After a five-hour climb* we arrived *at the top of Ben Nevis. Here* we first of all had a rest. *Then* we dug into our food. And *when* the fog lifted, we were rewarded by the most spectacular view of the Highland scenery *around* and *below* us.

or in giving direction:

> You take the road *north out of our village. When* you get to a junction *turn right, then the first left.* You continue *there for about a mile. Then* the castle will come into view.

Communicative action changes completely when symbols are anchored in the context of linguistic structure and are freed from situations. Let's assume that on 3 April 2005, the day after Pope John Paul II died, a passenger on a New York subway train says to the person beside him, 'The Pope's died', referring to what he has just read in the paper. This statement is removed from the place of the communicative situation between sender and receiver: it might have been made anywhere around the world (in the respective languages), but it is still linked to the time when the speaker makes it. In a proposition like 'Two times two is four' the time link is also severed. This is the self-contained synsemantic use of symbols in a symbolic field to refer to objects and factual relations, valid at all times and places, in statements of mathematics, logic and science.

As regards the intonation of such sentences in oral communicative actions, the occurrence of stepping pitch is all the more likely the stronger the sympractical deictic element. Synsemantic sentences have continuous pitch, rising-falling centered on 'Pope', and on the second 'two' in the above examples. If '↓The ↑Pope's died' is spoken with upward-stepping pitch, it may, for example, come from a newspaper seller in the street attracting the attention of people passing by ('Buy the paper, and read more about the news of the Pope'), i.e. a receiver-directed signal puts the synsemantic sentence into a pointing situation. Similarly, when saying the times tables by rote, for instance teacher-directed in class, an upward-stepping pattern will be given to the synsemantic sentence: '↓One times two is ↑two. ↓Two times two is ↑four. ↓Three times two is ↑six...', or shortened to '↓One two ↑two. ↓Two twos ↑four. ↓Three twos ↑six...'

There is another, quite different way of introducing pointing into the synsemantic symbolic field: anaphora (Bühler 1934, pp. 121ff, 385ff). It reinforces reference to the symbolic context because pointing occurs with backward or forward reference to the internal structure of developing talk in the symbolic field, not with reference to the external situation: the symbolic (linguistic) context functions as the pointing field. In Indo-European languages, the exponents are again the same deictics as for pointing in situations, supplemented by position and time adverbs, conjunctions, relative and third-person personal pronouns, fully integrated into the case system and syntax of the language. For examples from German illustrating the distinction between external situation and internal anaphoric pointing, see Abraham (2011, pp. xxiiff).

1.3   From Function to Form

1.3.1   *Bühler and Functional Linguistics of the Prague School*
Bühler places language functions at the centre of his theory of language and then looks at their mapping with linguistic form, for example in the discussion of the Indo-European case system as a formal device for representing objects and factual relations of the world with symbols in a symbolic field (Bühler 1934, pp. 249ff).

The model is thus eminently suited as a theoretical basis for a function-form approach. The notion of function has played a role in many structural theories of language that ask about the acts language users perform with the formal tools. Functional theories of grammar strive to define these functions and subsequently relate them to the structural carriers. The most elementary function is the differentiation of representational meaning, in its simplest form in functional phonetics. The Prague School linguists were the first to develop functional structuralism, starting with phonology, based on the principle of the distinction of lexical meaning, rather than on the principle of complementary distribution, as in American behaviourist structuralism.

Under the influence of Bühler's *Organon Model*, Trubetzkoy (1939, pp. 17ff) complemented the phonology of the REPRESENTATION function ('Darstellungsphonologie') by phonologies of the EXPRESSION and APPEAL (conative) functions ('Ausdrucks- und Kundgabephonologie'), which he did not always find easy to separate, and which, following Prague systematising, he allocated to a new discipline, called 'sound stylistics' ('Lautstilistik'), with two subsections. He subsumed vocalic lengthening, as in 'It's **won**derful!', and initial consonant lengthening, as in 'You're a **b**astard!', under the APPEAL function, because he maintained that the speaker signals to the listener to empathise with his/her feelings. Isačenko (1966) rightly criticised this solution as unacceptable psychologising and allocated such data to the EXPRESSION function, which I do likewise. Mathesius (1966) extended the functional perspective to lexical and syntactic form (beside accentuation and intonation) for INTENSIFICATION and for INFORMATION SELECTION AND WEIGHTING. Contrary to general usage, he called the latter *emphasis*. Since this term is used with a wide array of signification I shall avoid it altogether and refer to the two functions by the above pair of terms. An INTENSIFICATION scale will be incorporated into the *Organon Model* as the EXPRESSIVE LOW-TO-HIGH KEY function (see Chapter 5).

Jakobson (1960) took up the three functions of Bühler's model as *emotive*, *conative* and *referential*, oriented towards *addresser*, *addressee* and *message referent*. He derived a *magic, incantatory* function from the triadic model as a 'conversion of an absent or inanimate "third person" into an addressee of a conative message' (p. 355). Prayer comes under this heading. And he added another three functions (pp. 355ff):

- *phatic* serving to establish, prolong or discontinue communication: 'Can you hear me?' 'Not a bad day, is it?' – 'It isn't, is it, could be a lot worse' (an exchange between two hikers meeting in the Scottish hills on a foggy, drizzly day)
- *poetic* focusing on the message for its own sake: rhythmic effects make 'Joan and Margery' sound smoother than 'Margery and Joan';

the poetic device of paronomasia selects 'horrible' instead of 'terrible' in 'I **hate horrible Harry**'

- *metalingual*, language turning back on itself: 'What is a sophomore?' – 'A sophomore means a second-year student.'

Jakobson gives the following linguistic criteria for the poetic and metalingual functions:

> We must recall the two basic modes of arrangement used in verbal behavior, *selection* and *combination* ... *The poetic function projects the principle of equivalence from the axis of selection into the axis of combination.* Equivalence is promoted to the constitutive device of the sequence. In poetry one syllable is equalised with any other syllable of the same sequence; word stress is assumed to equal word stress, as unstress equals unstress ... Syllables are converted into units of measure, and so are morae or stresses ... in metalanguage the sequence is used to build an equation, whereas in poetry the equation is used to build a sequence.

Jakobson's additional communicative functions are an extension to Bühler's theory of language, but they are not on a par with the three functions of the *Organon Model*; rather, they are functions within the domains of the sender, the receiver and the referent. The phatic function is clearly receiver-directed and constitutes one type of signalling. The metalingual function belongs to the domain of objects and factual relations, and constitutes the essence of a symbolic speech act. The poetic function is not a function in the sense of the other two, i.e. of communicative action between a sender and a receiver. It is a device characterising a speech act or a language work. As such, it may have an aesthetic function to give sensuous pleasure, or a GUIDE function to increase intelligibility, or a rhetorical function to persuade, as in advertising, in all cases in the domain of the receiver. In the example of paronomasia given above, the poetic device has a speaker-focused EXPRESSION function, which it may also have in reciting lyrical poetry.

Garvin (1994, p. 64), in discussing Charles Morris's three branches of semiotics – syntactics, semantics, pragmatics – notes:

> In Bühler's field theory ... variants [of structural linguistic units] can be interpreted in terms of the field-derived properties of the units in question. In the Morrisian schema, I do not seem to be able to find a real place for this issue ... None of this, of course, means that I object to 'pragmatics' as a label of convenience for the discussion of certain of the phenomena that, as I have repeatedly asserted, Bühler's field theory handles more adequately, I only object to giving theoretical significance as a separate 'level' or 'component' ... the foundation of Bühler's theory is the ... Gestalt-psychological notion

of the figure–ground relation. Morris's foundations, on the other hand, are admittedly behaviorist ... There is no doubt about my preference for the Gestaltist position ... It is interesting to note that many of the linguists who have arrived at a total rejection of the behaviorist bases of descriptivist linguistics nevertheless have come to use the Morrisian schema, at least to the extent of accepting a pragmatics component for explaining certain phenomena.

In full agreement with Garvin's dictum, I also follow Bühler's theory of language. Building the theory, and the empirical analysis, of language on the *Organon Model* can immediately dispense with all the subdivisions of the field of speech science into separate disciplines, phonology versus phonetics, phonology versus sound stylistics, linguistics versus paralinguistics, pragmatics versus syntax and semantics, and relate units and structures across all linguistic levels of analysis to axiomatically postulated functions in speech communication – functions in the domains of Sender, Receiver and Referent, such as QUESTION, COMMAND, REQUEST, INFORMATION SELECTION AND WEIGHTING, INTENSIFICATION. In moving from these functions to the linguistic signs in their deictic and symbolic fields, speech science can capture all the formal phonetic, phonological and linguistic aspects related to them.

1.3.2   Halliday's Functional Systemic Linguistics

A few words need to be said about another, more recent functional framework that is also rooted in the European linguistic tradition, more particularly J. R. Firth's enquiry into systems of meaning (Firth 1957): Michael Halliday's *Systemic Functional Linguistics* (SFL) (Hasan 2009). It is conceived as systemic with reference to paradigmatic choices in language, and also as functional with regard to specific functions that these formal systems are to serve in communication. These functions are called metafunctions, comprising the *ideational* function (*experiential* and *logical*), the *interpersonal* function and the *textual* function. There are correspondences between Halliday's and Bühler's functions but also fundamental differences. Standing in the European tradition, Halliday and Hasan know Bühler's *Theory of Language*, but they do not always represent it correctly. Hasan (2009, p. 19) says:

> Bühler thought of functions as operating one at a time; further, his functions were hierarchically ordered, with the referential as the most important. The metafunctions in SFL are not hierarchised; they have equal status, and each is manifested in every act of language use: in fact, an important task for grammatics is to describe how the three metafunctions are woven together into the same linguistic unit.

The concept of 'function', when used in SFL with reference to the system of language as a whole, is critically different from the concept of 'function', as applied to a speech act such as promising, ordering, etc., or as applied to isolated utterances à la Bühler (1934) for the classification of children's utterances as referential, conative or expressive. SFL uses the term 'metafunction', to distinguish functions of langue system from the 'function' of an utterance.

As regards the first quotation, the discussion in this chapter will have made it clear that Bühler's three functions in the *Organon Model* do not operate one at a time, and they are not hierarchically ordered. His linguistic sign has the three functions of EXPRESSION, APPEAL and REPRESENTATION at any given moment, but depending on the type of communicative action their relative weighting changes. In the *Theory of Language*, he puts particular emphasis on the representational function, because this is the area linguistics had been dealing with predominantly during the nineteenth century and up to his time, and he felt a few principles that were generally applied needed to be put right.

The second quotation shows the reason for the misunderstanding. The fundamental difference between the two models is not that Halliday takes a global view of the system of language and Bühler refers to speech actions in isolated utterances. The difference is between a descriptive product model of language in SFL (Bühler's *Sprachwerk*), and a communicative process model of speech actions, which looks at communicative functions between speakers and listeners in speech interaction (Bühler's *Sprechhandlungen*). It is the difference between the linguist's versus the psychologist's view of speech and language. Halliday asks 'How does language work?', whereas Bühler asks 'How do speakers and listeners communicate about the world with linguistic signs in deictic and symbolic fields?' The *Organon Model* is system-oriented, not restricted to utterances, although the functions surface in utterance signals. Halliday's *interpersonal* function is part of all three *Organon* functions: social aspects of the speaker's expression, of attitudes and appeals to the listener, and of representation of the factual world. For Bühler, social relationships determine the communicative interaction between speakers and listeners about referents, i.e. they shape the three functions of the linguistic sign. For Halliday and Hasan, the interpersonal metalevel is a function at a linguistic level, the level of sociolinguistics. The two models are thus complementary perspectives; for a phonetician the process model is particularly attractive because it allows the modelling of speech communication in human interaction.

1.3.3   Discourse Representation Theory

More recent language theories have sprung up from logical semantics incorporating context dependence into the study of meaning. A prominent representative of this dynamic semantics is *Discourse Representation Theory* (DRT), developed by Kamp and co-workers (Kamp and Reyle 1993) over the past two decades. Utterances are regarded as interpretable only when the interpreter takes account of the contexts in which they are made, and the interaction between context and utterance is considered reciprocal. 'Each utterance contributes (via the interpretation which it is given) to the context in which it is made. It modifies the context into a new context, in which this contribution is reflected; and it is this new context which then informs the interpretation of whatever utterance comes next' (p. 4). This has resulted in moving away from the classical conception of formal semantics and replacing its central concept of truth by one of information: 'the meaning of a sentence is not its truth conditions but its "information change potential" – its capacity for modifying given contexts or information states into new ones' (Kamp, Genabith and Reyle 2011, p. 4). Anaphoric pronouns referring back to something that was introduced previously in the discourse are the most familiar and certainly the most thoroughly investigated kind of context dependence within this framework.

At first sight, this paradigm looks very similar to Bühler's, and, as its proponents and followers would maintain, is far superior because it is formalised, thus testable, and eminently suited to be applied to the automatic analysis of appropriately tagged corpora. But closer inspection reveals that the two are not compatible. DRT talks about utterances in context but means sentences in textual linguistic environments. However, it is *speech actions* that occur in everyday communication, and they occur not only in synsemantic contexts but, first and foremost, in contexts of situation in sympractical fields. Moreover, not all actions subserve information transmission, because there is *phatic communion* (Jakobson 1960; Malinowski 1923), and appeal to the receiver as well as expression of the sender, where referential meaning is subordinate to social and emotive interaction. DRT would need new categories and a change of perspective, going beyond information structure in texts, to provide explanations for exchanges by speech and gesture, such as the ones experienced on a Kiel bus or in a Scottish pub (cf. Introduction and 1.2.1.3). Here is another set of possible speech actions that illustrate the great communicative variety beyond information exchange in synsemantic text fields:

> I am about to leave the house to go to work, putting on my coat in the hall. My wife is in the adjoining open-plan sitting-room. She briefly looks out of the window and calls to me 'It's raining', with a downstepping level pitch pattern

on 'raining' (see 4.1), to draw my attention to the need to take protection against the weather. I thank her for warning me, grab my umbrella, say 'See you tonight' and leave.

After I have gone, she calls her sister in Edinburgh, and, following their exchanges of greetings, she goes on to talk about the weather, inevitable in British conversation, and asks, 'What's your weather like?', not because she wants to get meteorological information but as an interactional opening. She gets the answer 'It's raining', with a continuous, low falling pitch pattern across the utterance, suggesting 'What else do you expect?' This is followed by a reference to the Kiel weather and then by an appraisal that the recent terrible flooding in the North of England was much worse, so there is really no reason to complain. After this ritual, the two sisters exchange information about family and friends for another half hour, the goal of the telephone call.

After coming off the phone, she switches the radio on to get the 11 a.m. regional news. At the end, the weather forecast reports 'In Kiel regnet es heute' [It is raining in Kiel today]. This is now factual weather information, located in place and time, intended for an anonymous public, therefore removed from interaction between communicators, and since the individual recipient had looked out of the window, the speech action has no informative impact on her.

Each of these communicative interchanges serves a different, but very useful, communicative goal, with different values attributed to the information conveyed. DRT cannot model this diversity because the differently valued types of information are not simply the result of an incremental development of meaning evolving in linguistic contexts but depend on talk in interaction between communicators in contexts of situation. This fact is addressed by Ginzburg (2012) in the *Interactive Stance Model* (ISM).

1.3.4 Ginzburg's Interactive Stance Model

This is a theory of meaning in interaction that, on the one hand, is based on the DRT notion of dynamic semantics and, on the other, incorporates two concepts from Conversation Analysis (Schegloff, Jefferson and Sacks 1977) and from psycholinguistics (Clark 1996): *repair* and *grounding* of content in the communicators' common ground through interaction in contexts. Ginzburg defines the goal of his semantic theory as 'to characterize for any utterance type the contextual update that emerges in the aftermath of successful exchange and the range of possible clarification requests otherwise. This is, arguably, the early twenty-first-century analogue of truth conditions' (Ginzburg 2012, p. 8). This means that an adequate semantic theory must model imperfect communication just as much as successful communication. Besides giving meaning to indexicals 'I', 'you', 'here', 'there', 'now' through linguistic context in dynamic semantics, non-sentential units, such as 'yes', 'what?', 'where?', 'why?' etc., and repeated fragments of preceding utterances must receive their meanings through the interactive stance in contexts of situation. These are ideas that have been proposed, in a non-formalised way, by Bühler (1934) and Gardiner (1932), as well as by Firth (1957) and his followers in Britain to this day, e.g. John Local and Richard Ogden. None of this literature is cited, no doubt because it is considered outdated and surpassed by more testable and scientific models. However, careful study of the ideas of both camps reaches the opposite conclusion.

Ginzburg's theoretical proposition is that 'grammar and interaction are intrinsically bound' and that 'the right way to construe *grammar* is as a system that characterizes types of talk in interaction' (Ginzburg (2012), p. 349). The pivotal category in this interaction is *gameboards*, one for each participant, which make communicators keep track of unresolved issues in *questions under discussion* and allow for imperfect communication through mismatches. The corollary of the notion of the personal gameboard is that participants may not have equal access to the common ground, and contextual options available to one may be distinct from those available to the other(s). Ginzburg illustrates this with a constructed example of dialogue interaction under what he terms the Turn-Taking Puzzle (p. 23).

a.   A: Which members of this audience own a parakeet? Why?
                 (= Why own a parakeet?)
b.   A: Which members of this audience own a parakeet?
            B: Why? (= Why are you asking which members of this audience
                 own a parakeet?)
c.   A: Which members of this audience own a parakeet? Why am I
                 asking this question?

He explains the different meanings accorded to 'why' in the three contexts by referring them to who keeps, or takes over, the turn. 'The resolution that can be associated with "Why?" if A keeps the turn is unavailable to B were s/he to have taken over, and vice versa. c. shows that these facts cannot be reduced to coherence or plausibility – the resolution unavailable to A in a. yields a coherent follow-up to A's initial query if it is expressed by means of a non-elliptic form.'

These constructed dialogues are problematic, because they lack a sufficiently specified context of situation and violate rules of behavioural interaction beyond speech, and their interpretation by reference to turn-taking is flawed. The reference to 'members of *this audience*' in a book on the Interactive Stance indicates that the speaker must be contextualised as addressing, and interacting with, a group attending a talk, not as establishing contact for interaction with one or several individuals. Thus B, who is an individual that has not been addressed individually, will not call out from among the audience with non-sentential 'Why?' to ask why the speaker addressed the group with that question. There are three possible reactions from the audience. (1) There is a show of hands by those members who have a parakeet. (2) There is no gestural or vocal response, because nobody in the audience has a parakeet. (3) There may be a call from an obstreperous young attendee, something like 'What the heck are you asking that for? Get on with your subject.' Just as A did not establish interaction with individual members of the audience, speaker B in (3), in turn, does not intend to interact with A, but opposes interaction by refusing to answer A's question.

In response to the reactions, or the lack of a reaction, from the audience, A may continue with 'Why am I asking this question?' (in (2) after pausing for a couple of seconds). In all these cases, A starts a new turn, after a gestural turn from the audience in (1), after a speech turn from an individual member in (3) and after registering absence of a response in (2). A produces an *interrogative* form that is no longer a QUESTION because it lacks the APPEAL to somebody else to answer A's question. It actualises the content of a potential question that the members of the audience may have asked in (1), and particularly in (2), and did ask in (3). This is a QUESTION QUOTE (see 4.2.2.7). Since it is not a QUESTION APPEAL it cannot be reduced to the bare *lexical interrogative*, which presupposes the APPEAL function, and it has falling intonation. In German, the QUESTION QUOTE would be realised by *dependent-clause syntax* '(Sie mögen sich fragen) Warum ich diese Frage stelle?', instead of the *interrogative syntax* 'Warum stelle ich diese Frage?' The latter (as well as its English syntactic equivalent) has two communicative meanings: (a) A appeals to receivers to give an answer why they think A asks the question; (b) it is the speaker's exclamatory expression 'Why on earth am I asking this? (It does not get me anywhere!)' With meaning (b), the interrogative form does not code a question either, since A does not appeal reflexively to A to give an answer to a proposition A is querying. In traditional terminology it would be called a rhetorical question, but in terms of communicative function it is a speaker-centred EXPRESSION rather than a listener-directed APPEAL. Neither (a) nor (b) seem to have a behavioural likelihood in the interaction with an audience. Ginzburg's sequencing of INFORMATION QUESTION and QUESTION QUOTE in one turn in c. may therefore be considered an ill-formed representation of behavioural interaction. Before giving a QUESTION QUOTE to the audience, A must have assessed their reaction to the INFORMATION QUESTION A put to them.

There is a third possibility (c) of contextualising the German and English interrogative forms 'Warum stelle ich diese Frage?' and 'Why am I asking this question?' Here is a possible lecture context (let's assume A is male):

d.　　　A:　I would like to raise a question at the outset of my talk: 'How many of this audience keep parakeets at home?' Why am I asking this question? Well, let me explain. I would like to share experiences of parakeets' talking behaviour with you in the discussion after my talk. So, could I have a show of hands, please. 'Which of you have a parakeet?'

This constructed opening of a lecture illustrates the lecturer's ambivalent function of *reporter to* an audience and *communicator with* an audience. His main function is to report subject matter. In his role as a reporter, the lecturer may raise questions in connection with the topic of the talk, appealing to virtual recipients to give answers. In this reporting role, the lecturer does not enter into interaction with communicators in a real context of situation. He creates a virtual question–answer field in which he enacts interaction between virtual senders and receivers whom he brings to life through his mouth. He treats the audience as external observers of the reporter's question–answer field. This is *question–answer phantasma*, in an extension of Bühler's notion of *Deixis am Phantasma* (see the Introduction and Bühler 1934, pp. 121ff). The lecturer's second function is to enter into an interaction with the audience.

In d., lecturer A is first a reporter, then a communicator. A reports two questions for which virtual receivers are to provide answers in the lecture. The second question is immediately answered by the reporter. These questions differ from the question-in-interaction at the end by being non-interactive. The second question can be a virtual INFORMATION QUESTION with falling intonation, where the reporter enacts the sender and, at the same time, the receiver to give the answer. It may also be a virtual CONFIRMATION QUESTION, with high-rising intonation starting on 'why' (see 4.2.2.4), where the reporter enacts a virtual sender who reflects on his reasons for having asked, and a virtual receiver who is to confirm the reasons in the answer: 'Why am I asking this question really?' Ginzburg's interactive stance excludes both these questions from his context c., but he obviously explains c. in the non-interactive way of d. This problem must have been realised by the reviewer of Ginzburg (2012), Eleni Gregoromichelaki (2013), because she replaced 'this audience' by 'our team' in her discussion of Ginzburg's 'parakeet' example, which is now a question to individual communicators.

Ginzburg's sequencing of a general 'who?' and a more specific follow-up 'why?' INFORMATION QUESTION in one turn of a. is also a behaviourally

ill-formed representation. There must be some response to the first INFORMA-
TION QUESTION before the second one is asked in a new turn. Moreover, if the
first question is put to an audience, A needs to select an individual B, or several
individuals in succession, for an answer to the second question, because it can
no longer be gestural but must be vocal. There is the possibility of a double
question, 'Do you own a parakeet and why?', in the opening turn of an interaction with an individual.

Taking all these points together, there is no compelling reason to associate the
attribution of different meanings to non-sentential 'why?' with turn-holding or
turn-taking. Ginzburg's explication of this change of meaning in an interaction,
with reference to different options available to communicators in their respective
turns, is not convincing. He does not provide a sufficiently specified interactional setting, does not distinguish between interactions with a group and with an
individual, and fails to differentiate QUESTION function and *interrogative* form.
Furthermore, he does not acknowledge the occurrence of gestural beside vocal
turns, nor of two successive turns by the same speaker, only separated by a pause
for the assessment of the interactive point that has been reached. And, *last but
not least*, he discusses questions as if they are removed from interaction in spite
of their contextualisations. His concept of *interaction* does not model speech
action in communicative contexts in human behaviour but is derived *post festum*
from formal relations in written text, or spoken discourse that has been reduced
to writing, or in constructed dialogues dissociated from interaction.

Now let us give Ginzburg's interaction scenario a more precise definition
and develop the meanings of the two non-sentential 'why?'s in it.

> [General context of situation
> A famous member of the International Phonetic Association (P) is giving
> an invited talk to the Royal Zoological Society of Scotland on the subject
> 'Talking parakeets'. After the introduction by the host and giving thanks for
> the invitation, P opens his talk.]
>
> a. P(1): I suppose quite a few, if not all, of you have a parakeet at home.
>   P(2): [points to an elderly lady in the front row] What about you,
>   madam? Do you keep one?
>   S(1): I do. [may be accompanied, or replaced, by nodding]
>   Why?
>   P(3): Why am I asking you this question. Well, let me explain. I am
>   interested in how owners of parakeets communicate with their
>   pets.
> b. [same precursor as in a., then:]
>   S(1): I do.
>   P(3): Why?
>   S(2): Why? Well, because it keeps me company.

In a., P(2) asks a POLARITY QUESTION (see 4.2.2.2) whether the elderly lady keeps a parakeet in her home, most probably with a falling intonation because the speaker prejudges the answer 'yes'. S(1) answers in the affirmative and asks an INFORMATION QUESTION (see 4.2.2.3), appealing to P to tell her why he asked her. To establish rapport with P, S will use low-rising intonation in both her STATEMENT and her QUESTION. P(3) quotes the content of S's question (see 4.2.2.6), putting it in interrogative form to himself, as a theme for his rheme explanation of his original POLARITY QUESTION. Since the utterance is a factual report, lacking an appeal, the intonation falls. (In German it would be 'Warum ich Ihnen diese Frage stelle', again with falling intonation.) In b., P's POLARITY QUESTION is answered in the affirmative by S, as in a. This is followed by P asking a follow-up INFORMATION QUESTION about the lady's reasons for keeping a parakeet. The intonation may fall or rise, depending on whether P simply asks a factual question or, additionally, establishes rapport with S. This is, in turn, followed by S's CONFIRMATION QUESTION 'Are you asking me why?', with high-rising intonation on the *lexical interrogative* (see 4.2.2.4), in turn followed by her answer.

These examples illustrate communicative steps in a question–answer interaction field, made up of *declarative* and *interrogative* syntactic structures with varying intonation patterns as carriers of STATEMENTS and different types of QUESTION. Different functionally defined question types are bound to the semantic points reached at each step in the interaction and are not exchangeable without changing the semantic context. The crucial issue is that an *interrogative* form does not receive different meanings in different contexts of situation in interaction, as Ginzburg maintains. Rather, the transmission of meaning at different points in interaction necessitates functionally different QUESTIONS, which may be manifested by identical *interrogative* structure. This is the function-form approach proposed in this monograph, which also incorporates an important prosodic component to differentiate between lexically and syntactically identical utterances. Ginzburg's semantic modelling takes an infelicitous turn in three steps:

- He does not recognise *question function* beside *interrogative form*.
- He is forced to locate semantic differentiators in interaction contexts when syntactically identical interrogatives (disregarding utterance prosody), such as 'why', occur with different meanings, and he then incorporates the contexts into the grammar.
- He finally refers the semantic differences of these utterances to their turn-holding or turn-taking positions in dialogue.

The reason Ginzburg tries to resolve the semantic indeterminacy of formal grammar by incorporating context of interaction in it lies in the development of semantics in linguistic theory. The formal component of American Structuralism, as systematised by Zellig Harris (1951, 1960), became the morphosyntactic core of his pupil Noam Chomsky's Generative Grammar (1957, 1965), with a semantic and a phonological interpretive level attached at either end of the generative rule system. Within this generative framework, semantics gradually assumed an independent status, which culminated in DRT. With growing interest in spontaneous speech, the meaning of interaction elements that go beyond *linguistic* context variables had to be taken into account. This led to the inclusion of *situational* context in formal grammar, which became Ginzburg's research goal. It continues the preoccupation with form since the days of structuralism, now with an ever-increasing concern for meaning.

1.3.5   Developing a Model of Speech Communication
To really become an advanced semantic theory of the twenty-first century, the relationship between grammar and interaction would need to be reversed, with a form-in-function approach replacing interaction-in-grammar by grammar-in-interaction. Empirical research within a theory of speech communication can offer greater insight into the use of speech and language than systematising linguistic forms in discourse contexts with grammar-based formalisms. It is a task for the social sciences, including linguistics, to develop a comprehensive Theory of Human Interaction, which contains a sub-theory of Speech Communication, which in turn contains a Grammar of Human Language and Grammars of Languages. Herbert Clark has taken a big step towards this goal by advocating that:

> We must take ... an *action approach* to language use, which has distinct advantages over the more traditional *product approach* ... Language use arises in joint activities ... you take the joint activity to be primary, and the language ... used along the way to be secondary, a means to an end. To account for the language used, we need to understand the joint activities [for which a framework of interactional categories is proposed]. (Clark 1996, p. 29)

Influenced by the Language Philosophers Grice (1957), Austin (1962) and Searle (1969), he expanded their theory of meaning in action, *speech acts*, to a theory of meaning in joint activities and joint actions, which accords the listener an equally important role, beside the speaker, in establishing communicative meaning: 'There can be no communication without listeners taking actions too – without them understanding what speakers mean' (Clark 1996, p. 138). However, Clark is first and foremost concerned with *language$_u$*, the 'language' of language use, which he contrasts with *language_s*, the traditional conceptualisation of 'language' as language structure (p. 392). What we need is the incorporation of *language_s* into the theory of speech communication, including the AAA and GOV channels, and a powerful model of fine-graded prosodic systems and structures to signal communicative functions in *language_u*.

Since speech and language are anchored in the wider field of human inter-action, a communicative approach is the basis of a successful interdisciplinary linguistic science. The seminal thoughts that the psychologist Karl Bühler pub-lished on this topic eighty years ago are in no way outdated and inferior to more recent attempts at formalising interaction contexts in grammar. On the contrary, the product approaches of SFL, DRT and ISM, in the tradition of structural linguistics, deal with the formal results of interaction and lose sight of the functions controlling interaction processes, a distinction Bühler captured with *Sprachwerk* [*language work*] versus *Sprechhandlung* [*speech action*]. Since Bühler's theory is little known in the linguistic world, especially among an Anglophone readership, this chapter has given an overview of its main com-ponents, to bring them back into the arena of theoretical discussion in formal linguistics and measurement-driven phonetics. I shall pick up Bühler's threads in the following chapters to weave a tapestry of speech communication, and elaborate Bühler's model to a *function* network in human speech interaction to which communicative *form* across AAA and GVO channels will be relat-ed. More particularly, I shall provide subcategorisations of the functions of REPRESENTATION, APPEAL and EXPRESSION in Chapters 3, 4 and 5, and inte-grate prosody, the prime formal exponent of APPEAL and EXPRESSION, into the functional framework of the *Organon Model*. In adding the prosodic level to the analysis of speech interaction, which is largely missing from the formalised context-in-grammar accounts of DRT and ISM, I shall be relying on insights from extensive research on communicative phonetics carried out at Kiel Uni-versity over the past thirty years.

The communicative model starts from speech functions and integrates with them the production and perception of paradigmatic systems and syntagmatic structures in morpho-syntax, sounds and prosodies. Thus, the functional cat-egories of STATEMENT or QUESTION or COMMAND/REQUEST are separated conceptually and notationally from the syntactic structures of *declarative* or *interrogative* or *imperative*, with distinctive prosodic patterns coding fur-ther functional subcategorisations. In German and English, various syntac-tic structures can be used, with different connotations, of course, to code a COMMAND or a REQUEST:

imperative
with falling intonation for a COMMAND or rising intonation for a REQUEST
Mach (bitte) das Fenster zu!   Shut the window (please)!

interrogative
with falling intonation and reinforced accents for a COMMAND
Machst du endlich das Fenster zu!   Are you going to shut the window!
with rising intonation and default accents for a REQUEST
Würdest du bitte das Fenster   Would you like to shut the window!
zumachen!

declarative
with falling intonation and reinforced accentuation for a COMMAND
Du hast die Tür offen gelassen!   You have left the door open!
Du hast vergessen, die Tür   You forgot to shut the door!
zuzumachen!
Du machst jetzt das Fenster zu!   You are going to shut the window
                                      at once!

Or a QUESTION

interrogative
for a POLARITY QUESTION
Ist er nach Rom gefahren?   Has he gone to Rome?

declarative
with rising intonation or in high register for a CONFIRMATION QUESTION
Er ist nach Rom gefahren?   He's gone to Rome?

Furthermore, within STATEMENT or QUESTION or COMMAND/REQUEST, functional relations between semantic constituents are manifested by syntactic structures between formal elements. Both are enclosed in < >, the former in small capitals, the latter in italics (for some of the notional terminology, see Lyons 1968, pp. 340ff):

<ACTION/OCCURRENCE> <AGENT> <GOAL> <RECIPIENT> <TIME> <PLACE> <MANNER>
<verb> <subject> <direct object> <indirect object> <adverbial or prepositional phrases>

In the *active* versus *passive* constructions of Indo-European languages, <AGENT> is coded by *<subject>* and *<prepositional phrase>*, <GOAL> by *<object>* and *<subject>*, respectively.

<AGENT *subject* > <ACTION *verb*>   <GOAL *dir object*>
<Die Nachbarn>   <verprügelten>   <den Einbrecher>.
<The neighbours>   <beat up>   <the burglar>.

<GOAL *subject*>   <ACTION *verb infl*> <AGENT *prepos phrase*> <ACTION *verb uninfl*>
<Der Einbrecher>   <wurde>   <von den Nachbarn>   <verprügelt>.
<The burglar>   <was beaten up>   <by the neighbours>.

The <Action>, coded by the unitary <*verb*> 'verprügelten' or 'beat up', may be divided into the semantic dyad <Action> <Goal> coded by the <*verb*> <*direct object*> phrase 'verpassten eine gehörige Tracht Prügel' or 'gave a good beating', making 'Einbrecher' or 'burglar' the <Recipient *indirect object* > of <Action> <Goal>. *Active* can again be turned into *passive*.

<Agent *subject*>	<Action *verb*>	<Recipient *indir object*>	<Goal *dir object*>
<Die Nachbarn>	<verpassten>	<dem Einbrecher>	<eine Tracht Prügel>.
<The neighbours>	<gave>	<the burglar>	<a good beating>.

<Recipient *indir object*>	<Action *verb infl*>	<Agent *prepos phrase*>
<Dem Einbrecher>	<wurde>	<von den Nachbarn>
<Goal *subject*>	<Action *verb uninfl*>	
<eine Tracht Prügel>	<verpasst>.	
<Recipient *subject*>	<Action *verb*> <Goal *object*>	<Agent *prepos phrase*>
<The burglar>	<was given> <a good beating>	<by the neighbours>.

Finally, the passive patient construction may be lexical:

<Recipient *subject* ><Action *verb*><Agent *prepos phrase*>	<Goal *object*>
<Der Einbrecher> <erhielt> <von den Nachbarn>	<eine Tracht Prügel>
<Recipient *subject*> <Action *verb*><Goal *object*>	<Agent *prepos phrase*>
<The burglar> <got> <a good beating>	<from the neighbours>.

Another type of proposition centres on an <Event>, for instance meteorological events:

<Event>	<Time>/<Place>	<Place>/<Time>
<Es regnet/schneit>	<heute>	<in Paris>.
<It's raining/snowing>	<in Paris>	<today>.

In these cases, both the event and its occurrence are coded syntactically by the impersonal verb construction. But, more generally, the two semantic components are separated in syntactic structure, for instance as <*subject*> and <*verb*>, and German and English may go different ways, for example in:

Zur Zeit ist über Paris ein Unwetter.
<Event Occurrence>
<Es stürmt, hagelt, blitzt und donnert>

There is a heavy thunderstorm over Paris right now.
<Occurrence >   <Event>
<There are>   <gale-force winds, hail, thunder and lightning>

Before I move on, let me add a word of clarification concerning the difference, and the relationship, between communicative theory and linguistic discovery procedures. It is a well-established, very useful goal in linguistics to work out the systems and structures of distinctive phonetic sound units that are used to distinguish words in a language, including lexical tone, lexical stress and phonation type in tone, lexical stress and lexical voice quality languages. It is mandatory to base this investigation on the word removed from communicative context in interaction. There is an equally established and useful procedure to work out the morpho-syntactic elements and structures, as well as the accent and intonation patterns that carry distinctive sentential meaning. This puts the sentence removed from communicative context in focus. In the initial analysis stages of an unknown, hitherto uninvestigated language, these phonological and syntactic discovery procedures produce context-free word and sentence representations, which will have to be adjusted as the investigation continues and more and more context is introduced in a series of procedural steps. But it will not be possible to base the phonetic or syntactic analysis on talk in interaction for a long time yet. The procedural product approach makes it possible to reduce a language to writing, and to compile grammars, as well as dictionaries, that link graphemic, phonetic and semantic information for speakers and learners of the language to consult for text writing and speaking. The product approach to language forms also provides useful procedural tools for language and dialect comparison, dialect geography, language typology and historical linguistics.

But the situation changes when languages have been investigated for a very long time, such as English, German, French, Spanish, Arabic, Hindi, Japanese and Mandarin Chinese. When sound representations of words and structural representations of words in sentences have been put in systematic descriptive linguistic formats in such languages, linguistic pursuits may proceed in two different ways.

(1)   The formal representations may acquire a purpose in themselves and assume the status of the 'real' thing they are supposed to map. Then proponents of another linguistic paradigm may recycle the same data in a different format of their own, suggesting that it increases the explanatory power for the 'real' thing. So, we experience recycling of the same data from Structural Linguistics to Generative Grammar to Government and Binding, to Head-driven Phrase Structure Grammar to Role and Representation Grammar, and so on. An example from phonology is the treatment of Turkish vowel harmony in the frameworks of structural phonemics, generative phonology and Firthian prosodic analysis (Lees 1961; Voegelin and Ellinghausen 1943; Waterson 1956). The contribution of such *l'art pour l'art* linguistics to

the understanding of speech communication in human interaction is limited.

(2)   On the other hand, it may be considered timely to renew theoretical reflection on how speakers and listeners interact with each other, using language beside other communicative means in contexts of situation. The forms obtained through a linguistic product approach will now be studied as manifestations of communicative functions in interactive language use. SFL, DRT and ISM are no longer discovery procedures, but theoretical models. They stop short, however, of reaching the dynamic level of speech interaction because they are still product-oriented and incorporate interaction context statically into structural representation.

Future research will benefit from advancing models of speech communication in interaction for at least some of the well-studied languages of the world. This monograph is an attempt in this direction, focusing primarily on German and English, but additionally including other languages in the discussion of selected communicative aspects. The results of this action approach can, in turn, be fed back into the product approach of language description and comparison. For example, in traditional language descriptions interrogative structures are compared between languages with regard to some vague 'question' concept. In the action approach, different types of question are postulated as different APPEAL functions in human interaction, and the *interrogative* forms found in different languages are related to these functions. This will have a great effect on making language teaching and language learning, based on linguistic descriptions of languages, more efficient.

Since, in addition to the syntactic structures, prosody is another central formal device in this functional framework, a prosodic model needs to be selected that guarantees observational and explanatory adequacy for the communicative perspective. This goal can best be achieved when the choice follows from a critical comparative overview of the most influential descriptive paradigms that have been proposed in the past. Therefore, the remaining section of this chapter provides such an historical survey to prepare the exposition, in Chapter 2, of the prosodic model adopted for integration in the *Organon Model*.

1.4   Descriptive Modelling of Prosody – An Overview of Paradigms

The study of prosody has concentrated on intonation and, with few exceptions, such as Bolinger's work (1978, 1986), has focused on the formal elements and structures of auditory pitch of acoustic F0 patterns. Questions of meaning and the function of these patterns were raised *post hoc*, above all in relation to syntactic structures, sentence mode, phrasing and focus. Two influential paradigms in the study of prosody, the British and the American approach, are briefly discussed here, as a basis for the exposition of the Kiel Intonation Model (KIM), the former because KIM is an offspring of it, the latter in order to show and explain the divergence of KIM from present-day mainstream prosody research. Examples will, in each case, be presented in original notations, as well as in KIM/PROLAB symbolisations (cf. the list at the end of the Introduction), for cross-reference.

1.4.1   The Study of Intonation in the London School of Phonetics
Descriptions of intonation by the London School of Phonetics (Allen 1954; Armstrong and Ward 1931; Cruttenden 1974, 1986 (2nd edn 1997); Jones 1956; Kingdon 1958; Lee 1956; O'Connor and Arnold 1961; Palmer 1924; Palmer and Blandford 1939; Schubiger 1958; Wells 2006) relied on auditory observation and introspection for practical application in teaching English as a foreign language. Armstrong and Ward (1931) and Jones (1956) set up two basic tunes for English, imposed on stress patterns and represented by dots and dashes and curves: Tune I falling, associated with statements, commands and *wh* questions, Tune II rising, associated with requests and word-order questions. Modifications of these generate falling-rising and rising-falling, as well as pitch-expanded and compressed, patterns, signalling emphasis for contrast and intensity.

Palmer, Kingdon, and O'Connor and Arnold elaborated this basic two-tune concept by differentiating tunes according to falling, low-rising, high-rising, falling-rising and rising-falling patterns. Palmer introduced tonetic marks in orthographic text to represent the significant points of a tune, rather than marking every syllable. This was a move towards a phonological assessment of prosodic substance. The tune was also divided into syntagmatic constituents. O'Connor and Arnold's practical introduction became the standard textbook of Standard Southern British English intonation, proposing a division of tunes, now called tone groups, first into nucleus and prenucleus, then into nuclear tune and tail, and into head and prehead, respectively. These structural parts, with their paradigmatic elements, are combined into ten Tone Groups, five with falling, five with rising tunes at the nucleus. The intonation patterns are, in turn, related to four grammatical structures – statements, questions, commands and interjections. These are formal syntactic structures: declarative syntax, lexical interrogative (called special questions), word-order interrogative syntax (called general questions), imperative syntax and interjectional ellipsis. High-rising nuclear tunes in declarative syntax ('You like him?') are discussed under the formal heading of statements, though referred to as 'questions' in a functional sense. Similarly, low-falling nuclear tunes in word-order question syntax ('Will you be quiet!', 'Stand still, will you!', with a high head, or 'Aren't you lucky!', with a low head) are discussed under the formal category of 'general questions', though referred to as 'commands' or 'exclamations' in a functional sense. This highlights the formal point of departure of intonation analysis. However, the formal description is followed by a discussion of fine shades of meaning carried by the ten tone groups in their four syntactic environments. This discussion is couched in descriptive ordinary-language word labels (e.g. 'Tone Group 2 is used to give a *categorical, considered, weighty, judicial, dispassionate* character to statements'), not in terms of a semantic theory of speech functions. The result is a mix of the formal elements and structures of intonation and syntax in English with *ad hoc* semantic interpretations. The descriptive semantic additions include attitudinal and expressive meaning over and above the meaning of syntax-dependent sentence modes, i.e. they are treated inside linguistics, not relegated to paralinguistics.

The phoneticians of the London School were excellent observers, with well-trained analytic ears. Although they did not have the concept of *alignment* of pitch accents with stressed syllables, and did not separate *edge tones* from *pitch accents*, central premises in AM Phonology, they described the auditory differences in minute, accurate detail. What AM Phonology later categorised as H+L*, H* or L+H*, L*+H pitch accents, combined with L-L% edge tones, are separate unitary pitch contours in the taxonomic system of the London School: low fall, high fall, rise-fall. AM/ToBI H* and L+H*/L*+H, combined with L-H%, are fall-rise and rise-fall-rise. Ladd (1996, p. 44f, 122f, 291 n.6, 132ff) accepts this contour approach as observationally adequate but does not consider it descriptively adequate, because it does not separate edge tones from pitch accents and does not associate the latter with stresses in various alignments.

In Ladd's view, a lack of insight into prosodic structures is most obvious in the way the London School phoneticians treat (rise-)fall-rises in British English. He argues that a rise-fall-rise pattern is compressed into a monosyllabic utterance, but is not spread out across syllables following a stressed syllable. In this case, the fall occurs on the nuclear syllable, the rise at the end of the utterance, with syllables on low pitch in between. To illustrate this he gives the example:

i.   A: I hear Sue's taking a course to become a driving instructor.
      (a)   B: Sue!? [L*HL-H%].
                    PROLAB: **2**(Sue **&.**, **&PG**

                    A [L*+H] driving instructor [L-H%]!?
                    PROLAB: A **2**(driving instructor **&.**, **&PG**

The low tone of the combined pitch accent L*+H is associated with the stressed syllable of 'driving', the trailing high tone with this stressed and the following unstressed syllable. The low tone of the phrase accent L- is associated with the second syllable of 'driving' and the first two syllables of 'instructor', creating a long low stretch, and the high tone of the boundary tone H% is linked to the final syllable. This shows, according to Ladd, that the edge tones L-H% must be separated from the pitch accent in both cases, although they form an observable complex pitch contour on the monosyllable. The analysis with AM categories and ToBI symbols leaves out an important aspect of the actual realisation, which can be derived from this phonological representation in combination with the impressionistic pitch curve that Ladd provides. The final-syllable pitch rise after a stretch of low pitch gives the stressed syllable of 'instructor' extra prominence, partially accenting the word. The pitch pattern is thus turned into a rise-fall on main-accent 'driving', followed by a rise on partially accented 'instructor'.

i.   (b)   B: *PROLAB:* A **2**(dr'iving **&2.** **&1**[instr'uctor **&**, **&PG**

This is no longer the same pattern as the rise-fall-rise on the monosyllabic utterance, and would not convey the same intended meaning. Therefore, Ladd's line of argument is no proof of a need to separate edge tones from pitch accents in intonational phonology.

    The structurally adequate systematisation of rise-fall-rise intonations in English becomes a problem in Ladd's analysis, rather than in that of the English phoneticians, because, in the wake of AM Phonology, Ladd does not distinguish between unitary fall-rise and sequential fall+rise intonation patterns, which were separated as meaningful contrasts by the London School, especially by Sharp (1958). Prosodically the two patterns differ in the pitch end points of the fall and of the following rise, being lower for both in the sequence F+R than for the unitary FR, and they also differ in rhythmic prominence on the rise of F+R, as against FR, resulting in a partial accent on the word containing the rise. If the partial accent is put on a function word it naturally has a strong form, whereas in FR a weaker form occurs. This is an additional manifestation of greater prominence in the rise of F+R. Sharp provides an extensive list of examples for both patterns, predominantly in statements and requests, a few in information and polarity questions, and some miscellaneous cases. He is less sure about the occurrence of FR in questions, but maintains, against Lee (1956, p. 70) and Palmer (1924, p. 82), who mention its absence from this sentence mode, that it does occur, but less frequently than in the other modes. It seems to be perfectly clear, however, 'that in both "yes-no" questions and "special" questions at least one focus for the patterns is quite common: the *first* word [of the question]. FR, in these circumstances, asks for confirmation or repetition, F+R pleads for an answer (or for action)' (Sharp 1958, p. 143). Sharp does not give any examples 'for these circumstances', but from the general functional description he has given for FR and F+T in questions, the following typical instances may be constructed:

ii.   (a)   [FR] What did you say?
                   'I did not catch that, please repeat.'
                   PROLAB: **&2**^What did you say **&., &PG**
                   The fall before the rise adds insistence to the request for repetition,
                   which is absent in a simple rise starting on 'what':
                   PROLAB: **&2**]What did you say **&, &PG**

             (b)   [F] What did you [R] say?
                   'Give me the content of what you said (when he asked you).'
                   PROLAB: **&2**^What did you **&2. &1**]say **&, &PG**

             (c)   But a full accent on the rise is more likely:
                   'Tell me what you said (when he asked you).'
                   PROLAB: **&2**^What did you **&2. &2**[say **&, &PG**

       The fall before the rise in (b) and (c) adds insistence to the request for
       information, which is absent when the rise on 'say' is preceded by a
       high, instead of a falling, prenucleus:
             PROLAB: **&2**^What did you **&0. &2**] say **&, &PG**

iii.   (a)   [FR] Are you going to tell him?
                   'He needs to be told, please confirm.'
                   PROLAB: **&2**^Are you going to tell him **&., &PG**
                   The fall before the rise adds insistence to the request for
                   confirmation, which is absent in a simple rise starting on 'are':
                   PROLAB: **&2**]Are you going to tell him **&, &PG**

             (b)   [F] Are you going to [R] tell him?
                   'Inform me whether you will tell him.'
                   PROLAB: **&2**^Are you going to **&2. &1**]tell him **&, &PG**

             (c)   But a full accent on the rise is more likely:
                   PROLAB: **&2**^Are you going to **&2. &2**[tell him **&, &PG**

The fall before the rise in (b) and (c) adds insistence to the request for information, which is absent when the rise on 'tell' is preceded by a high, instead of a falling, prenucleus:

PROLAB: **&2^**Are you going to **&0. &2**]tell him **&, &PG**

In examples (ii.a) and (iii.a), the peak of FR has medial alignment with the accented syllable, AM H*, PROLAB **&2^**. In (ii.b) and (iii.b), a partial accent is possible for the rise of F+R on 'say' or 'tell him', but the full accent in (c) conveys the given meaning more clearly. The increased prominence that signals it is produced by the F0 onset of the rise in the accented syllable being critically below the end point of the preceding fall. This difference between a partially and a fully accented rise in F+R cannot be represented in the London School framework because accent is not a separate category from intonation and rhythmic structure. The examples in (ii.) and (iii.) have been constructed on the basis of Sharp's description. There are one or two examples in his list of the FR and F+R distinction in initial focus position of questions, but they are different from the ones in (ii.) and (iii.); they represent his standard patterns of medial-to-late FR alignment and F+R accentuation.

iv.   (a)   [FR] What's his name?
                  a 'I have forgotten.' *b* 'I am incredulous.'
                  PROLAB: **&2^-**(What's his name **&., &PG**

           (b)   [F] What shall I [R] tell him?
                  'I really cannot think of anything.'
                  PROLAB: **&2^**What shall I **&2. &1**]tell him **&, &PG**
                  Accent **&2**[is possible as well when 'tell' is given a second major information point.

v.   [F] Are you [R] coming?
           'Do tell me whether you are coming.' 'Must I wait here for ever?'
           (Despair)
           PROLAB: **&2^**Are you **&2. &1**]coming **&, &PG**

Sharp did not distinguish clearly between two different alignments of FR. Except for the cases illustrated in (ii.) and (iii.), his examples refer to medial-to-late alignment of FR with the accented syllable. His FR data also appear to be all of the non-intensified type of (rise-)fall-rise, and therefore do not correspond to the AM category L*+HL-H% in Ladd's emphatic example, but to (L+)H*L-H% (*PROLAB:* **&2^**...**&.,** versus **&2^-**(...**&.,**). The general meanings of F+R and FR may be given as 'associative' versus 'dissociative' reference to alternatives in preceding speech actions. Here are two sets of examples:

vi.   A: Look, there's Peter.

             B: I've seen him.

            (a) [aɪv FR siːn ɪm] 'I saw him before you even pointed him out.'
                 PROLAB: [aɪv **&2^-**(siːn ɪm **&., &PG**]

            (b) [aɪv F siːn R hɪm] 'I have spotted the person you are pointing to.'
                 PROLAB: [aɪv **&2^**siːn **&2. &1**]hɪm **&, &PG**]

            (c) [aɪv FR siːn R hɪm] 'I saw the person you are pointing to without
                 you mentioning it.'
                 PROLAB: [aɪv *2^-*(siːn **&., &1**]hɪm **&, &PG**]

In FR of (a) 'him' has its weak form, in F+R of (b) its strong form. (c) shows that an FR on 'seen' may be followed by a simple rise on 'him' [hɪm] (again in its strong form, as in (b)), giving it more prominence, and partially accenting and foregrounding it. This rules out an association of the rise of the (rise-)fall-rise with an edge tone and is therefore outside the scope of AM Phonology.

    There are further possibilities:

vi.   (d) [aɪv F siːn ɪm], 'reporting the fact that I have seen him'
                 PROLAB: [aɪv **&2^**siːn ɪm **&2. &PG**]

            (e) [aɪv F siːn hɪm]
                 with partial accent on 'him', like (d) but foregrounding 'him'.
                 PROLAB: [aɪv **&2^**siːn **&2. &1**)hɪm **&2. &PG**]

               (d) and (e) differ from (a) and (c) by only reporting speaker-oriented
               facts, whereas the latter involve the dialogue partner.

vii.   A: You chaired the appointment committee for the chair of phonetics.
                 The committee decided to take the applicant from down-under. Was
                 it a good choice?

             B: I [F] thought [R] so. 'That was my opinion and it still is.'
                 PROLAB: I **&2^**thought **&2. &1**]so **&, &PG**
                 I [FR] thought so. 'That was my opinion at the time, but I have
                 changed my mind.'
                 PROLAB: I **&2^-**(thought so **&., &PG**

    These data, analysed with observational as well as descriptive adequacy in the London School of Phonetics, cannot be handled in the AM Phonology framework, precisely because it links the rise to edge tones. Intermediate phrase boundaries cannot be introduced to solve the problem because there are no phonetic grounds for them. This had already been pointed out with reference to German data in Kohler (2006b, pp. 127ff), cf. 2.7. In addition to pitch accent L*+H, followed by the edge tones L-H%, Ladd (1996, p. 122) discusses some examples in British English for which he postulates pitch accent H*:

viii.   (a1)   Could I [H*] have the [H*] bill please [L-H%]?
                PROLAB: Could I **&2^**have the **&0. &2^**bill please **&., &PG**

        (b1)   Is your [H*] mother there [L-H%]?
                PROLAB: Is your **&2^**mother there **&., &PG**

They sound 'condescending or peremptory' to speakers of North American English, where a high-rising nucleus + edge tones, H*H-H%, would be used instead:

viii.   (a2)   Could I [H*] have the [H*] bill please [H-H%,]?
                PROLAB: Could I **&2^**have the **&1. &2]**bill please **&? &PG**

        (b2)   Is your [H*] mother there [H-H%]?
                PROLAB: Is your **&2]**mother there **&? &PG**

The reference to Halliday's broken Tone 2 in viii. (p. 291 n.6) makes it clear that Ladd is referring to a fall (not a rise-fall) on the accent of 'bill' or 'mother', followed by a rise on unaccented 'please' or 'there' in word-order questions. The pattern is a unitary *fall-rise*, making an *associative* reference to preceding actions of the type 'I've been served, I've eaten, I want to pay now' in (a), and 'I would like to speak to your mother. Is she in?' in (b). In both cases the rise establishes contact with the person spoken to; a simple fall would lack this and sound abrupt.

These examples could, of course, also be spoken with a unitary *rise-fall-rise*, and would then make *dissociative* references, (a) 'Waiter, I've been trying to catch your attention but you are constantly dealing with other customers, I am in a hurry' (b) 'Sorry, it's not you I have come to see, but your mother.' And in (a), 'please' may get extra prominence, giving it a secondary accent, in a separate rise after a fall or a fall-rise, creating F+R or FR+R and adding insistence to the request.

viii.   (a3)   *PROLAB:* Could I **&2^**have the **&1. &2^-(**bill please **&., &PG**
        (a4)   *PROLAB:* Could I **&2^**have the **&1. &2^**bill **&2. &1]**please **&, &PG**
        (a5)   *PROLAB:* Could I **&2^**have the **&1. &2^-(**bill **&., &1]**please **&, &PG**
        (b3)   *PROLAB:* Is your **&2^-(**mother there **&., &PG**

Parallel to the British English example (viii.b1) 'Is your mother there?', Ladd (1996, p. 122) discusses the German equivalent in the AM Phonology framework:

ix.   (a1)   Ist deine [H*] Mutter da [L-H%]?
              probably based on an exponency classifiable as
              Ist deine [FR] Mutter da?

and as *PROLAB:* Ist deine **&2^Mutter da &., &PG**
But there are other possible realisations.

(b1)   Ist deine [F] Mutter [R]da?
PROLAB: Ist deine **&2^Mutter &2. &1]da &, &PG**
partially foregrounding 'being *present*' as a minor information
point beside the main information point 'your mother'

(a2)   *PROLAB:* Ist deine **&2^-(Mutter da &., &PG**

(b2)   *PROLAB:* Ist deine **&2^-(Mutter &,. &1]da &, &PG**

The functional interpretations of these patterns are the same as in the
English equivalents.

1.4.2   Halliday's Intonational Phonology

Halliday followed the tradition of the London School of Phonetics, but he incorporated the phonetic analysis of intonation in a phonological framework
within his categories of a theory of grammar (Halliday 1961). In two complementary papers (1963a,b), which were republished in adapted and more
widely distributed book form in 1967, he described intonation as a complex of
three phonological systemic variables, *tonality*, *tonicity* and *tone*, interrelated
with a fourth variable, *rhythm*. Tonality refers to the division of speech events
into melodic units, *tone groups*. The tone group enters into a hierarchy of four
phonological units together with, in descending order, the *rhythmic foot*, the
syllable and the *phoneme*, each element of a higher-order unit consisting of
one or more elements of the unit immediately below, without residue. The
rhythmic feet in a tone group form a syntagmatic structure of an obligatory
tonic preceded by an optional *pretonic*, each consisting of one or more feet.
This structure is determined by the tonicity variable, which marks one foot in
the foot sequence of a tone group as the *tonic foot*, by selecting one of a system of five tonal contrasts, the *tones* 1 fall, 2 high rise, 3 low rise, 4 fall-rise,
5 rise-fall. Feet following the tonic foot in the tonic of a tone group generally
follow the pitch course set by the tone of the tonic. Besides these single tonics
there are the *double tonics* 13 and 53, uniting tone 1 or 5 with tone 3 in two
successive tonic feet of the tonic section of one tone group. They form major
and minor information points and correspond to F+R versus FR in tone 4.

Tied to the tone selection at the tonic there are further tone selections at
the pretonic. At both elements of tone group structure, a principle of delicacy
determines finer specifications, such as different extensions of the fall in tone 1
(1+ high, 1 mid, 1- low), different high-rising patterns for tone 2 (2 simple rise,
2 rise preceded by high fall: broken tone 2), and different extensions of the fall
in tone 4 (4 mid fall-rise, 4 low fall-rise). Each rhythmic foot has a syntagmatic
structure of obligatory *ictus*, followed by optional *remiss*; the former is filled

by a strong syllable, the latter by one or more weak syllables. Halliday follows Abercrombie (1964) in assuming stress-timed isochronicity for English, and that the ictus may be silent ('silent stress') 'if the foot follows a pause or has initial position in the tone group' (Halliday 1963a, p. 6).

Halliday integrates his intonational phonology into the grammar of spoken English, where the intonational systems operate side by side with non-intonational ones in morphology and syntax, at many different places in the coding of meaningful grammatical contrasts. In the 1963a paper, he looked from phonological contrasts to distinctive grammatical sets, asking 'What are the resources of intonation that expound grammatical meaning?', whereas in the 1963b paper, he looked at the phonological contrasts from the grammatical end, asking 'What are the grammatical systems that are expounded by intonation?' With this approach, Halliday took a step towards a functional view of phonological and grammatical form, which he has been concerned with ever since in the development of a coherent framework of *Systemic Functional Linguistics* (SFL).

Pheby (1975) and Kohler (1977 (1st edn)) applied Halliday's framework to German. They were an advance on von Essen (1964), who delimited three basic pitch patterns with reference to vaguely defined functional terms – terminal, continuative, interrogative intonation – and was then forced to state that *yes-no* questions have rising intonation, question-word questions and statements terminal intonation, and syntactically unfinished sentences continuation rises. This analysis, quite apart from being superficial and incomplete, mixed up the formal and functional levels of intonation right from the start, which the British colleagues and Kohler (1977, 1995, 2004, 2013b) did not; they knew, and said so, that both question forms can have either terminal or rising pitch with finer shades of meaning.

The more recent publication by Halliday and Greaves (2008) expounds the Hallidayan intonation framework in greater detail and reflects its integration with grammar in the very title. Whereas the earlier publications described the intonation of Standard Southern British English (RP), the later one includes Australian and Canadian English, thus taking 'English' in a more global sense, and it illustrates the descriptions with Praat graphics in the text and with sound files of isolated but grammatically contextualised utterances, as well as of dialogues, on an accompanying CDROM. Meaning as carried by intonation is now related to three of Halliday's four metafunctions: the interpersonal, the textual and the logical. The systems of *tonality* and *tonicity* are linked to textual meanings, the systems of *tone* to interpersonal meanings. The phonological rank scale is paralleled by a grammatical rank scale of *sentence, clause, group/phrase*, *word*, *morpheme*, linking to experiential, interpersonal and textual meanings. Setting up separate systems for intonation and grammatical structure is a good principle because it avoids the conflation of falling or rising tonal movement with declarative and two types of interrogative structure, as has been quite common. But cutting across this grammatical rank scale is the *information unit*, which is not independently defined, and seems to be in a circular-argument relationship with the phonological unit of the tone group, since by default one tone group is mapped onto one information unit: 'Thus the two units, the phonological "tone unit" and the grammatical "information unit" correspond one to one; but since they are located on different strata, their boundaries do not correspond exactly. In fact, both are fuzzy: the boundaries are not clearly defined in either case' (Halliday and Greaves (2008), p. 99). This means that adding yet another unit to the extremely complex taxonomic intonation-grammar system does not seem to serve a useful purpose, and Crystal (1969b) had already criticised the concept in his review of Halliday (1967).

Another weak point of Halliday's intonational phonology concerns the division of the stream of sound into tone groups and of these into rhythmic feet. Although Halliday and Greaves gave up the doubtful isochrony principle and no longer quote Abercrombie (1964), rhythmic regularity is still the building principle of the tone group: 'When you listen carefully to continuously flowing English speech, you find there is a tendency for salient syllables to occur at fairly regular intervals, and this affects the syllables in between: the more of them there are, the more they will be squashed together to maintain the tempo' (Halliday and Greaves (2008), p. 55). This can be a useful heuristics when dealing with isolated sentences in foreign language teaching, even more so for learners whose native languages have totally different rhythmic structures from English, such as French. Teaching English as a Foreign Language was a prominent field of application of a large part of intonation analysis in the London School of Phonetics. Halliday, likewise, worked out his system of intonational phonology for the *Edinburgh Course in Spoken English* (1961) by R. Mackin, M. A. K. Halliday, K. Albrow and J. McH. Sinclair, later published by Oxford University Press (see Halliday 1970). The *Intonation Exercises* of this course were reproduced as teaching materials at the Edinburgh Phonetics Department Summer Vacation Course on the Phonetics of English for foreign students. In 1965 and 1966, I was asked to give these intonation tutorials.

But the rhythmic foot analysis of the tone group does not really provide a good basis for analysing continuous speech. Moreover, Halliday's intonational phonology lacks the category of a phrase boundary. Such a prosodic phrase marker encapsulates a bundle of pitch, duration, energy and phonation features to signal a break, which may, but need not, coincide with grammatical boundaries and with the boundaries Halliday sets up for his tone groups. In sequences of rhythmic feet, Halliday earmarks those that contain one of his five tones, the tonic feet, constituting the tonics of tone groups. Since by arbitrary definition any one tone group can only have one tonic (except for the major+minor tonic compounds 13 and 53), there must be a tone group boundary between two succeeding tonics. Where this boundary is put is again arbitrary in view of the fuzziness Halliday and Greaves refer to in the quotation above, i.e. due to the lack of a phonetic criterion that determines a phrase boundary. This was again pointed out by Crystal (1969b). In many cases, Halliday no doubt takes the grammatical structure into account when deciding on the positions of tone group boundaries. But this is against his principle of setting up separate phonological- and grammatical-rank scales and relating them afterwards, and the violation of this principle borders on circularity.

And, finally, giving tone groups a rhythmic foot structure conflates rhythmic grouping into ictus and remiss with meaning-related phrasal accentuation. Halliday's framework does not provide a separate accent category outside the tonic, and in the latter it is the pitch-related tone category that determines the tonic foot and the tonic syllable, and thus constitutes a phrasal accent. The syllable string preceding the tonic may contain meaning-related phrasal accents, but not all ictus syllables of a postulated rhythmic foot structure are accented. A tonic foot may be preceded by a multisyllable *prehead*, which contains no accent, but may be perceived as a sequence of strong and weak syllables due to timing and vowel quality, for example before a tonic containing tone 3 in:

> // 3 don't stay / out too */ **long** // (Halliday and Greaves (2008), p. 119; see Figure 1.2a)

In Hallidayan notation 'don't' and 'out' are treated as ictus syllables in two rhythmic feet of the pretonic and a tone-3 tonic. But, when listening to the .wav file (supplied on the CDROM), no accent can be detected in the pretonic syllable sequence, and the perception of rhythmic structure fluctuates between the one noted and /don't stay out too/. The vocalic elements in all four syllables have durations between 120 and 130 ms. Duration would be considerably longer in an accented syllable containing a diphthongal element.

What the (male) speaker realises here is a high prehead before the (only) sentence accent, in a *high register* at a pitch level around 180 Hz, which at the same time increases the *pitch range* down to the following low rise. The speaker could, of course, have used a high prehead without going into a high register

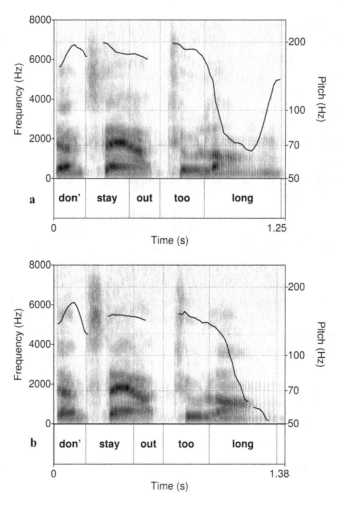

Figure 1.2. Spectrograms and F0 traces (log scale) of *a* // 3 don't stay / out too */ long // – audio file 5_2_2_4a3.wav, and *b* // 1 don't stay / out too */ long // – audio file 5_2_2_4a4.wav, from Halliday and Greaves (2008), p. 119. Standard Southern British English, male speaker (M. A. K. Halliday)

and thus without increasing the pitch range. In the high prehead, F0 fluctuation is largely conditioned by vowel-intrinsic and consonant-vowel coarticulatory microprosody: only the initial 'don't' has a more extensive rise, which, just like vowel duration, is not large enough to signal a phrasal accent. The listener may then structure the prehead rhythmically in variable ways. Halliday differs from the London School of Phonetics, e.g. O'Connor and Arnold (1961), by not having the category of prehead. The composition of tone groups by rhythmic feet with an obligatory ictus syllable that may be silent precludes it.

How serious this omission is in a systemic functional approach to intonation is shown by the example:

> // 1 don't stay / out too */ **long** // (Halliday and Greaves (2008), p. 119; see Figure 1.2b)

The notation given for this tone group differs from the previous one only by having tone 1 instead of tone 3. But listening to the .wav file reveals two differences: (1) 'don't' is accented because its prominence is greater, due to longer duration of its sonorous part, and to more extensive F0 movement, well above the pitch level of the following syllables, so the pretonic sequence is not a prehead; (2) the pretonic sequence is at a much lower pitch level of 150 Hz – even the peak in 'don't' only reaches 170 Hz. The accent on 'don't', combined with the lower pitch level preceding the final fall, intensifies the meaning of a command, whereas the unaccented, but high prehead preceding the final low rise intensifies the meaning of a request, and the high register adds a note of entreaty. These are important aspects of the transmitted meanings, which are not reflected by different tonal categorisation in Halliday's notation: the two pretonics are identical because they are given the same rhythmic structure. But this rhythmic structure is an additional overlay on accentuation, register and range, and may surface perceptually in variable ways in both utterances. In PROLAB, the two utterances are differentiated as:

> **&HP &HR** don't stay out too **&2[**long **&, &PG**
> **&2^**don't stay out too **&0. &2^**long **&2. &PG**

The additional rhythmic structure is captured at the level of segmental spectrum and timing.

The following postulates of Halliday's intonational phonology can be taken as essential for any prosodic framework:

- English intonation is based on a system of contour-defined contrastive tones.
- Parallel to the phonological tone system there are lexicogrammatical systems.
- Phonological form is part of the grammar as another exponent of meaning in language functions.

But to be applicable to the analysis and description of prosodic systems in connected speech, more particularly spontaneous speech, and in text-to-speech synthesis, several weak points of Halliday's systemic functional approach need adjusting.

- The nesting rank scale of phonological units, as well as the immediate constituents division of tone groups into tonic and pretonic, do not provide an adequate representation of prosodic structures – especially, the composition of the unit of the tone group by elements of the unit of the rhythmic foot cannot cope with the dynamic flow of speech and rhythmic disturbances such as hesitations, false starts, repetitions. Instead we need an accent category with several levels, based on degrees of prominence, to which tones are linked. In between successive accents, pitch is organised into distinctive concatenation patterns.
- Speech is organised into prosodic phrases, so prosodic phrase boundaries need to be determined by bundles of phonetic features.
- In prosodic phrases, the first accent may be preceded by unaccented preheads, and they form a system of mean, low and high pitch.
- Register needs to be introduced to set the pitch level of prosodic phrases, or of the part up to the final accent-linked pitch turn (thus also determining pitch range), or of sequences of prosodic phrases.

When these weaknesses of Halliday's intonational phonology became relevant in the Kiel TTS development (Kohler 1991a,b) and in spontaneous speech annotation for the Verbmobil project (Kohler, Pätzold and Simpson 1995), the description of German intonation, given in Hallidayan terms in the first edition of Kohler (1977), was put on a new basis developed for the tasks: the *Kiel Intonation Model*. It was presented in Kohler (1991a,b), then in the second edition of Kohler (1995) and in Kohler (1997a,b), and will be set out in Chapter 2. Subsequent chapters will take Halliday's form and function perspective one step further. Whereas Halliday looked from phonology to grammar and from grammar to phonology in the early papers, and later related phonological form in grammar to metalinguistic functions, I shall reverse the relationship, set up a few basic communicative functions within Bühler's model and then investigate language-specific prosodic, syntactic and lexical carriers for them.

1.4.3   Pike's Level Analysis

Pike laid the foundation for the analysis of American English intonation on a different descriptive basis, auditorily referring significant points of pitch contours – starting and ending points, and points of direction changes, in relation to stressed syllables – to four pitch levels, 1–4 from highest to lowest. Not every unstressed syllable gets a significant pitch point but may have its pitch interpolated between neighbouring pitch points. On the other hand, a syllable may get more than one significant point to represent the stress-related pitch contour, or even more than two, when a contour changes direction and is compressed into a single stressed syllable. Pike gives a detailed formal account of the resulting pitch-level contours of American English and relates them to syntactic structures. He points out that the contours found in statements can also occur in questions and vice versa, and he provides a wealth of *ad hoc* references to attitudinal and expressive shades of meaning added to utterances by pitch contours. His analysis thus parallels the one by O'Connor and Arnold with a different paradigm for a different variety of English.

1.4.4   Intonation in AM Phonology and ToBI

As Halliday provided a phonological framework within structuralist grammar for the intonation analysis of the London School of Phonetics, Pierrehumbert put the Pikean level analysis of intonation into a framework of Autosegmental Metrical (AM) Phonology. The distinctive pitch levels were reduced to two, H and L, which, on their own and in the sequence H+L and L+H, form systems of pitch accents, phrase accents and boundary tones. In pitch accents, H and L are associated with stressed syllables indicated by *, but they may have leading or trailing H or L, yielding H*, L*, H+L*, H*+L, L+H*, L*+H. The separation of H* and L+H* was a problematic alignment category in AM Phonology and ToBI because a dip between two H* accents requires an L tone attached to an H* tone, given the principle of linear phonetic interpolation between pitch accents.

   Falling, rising or (rising-)falling-rising nuclear pitch contours (of the London School), which in the extreme case are compressed into a one-syllable utterance, such as 'yes', are decomposed into three elements: a pitch accent, followed by a phrase accent and, then, by a boundary tone, in each case with selection of H or L. All three must always be represented, e.g. H*L-L%, H*H-H%, L*H-H%, H*L-H%, L+H*L-H%, L*+HL-H%. Since falling-rising contours are defined by three pitch points, three types of syntagmatic element are needed to represent them. AM Phonology selects them from the three accent and boundary categories and extrapolates them to all contours, including monotonic falls and rises. These phonological elements are associated with syllables and phrase boundaries, linked to F0 traces and aligned with segmental syllable structure in spectrograms. The confounding of pitch accents with edge tones has already been reviewed in the discussion of AM solutions for FR and F+R patterns of the London School in 1.4.1.

AM Phonology is a highly sophisticated formal framework, which, beyond the basic premises sketched here, has been undergoing continual change over the years, and right from the outset the focus has been on form, not on function and meaning. When the AM phonological framework became the basis for a transcription system, ToBI, the original strict language-dependent systemic approach began to get lost, phonetic measurement was squeezed into the preset categories, which were transposed to other languages, and the transcription tool was elevated to the status of a model.

Questions of meaning of the formal intonation structures have been raised, but *post festum*, for example by Pierrehumbert and Hirschberg (1990), who propose a compositional theory of intonational meaning related to pitch accents, phrase accents and boundary tones. Another, very influential example of linking intonational form to meaning is Ward and Hirschberg (1985), where the rise-fall-rise contour, based on the AM representation L*+HL-H%, is analysed as a context-independent contribution to conveying speaker *uncertainty*. It appears, however, that most of the examples discussed by Ward and Hirschberg are not instances of L*+HL-H%, but of L+H*L-H%, which they explicitly exclude as the phonological representation of their rise-fall-rise. With the L*+HL-H% pattern, a speaker is said to relate an utterance element to a scale of alternative values and to indicate not being certain whether the hearer can accept the allocation as valid. For example, in:

> B: I'm so excited. My girlfriend is coming to visit tonight.
> A: From far afield?
> a.   B: From suburban Phila\del/phia.
> b.   B: *From next \door/. (p. 766)

'[T]he speaker, a West Philadelphia resident, conveys uncertainty about whether, on a distance scale, *suburban Philadelphia* is *far away* from the speaker's location. ... b. is distinctly odd, given the implausibility of B's uncertainty whether *next door* is *far away*' (p. 766).

The authors provide an analysis in terms of logical semantics at the Representation level, which considerably narrows the field of speech communication, and may thus make it difficult to capture the full range of the communicative function of the fall-rise pattern in English. If, in the above example, B were to give a facetious answer, with a smile on his face, b. would not be odd at all, but would be understood as an ironic reply to A's enquiry about distance. It would still be an instance of what Sharp (1958) called the dissociative reference to alternatives in his fall-rise FR. The semantic-prosodic distinction between this pattern and Sharp's F+R is nicely illustrated by the two versions

of the sentence 'I thought so' discussed in 1.4.1. The speaker expresses association with, or dissociation from, the earlier belief, using either F+R or FR, and
is certain about that in both cases. With FR, the speaker is, on the one hand,
definite about having changed his mind, by using a peak pattern, but on the other hand, plays it down in social interaction conforming to a behavioural code,
by adding a rise to alleviate the categoricalness in an appeal to the listener to
accept the change of mind. If the speaker makes a statement about the present
opinion without associative or dissociative reference to the past, it may be 'I
[F/R] think so', with either a fall or a low rise for a definite or a non-committal
response.

Whereas all the Ward and Hirschberg examples of American English have
their fall-rise equivalents in Standard Southern British English, this may not
hold for transposing Sharp's British English examples to American English.
If the pattern distinctions do apply to both varieties, the conflation of pitch
accents with edge tones and the lack of an accent category, separate from pitch,
preclude the distinctive representations of the semantic-prosodic subtleties
related to fall-rise pitch patterns. This may be illustrated by the following
contextualisations:

> To provide sufficient seating at a family get-together, father A says
> to his two boys B and C

A   We need more chairs in the sitting-room. Go and get two from the
     kitchen and a couple more from the dining-room.
B   [Goes to the kitchen, comes back with two chairs, says to A]
   (a)   There's [FR] another one in the kitchen.
         PROLAB: There's **&2^**another one in the kitchen **&., &PG**

   (b)   There's [F+R] another one in the kitchen.
         PROLAB: There's **&2^**another one in the **&2. &1]**kitchen **&,
         &PG**

   (c)   There's [FR] another one in the [R] kitchen.
         PROLAB: There's **&2^**another one in the **&., &1]** kitchen **&,
         &PG**

C   [Goes to the dining-room, gets two chairs, comes back via the
     kitchen, says to A]
   (d)   There's [F] another one in the [R] kitchen.
         PROLAB: There's **&2^**another one in the **&2. &2[**kitchen **&,
         &PG**

   (e)   There's [FR] another one in the [FR] kitchen.
         PROLAB: There's **&2^**another one in the **&., &2^**kitchen
         &., &PG

In (a), B uses a rise-fall-rise that falls sharply to a low level on 'another', and then immediately rises again to mid-level at the end of 'kitchen', which is unaccented because it is integrated in a monotonic rise from 'one' onwards. This is Sharp's unitary FR, Halliday's tone 4, and L+H*L-H% in AM Phonology. B transmits the meaning 'There's an additional chair in the kitchen, besides the two I have just brought from there, although Dad thought there were only two', a dissociative reference to alternatives.

In (b), the rise after the low-level fall on 'another' is delayed until 'kitchen', which is partially foregrounded with a partial accent. This is Sharp's compound F+R, and Halliday's double-tonic with tone 13. However, the pattern cannot be represented in AM Phonology because the categorisation L+H* L*L-H% for a fall followed by a rise, with two pitch accents and final edge tones, allocates two full accents to the phrase, and therefore does not distinguish (b) from (d). The F+R pattern makes an associative reference to alternatives; it does not have the contrastive reference to A's mention of 'two chairs from the kitchen'.

In (c), B makes the same dissociative reference to alternatives as in (a) but partially foregrounds 'kitchen', giving it a partial accent by breaking the rising contour of the fall-rise and by starting another rise from a lower level within the same intonation phrase. In Sharp's analysis, 'another' would receive a fall-rise FR, 'kitchen' a simple rise. Similarly, Halliday would have tone 4 followed by tone 3 in two tone groups. AM Phonology cannot represent this pattern because an intermediate intonation phrase would have to be postulated even in the absence of any phonetic boundary marker. If the pitch break were to be taken as the indication of such a phrase boundary, from which the presence of edge tones would in turn be deduced, the argument becomes circular. In all three descriptive frames, the different accent level of 'kitchen' versus that of 'another' would not be marked, and therefore the different meaning from (d) and (e) could not be captured.

Since C has brought chairs from the dining-room he refers contrastively to an additional chair in the kitchen, and gives 'kitchen' a full accent. In (d), Sharp's F+R is separated into F and R linked to the two accents, with associative reference to alternatives. Halliday would have to have two tone groups //1 There's an<u>o</u>ther one //3 in the <u>kitchen.</u>// This analysis is independent of the presence or absence of phonetic boundary markers. In AM Phonology, the pattern may be represented by two pitch accents in one intonation phrase, L+H* L*L-H%, because the L of the second pitch accent provides the right-hand pitch point for linear interpolation of the fall from the H of the first pitch accent. In (e), there are dissociative references to an alternative number of chairs and to an alternative locality, by two rise-fall-rises linked to the two accents. As in (c), there may again be a single prosodic phrase. Sharp's analysis would simply have FR in both positions; Halliday would again need two tone groups, each with tone 4. In AM Phonology, two intonation phrases with L+H*L-H% would be necessary to generate the four-point rise-fall-rise contours, each with two intonation-phrase edge tones in addition to two pitch-accent tones, irrespective of the potential absence of phonetic boundary markers between them.

Thus, the AM phonological representations in (d) and (e) of C differ in the relative allocation of prosodic information to the theoretical categories of paradigmatic *pitch accent* and syntagmatic *intonation phrasing*. This different allocation is conditioned by constraints in the canonical AM definitions of prosodic categories:

- Pitch accents are defined by up to two sequential H or L tones.
- In a sequence of pitch accents, the pitch contour between abutting tones is the result of linear phonetic interpolation between the phonological pitch-accent tones. Therefore, for example, in two successive peak patterns, a distinctive pitch dip between two H* necessitates postulating a bitonal pitch accent, either a trailing L tone in the first, or a leading L tone in the second.
- The pitch contour between the last pitch-accent tone and the end of the intonation phrase is represented by two sequential H or L edge tones, a phrase accent and a boundary tone.
- A rise-fall-rise intonation contour around an accented syllable, with four distinctive pitch points, must be represented by a bitonal pitch accent followed by two edge tones.
- If a rise-fall-rise contour occurs utterance-internal, it must be followed by an intonation phrase boundary.
- If there are no phonetic boundary markers indicating such a boundary, such as segmental lengthening, with or without a following pause, there are no pitch-independent reasons for postulating such a boundary, or the argumentation becomes circular by using pitch as the defining feature for the postulated boundary, which in turn determines the edge tones before it.

These constraints on the phonological representation of intonation contours in AM Phonology reduce descriptive and explanatory adequacy in prosodic data interpretation, compared with the accounts provided by the London School and Halliday.

1.4.4.1 Alignment of Rise-Fall-Rises in English

AM Phonology conceptualises English L*+HL-H% and L+H*L-H% rise-fall-rise patterns as different alignments of the L and H tones of the rise-fall pitch accent with the stressed syllable: either L or H is aligned with it, H trailing L* and L leading H*, producing later (delayed) or earlier association of the pitch accent with the stressed syllable. An even earlier alignment is given as H*L-H%, and there is a fourth possibility – H+L*L-H%, where alignment occurs with the syllable preceding the stressed one, which appears not to be discussed in the AM literature. KIM treats these pitch patterns as distinctive points on a scale of synchronisation, from *early* to *late*, of F0 peak maximum with vocal-tract timing, and uses the PROLAB notations <&2) &.,>, <&2^ &.,>, <&2^-(&.,>, <&2(&.,> (see 2.7).

Pierrehumbert and Steele (1987, 1989) raised the question as to whether the L+H*L-H% versus L*+HL-H% distinction is discrete or scalar. They based their investigation on the utterance 'Only a millionaire', with initial stress on the noun and F0 peaking earlier or later in relation to the offset of /m/. They contextualised the two versions in a scenario of a fund-raising campaign targeting the richest. A potential donor, when approached as a billionaire in a telephone call, replies, 'Oh, no. Only a millionaire', with L+H*L-H%, whereupon the charity representative expresses his incredulity and uncertainty with the later peak alignment L*+HL-H%. To decide on the discrete versus scalar issue, the authors performed a perception-production experiment. They took a natural production of a L+H*L-H% utterance as the point of departure for LPC synthesis, shifting the stylised rise-fall pattern in 20 ms steps through the utterance, with peak positions ranging from 35 ms to 315 ms after /m/ offset.

Five subjects were asked to listen to each of the fifteen stimuli in fifteen randomised blocks, and to imitate what they had heard. These imitations were recorded and analysed with the hypothesis that, if the categories are discrete, the ideal speaker/listener will allocate the percepts to two different categories and then reproduce them in such a way that the realisations will show a bimodal clustering. The statistical basis of this experiment is weak, not only because of the insufficient number of subjects, but more particularly since one hearer-speaker was the junior author, who, of course, knew what the test categories were and sounded like, and who produced the clearest bimodal pattern. Furthermore, one subject failed to produce even a vague resemblance of bimodality.

The authors' conclusion that the two phonological categorisations of rise-fall-rise patterns in AM Phonology represent a discrete contrast can therefore not be accepted as having been proved. It is to be assumed that peak shifts in rise-fall-rise patterns are perceptually processed in similar ways to *peak* shifts in rise-fall patterns, as obtained for English and German (see 2.8). These data show that the perception of peak synchronisation only changes categorically from *early* (pre-accent) to *medial* (in-accent) position, but not for peak shift inside the accented vowel, from *medial* to *late*, where changes are perceived along a continuum. Since the Pierrehumbert and Steele experiment only dealt with the in-accent shift, the potential categorical change from pre-accent to in-accent could not become a research issue, and in view of the weakness of the experimental paradigm, the results do not support discrete patterning. The perceptual and cognitive processing of rise-fall-rise peak shifts may be considered parallel to that observed for rise-falls, with the addition of an interactional rapport feature carried by final rising pitch. Whereas in a shift from *early* to *medial* peak there is a discrete semantic change from FINALITY to OPENNESS, coupled with a categorical perceptual change (see 2.8), the shift from *medial* to *late peak* successively adds degrees of CONTRAST and of the expression of UNEXPECTEDNESS along a continuum of peak synchronisation. Furthermore, this expression includes other prosodic variables besides F0 alignment, i.e. F0 peak height, timing, energy and more breathy phonation.

This issue was investigated by Hirschberg and Ward (1992). They report recording the pattern L+H*L-H% with eight utterances in an 'uncertainty' as well as in an 'incredulity' context, where the latter was hypothesised to generate an expanded pitch range, different timing, amplitude and spectral characteristics. The utterances differed widely in the stretch of speech over which the rise-fall-rise was spread, with 'ELEVEN in the morning' at one end of the scale and 'Nine MILLION' at the other. For the former, the two contexts, as well as the F0 displays of the two data samples produced, are provided:

'uncertainty'   A   So, do you tend to come in pretty late then?
                B   \ELEVEN in the morning/.
'incredulity'   A   I'd like you here tomorrow morning at eleven.
                B   !ELEVEN in the morning!

! ! is to symbolise the incredulity version of the utterance with the same pitch-accent and edge-tone pattern L*+HL-H% as in the uncertainty version \/. The two figures provided show that F0 sets in low and starts rising at the end of the stressed vowel of 'eleven', peaks at the end of the accented word, stays high during the following vowel and then descends to a low level in 'the'. There follows a further small F0 drop in the stressed vowel of 'morning', before F0 rises again in the final syllable. The two displays differ only in the F0 range, which is wider in the 'incredulity' version, with a slightly higher precursor and considerably higher peak and end points. These F0 patterns suggest that 'morning' received extra prominence and was accented in both cases. This would also be a more plausible realisation of the utterance in the two contexts than the one with a single accent on 'eleven' and a much earlier rise, start-ing somewhere around 'the'. So, this pattern looks different from a single-accent rise-fall-rise in 'million' and does not seem to be L*+HL-H%, but L*+HL*L-H%, a fall followed by a rise, as in (b) or (d) of 'There's another one in the kitchen' in 1.4.4. This would mean that 'incredulity' is signalled by the expanded pitch ranges of the *late peak*, which signals expressively evaluated CONTRAST, and of the *final rise*, probably supported by non-modal phonation. A double-accent fall-rise in the 'uncertainty' context does not make a dissocia-tive reference to other alternatives, as the single-accent rise-fall-rise would. But the *late peak* contrasts, and expressively evaluates, B's time reference with A's question about coming in 'pretty late', and the *final rise* establishes contact with the dialogue partner and alleviates the categoricalness of a *late peak*.

   Hirschberg and Ward used the recordings of the eight contextualised utter-ances to generate two sets of stimuli, categorised as conveying 'uncertainty' and 'incredulity' for a listening experiment, where subjects had to allocate each stimulus to one of the two categories. Since the pitch patterns were most probably not homogeneous, and since such context-free semantic allocations are difficult, especially in view of the somewhat opaque meaning of 'uncer-tainty', the conclusions about the physical properties that cue 'uncertainty' or 'incredulity' are not so clear as they are made out to be.

1.4.5 A New Paradigm

The critical historical survey in 1.4 has prepared the ground, and provided the rationale, for presenting a new paradigm. The following chapters model prosody in relation to communicative functions of speech interaction, on the basis of the Kiel Intonation Model (KIM) in a broad linguistic-paralinguistic setting. The concern for function in prosody research at Kiel University goes back to Bill Barry's paper 'Prosodic functions revisited again!' (Barry 1981), following Brazil (1975, 1978). The function perspective guided the analysis, in production and perception, of prosody in general, and of intonation in par-ticular, from the early 1980s onwards, converging on the development of a prosodic model (Kohler 1991a,b, 1997b, 2006b, 2009b).

The idea behind KIM is that modelling prosody should mirror its use by speakers and listeners in communicative action, i.e. prosodic categories must be an integral part of communication processes rather than just static elements in a linguistic description. Speakers use prosody to structure the flow of sound for the transmission of meaning to listeners. In a synsemantic field, prosody operates on linguistic signs in parallel to morphological and syntactic patterning for propositional representation, and in a sympractical deictic field it signals Speaker-Listener-Situation relations. Finally, speakers use prosody to express their emotions and attitudes, and to signal their appeals to listeners. The prosodic model is to be structured in such a way that it can capture and adequately represent all these communicative functions in speaker–listener interaction. This also implies that the model needs to be integrated into a theory of speech and language together with all the other formal means – segmental-phonetic, lexical, morphological, syntactic – contributing in varying proportions as carriers of these functions. The model must be oriented towards basic communicative functions of *homo loquens*, and at the same time it must take into account psycho-physical components of the human-speech producing, perceiving and understanding mechanisms, irrespective of any particular language form that organises the general psycho-physical prerequisites for communicative purposes in language-specific ways.

KIM follows the European tradition of postulating a system of distinctive global pitch contours – *peak*, *valley*, combined *peak-valley* and *level* patterns. The model sets out how these patterns are synchronised with vocal-tract articulation, how they are concatenated into a hierarchy of larger units from phrase to utterance to paragraph in reading or to turn in dialogue, and how they are embedded in other prosodic patterns – vocal-tract dynamics, prominence and phonation, paying attention to both the production and the perception of prosody in communicative function. The model was developed over many years, starting with a project in the German Research Council programme 'Forms and Functions of Intonation' in the 1980s (Kohler 1991c), continuing with its implementation in the INFOVOX TTS system (Kohler 1997a) and with the development of a data acquisition and annotation platform in the PHONDAT and VERBMOBIL projects of the German Ministry of Research and Technology (Kohler, Pätzold and Simpson 1995; Scheffers and Rettstadt 1997). In this research environment, large databases of read and spontaneous German speech were collected (IPDS 1994–2006; Kohler, Peters and Scheffers 2017a–b) and annotated segmentally and prosodically with the help of the PRO[sodic]LAB[elling] tool (Kohler 1997b; Kohler, Peters and Scheffers 2017a–b), which was devised to symbolise the prosodic systems and structures of KIM for computer processing of the German corpora. In a subsequent German Research Council project, 'Sound Patterns of German Spontaneous Speech', various prosodic aspects of the corpus data were analysed in the KIM-PROLAB frame (Kohler, Kleber and Peters 2005). PhD theses by Benno Peters (2006) and Oliver Niebuhr (2007b) followed, and there has been a continuous flow of prosodic research within this paradigm in Kiel.

2 Prosody in a Functional Framework: The Kiel Intonation Model (KIM)

The following sections will successively build up the concepts of KIM: *Prominence* (2.1), *Sentence accent* (2.2, 2.3), *Declination, downstep and upstep* (2.4), *Lexical stress* (2.5, 2.6), *Intonation* (2.7, 2.8), *Concatenation of pitch patterns* (2.9), *Contour-internal F0 timing in falls and rises* (2.10*), Prehead and register* (2.11), *Prosodic phrasing* (2.12) and *Microprosody* (2.13). In each case, the PROLAB symbolisation will be introduced in parallel to the categories. The chapter is rounded off by a section on level-pitch *stepping patterns* (2.14), followed by an overview of *Time-windows in speech production* (2.15).

2.1   Prominence

In any language, the flow of syllables produced by a speaker varies along a scale of salience. This fluctuation is referred to by the concept of *prominence*, i.e. the listener's perception of relative weight in the acoustic intermediary generated by the articulatory mechanism. In Metrical Phonology, prominence is a qualitative, phonological category whose levels are derived from linguistic structures (Liberman and Prince 1977), largely based on native speakers' intuition. Fant and Kruckenberg (1989, 1999) proposed a quantification of prominence on a perceptual scale from 0 to 30 (the 1999 paper erroneously refers to an upper end of 35), by asking subjects to mark each syllable in the recording of a read text on the given scale. They then correlated the perceptual syllable judgements with the physical syllable parameters of sub- and supra-glottal pressure, syllable duration, F0 and sound-pressure level with and without high-frequency pre-emphasis. Duration turned out to be a very robust indicator of perceptual prominence. The quantified concept of perceptual prominence was pursued further in Wagner (2002), but now based on a scale from 0 to 31.

The problem with this type of quantitative scaling is that, on the one hand, it is too detailed and puts high demands on subjects, which they are only able to meet somehow because they are biased by being told that typical values are 10 units for unstressed syllables and 20 units for stressed syllables. On the other hand, the detail is not only unnecessary for a proper assessment of prominence variation in running speech, it also blurs the relation to the significant production patterns that create the acoustic signals that listeners have to judge on a perceptual prominence scale.

By way of illustration, let us look at the German CONFIRMATION QUESTION 'Wie weit ist es bis Hamburg?' [How far is it to Hamburg?] in Figure 2.1a. In the F0 trace inside the spectrogram, there is a monotonic F0 rise throughout the sentence (plain line), only disturbed by microprosodic effects at vowel-consonant-vowel transitions (see 2.13). This global F0 pattern gives high prominence to the initial syllable and lower prominence to all the following ones. In terms of discrete prosodic categories, we say that the former receives a *sentence accent* and the latter are *unaccented* (see 2.2). Combined with question-word structure, this pattern signals that the information about 'distance to' has already been given by a dialogue partner; and that the speaker is asking for confirmation, backgrounding the locality. If 'Hamburg' is replaced by 'Halle' [ˈhalə], the prominence relations in the syllable chain remain the same but both [ˈha] and [lə] have lower values because of reduced articulatory syllable complexity leading to shorter durations and less acoustic change. On the other hand, replacing 'Hamburg' with 'Flensburg' [ˈflɛnsbʊɐk] increases the prominence of the penultimate syllable, within the same prominence profile, because of the greater articulatory complexity of 'Flens-'.

The perceptual syllable prominence relations are, from high to low, 'wie', 'weit', 'Ham-', '-burg', 'ist'/'bis', 'es', reflected in their relative durations.

However, if the monotonic F0 rise is broken by the rise starting afresh from a slightly lower level on 'Hamburg' (dashed line in Figure 2.1a), the locality is weakly foregrounded as a specific reference in the CONFIRMATION QUESTION, changing the prominence profile of the utterance: 'Ham-' is now at the second-highest prominence level. In categorical terms it is *partially deaccented* (see 2.2). If a more substantial break of the monotonic rise is effected by a larger F0 drop at the beginning of 'Hamburg' (dotted line), the prominence level is raised to that of 'wie', and the sentence mode changes from CONFIRMATION QUESTION to INFORMATION QUESTION. The speaker no longer asks the listener to repeat information that has already been provided, but solicits new information about both distance and locality, with two discrete *sentence accents* (see 2.2), for example in the dialogue context:

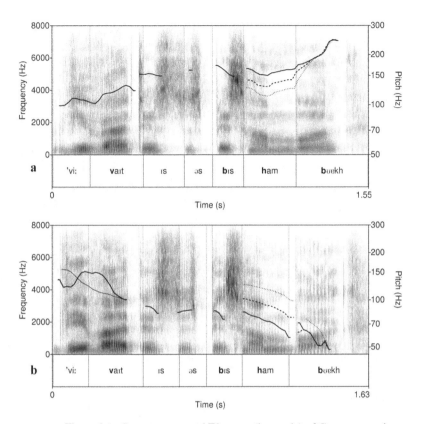

Figure 2.1. Spectrograms and F0 traces (log scale) of German question-word interrogative 'Wie weit ist es bis Hamburg?': **a**, CONFIRMATION QUESTION with rising F0 starting on 'wie'; **b**, INFORMATION QUESTION with rising-falling F0 starting around 'wie'. In each panel, spectrogram and thick plain F0 trace from original, naturally produced utterance **a** or **b**. Dashed and dotted F0 traces derived from original utterances in Praat by systematic pointwise manual modification across the two final syllables to test prominence changes in psola resynthesis. Likewise, continuously falling F0 contour (thin line in **b**) generated from the original rising-falling one. Standard German, male speaker (KJK).

A: Für die Fahrt nach Hannover werden wir etwa drei Stunden brauchen. Wir können dazwischen ohne weiteres einen Einkaufsbummel in Hamburg einplanen.
       [Driving to Hanover will take about three hours. We can easily stop on the way for a shopping spree in Hamburg.]

B: Wie weit ist es bis Hamburg?
       [How far is it to Hamburg?]

The same changes apply when 'Halle' or 'Flensburg' are weakly foregrounded or given full foreground weight, relative to lowered or raised prominence levels of their different syllable complexities.

Attributing prominence levels to the two final syllables in the monotonic F0 rise pattern of the CONFIRMATION QUESTION does not add any information that is not already contained in the articulatory make-up of the lexical items and their acoustic transforms. But the F0-related prominence increases utterance-initially and -finally have such additional information value because they are intentionally introduced by the speaker to perform communicative functions. Similarly, the low prominence levels of the function words 'ist', 'es', 'bis' reflect articulatory reduction in low-key speech stretches. Prominence may thus either be determined by articulatory complexity of syllables at the lexical level, or it may be derived from prosodic structuring reflecting communicative functions in speech interaction. It may be regarded as a production category, linked directly to its physical parameters. Setting up acoustic databases annotated by instructed or trained listeners on a syllable prominence scale, and correlating these perceptual measures with physical production parameters is an indirect way of making statements about the physical exponents of weight fluctuation in speech production. It is an attempt to replace the discrete prominence categories of metrical phonology with an objective measure along a continuous scale. But the reliability of this measure as an objective mapping of syllable prominence perception is questionable, because prominence profiles are generated in subjective auditory evaluation by a small number of specially instructed listeners, and there is no guarantee that they actually apply purely auditory criteria, uninfluenced by syntactic and semantic considerations.

I relate the prominence concept to varying degrees of articulatory weight that speakers give to syllables in the speech flow in order to make specific syllables more salient against their neighbours for the listener. This is achieved by a hierarchy, from most to least important, of the physical parameters of F0 change, syllabic duration ratio, acoustic energy ratio and spectra of more peripheral versus more central vowels in adjacent syllables. In non-tone languages, like German or English, where pitch is not distinctive at the level of the lexical syllable and therefore free to vary across syllables at the phrase level, F0 gliding up or down through a syllable, or changing gliding direction, or a flat F0 contour getting broken by stepping up or down from one syllable to the next, are strong markers of prominence. If monotonic upward gliding continues through subsequent syllables to the end of a phrase, F0 does not mark any further prominent syllables. But if the monotonic gliding is broken by a renewed rising movement, this marks another prominent syllable, with two distinctive degrees of prominence, depending on the extent of the F0 drop relative to a threshold (see Figure 2.1a).

Similarly, monotonic downward gliding into low trailing off does not generate further prominences, but breaking the monotonic gliding by a renewed falling movement does, again in two distinctive degrees. The F0 traces inside the spectrogram of Figure 2.1b illustrate this: 'wie' is made strongly prominent either by an F0 fall (thin plain line), or a rise-fall straddling 'wie weit' (thick plain line). In both cases, the thick line continuing to the end of 'Hamburg' marks the low-prominence trailing off, only disturbed by consonant-vowel-consonant microprosodies.

The global F0 fall signals that the speaker requests more precise information about the distance of the locality than the dialogue partner has provided, for example in the context:

A: Von Kiel nach Hamburg ist es nicht weit.
    [It is not far from Kiel to Hamburg.]
B: Wie weit ist es bis Hamburg?

Breaking the monotonic downward trend by a restart from a slightly higher F0 level, as shown by the dashed line, again gives the syllable 'Ham-' extra prominence, second to 'wie'. This puts the word 'Hamburg' in the prosodic category of *partial deaccentuation* (see 2.2). Its function is to weakly foreground 'Hamburg' as an explicit reference to the requested distance information, which is also possible in the above context. A more extensive F0 break, shown by the dotted line, puts the prominence of 'Ham-' on a par with the one of 'wie', creating a second *sentence accent* on a downtrend line of successive peaks (see 2.4). This prosodic pattern is no longer possible in the above context because it singles out the locality 'Hamburg' among alternatives and asks something specific about it.

In the utterances of Figures 2.1b and 2.2a, the initial interrogative word 'wie' is made prominent by gliding F0 movement across it, which links it to a sentence accent. But this movement varies within a wide range. In Figure 2.1b, it either falls from syllable onset, thus has its peak maximum early and lowers the pitch percept of the prominent syllable nucleus, or it rises to its maximum within the prominent syllable before falling across the following syllable 'weit', thus shifting the pitch percept of the prominent syllable upwards. In Figure 2.2a, F0 rises up to its maximum at the vowel onset of 'weit', where the fall starts. So, we notice a progressive rightward shift of the peak maximum synchronisation (see 2.7, 2.8). This shift does not alter the position of prominence in the syllable chain and the sentence accent in the sentence; it changes

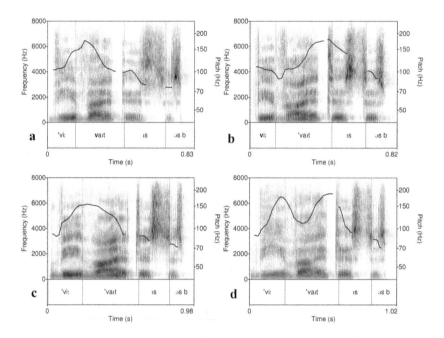

Figure 2.2. Spectrograms and F0 traces (log scale) of four functionally different types of accentuation in the German INFORMATION QUESTION 'Wie weit ist es (bis)?' They are all rising-falling F0 patterns synchronised around different words in the sentence: **a**, rise on 'wie', fall on 'weit', single accent on 'wie'; **b**, rise on 'weit', fall on 'ist', single accent on 'weit'; **c**, rise on 'wie', fall stretched out across lengthened 'weit', two-accent *hat pattern*; **d**, rise on 'wie', followed by fall into 'weit', new rise in 'weit', followed by fall on 'ist', two-accent double-peak pattern. Standard German, male speaker (KJK).

the intonation pattern as an exponent of different expressive and attitudinal functions. But a further move to the right in Figure 2.2b does shift prominence from 'wie' to 'weit'. This means that in German certain F0 contours not only function as carriers of perceived pitch patterns, as F0 generally does, but, over and above that, they function as carriers of perceived prominence patterns. In the IPO perception model of intonation this was termed 'prominence lending' ('t Hart, Collier and Cohen 1990).

Prominence-lending F0 is supported by timing. The comparison of Figures 2.2a,b shows that prominence goes together with a change of the duration ratio of the prominent and non-prominent syllable nuclei [iː] and [aɪ]: 96 ms: 135 ms and 80 ms: 175 ms. The integration of a fall with a preceding rise into one prominent F0 peak contour around the syllable containing the rise presupposes that the two movements must not exceed a certain time-window, which is set by the overall speech rate, the syllable complexity and short or long vowel quantities. The single rise-fall pattern in Figure 2.2a has a width of about 220 ms from the left to the right low F0 base point. This time-window is doubled in the rise-fall pattern of Figure 2.2c on the same segmental string. Here the rise on 'wie' and the fall on the lengthened nucleus of 'weit' become dissociated into two prominences in a two-accent *hat pattern* (see 2.9). The time-window for the rise-fall needs to be above a duration threshold to signal two separate prominences for the fall and for the rise. If the *hat pattern* is broken up into two rise-falls, as in Figure 2.2d, each has its own time-window for two separate prominences leading to two accents.

An utterance such as 'Die Uhr tickt' [The clock is ticking], intended as a double-accent *hat pattern* with a late rise on 'Uhr' and an early fall on 'tickt', may become ambiguous with a single-accent late peak contour spanning 'Uhr tickt'. Ambiguity arises in sequences of two accented monosyllabic words where the second one does not provide much leeway for temporal expansion of the falling F0 branch, particularly when, as in the present case, the short vowel [ɪ] in the voiceless obstruent context puts heavy limitations on the F0 time-window for a double-prominence rise-fall (Hertrich 1991). This problem does not arise in the rise-fall pattern of Figure 2.2b, although the time-window between the left and right F0 base points spans 'weit ist es' with a duration of >400 ms. In spite of this expansion, only one prominence is perceived, associated with 'weit'. This is due, first of all, to the very short durations of the vowels in the function words 'ist' and 'es', which cannot create prominences. Secondly, the F0 fall is curtailed at the long obstruent sequence 'st', and there are, furthermore, microprosodic disturbances in the consonant-vowel sequences '-t ist e-' delaying the F0 descent. The perception mechanism must take all these variables into account to arrive at just one prominence in a single accented word.

The prominence-lending function of F0 applies to all the West-Germanic languages. The discussion of the German data can therefore be extrapolated to the English equivalents. And the principle still holds in all languages that mark sentence accents by gliding F0. French does not seem to fit into this set (see 2.2). The conditions change completely in tone languages where F0 does not have the same freedom of variation across syllable chains, and therefore F0 gliding to mark prominence cannot operate in the same way. It is an empirical question to investigate the concept of prominence in contour and register tone languages of East Asia and sub-Saharan Africa, respectively, to find out to

what extent F0 can play a role in generating prominences and how other phonetic variables, especially vowel duration and spectral features, take over the
prominence-lending function. The question remains as to whether prominence
relations are used at all to signal sentence accentuation, or whether syntactic
and lexical forms are used instead. One thing is already certain: the perceptual
prominence scaling proposed by Fant and Kruckenberg on the basis of prosody
relations in Swedish syllable sequences cannot apply to tone languages and has
no status as a language-independent measure.

2.2   Sentence Accent

In the synsemantic field, speakers select objects and weight factual relations
between them by choosing lexical items and putting them in morpho-syntactic
and prosodic structures to mark their relative importance (see Chapter 3). The
prosodic category that fulfils this function besides phrase structure is *sentence
accent*. It needs to be given a separate status in its own right in the prosodic
model, independent of intonation and the metrical structure of words and
phrases. Four distinctive levels of sentence accent, based on levels of prominence, are distinguished to bring out relations between words in phrase structures.

Label	Prosodic category
&0	*unaccented (defocused)*
&1	*(partially) deaccented (partially foregrounded)*
&2	*default accent*
&3	*reinforced accent*

In prosodic notation, accented words are prefixed by one of the accent labels.
Accent labels, and all other prosodic labels introduced in subsequent sections,
are marked by **&**.

These accent levels are manifested by scaling and summing the prominence
variables of F0 change, syllabic duration ratio, acoustic energy ratio and spectrum between neighbouring syllables. They form a perceptual hierarchy from
most to least important (Kohler 2012). Accent levels **&0-&2** are discrete prosodic categories; accent level **&3** is graded depending on the degree of intensification. At the *unaccented* level, F0 change does not exceed a critical threshold, but is integrated in the F0 pattern associated with a neighbouring sentence
accent, e.g. the low trailing off after a peak contour, or the monotonic continuation of a valley rise (see 2.1). All languages have a sentence-accent category,
but they vary greatly in its use beside morpho-syntactic structure. They also
differ in the way the physical properties are docked in the flow of words.

In all the West Germanic languages, any word in an utterance can be put in focus by a sentence accent, thus weighting the object or factual relation it represents. For example, in English, a Speaker A, in talking about the guests at a party, may say:

&2Anna &0came &0with &2Manny.

(cf. Liberman and Pierrehumbert 1984), attributing equal information weight to both 'Anna' and 'Manny' by giving each a *default accent*. Then Speaker B may reply:

&2No. &2Alice &0came &0with &1/&0Manny.

with a *default accent* on 'Alice' and just partially foregrounding 'Manny' by *partial deaccentuation*, or defocusing it altogether by *complete deaccentuation*. On the other hand, Speaker B may reply:

&2No. &1Anna &0came &0with &2Morris.

with the reversed sentence-accent patterns on 'Morris' and 'Anna'. In such contradictory statements, the names may get a *reinforced accent* **&3**. In all these cases, patterns of F0-change, increased duration, more peripheral vowel articulation and greater acoustic energy are docked at the lexically stressed initial syllables (see 2.5) of the accented or partially deaccented words, raising their prominences.

Prominence-lending F0 gliding over words to be highlighted is a powerful indicator of sentence accents (see 2.1), but their specific pitch patterns depend on the distinctive *intonation* elements selected at each *sentence accent* (see 2.7). One possibility is a rising-falling *peak* pattern at each accent, with downstep from peak to peak, to signal equal prominence for equal information weight. In the case of two successive accents, they may either be implemented as a *double F0 peak* or as an *F0 hat pattern* (see 2.1, 2.9), depending on linked or separated information weighting (see 2.9). The *hat pattern* is a broadened rise-fall, which is conceptualised as containing the rise for the first accent and the fall for the second, i.e. a concatenation of two peaks, without a first fall and a second rise. Downstepping, which creates default accents in peak sequences, also applies to the *hat pattern*. This was illustrated in the double prominence *hat pattern* of Figure 2.2c; the double-peak pattern of Figure 2.2d, however, lacks this downstep and consequently creates greater prominence on the second peak, which becomes a *reinforced accent*. In a **&3** peak, the extent of F0 change is graded for degrees of intensification. For further discussion of the concept of downstep, see 2.4.

Information selection and weighting by prosodic sentence accentuation is not possible in French. The French equivalent of Speaker A's double-accent utterance '[Annie] [est venue] [avec Michel]' is organised in two or three prosodic phrases, each with a rising syllable series. In the last prosodic phrase, it ends on the penultimate and is followed by an abrupt descent on the final syllable. In each prosodic phrase, the final syllable is made more prominent than the preceding ones because of the break in the rising pitch series, either due to the restart in the next phrase or due to the utterance-final drop. In the case of three prosodic phrases, 'Annie' gets its own informational weight; in the case of two phrases, it is subordinated to the information 'est venue'. The phrase-final accentuation highlights information structure in prosodic phrasing; it does not weight lexical elements, which lose their phonetic boundary identity in these prosodic phrases. This, in turn, means that focusing on selected words requires formal means other than the prosodic patterns of *sentence accent*, i.e. cleft sentence construction. So, the French equivalents of Speaker B's one-accent utterances would be 'Non, c'est Alice (qui est venue avec Michel)', and 'Non, c'est avec Maurice (qu'Annie est venue).' In each utterance, the first part is a self-contained statement, with an abrupt pitch drop on the last syllable. The second part is usually skipped; if it is present, it is backgrounded by a narrower pitch range of the rising-falling phrase pattern. In English, Speaker A may also contradict Speaker B's negation by **&2**No, **&2**no. **&2**Anna **&3**did **&0**come **&0**with **&0**Manny with one *sentence accent* on the verb phrase, structurally intensified by 'did': the focus pattern is further reinforced syntactically. In French, this would be rendered by 'Non, non, Annie est venue avec Michel' with the same prosodic structuring as in the neutral statement, but with intensification of 'est' (*accent d'insistance*) by an initial glottal stop and vowel lengthening, and by retaining the [ə], in the first syllable of 'venue' as well as by pitch range expansion of the prosodic phrases.

In the German sentence 'Aber der Leo säuft' [But Leo drinks], either the person or the fact that he drinks may be highlighted by positioning a rising-falling peak pattern around the lexical items 'Leo' or 'säuft', giving the one or the other a default sentence accent **&2**. The rise-fall peak pattern may also span both items and thus generate default sentence accents **&2** on both. To test the cue value of peak pattern synchronisation with vocal-tract articulation, stimuli were generated for a perception experiment by systematically shifting a rise-fall F0 contour through that utterance.

Based on the original stimulus shown in Figure 2.3, nineteen stimuli were LPC-synthesised (for further details see Kohler 1991a). The original F0 peak contour was shifted in 30 ms steps, 7 to the left and 11 to the right. In the

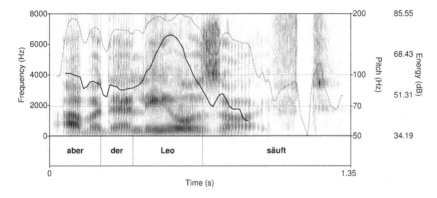

Figure 2.3. Spectrogram, F0 (log scale) and energy traces, and orthographically annotated word segmentation of the original utterance of the German sentence 'Aber der Leo säuft', with a position of the rise-fall F0 peak pattern in the centre of the accented syllable 'Leo'. Standard German speaker (KJK).

left shift, the rising branch was moved and the falling branch was expanded between the new maximum position and the old right base point. In the right shift, the complete peak contour was moved in parallel. Figure 2.4 shows the peak synchronisations for the 1st, 4th, 5th, 8th, 11th, 13th and 16th stimuli in the left to right series. The nineteen stimuli entered a standardised perception experiment, asking subjects which word, 'Leo' or 'säuft', they perceived as more accented (for details, see Kohler 1991a). Figure 2.5 presents the results. Stimuli 1–11 in the series from left to right, where the rising-falling F0 peak contour is in *early, medial* or *late* synchronisation with the word 'Leo', and where a substantial part of the F0 fall occurs in its vowel, were almost unanimously judged as having the sentence accent on 'Leo'. In stimuli 15–19, where F0 rises into, and then falls in, the vowel of 'säuft', this word is almost unanimously perceived as accented. Stimuli 12–14 form a transition range, and stimulus 13 is divided between the judgements, pointing to a two-accent *hat pattern*, as it straddles both monosyllabic words, the rise occurring in 'Leo', the fall in 'säuft'. In the left peak shift the falling branch was flattened to avoid too long a low F0 trail, which would have generated poor LPC synthesis quality. Since the precursor to the F0 peak was stretched as a whole in the right shift, the microprosodic F0 effects were displaced, which influenced the acoustic quality of the synthesised stimuli, and the large F0 inflections on the original low F0 stretch in stimuli 16–19 also degraded their acoustic quality. But this did not affect accent perception.

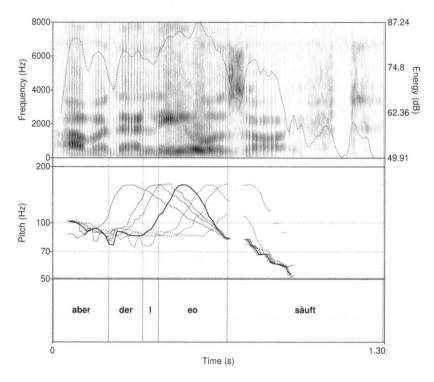

Figure 2.4. Spectrogram with energy trace of LPC resynthesised original utterance 'Aber der Leo säuft', as well as F0 traces (log scale) of the original (thick line) and of the 1st, 4th and 5th positions of the left F0 shift (thin lines), and the 11th, 13th and 16th positions of the right F0 shift (dotted lines). In the 4th position, the F0 maximum is located at the transition from [l] to the stressed vowel of 'Leo'; the 5th position is the first where the F0 maximum is in the vowel. Orthographic annotation, segmented at word boundaries and at consonant-vowel transition in 'Leo'.

2.3   Sentence Accents in Syntagmatic Prominence Patterns

In 2.2, accent levels **&1–3** were determined by local prominences related to physical properties, especially F0 gliding, in the accented words. But accent perception is also influenced by the occurrence of these word-bound properties in broader syntagmatic prominence patterns. This can be illustrated with the German sentence 'Anna kam mit Menne', the equivalent of 'Anna came with Manny' (see 2.2). The sentence was produced in four versions:

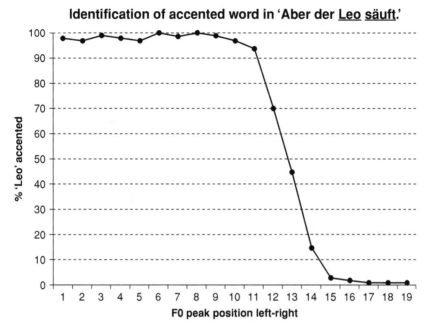

Figure 2.5. Identification function showing percentage of 'Leo' stressed judgements for nineteen LPC synthesised stimuli of 'Aber der Leo säuft', with F0 peak shift, ordered from left to right. Thirty-one subjects, n = 155 at each data point.

(1) **&3**Anna **&0**kam **&0**mit **&1**Menne.
(2) **&2**Anna **&0**kam **&0**mit **&2**Menne.
(3) **&2**Anna **&1**kam **&0**mit **&2**Menne.
(*late low-rising valley* contour on 'Menne' in all three cases)
(4) **&2**Anna **&0**kam **&0**mit **&2**Menne.
(*early low-rising valley* contour on 'Menne').

All four utterances sounded as intended, especially as regards the accent level **&1** or **&2** on 'Menne'. Version (2) may oscillate between **&2/&1**Menne. The *late low-rising valleys* were all very similar. An identical rising pattern was created in all three by replacing the 'Menne' sections of (2) and (3) with that of (1). Original (1) and modified (2) and (3) are shown in Figures 2.6a,b,c. A parallel set was then created in the same frames (1)–(3) by replacing their late-valley 'Menne' with the *early valley* of (4); it is displayed in Figures 2.6d,e,f.

The identical 'Menne' stimulus of the original frame (1), spliced into frames (2)–(3), is perceived as accent level **&1** in the utterance of Figure 2.6a, but as accent level **&2** in the utterance of Figure 2.6c, and as oscillating between

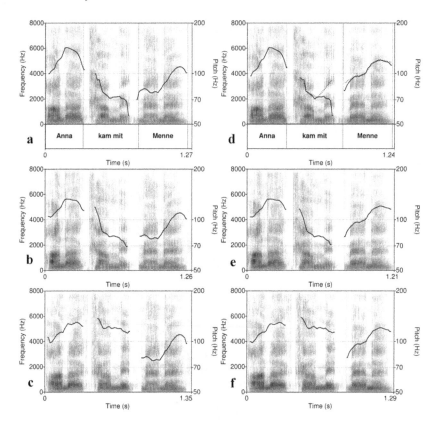

Figure 2.6. Spectrograms, F0 traces (log scale) and orthographic word annotations of the German sentence 'Anna kam mit Menne': **a** original utterance (1); **b, c** 'Menne' of (1) with late low-rising valley spliced into (2) and (3); **d, e, f** 'Menne' of (4) with early low-rising valley spliced into (1), (2) and (3). F0 jump from 'mit' to 'Menne' was additionally adjusted to a smooth rise in **d** (dotted line). Standard German speaker (KJK).

&2 and **&1** in the utterance of Figure 2.6b. The reason for the different accent perception of an identical physical stimulus must reside in its embedding in different prosodic contexts. When 'kam mit Menne' is excerpted from each utterance, 'Menne' has the same default accent in all three excerpts. So the difference must be due to the prominence relation of 'Menne' to 'Anna'. In 2.6a, 'Anna' has a high-maximum peak pattern, with F0 falling quickly from 142 Hz in the accented vowel of 'Anna' to 72 Hz in [mɪ] of 'kam mit', corresponding to 12 st, followed by glottalisation for [tm]. These are the physical exponents of a *reinforced* accent. The rise in 'Menne' starts at 79 Hz and moves up to a maximum of 109 Hz, corresponding to 6 st. The upward gliding is considerably smaller than the preceding downward gliding and consequently has less prominence-lending power in syntagmatic comparison, which is perceived as *partial deaccentuation*. In 2.6c, there is a pitch drop from 113 Hz of the plateau to 79 Hz at the beginning of the rise (= 6 st), giving comparable prominence and independent accent status to the rise. The stimulus of Figure 2.6b has an F0 maximum of 132 Hz, dropping more slowly than in 2.6a to 80 Hz in [m] of 'kam mit' (= 8.8 st), and it does not end in glottalisation. The physical parameters are the exponents of a *default*, not a reinforced, accent on 'Anna'. The extensions of downward and upward gliding are closer than in 2.6a, and the accentuation of 'Menne' is in between the stimuli of 2.6a,c, but closer to the latter. Perception oscillates between **&2** and **&1**.

In the *early-valley* 'Menne' of Figures 2.6d, e, f, F0 starts at 80 Hz and moves up to 120 Hz (= 7 st). This is a higher and more extensive rise than the *late-valley* rise in Figures 2.6a, b, c. In 2.6e, the extensions of the upward and the downward gliding are more similar than in 2.6b, and accentuation is now perceived as a clear **&2**. The *early-valley* 'Menne' of 2.6f also produces a clear *default accent*; like the *late-valley* 'Menne' in 2.6c, it has the same prominence lending. The *early valley* in 2.6d reduces the prominence of 'Menne', but not to the same extent as the *late valley* in 2.6b. There is still a considerable F0 jump up from the end of voicing in 'mit' to the beginning of 'Menne', which gives 'Menne' more prominence. If this is corrected by synthesising a rise through 'mit', shown by the dotted line in 2.6d, the prominence of 'Menne' gets further reduced to *partial deaccentuation*.

Figure 2.7 provides two natural productions of 'Anne kam mit Menne', with a wide and a narrow low F0 fall in 'Menne'. In 2.7a, the F0 maximum in 'Anne' is at 151 Hz; across 'kam mit' it ends at 103 Hz; its onset in 'Menne' is at 117 Hz, its offset at 60 Hz. In this constellation, 'Menne' is clearly perceived as *partially deaccented* and backgrounded. In 2.7b, the F0 maximum in 'Anne' is at 153 Hz; across 'kam mit' it ends at 82 Hz; its onset in 'Menne' is at 94 Hz, its offset at 67 Hz. In this acoustic setting, 'Menne' is also clearly perceived as *partially deaccented* and backgrounded. In both cases, the jump up from the F0 offset in 'mit' to the F0 onset in 'Menne' are comparable (about 2 st).

The original utterance (plain line in Figure 2.7a) has a continuous F0 fall through '-ne kam' if the microprosodic lowering into the voiceless stop and raising out of the strong aspiration is taken into account (see 2.13). This setting

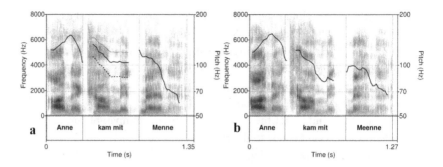

Figure 2.7. Spectrograms, F0 traces (log scale) and orthographic word annotations of the German sentence 'Anne kam mit Menne': **a**, wide low F0 fall in 'Menne', original utterance (plain line), central F0 section in 'kam mit' raised (dotted line) and lowered (dashed line); **b**, narrow low F0 fall in 'Menne'. Standard German speaker (KJK).

generates the accentual pattern **&2**Anne **&0**kam **&0**mit **&1**Menne. When the F0 contour across 'kam mit' is raised, both 'kam' and 'Menne' move up by one accent level: **&1**kam, **&2**Menne. When it is lowered, the two flanking words become more prominent: **&3**Anne **&0**kam **&0**mit **&2**Menne.

'Menne' with the larger fall in Figure 2.7a was also spliced into the three frames of Figures 2.6a,b,c, replacing the final rise. *Default accent* is perceived in all. In 2.6a and 2.6b, the F0 offset in 'mit' around 70 Hz generates a large jump up to the fall onset of spliced 'Menne'. The F0 fall in 'Menne' is thus above the threshold for *default accentuation* in relation to the preceding utterance section. Spliced into 2.6c, the fall in 'Menne' forms the falling section of a *hat pattern* and is therefore a *default accent*.

Finally, 'Menne' with the smaller fall in Figure 2.7b was spliced into the three frames of Figure 2.6a,b,c. Now *partial deaccentuation* occurs in 2.6a and 2.6b. Here the jump up to the lower F0 onset in 'Menne' is much smaller than in the larger fall on 'Menne'. The F0 fall in 'Menne' is below the threshold for accentuation in relation to the preceding utterance section. In 2.6c, the fall on 'Menne' again forms the falling section of a *hat pattern* and is therefore a *default accent*.

The description of these data relies on observation by a trained phonetician and an experienced speech analyst. The analysis lacks experimental validation by large populations of listeners in formal perceptual testing. But the observational hypotheses can easily be supported or falsified by future research that takes the next step in the speech scientist's contribution to a theory of communication. The data have already demonstrated that the prominence-lending aspect of F0 is complex. It may be implemented by a break in monotonic rising or falling movement, or by the extension of movement or by the integration of local, word-bound physical properties in larger prominence patterns. A perception-based prosodic category is needed that can relate physical parameters, most prominently F0 change, to distinctive salience relations in INFORMATION SELECTION AND WEIGHTING. This category is the four-level *sentence accentuation* of words in syntax and information structures proposed here. Accent levels are perceived by summing pitch and other signal properties over variable windows. The finding that the same physical F0 rise or fall in different global pitch patterns can change the perception and cognitive processing of words between foregrounding and backgrounding presupposes a separate sentence-accent category, independent of intonation proper, i.e. non-prominence-lending F0, and of metrics. The concept of accentuation in KIM is thus different from L-H related pitch accents in AM Phonology.

2.4 Declination, Downstep and Upstep

Phonetic research has proved that, to create equal prominences, successive F0 peaks need to form a descending sequence. This was called *declination* in the IPO intonation model (Adriaens 1991, Cohen and 't Hart 1967), and the term was taken over generally, among others by AM Phonology, to differentiate it as a phonetic process from phonological *downstep* of H tones in the vicinity of L tones, a feature adopted from African tone languages for intonation analysis of English and other languages. Kohler (1991a,b) argued against the use of the term *declination* for this downscaling of successive, equally prominent peaks. It was defined on a time basis in the IPO model, and this phonetic definition has been retained by all scholars using it, opposing it to phonological prosodic categories. This means that the F0 downtrend is considered a linear lowering of successive F0 peaks through an utterance, proportionate with the temporal distance between peaks, but even the IPO model introduced F0 reset when utterances were too long and F0 descended unnaturally low in the application to speech synthesis. The concept of time-based declination has to be rejected if it can be shown that (a) there are naturally produced data where the same maxima steps in differently spaced successive peaks are perceived as equal in prominence, and (b) the application of linear proportionate lowering generates different pitch levels and prominences in successive peaks.

Figure 2.8 presents stimuli for test criteria (a) and (b). In 2.8a, the naturally produced German sentences are 'Die Wähler wählen' [The male voters vote] and 'Die Wählerinnen wählen' [The female voters vote], each with two default

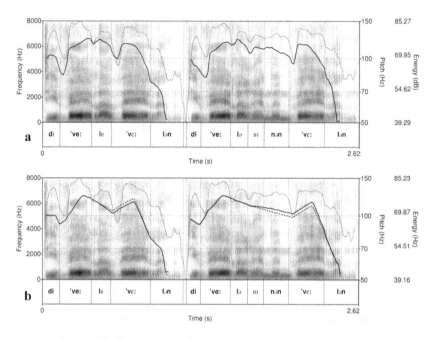

Figure 2.8. Spectrograms, F0 (log scale, plain lines) and energy traces (dotted lines), syllabic segmentations and transcriptions of the German sentences 'Die Wähler(innen) wählen': **a**, natural production; **b**, resynthesis with stylised F0 patterns. The dashed F0 lines represent the time-based F0 declination of the shorter sentence adjusted to the longer sentence, and vice versa. Standard German, male speaker (KJK).

accents **&2** on 'Wähler(innen)' and 'wählen'. In both sentences, the two peak contours associated with the two accents have their maxima at 123 Hz and 117 Hz, spaced at 284 ms and 510 ms in the shorter and the longer sentence, respectively, but they are perceived as the same sequence of pitch levels and prominences. Moreover, the low left base points of the first and the second peak are also very similar, at 86 Hz/82 Hz and at 100 Hz/97 Hz, and so are the right base points of the second peak, at 83 Hz/85 Hz, before the final low trailing off. In Figure 2.8b, the pitch contours in the two sentences have been stylised, using Praat, as prototypical *medial peak* sequences (see 2.7), according to the model in Kohler (1991b). In both sentences, the first peak maximum of 125 Hz is at 60% of the duration of the accented vowel in 'Wähler(innen)', the second peak maximum of 117 Hz at the same duration ratio in the accented vowel of 'wählen', an interval of 1.1 st. The first left base point (90 Hz) is at the onset of the initial consonant of the accented syllable, the right base point of the second peak (80 Hz) 120 ms after the maximum. The inter-peak base point (102 Hz) is at the onset of the initial consonant of 'wählen', which is 2.4 st below the following maximum. The psola synthesis with these values sounds perfectly natural, with comparable pitch levels and prominences in both sentences, irrespective of the difference of peak maxima spacing of 420 ms versus 730 ms.

The dashed F0 contours in Figure 2.8b show the time-based F0 adjustments of the two maxima and the inter-peak base point in:

(1)   'Die Wähler wählen',
       on the basis of stylised 'Die Wählerinnen wählen' with longer maximum
       spacing,
(2)   'Die Wählerinnen wählen',
       on the basis of stylised 'Die Wähler wählen' with shorter maximum
       spacing.

In (1) the interval of 1.1 st between the two maxima is scaled down with the proportion of the shorter to the longer distance, i.e. 1.1*420/730 = 0.63 st, which sets the second peak maximum at 121 Hz, and the inter-peak base point 2.4 st down at 105 Hz. In (2), the interval is scaled up with the reversed proportion, i.e. 1.1*730/430 = 1.91 st, which sets the second peak maximum at 112 Hz, and the inter-peak base point 2.4 st down at 98 Hz. When rescaled 'Die Wähler wählen' is auditorily compared with stylised 'Die Wählerinnen wählen' of Figure 2.8b, the succession of peaks no longer sounds the same in the two sentences: 'wählen' in 'Die Wähler wählen' is higher in pitch, getting more closely linked with the first peak, and therefore has its prominence perceptually reduced. On the other hand, when rescaled 'Die Wählerinnen wählen' is auditorily compared with stylised 'Die Wähler wählen' of Figure 2.8b, the opposite happens: 'wählen' in 'Die Wählerinnen wählen' is lower in pitch, becoming more independent from the first peak, and thus has its prominence perceptually increased.

The phenomenon we are dealing with here is not a phonetic, as against a phonological, feature but is a distinctively applied mechanism to create equal prominences irrespective of the time that elapses between peaks. The F0 downtrend to safeguard perceptual prominence equality of successive peaks has a functional, not a temporal, basis; I therefore use the category of *downstep* to refer to it. Perception orientates itself at structurally positioned and downstepped peaks, not at time-based declination. Furthermore, in natural speech production, especially in spontaneous interaction, downstep may be interrupted and restarted with an upstep at any structural point to reflect the

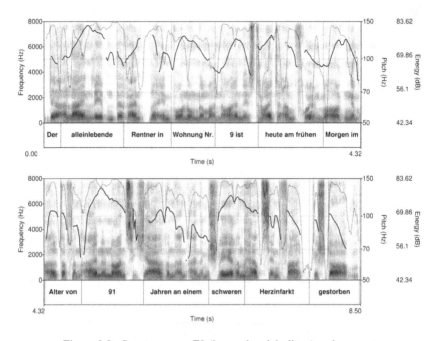

Figure 2.9. Spectrograms, F0 (log scale, plain lines) and energy traces (dotted lines), accent-unit segmentations and orthographic annotations of the German long complex single-sentence syntactic structure 'Der alleinlebende Rentner in Wohnung Nummer Neun ist heute am frühen Morgen im Alter von einundneunzig Jahren an einem schweren Herzinfarkt gestorben', in two approximately equal successive time-windows. F0 resets for selecting and weighting the information units 'alleinlebende Rentner', 'Wohnung Nr. 9', 'heute am frühen Morgen', '91 Jahren', 'schweren Herzinfarkt gestorben'. Standard German, male speaker (KJK).

information weighting and phrasing speakers want to transmit to listeners. It is symbolised by | in **&|2** or **&|3**.

Figure 2.9 provides an example of a long string of INFORMATION SELECTION AND WEIGHTING integrated into the German sentence:

> **&0**Der **&2**alleinlebende **&2**Rentner **&0**in **&|2**Wohnung **&1**Nummer **&2**Neun **&0**ist **&|2**heute **&0**am **&1**frühen **&2**Morgen **&0**im **&2**Alter **&0**von **&|3**einundneunzig **&2**Jahren **&0**an **&0**einem **&|2**schweren **&2**Herzinfarkt **&2**gestorben.
> [The pensioner living on his own in flat number 9 died of a massive heart attack early this morning at the age of 91.]

It has a complex syntactic structure of:

> subject phrase:
> [[Der alleinlebende] (Rentner) [in Wohnung Nummer 9]],

with (Rentner) as the head, and two qualifiers in the form of further structured adjectival and prepositional phrases, and:

> predicate phrase
> [(ist) [[heute] [am frühen Morgen]] [im Alter [von 91 Jahren]] [an einem schweren Herzinfarkt] (gestorben)].

with (ist) … (gestorben) as the head, and an adverbial and three further structured prepositional phrases as qualifiers.

Although constructed, the sentence is perfectly natural and could be part of a police report. When it is read out competently following its information structure, rather than its syntactic grouping, one way is to realise the sentence with a succession of downstepped accent sequences in accordance with the number of information units to be transmitted, and to mark the beginning of these prosodic phrases solely by F0 upstep above, or at least at, the level of the preceding accent. In Figure 2.9, the speaker marks five information units in this downstep-upstep way: 'alleinlebende Rentner' [pensioner living on his own] (2 downstepped accents), 'Wohnung Nr. 9' [flat no. 9] (2 downstepped accents 'Wohnung' and '9'), 'heute am frühen Morgen' [today early in the morning] (2 downstepped accents 'heute' and 'Morgen'), '91 Jahren' [91 years] (2 downstepped accents), 'schweren Herzinfarkt gestorben' [massive heart attack died] (3 downstepped accents, the first two forming a *hat pattern*). None of the upsteps in this example reach the F0 level of the utterance-initial accent; the degree of upstep varies with the relative importance attached to each information unit, which is greatest for '91', preceded and followed by downward trends of F0 upsteps.

The first, unstressed syllable of 'alleinlebende' is part of the up-beat, together with 'Der', but the left accent segmentation point was uniformly put at the word boundary, similarly in 'gestorben', where the accent is docked at the stressed, second syllable. The unaccented function words 'in' (preposition in accent unit 2), 'ist' (auxiliary verb in accent unit 4), 'im', 'von' (prepositions in accent units 6 and 7) and 'an einem' (preposition and indefinite article in accent unit 9) are integrated prosodically in the F0 contours of their preceding accents, with which they form accent units, although there is a syntactic, but prosodically unmarked boundary before them. This example shows that prosodic phrasing following information structure may diverge from syntactic grouping, and upsteps in prosodic phrasing may cut across information units.

'Alter von' is prosodically part of the preceding downstep sequence 'heute am frühen Morgen', resulting in a sequence of three downstepped accents, in spite of forming an information unit together with '91 Jahren'. If syntactic boundaries are signalled by prosodic phrase boundaries in addition to information selecting upstep, this is achieved (1) by syllabic lengthening before the syntactic boundary, (2) by valley or combined peak-valley, instead of simple peak patterns (see 2.7) and (3) by pausing, with increasing boundary strength in combinations of (1) and (3) (see 2.12).

The interpretation of the pitch patterns in Figure 2.9 has to take microprosodic effects into account. Glottalisation of word-initial vowels lowers the analysed F0 trace drastically or cuts it out altogether; glottis opening into voiceless fricatives lowers the frequency of vocal fold vibration, and glottal closing out of voiceless obstruents raises it. This is shown very clearly in the F0 trace for 'Herzinfarkt gestorben'. The macroprosodic falling F0 contour in the double-accent *hat pattern* of 'schweren Herzinfarkt' is microprosodically lowered preceding the syllable '-farkt', and then raised at voice onset, disturbing the continuous fall. But accent perception is not influenced by this disturbance: '-farkt' is not accented. F0 is raised again after the voiceless obstruents of the syllables 'ge-' and '-stor-'. Macroprosodically, 'ge-' represents the low-level tail of the preceding accent contour, '-storben' a new accent contour with an F0 maximum above the tail and below the maximum of the preceding accent contour on 'Herzinfarkt', so 'gestorben' is perceived as *accented* but not upstepped.

A further possibility of rendering this German sentence is to mark neither information nor syntactic structure prosodically but to realise the twelve accent units as a continuous sequence of downsteps, i.e. a purely rhythmic structure of feet, which may, for example, be produced by a police officer monotonously reading out a prepared statement at a press conference. Figure 2.10 illustrates this. The accent of '91' moves out of this downstep sequence, but this reinforces the accent rather than marking an information structure, so it is **&3**. The microprosodic rise of the F0 onset in the syllable '-stor-' does not produce an upstep; 'gestorben' remains in the downstepped sequence macroprosodically and is perceived with equal prominence as the preceding accent.

Figure 2.10 also supports the view that pitch in peak contours points downwards in the individual peak pattern and, by default, globally in peak sequences. If this global downward trend is broken by setting a peak maximum at the level of the preceding maximum or above it, the word associated with this upstep is made more prominent. There is a broad margin of variability in the steepness of the downward trend to cope with speech rate, overall volume and attitudes. As long as the downward trend is not broken, the perceptual prominence

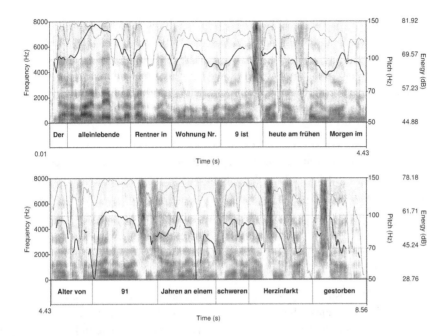

Figure 2.10. Spectrograms, F0 (log scale, plain lines) and energy traces (dotted lines), accent-unit segmentation and orthographic annotation of the same German sentence as in Figure 2.9, again in two approximately equal successive time-windows, but spoken in a continuous sequence of downsteps. Standard German, male speaker (KJK).

relations between successive peaks remain stable within the global frame of utterance prominence. The longer the downstepped sequence, the more monotonous, routine-like and dull speech sounds, and since this very simple prosodic structuring cannot reflect complex content structure adequately, it interferes with intelligibility. Repetitive downstep patterns are typical of inexperienced readers and public announcers, for example at airports, on planes or on trains, who reel off routine tasks without giving much thought to effective information transmission.

Valley contours, on the other hand, point upwards, in the individual valley pattern and globally in valley sequences. If, for instance in counting, the minima of successive valleys follow an upward trend, their prominences remain stable. But if the upward movement is broken by the valley minima returning to a low position, extra prominence is put on the words associated with the downstep. Thus downstep as found in peak sequences for perceptual prominence equality does not apply to valleys.

What has been said about downstep and upstep in German also applies to English and all the Germanic languages. It is most likely a language universal of pitch perception. The question simply is as to how individual languages make use of global downstep peak and upstep valley sequences. The former is characteristic of the Germanic languages, the latter of French.

2.5   Lexical Stress

There are languages which, in addition to *sentence accent*, have the category of *lexical stress*, e.g. a 2×2 binary syllable feature of the phonology of the word in English and German:

Label (put before syllable nucleus)	**Prosodic category**
'	*stressed – primary*
''	*stressed – secondary*
(unmarked)	*unstressed*

stressed is an abstract phonological position marker in the syllable chain of words and compounds where sentence accents dock by default. The position is either fixed (on the first syllable in Czech, or the penultimate in Polish), or in part conditioned morphologically in English and German, or free in Russian. In English and German, *stressed* may be either *primary* or *secondary*, e.g. 'b'uttercup' [flower] versus 'b'utter-c''up' [butter dish], and 'R'ücksicht' [consideration] versus 'R'ück-s''icht' [view to the back]. They are formal compounds, but only the second item in each pair is also a functional compound; the other is functionally a simplex word. Following from this functional difference the pairs are distinguished by 'cup' and 'sicht' being unstressed or having secondary stress, with consequences on the timing of the words in sentence-accent frames. *Lexical stress* does not have physical exponents by itself, but only receives them through one of the sentence-accent levels docking at the stress-place markers. The combination of stress-place marker and sentence-accent level determines the temporal and spectral manifestations of vowels and consonants in the specified syllable, as well as prominence-related F0 and energy patterns at the marked place in a syllable chain. Most of the investigations into the hierarchy of physical properties of *stress* since Fry (1955, 1958, 1965) actually deal with *accent* manifestations in word citation.

In English and German, there is also a distinction between *double* and *single lexical stress*, besides *primary* and *secondary*, to differentiate simplex and compound words, as well as syntagmas, cf. Kingdon (1965: §70; §50) for English: m'oving v''an [removal van], m'oving v'an [van in motion]; st'onebl'ind (_c'old, _d'ead, _d'eaf), d'irtch'eap (double stress: the first word intensifies the meaning of the second); and Kohler (1995: pp. 114ff, 186ff) for German: bl'ut''arm [anaemic], bl'ut'arm – st'einr'eich [very poor/rich] (double stress: the first word intensifies the meaning of the second, as in English).

In the West Germanic languages, lexical stresses mark low-level syntagmatic structures, binding syllables in words, words in compounds and in syntactic constructions. Lexical stress indexes a specific syllable of a word that receives the physical manifestations of accentuation when the word is accented in an utterance. The *lexical stress* position is stable, although there may be differences between dialectal varieties, and stress patterns may be restructured for rhythmical reasons. This is found in English words with *double* stress, e.g. numerals in '_t'een' or words like 'pr'inc'ess', 'P'iccad'illy'. In the context of another lexical stress in an immediately preceding or following word, forming a close syntagma with the double-stress word, stress is reorganised into a new double-stress pattern at the initial and the final stress position of the syntagma, creating regular 2-beat rhythmical prominence profiles: 'j'ust eight'een', ''eighteen y'ears', or 'a 'y'oung princ'ess', 'Pr'incess 'Anne'. The stressed syllables need not be contiguous for this to apply: 'a r'oyal princ'ess', 'Pr'incess Vict'oria', 'cl'ose to Piccad'illy', 'P'iccadilly C'ircus'. The latter examples speak against the concept of *stress clash* (e.g. Liberman and Prince 1977), which refers to the reduction of two contiguous stresses to a single stress under rhythmical conditions. In the quoted examples, the stresses are not contiguous, but reduction occurs nevertheless, i.e. this is phonological reorganisation of *double* stress at the word level in cohesive syntagmatic structures, irrespective of stress contiguity.

Different from the West Germanic languages, French is a language without lexical stress. The word is integrated into the phrase prosodically and segmentally: the last non-schwa syllable of the prosodic phrase receives an accent, and words lose their phonological identity in the phrase, leading to a rich source of puns in 'mots phonétiques'. Tone languages (contour-tone Mandarin, register-tone Yoruba) have lexical tone instead of lexical stress as the prosodic feature of word phonology, and finally, there are languages (Swedish, Norwegian) where certain types of lexically stressed syllables are additionally marked by distinctive tonal accent.

This handling of accent and stress in KIM differs from prosody modelling in AM Phonology. There, firstly, accents are linked to pitch (*pitch accent*) as part of intonational phonology, thus mixing two prosodic variables, accentuation and intonation. Moreover, the theory of pitch accents was worked out on the basis of English and, in view of the discussion above, cannot be applied to

French, although it has been attempted (Jun and Fougeron 2002). Secondly, stress patterns in words and sentences enter the prosody of, e.g., English phonology as relative prominence patterns defined in relation to phrase structure and aligned with the metrical grid of linguistic rhythm in Metrical Phonology (Liberman and Prince 1977). This concept of stress goes back, in the last resort, to the traditional view of a multi-graded feature of prominence, and is a theoretical reorientation of the anchoring of perceptual stress in phrase structure and of its formal representation by the transformational cycle in Generative Phonology (Chomsky and Halle 1968). In Metrical Phonology, however, relative prominence is no longer represented in terms of some feature of the vowel or syllable, but is defined on constituents as s(trong)w(eak) or w(eak)s(trong) relations. Liberman and Prince thus recognised the need for a stress category in English in addition to pitch accents, but, following the tradition of the structuralists and the generative phonologists, they extended the notion of stress beyond the word to the phrase level. This was already criticised by Bolinger (1986). In KIM, *stress* is treated as a *primary* or *secondary* place marker in simplex and compound word phonology for the potential docking of sentence accents. The physical manifestation of sentence-accent level at this stress position marker, in association with separately selected intonation patterns, can account for all and only the functionally relevant prominence relations in utterances in English and German, or any other stress language. No readjustment rules are necessary to level out over-differentiated relative prominence patterns generated by descriptive rules from elaborate phrase constructions. Stress, accent and intonation are derived from speech and language functions and are part of a dynamic model of speech communication instead.

German has minimal verb pairs with either prefix- or stem-stress, which can occur in the same sentence frame, e.g. 'Er wird's wohl umlagern', with stress either on the prefix 'um-' [ʊm], meaning 'verlagern' [I suppose he will relocate it], or on '-la-' [laː], meaning 'belagern' [I suppose he will surround it]. This allows us to apply the same peak-shift paradigm that was used to determine the prosodic manifestations of sentence accents in syntagmatic structures (see 2.2) to different stress positions in word pairs that may be represented with the same segmental phonology. This was the basis for an experimental examination of the relative ranking of F0 change and syllable-duration ratio in the signalling of sentence accent in different lexical stress positions in German (Kohler 1987a, 1990a, 1991b). The results gave an important insight into the signalling of lexical stress by F0 peak position and syllable duration, as well as into accent and intonation interaction. They are therefore discussed here in some detail.

2.6   Experiments in Lexical Stress Perception in German

2.6.1   *Test Construction*

Repeated utterances of the sentence pair 'Er wird's wohl umlagern' were ana-lysed, and one pair was selected for experimentation: (a) with the accent on the stressed syllable 'um-' and a *medial-to-late intonation peak* (see 2.7) on this syllable; (b) with the accent on the stressed syllable '-la-' and an *early intonation peak* (see 2.7), which is actually located in the syllable 'um-'. Figures 2.11a,b present the spectrograms together with F0 displays. The F0 peak positions in the two utterances are practically identical as regards their relations to the syllable structures of 'umlagern': they occur at approximately the same time distance just before the beginning of [l]. The utterances differ in the shapes of the F0 peak contours and in the syllable durations. In the utterance with stem-stress in Figure 2.11b, the post-peak F0 descent is more gradual, and the syllable 'um-' is shorter (135 ms in Figure 2.11b versus 222 ms in Figure 2.11a). F0 rises faster,

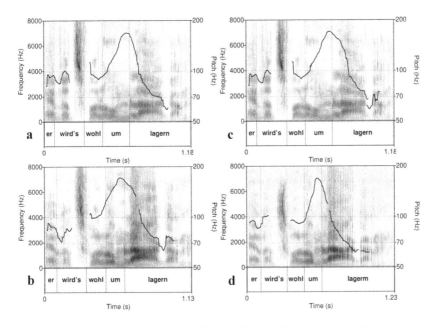

Figure 2.11. Spectrograms, F0 traces (log scale) and orthographic segmentations of words and of the 'um-' syllable in the German sentence 'Er wird's wohl umlagern': original stimuli **a**, prefix-stress with *medial-to-late peak*; **b**, stem-stress with *early peak*; derived stimuli with exchanged and time-warped F0 contours of the originals **c**, stem F0 on prefix-word; **d**, prefix F0 on stem-word. Standard German, male speaker (KJK).

starting at a structurally earlier point (beginning of the [l] in 'wohl', rather than at the 'um-' syllable onset of prefix-stress). The '-la-' syllables in the stem and prefix-stress words, on the other hand, have very similar durations (268 ms in Figure 2.11b versus 258 ms in Figure 2.11a). Two further stimuli were generated by LPC synthesis (see Kohler 1990a, 1991a) from the ones in Figures 2.11a,b by exchanging the F0 contours. They are shown in Figures 2.11c,d. These four stimuli (ST1 – ST4) were the basis for generating four series of F0 peak shifts (PI – P4):

- P1 – a series of 12: 6 left shifts (parallel transposition of the left branch and time expansion of the right branch), and 5 complete parallel right shifts, of 30 ms each in the utterance of Figure 2.11a
- P2 – a series of 9: 8 complete parallel left shifts of 30 ms each in the utterance of Figure 2.11b
- P3 – a series of 12 in the utterance of Figure 2.11c, following the procedure in P1
- P4 – a series of 9 in the utterance of Figure 2.11d, following the procedure in P2.

P1 and P3 are based on the original prefix-stress, P4 and P2 on the original stem-stress utterance, and in each pairing the series form an opposition between more abruptly and more slowly falling F0 peak contours. From these four sets of stimuli two test tapes were compiled: Test I combined the more sharply falling sets P1 and P4, Test II the slowly falling sets P2 and P3. Subjects were asked to identify the stimuli with the meanings of either 'belagern' (stem-stress) or 'verlagern' (prefix-stress).

2.6.2   Results

Figures 2.12 and 2.13 present the data of the two identification tests for the original prefix and stem-stress series, respectively, each with slow and more sharply falling peak contours. In the shift of the more sharply falling F0 peak contour through the original prefix-stress utterance (series P1) there is a clear change from prefix- to stem-stress, in spite of the duration of 'um-' pointing to the former. F0 can thus override duration, particularly since the duration of unstressed '-la-' in the original utterance is very close to its duration under stress. In stimulus 10, which is the first in the ordering from 1 to 12 to yield an unequivocal stem-stress categorisation with over 80% responses, the F0 peak position is 30 ms into the vowel of the syllable '-la-'. That the change from one stress position to the other is gradual rather than categorical may be due to a residue of the duration cue. There may also be some interaction between the

Stress identification in 'umlagern'
F0 peak shift in orig. prefix-word

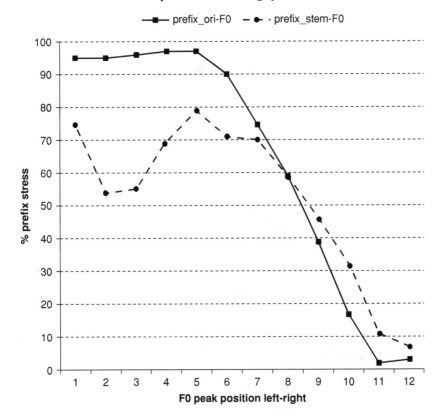

Figure 2.12. Percentage of prefix-stress responses for 'umlagern' in the series of twelve F0 peak-shift positions (from left to right) in the original prefix-stress utterance of 'Er wird's wohl 'umlagern' (no. 7 is approximately the naturally produced original peak position). Plain line = P I, sharply falling peak contour, Figure 2.11a (n = 185 at each data point); broken line = P3, slowly falling peak contour, Figure 2.11c (n = 80 at each data point).

accent and intonation functions of F0 because the F0 peak assumes positions before the beginning of the syllable nucleus of '-la-' that can simultaneously function as the *medial-to-late intonation peak* in stressed 'um-' and as the *early intonation peak* in stressed '-la-'. The relevance of this intonation interference with accent is confirmed by the finding that when the more slowly falling F0 peak is substituted (series P3), the prefix-stress category is not represented so

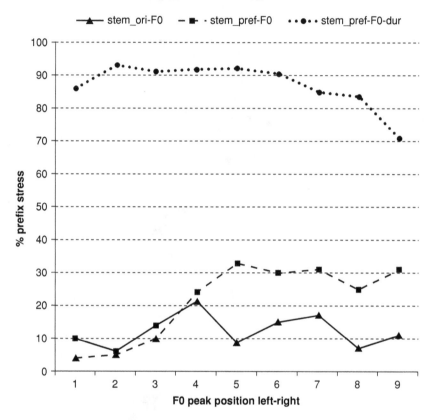

Figure 2.13. Percentage of prefix-stress responses for 'umlagern' in the series of nine F0 peak-shift positions (from left to right) in the original stem-stress utterance 'Er wird's wohl uml'agern' (no. 9 approximately original peak position). Plain line = P2, slowly falling peak contour, Figure 2.11b (n = 80 at each data point), broken line = P4, sharply falling peak contour, Figure 2.11d (n = 185 at each data point), dotted line = P4´, sharply falling peak contour and durations of prefix-stress (n = 170 at each data point).

clearly: in this case, the interpretation of an *early intonation peak* for stem-stress is never completely ruled out.

When the F0 peak contour is shifted through the original stem-stress utterance (series P2) there is no change of stress category (Figure 2.13): the responses remain predominantly in favour of stem-stress. In this case, F0 cannot override the duration cue because 'um-' is too short in relation to '-la-' to signal initial stress. There is some effect of F0 when the more sharply falling F0 peak (series P4) occurs within the syllable 'um-'. In stimuli 1 to 5, the F0 peak is shifted leftward into the preceding syllable 'wohl', but it stays within the boundaries of the prefix syllable 'um-' in stimuli 6 to 8; there are up to 30% judgements of prefix-stress. This suggests that the overriding salience of duration for prefix-stress perception is checked when the characteristic sharply falling contour occurs in the prefix syllable and is more narrowly limited to it. It supports recognition of a *medial-to-late peak* on 'um-', rather than an *early peak* on the following '-la'. This is prevented in series P2, due to the wider span of the F0 peak descent.

Two conclusions may be drawn from the results:

- An F0 peak shift by itself is sufficient to bring about a clear change from one stress position to another, provided the duration of the stressed-syllable-to-be towards which the F0 peak is shifted is not too short; but even when it is, there is a residual F0 effect.
- The intonation function of F0 interferes with its accent function if it is not supported by duration. This shows up in a gradual change between stress positions in abutting syllables where an ambiguity can arise between a *medial-to-late intonation peak* in one syllable and an *early intonation peak* related to a subsequent one. This interaction gets stronger when the shape of the F0 peak contour is the more slowly falling one.

The importance of duration for stress perception was further investigated in an experiment with a modified peak series P4´. A new base stimulus ST4´ was generated by adjusting the durations of the syllable 'um-' and of the vowel in the syllable '-la-' of base stimulus ST4 to the same values of base stimulus ST1. By repeating periods in [ʊm] and deleting some in [aː], [ʊ] was lengthened from 70 ms to 117 ms, [m] from 65 ms to 105 ms and [aː] reduced from 210 ms to 189 ms. Then the F0 contour of base stimulus ST1 (see Figure 2.11d) was transferred – sound segment by sound segment – to the modified base stimulus ST4´. Series P4´ was generated by shifting the F0 peak to the left as for P4. The first seven stimuli of P1 and the last seven of P4´ occupy the same ranges of F0 peak positions, and have very similar segment durations ([ʊm] and [aː] being identical in both) and comparable F0 contours, but they differ in the base stimuli, which are either the original prefix-stress utterance in P1 or the original stem-stress utterance in P4´ with spectral and energy differences.

The hypothesis was that the change of segment durations in P4´ versus P4 is sufficient to reverse judgement from stem-stress to prefix-stress in all cases of the series, resulting in similar response functions for stimuli 1–7 of P1 and for stimuli 3–9 of P4´. This result will also show the low relevance of spectral and energy features in German stress perception in these prosodic frames. The dotted line in Figure 2.13 confirms this hypothesis.

In a later experiment (see Kohler 2012 for details), the effect of duration was examined in different F0 frames in the German utterances 'Wir treffen uns **&2**regelmäßig beim **&1**K'affee/**&1**Caf'é dort an der **&1/&2**Ecke' [We **&2**regularly meet for **&1**coffee/at the **&1**café on the **&1/&2**corner]. There is a default accent **&2** on 'regelmäßig'; the test items 'K'affee/Caf'é', with lexical stress on the first or second syllable, respectively, are partially deaccented **&1**. They occur either in a low F0 tail, with partial deaccentuation also of the sentence-final word 'Ecke', or in a high F0 plateau, spanning 'regelmäßig beim K'affee/Caf'é dort an der', followed by an F0 fall for default accent **&2**Ecke. These prosodic frames exclude critical F0 change on the test items. Vowel duration was manipulated in a complementary fashion across the two syllables in five steps, spanning the continuum from initial to final stress in each word and in each frame. The different spectral properties of the stressed and unstressed vowels in the original productions of 'Kaffee' [k'afe˙] and 'Café' [kafe:] were an additional variable besides duration in this experiment. Vowel duration, intervocalic fricative duration and vowel quality turned out to be strong significant main effects in shaping the stress response profiles for German 'Kaffee' versus 'Café' along the duration scale, but there are only marginal effects of the prosodic frame on stress perception. These data show that the rank scale of acoustic properties in lexical stress perception, descending from F0 to duration to vowel quality to energy, which was first set up for English by Fry (1955, 1958, 1965), needs to take prosodic settings into account. As F0 on test items is levelled in a low tail or a high-plateau *hat pattern*, F0 itself is a minor cue in lexical stress perception; on the other hand, vowel quality becomes important, further enhanced by the duration/strength of an intervocalic consonant. The combined cue force of these two parameters can even outweigh the effect of vowel duration.

2.7   Intonation

Critical F0 change is one of the prominence-lending variables in the signalling of *sentence accent* (2.1, 2.2). But the essential signalling power of F0 is to relate specific contour aspects to *intonation*. At sentence-accent levels **&1–3**, functionally determined pitch patterns are selected from a system of distinctive contrasts. Each contour is defined by two aspects: (a) the direction of pitch movement and its time course to the next sentence accent or a phrase boundary, and (b) the synchronisation of pitch maxima or minima of these contours with the sentence-accented word, and (in English or German) the lexical-stress syllable. Here are the four direction categories and the symbolisations of their pitch movements:

Label	Prosodic category
&2./1./0.	*peak*
&,/&?	*valley: low or high rising*
&./&.?	*peak-valley: low or high rising*
&- &0.	*level*

The symbol is put before the next accent or a **PhrasinG** marker **[&PG]** (see 2.12).

A rising-falling-rising *peak-valley* pitch pattern in English 'Yes **&., &PG**', expressing reserved agreement, is a global intonation unit in contrast with a rising-falling *peak* pattern 'Yes **&2. &PG**' for decided agreement, or with a rising *valley* pattern, either a *low rise* 'Yes **&, &PG**', meaning 'I agree, carry on', or a *high rise* 'Yes **&? &PG**', meaning 'really? is that so?', or finally with a *level* pitch pattern '**&-**Yes **&0. &PG**', expressing hesitation or indecision. Peak patterns differ in the extent of the fall that follows the rise: a fall to the speaker's low pitch range **&2. &PG**, a small drop to a middle range **&1. &PG** or levelling out at high pitch in **&0. &PG**.

There are different synchronisations of the F0 time courses of the four intonation patterns with vocal-tract timing of accented words. The synchronisation symbols are put after the accent marker before the word. In level patterns, there can only be one synchronisation category, symbolised as **&-**, with one of the accent levels **&1–3**. Peak patterns synchronise their F0 maximum with accented-vowel onset in three different ways:

Label	Prosodic category	
&3)/&2)/&1)	*early*	(fall begins at or before accented-vowel onset)
&3^/&2^/&1^	*medial*	(central rise-fall in the accented vowel)
&3(/&2(/&1(	*late*	(late fall in the accented vowel, or in a following syllable, depending on timing constraints, preceded by extensive rise)

These synchronisations also apply to peak-valley patterns.

The space between *medial* and *late* synchronisation forms a continuum of increasing low-high F0 movement in time and frequency; the speaker signals scalar argumentative weighting of information contained in the accented word. Near the *medial* end of this continuum, argumentation simply gives the information a *newness* value. This new value is *contrasted* implicitly with an old one as synchronisation shifts to later positions; modal particles such as 'ja', 'doch', 'aber', in German, may make this contrast verbally explicit. Near the *late* end, ARGUMENTATION turns into the *expression of unexpectedness*. Since these are three quite different types of ARGUMENTATION weighting, a *medial-to-late* category has been added to the KIM system of synchronisations, with the PROLAB notation &^-(.

Valley patterns synchronise their F0 minimum with accented-vowel onset in two different ways:

Label	Prosodic category	
&3]/&2]/&1]	*early*	(rise begins at or before accented-vowel onset)
&3[/&2[/&1[	*late*	(rise begins in the accented vowel)

The different synchronisations are perceptually distinctive (see 2.8). Distinctive phonological synchronisation categories are different from variation in phonetic alignment of significant points of F0 contours in syllables, for example in the comparison of synchronisation categories across languages. Accent-synchronised intonation movements are produced and perceived holistically and are rooted as such in the semantics and pragmatics of different communicative functions. Some of these functions will be discussed in Chapters 3–6.

The symbolisation of pitch movement and synchronisation of intonation patterns can now be added to the prosodic annotation of the examples in Figures 2.1–2.4, 2.6–2.11. By convention sequences of peak contours &2)/^/(are downstepped, only upstep is marked, by &|2. Downstep also affects the falling pitch movement &1. or &2.

2.1a   &2]Wie &0weit &0ist &0es &0bis &0H'amburg&? &PG
      &2]Wie &0weit &0ist &0es &0bis &, &1[H'amburg &? &PG
      &2]Wie &0weit &0ist &0es &0bis &, &2[H'amburg &? &PG

2.1b   &2)/(Wie &0weit &0ist &0es &0bis &0H'amburg &2. &PG
      &2)/(Wie &0weit &0ist &0es &0bis &2. &1^H'amburg &2. &PG
      &2)/(Wie &0weit &0ist &0es &0bis &2. &2^H'amburg &2. &PG
      Although the direction marker &2. is, by convention, put before the next accent marker or a phrase boundary, the intervening &0 accents imply, again by convention, that the low F0 fall of a peak contour occurs close to the synchronisation syllable. After this, the low fall F0 trails off, lowering slightly, to the phrase boundary if there is no intervening accent.

2.2a   &2(Wie &0weit &0ist &0es &0bis … &2. &PG
2.2b   &0Wie &2(weit &0ist &0es &0bis … &2. &PG
2.2c   &2(Wie &0. &2)weit &0ist &0es &0bis … &2. &PG
2.2d   &2(Wie &2. &|2(weit &0ist &0es &0bis … &2. &PG

2.3   &0Aber &0der &2^Leo &0säuft &2. &PG

2.4   &0Aber &0der &2)/^/)Leo &0säuft &2. &PG
        &0Aber &0der &2^/(Leo &0. &2)säuft &2. &PG
        &0Aber &0der &0Leo &2)/^/(säuft &2. &PG

2.6a   &3^'Anna &0kam &0mit &2. &1[M'enne &, &PG
2.6b   &2^'Anna &0kam &0mit &2. &2[M'enne &, &PG
2.6c   &2^'Anna &0. &1^kam &0mit &2. &2[M'enne &, &PG
2.6d   &3^'Anna &0kam &0mit &2. &1]M'enne &, &PG
2.6e   &2^'Anna &0kam &0mit &2. &2]M'enne &, &PG
2.6f   &2^'Anna &0. &1^kam &0mit &0. &2]M'enne &, &PG

2.7a   &2^'Anne &0kam &0mit &1. &1^M'enne &2. &PG
        &2^'Anne &0. &1^kam &0mit &0. &2^M'enne &2. &PG
        &3^'Anne &0kam &0mit &2. &2^M'enne &2. &PG
2.7b   &3^'Anne &0kam &0mit &2. &1^M'enne &2. &PG

2.8   &0Die &2^W'ähler(innen) &1. &2^w'ählen &2. &PG

2.9   &0Der &2^-(all'einlebende &1. &2^-(R'entner &0in &1. &|2^W'ohnung
        &0. &1)N'ummer &2. &2^-(neun &0ist &2. &|2^h'eute &0am &0frühen
        &1. &2(M'orgen &0im &1. &2^'Alter &0von &2. &|3^-('einundneunzig
        &1. &2(J'ahren &0an &0einem &2. &|2^schw'eren &0. &2)H'erzinfarkt
        &2. &2^gest'orben &2. &PG

2.10   &0Der &2^-(all'einlebende &1. &2^-(R'entner &0in &1. &2^W'ohnung
        &0. &1)N'ummer &1. &2^-(neun &0ist &2. &2^h'eute &0am &0frühen
        &1. &2(M'orgen &0im &1. &2^'Alter &0von &2. &|2^'einundneunzig
        &1. &2(J'ahren &0an &0einem &2. &2^schw'eren &0. &2)H'erzinfarkt
        &2. &2^gest'orben &2. &PG

2.11a   &0Er &0wird's &0wohl &2^-('umlagern &2. &PG
2.11b   &0Er &0wird's &0wohl &2)uml'agern &2. &PG

KIM conceptualises observable global *peak*, *valley*, combined *peak-valley*
and *level* F0 patterns as unitary prosodic categories, linked to the category
of sentence accents and consisting of features of movement direction and of
synchronisation with articulation. The pitch-accent concept of AM Phonology
separates the feature of movement direction and attributes it to the categories
of phrase accent and boundary tone. This means that the same type of peak

contours are categorised differently in phrase-internal and phrase-final positions. For example, in GToBI representation of

&0Die **&2^W'ähler &2. &2**^w'ählen**&2. &PG**
Die L+H*Wähler L+H*wählen L-L%

(cf. Grice and Bauman 2002; Grice, Baumann and Benzmüller 2005), the pitch accent L+H* receives its fall by linear interpolation between its high tone and the low tone of the following bitonal pitch accent L+H*, whereas the fall of the latter is captured by the boundary tones L-L%, not by a pitch-accent tone. In KIM, both are peak contours, and it is only the lower trailing off of F0 in the final peak pattern, compared with the non-final one, that is related to **&PG**. Intonation effects on sentence accents are thus separated from phrasing effects. Non-terminal falls of internal and final pitch movements are treated in the same inconsistent way in AM/ToBI, for example:

GToBI   Die L+H*Wähler L+H*wählen !H-H%
for   KIM/PROLAB &0Die **&2**^W'ähler**&1. &2**^w'ählen **&1. &PG**
(It is not clear how internal **&1.** and **&2.** would be distinguished in GToBI.)

Furthermore, H* is not only a pitch accent in a falling pattern H*L-L%, but it can also be one in a rising pattern H*H-^H%. The fundamental difference between a *peak* and a *valley* contour is handled by different boundary tones, although the same type of rising patterns can occur internally as well, e.g. in the insisting question addressed to a child:

&2[Kommst du **&, &2**[mit uns **&, &2**[mit **&, &PG**
&2[Are you **&, &2**[coming **&, &2**[with us **&, &PG**

There are cases of pitch distinctions at the pitch-accent level that can no longer be represented by moving the categorisation of pitch features to boundary tones, because there are no boundaries. This point was illustrated in Kohler (2006b, pp. 126ff) with pitch patterns in the German sentence 'War er das wirklich?' There are four distinctive possibilities involving rises:

(1) one accent with a *medial peak-valley* pattern; a rise-fall occurs on 'war er' and is continued up to the end of the sentence; 'war' is accented, 'wirklich' unaccented:

&2^war **&0**er **&0**das **&0**w'irklich**&.? &PG**
&2^was **&0**it **&0**r'eally **&0**him **&.? &PG**

(2) two accents with a *medial peak-valley* on accented 'war', and a *late-valley* pattern on accented 'wirklich'; the rise-fall of the *peak-valley* occurs on 'war er', its rise on 'das', followed by a separate rise on 'wirklich':

&2^war &0er &0das &., &2[w'irklich &? &PG
&2^was &0it &0him &., &2[r'eally &? &PG

(3) two accents with a prosodic boundary between the *peak-valley* and *valley* patterns of (2):

&2^war &0er &0das&., &PG &2[w'irklich &? &PG
&2^was &0it &0him &., &PG &2[r'eally &? &PG

(4) two accents with a *medial peak* pattern on accented 'war', and a *late-valley* pattern on accented 'wirklich'; the rise-fall occurs on 'war er', trailing off low on 'das', followed by a rise on 'wirklich':

&2^war &0er &0das &2. &2[w'irklich &? &PG
&2^was &0it &0him &2. &2[r'eally &? &PG

In (1), as against (2)–(4), 'wirklich' loses its reinforced meaning 'in reality' and becomes a modal particle, just like 'really' in the English translation. There are no perceivable exponents of internal phrase boundaries required in (2) and (4), nor in their English translations. In (2) the POLARITY QUESTION is asked with an expression of disbelief that 'it might have been him', whereas the POLARITY QUESTION in (4) insists on finding out whether 'it was him or not'. This also applies to the English translations. The introduction of an internal phrase boundary after 'das' (or 'him' in the English translation) in (3) may be achieved simply by lengthening 'das' (or 'him'); a pause is not necessary. This break turns (2) into a succession of two questions, with increased disbelief.

AM/ToBI marking of (1) would give 'war' (or 'was') the bitonal pitch accent L+H* and attribute the fall-rise to a phrase accent and boundary tone L-H%, with linear interpolation between H* of the pitch accent and the phrase accent L-. In (4), 'wirklich' would receive an additional pitch accent L*, with linear interpolation as in (1). In (3), there would be two intonation phrases 'war er das' with L+H* L-H% and 'wirklich' with L* H-H%, again with linear interpolation H-L and L-H. The empirically found intonation patterning in (2) cannot be represented in AM/ToBI. Pitch accents being limited to bitonal combinations and movement direction being associated with phrase accents and boundary tones make it impossible to represent the fall-rise of the first pitch accent in the absence of an internal phrase boundary. Either a phrase boundary would have to be created, blurring the meaningful distinction between (2) and (3), or the bitonal restriction on pitch accents would have to be given up, thus moving pitch information back from the edge tones to the pitch accents.

Grice (1995) allowed more than two tones in a single pitch accent in order to account for distinctive pitch phenomena, without theoretical reasoning, just as the original bitonal restriction was not theoretically motivated. This is circular argumentation, because the empirical data trigger the expansion of the categorical repertoire, and the revised underlying representation is then supposed to provide an explanatorily adequate account of the same empirical data. Moreover, in such a data-driven approach, underlying categories are no longer falsifiable, since they are adjustable in an *ad hoc* way to meet empirical findings, instead of being set up by considerations that lie outside the data they are to provide a theoretical framework for.

The division of tonal features of global accent-related pitch patterns between pitch accents and edge tones disrupts the unity of sets of direction-defined contours and their synchronisation with articulation. Perceptual experiments have shown (see 2.8) that shifting a *peak* or a *valley* pattern through the environment of an accented word in an utterance creates a continuum from *early* via *medial* to *late peak*, or from *early-* to *late-valley* synchronisation, which is to be given theoretical status in a model of intonation. This means that movement direction should be part of the definition of intonation patterns linked to sentence accents. It provides the unifying feature within which different synchronisations with articulation lead to pattern subcategorisation.

2.8   Experiments in Peak and Valley Synchronisation

2.8.1   *Signal Analysis of Peak Patterns*
Figure 2.14 illustrates the three synchronisation patterns of F0 with the accented syllable in the German sentence:

> **&0**Sie **&0**hat **&0**ja **&2**)/^/(gel'ogen **&2. &PG**   [She's been lying.]

The F0 and overall energy patterns are clearly distinguished and are associated with different meanings. The *medial peak* in **a** signals the OPENING of an ARGUMENTATION ('Now I understand. She's been lying'), the *early peak* in **b** signals the CONCLUSION of an ARGUMENTATION ('That's it then. She's been lying'), and the *late peak* in **c** adds UNEXPECTEDNESS to OPENING ARGUMENTATION ('Oh! She's been lying').

In a *medial peak*, F0 enters the nucleus of the stressed syllable [loː] in the accented word 'gelogen' as a rise to the maximum F0 point in the centre of the vowel, from which it falls to a low level. In an *early peak*, F0 enters the stressed syllable as a fall from a higher pre-accent level. This reversal of pitch movement into the vowel between *medial* and *early peaks* is coupled with an

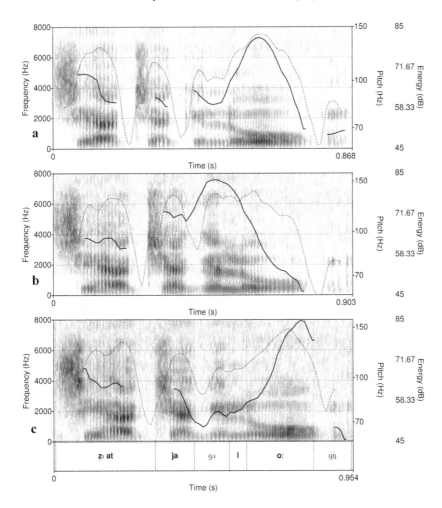

Figure 2.14. Spectrograms, F0 traces (log scale, plain lines) and energy traces (dotted lines) of natural productions of **a** *medial peak* **b** *early peak* **c** *late peak* in the German utterance 'Sie hat ja gelogen' [She's been lying]. Phonetic segmentation of syllables, and segments [l] and [oː] in **c**, adjustable to the different timing in **a** and **b**. Standard German, male speaker (KJK).

increase of acoustic energy as the vocal tract opens, especially if there is a consonant syllable onset. This highlights the pitch difference and creates a distinctive acoustic contrast. In a *late peak*, there is not the same acoustic strength contrasting it with medial synchronisation or any peak position in between: the F0 rise across the accented vowel has a progressively lower start and greater extension, and the fall does not occur until the vowel offset, or even in a following unstressed syllable. This creates a pitch continuum from *medial* to *late*.

Unaccented syllables before the accent syllable can make the pitch reversal across the accent-syllable boundary still more salient if the immediately preceding one is either high or low pitch for *early* and *medial*, respectively. When the accent syllable is utterance initial, the *early peak* F0 contour is still low falling in the critical transition period, as against rising or high level before the subsequent fall in the *medial peak*. The essential difference between the two synchronisations then becomes one of pitch scaling: in the *early peak*, pitch is lowered in a narrow time-window after the accented-vowel onset, whereas in the *medial peak* it is raised.

The *medial peak* pitch-level contrast *low-high* across an accented-syllable boundary can also be generated in a peak contour with an early F0 maximum synchronisation. In Figure 2.15, panel **a** shows the stylised version of a natural *medial peak* production (plain line) of the sentence 'Sie hat ja gelogen', and the parallel left shift to synchronise the peak maximum with the [l]–[o:] transition (dashed line). In each case, the ascending and descending branches occur in time-windows of about 120 ms. The left shift is perceived as an *early peak*. When the descending branch of this shifted peak is raised and the ascending branch dipped, generating a *low-high* contrast across the accented-syllable boundary, as shown in panel **b** (dotted lines), the percept becomes a *medial peak*. If only one branch is changed, the percept is neither a proper *early* nor a proper *medial peak*. Contrariwise, a peak that is synchronised 30 ms into the accented vowel, and is perceived as a *medial peak* (panel **c**, dashed line), can be changed to an *early peak* percept by raising the ascending branch and dipping the descending one (dotted lines), generating a *high–low* contrast across the accented-syllable boundary. Again the perceptual change depends on both branches being modified simultaneously. A change of *medial peak* synchronisation to a perceived *early peak* by on-branch raising and off-branch dipping cannot be effected if the peak maximum is moved into the vowel by more than about 60 ms, for example, at the position in the original utterance. This is so because F0 would be raised more in the critical time-window *after*, rather than before, the accented-vowel onset, which supports *medial peak* perception. Likewise, the reverse change of *early peak* synchronisation to *medial peak* perception by on-branch dipping and off-branch raising is not possible if it occurs in the critical time-window *before* the accented-vowel onset. These data show that the pitch contrast across the accented-vowel onset in pre- and post-boundary windows of about 60 ms (in the case of a long vowel) is essential for signalling *early* or *medial peak* synchronisation.

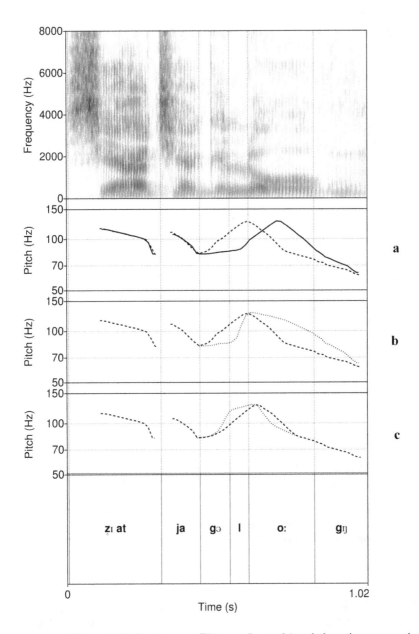

Figure 2.15. Spectrogram, F0 traces (log scale) and phonetic segmentation
of syllables and segments [l] and [oː], in the German utterance 'Sie hat
ja gelogen': **a**, stylised original F0 contour (plain line) and peak shift to
synchronise F0 maximum with [l]–[oː] transition (dashed line); **b**, raising
the descending, and/or dipping the ascending branch (dotted line) of the
shifted F0 peak contour (dashed line); **c**, F0 peak shift 30 ms into the
accented vowel (dashed line), dipping the descending and/or raising the
ascending branch (dotted line). Standard German, male speaker (KJK).

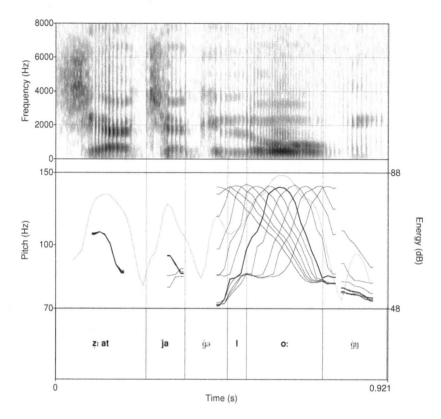

Figure 2.16. Spectrogram of the German *medial-peak* utterance 'Sie hat ja gelogen' and its F0 trace (log scale, thick line). F0 traces (log scale) of six left and four right shifts (thin lines) and the energy trace of the original utterance (dotted line) in a separate Pitch/Energy panel, used for LPC synthesis of an eleven-stimulus peak-shift continuum from *early* to *late*. Segmented and phonetically annotated. Standard German, male speaker (KJK).

2.8.2   *Discrimination and Identification Tests with Peak Patterns*

The peak-shift paradigm that was used to investigate *sentence accent* and *lexical stress* perception (2.2, 2.6) was also applied to the perceptual catego-risation of *early-medial-late peak* synchronisation (for experimental details, see Kohler 1987b, 1991a). Taking the medial F0 peak position of the original utterance 'Sie hat ja gelogen' in Figure 2.14a as a point of departure, the peak rise-fall contour was moved along the time axis in 6 equal steps of 30 ms each to the left and 4 corresponding steps to the right. In the right shift, both branches were moved in parallel. In the left shift, only the rising branch was:

Table 2.1. *Frequency distribution of 'change has occurred' responses by sixty listeners in the left-right sequence of the* serial discrimination test *across the eleven stimuli with F0 peak shifts in 'Sie hat ja gelogen' (1 = left-most, 11 = right-most position).*

	Stimulus								
	3	**4**	**5**	**6**	**7**	**8**	**9**	**10**	**11**
First change perceived	1	4	39	16					
Further changes perceived			1	5	11	15	21	22	11
Total	1	4	40	21	11	15	21	22	11

the falling one was expanded between the new maximum position and the original right base point, and was thus given a less steep slope. This approached the natural production of an early peak (Figure 2.14b) and generated better LPC synthesis than a parallel left shift, avoiding too long and too low an F0 stretch. Figure 2.16 shows the set of eleven F0 peak patterns from *early* to *late*, synchronised with the spectral timing in the spectrogram of the original medial-peak utterance; the thick F0 trace marks its original F0 contour. The dotted line is the energy trace of the original utterance. Sections of the shifted peak patterns that coincided with voiceless stretches had F0 masked. The peak maximum of stimulus 4 (from the left) was synchronised with the [l]-[oː] transition; stimulus 5 was the first that had its peak maximum inside the accented vowel.

In a *serial discrimination test*, listeners were presented with the ordered series of peak-shift stimuli from left to right and asked at which stimulus in the series they perceived the first melodic change and at which stimuli they perceived further changes. Table 2.1 presents the responses by sixty listeners. Subjects were also asked to paraphrase the meanings (a) of the initial utterance of the series, (b) of the first change and (c) of a later change; for each question the series was repeated. Typical answers were: (a) knowing, summarising, concluding; (b) observing, recognising facts and events, opening an argument; (c) like (b) but, contrary to expectation, with surprise. These pragmatic descriptions formed the basis for the context construction in an identification test.

In a formal *randomised paired discrimination test*, all the pairs of two-step distances from the ordered peak-shift series in ascending or descending order were presented for 'same/different' judgements. The test was carried out with a group of thirty-nine subjects in ascending order and with a different group

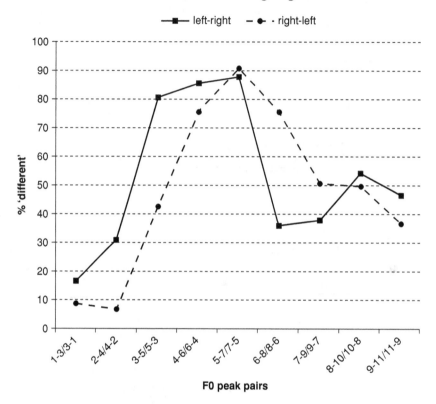

Figure 2.17. Discrimination functions in the *randomised paired discrimination test*, showing percentage of 'different' judgements for utterance pairs of 'Sie hat ja gelogen' with two-step distances of F0 peak positions, in the ordering left-right (plain line) or right-left (dashed line). Thirty-nine subjects, n = 78 in the left-to-right ordering; thirty-four subjects, n = 68 in the right-to-left ordering.

of thirty-four subjects in descending order. Figure 2.17 shows the response functions.

Both types of test converge in demonstrating a major and a minor peak in the discrimination function, around stimuli 5/6 and 9/10, respectively. In the paired discrimination test, differentiation is sharpest, and equally so in both orderings of stimuli, when the 60 ms peak-maximum distance between the paired stimuli is located early rather than late in the critical time-window after accented-vowel onset, or inside rather than outside it, i.e. in the pairs 4–6,

5–7 and 7–5, 6–4. But there is also a strong order effect, as 3–5 and 8–6 show sharp discrimination as well, but 5–3 and 6–8 do not. In 3–5 the F0 maxima positions straddle the accented-vowel onset; in 6–8 they are outside the critical time-window. Therefore, discrimination is expected to be strong in the former, weak in the latter. But when stimulus 5, with its F0 maximum only 30 ms into the vowel, is heard first, it appears to be perceptually represented closer to an *early peak*, and stimulus 3 is then not sufficiently different. When stimulus 8, being 120 ms into the vowel, is heard first, it gets a perceptual representation as a clear medial peak, from which stimulus 6 on the edge of the critical time-window may be sufficiently different.

The paired discrimination test on the set of 'Sie hat ja gelogen' utterances was supplemented by an *identification test*, prefixing each of the first eight peak-shift stimuli (from *early* to *medial*) with the context stimulus 'Jetzt versteh ich das erst' [Now I understand], spoken by the same speaker (KJK); it imparts OPENNESS OF ARGUMENTATION. And nineteen listeners were asked to judge, in a forced-choice response, whether the melody of the test stimulus matched the context or not. This is an indirect way of assessing the communicative functions of *medial peaks* and, by exclusion, of *early peaks* in German. Figure 2.18 presents the identification function. The stimuli with F0-maximum synchronisation up to the [l]-[oː] transition, i.e. the *early* set, are almost unanimously perceived as not matching, and, likewise, the stimuli with F0 maximum ≥60 ms inside the accented vowel, i.e. the *medial* set, as matching. Stimulus 5, with its F0 maximum inside the critical transition time-window, is in between the two perceptual and functional categories. Taking the discrimination and the identification function together provides a case for categorical pitch perception, i.e. increased sensitivity across the prosodic division between *early* and *non-early peaks*, resulting in discrete category attribution. There is also perceptual prosody-function categorisation among *non-early peaks*, and it is no longer discrete categorical but, rather, continuous.

The *serial discrimination test* was also applied to the first ten stimuli of the corresponding F0 peak shift in 'Aber der Leo säuft', where the F0 peak position moved from *early* to *late* in accented 'Leo' (2.2). The data, shown in Table 2.2, replicate those found in 'Sie hat ja gelogen', with a peak in the discrimination function at the same shift-series point (stimuli 5–6).

The nine-point peak-shift paradigm was also applied to 'Es ist ja gelungen' [It has been successful], where the accented vowel is short. The step size was again 30 ms, and one peak maximum was located at the [l]-[ʊ] boundary of the accented word 'gelungen', three to its left and five to its right. Table 2.3

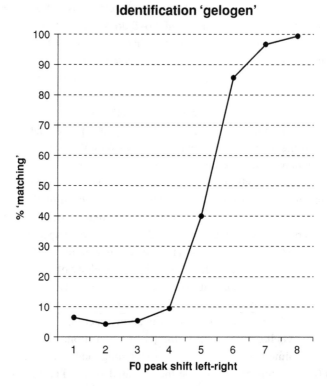

Figure 2.18. Identification function in the *identification test*, showing percentage of 'matching' judgements for eight stimuli 'Sie hat ja gelogen' with F0 peak shift from left to right in the context 'Jetzt versteh ich das erst.' Nineteen subjects; for each stimulus n = 190.

Table 2.2. *Frequency distribution of 'change has occurred' responses by thirty-two listeners in the left-right sequence of the* serial discrimination test *across the first ten stimuli of the F0 peak shift in 'Aber der Leo säuft' (1 = left-most, 10 = right-most position; two listeners perceived no change).*

	Stimulus							
	2	**4**	**5**	**6**	**7**	**8**	**9**	**10**
First change perceived	1	5	12	10	2			
Further changes perceived				4	7	5	7	7
Total	1	5	12	14	9	5	7	7

Table 2.3. *Frequency distribution of 'change has occurred' responses by twenty-nine listeners in the left-right sequence of the* serial discrimination test *across the nine stimuli of F0 peak shift in 'Es ist ja gelungen' (1 = leftmost, 9 = right-most position).*

	Stimulus					
	4	**5**	**6**	**7**	**8**	**9**
First change perceived	5	19	5			
Further changes perceived		2	5	3	3	0
Total	5	21	10	5	3	0

presents the results. The response function again peaks at the same position in the series for stimuli 5–6.

Gartenberg and Panzlaff-Reuter (1991) have shown that syllable structure influences production and perception of F0 peak synchronisation. In short vowels, medial peaks have their maxima closer to the accented-vowel offset. This may point to the same absolute transition time-window for long and short vowels, but the critical time-window in short accented vowels may also be smaller than for long vowels, and a narrower peak-shift step may have shown a perceptual change earlier in the vowel of 'gelungen'. Moreover, the late synchronisation was not reached in the peak shift of 'Es ist ja gelungen'; the maximum would have to be moved into the following unstressed [ə]. These are open issues.

In the various peak-shift series, the sharp change in discrimination for stimuli with F0 maxima moving 30–60 ms into the accented vowel contrasts with low discrimination before and after. These perceptual data can be linked to an acoustic change from high-low to low-high F0 across the accented-vowel onset, on the one hand, and to a shift along a high-low or a low-high monotonic F0 continuum before or after the transition, on the other. This acoustic-perceptual link points to a psychophonetic principle of pitch perception, which may be assumed to be universal in speech communication across the languages of the world.

Such a general psychophonetic principle would operate in the perception of F0 patterns in human speech, irrespective of the phonological categorisation and the linguistic functions it may serve in any particular language. This means that native speakers of languages other than German should be able to detect changes in F0 peak positions in relation to general human articulatory sequences when they listen to the same German utterances without knowing any German at all, and thus without assessing the stimuli semantically, but simply on the basis of the general phonetic properties of human speech. If the results of such listening tests coincide with the results from German listeners, this will be strong support for a language-independent psychophonetic principle. As a first step, the serial discrimination test in the ascending ordering was run with two groups of non-German speakers.

(a)   At talks I gave about the modelling of intonation to native English audiences at the British Phonetics Colloquium in Edinburgh in 1984 and at AT&T Bell Labs, Murray Hill, in 1986, I informally presented the eleven-point peak-shift series of 'Sie hat ja gelogen' and asked listeners, most of whom had no knowledge of German, to decide when they heard the first melodic difference. The answers clearly pointed to stimuli 5 and 6.

At Bell Labs, there was a Chinese speaker among the audience, Chilin Shih, a research worker in the lab at the time, who was able to classify the eleven stimuli of the left-right series tonally, although she had no knowledge of German. Without the slightest doubt, she associated stimuli 1–4 with Mandarin tone 3, stimulus 5 with tone 4; later in the series, tone 4 changed to the combined tones 2+4. Whereas the switch from tone 3 to tone 4 occurred abruptly in the succession of stimuli 4 and 5, the change from tone 4 to tones 2+4 was gradual and could be less easily located (at stimulus 9 the change had definitely taken place). This informal test shows (1) that tones 3 and 4 in Mandarin Chinese are differentiated by the F0 maximum relative to the vowel onset, prenuclear higher F0 signalling the former, nuclear higher F0 the latter, and (2) that these categorisations are possible on the language-independent basis of human speech perception in general. See also Gårding, Kratochvil, Svantesson and Zhang (1985).

(b)   The second group was made up of twenty-five Russian speakers in Leningrad, who had no knowledge of German and who worked on Russian, English or French phonetics (eleven), or were students in their first or second year in the Philology Faculty (fourteen). The eleven-point peak-shift series, from left to right of 'Sie hat ja gelogen' was played to them. The subjects listened to the series twice and crossed, on a prepared answer sheet, the number of the stimulus in the series that they perceived as being most clearly different from the rest. The test was carried out by Natalia Svetozarova, Chair of Phonetics at Leningrad University, in 1988. Table 2.4 presents the results. Although the instruction requested a single response, some subjects indicated more than one stimulus as being clearly different.

Both the phoneticians and the non-phoneticians in the Russian group converged in having a clear maximum of the response function for stimulus 6. This is a higher position than for the German listeners, who favoured stimulus 5, but who also provided a substantial portion of their answers for stimulus 6. These results are a very strong indication that the dichotomy between an *early* and *medial peak* position is indeed a general psychophonetic, language-independent phenomenon, which is then incorporated into the language-specific phonology at different levels.

The acoustic continuum of F0 peak shift is thus perceptually partitioned into two clearly delimited sections with the boundary occurring around stimuli with their F0 maximum 0–60 ms into the accented vowel, and this perceptual division coincides with an acoustic change from *high-low* to *low-high* F0 across the vowel onset. Around the boundary between these two sections, discrimination is sharpest. The question then is to find out how different languages incorporate this acoustic-perceptual principle at different levels in speech communication. It has already been pointed out in the discussion of Figure 2.14 that in German the two perceptually determined sections of the acoustic continuum correspond to two communicative functions: FINALITY and OPENNESS in ARGUMENTATION. A further F0 peak shift along the acoustic continuum results in a more gradual auditory change which in German is correlated with a more gradual change of communicative function, expressing degrees of distance that speakers establish

Table 2.4. *Frequency distribution of 'clearly different' responses by twenty-five Russian listeners without any knowledge of German in the left-right sequence of the serial discrimination test across the eleven stimuli with F0 peak shifts in 'Sie hat ja gelogen' (1 = left-most, 11 = right-most position).*

	Stimulus							
	2	4	5	6	7	8	9	10
Phoneticians (11)		1	1	7	4	1	1	1
Non-phoneticians (14)	1	1	2	11	3	1	1	
Total	1	2	3	18	7	2	2	1

between themselves and the world as it presents itself to them, successively superimposing degrees of CONTRAST and UNEXPECTEDNESS/INCREDULITY upon OPENNESS in ARGUMENTATION. This degree of distance is the semantic basis of the *medial* to *late peak positions*, whereas degrees of INTENSIFICATION in *reinforced accents* (see 2.2) are correlated with another F0 continuum of *extension of F0 change*.

The association of the *early-medial-late* synchronisation with different communicative functions was further investigated experimentally. On the basis of the discrimination test results and of hypotheses concerning the communicative functions of *early*, *medial* and *late peaks*, three contexts were constructed:

(1)   'Wer einmal lügt, dem glaubt man nicht, auch wenn er gleich die Wahrheit spricht. Das gilt auch für Anna.' [Once a liar, always a liar. This also applies to Anne.]
        This context sets the frame for summing up and bringing an argument to a close.

(2)   'Jetzt versteh ich das erst.' [Now I understand.]
        This context presents a new fact and opens a new argument.

(3)   'Oh.' This context introduces speakers distancing themselves from observed facts and expresses contrast and unexpectedness.

Each of these contexts was produced naturally (by KJK) and paired with each of the three naturally produced peaks in the sentence 'Sie hat ja gelogen' of Figure 2.14 in a forced-choice *natural-stimuli identification test* for listeners to judge whether the test stimulus matched the context or not. Table 2.5 presents the results.

Table 2.5. *Percentages of 'matching' responses for combinations of three contexts and* early, medial *or* late *F0 peaks in the sentence 'Sie hat ja gelogen' in a natural-stimuli identification test. Eighty-eight subjects.*

	Context		
	(1) Wer	**(2) Jetzt**	**(3) Oh**
Peak position			
early	87.5	27.3	8.0
medial	26.1	70.5	72.7
late	13.6	67.0	76.1

The *early peak* matches well with context (1), but with no other, least of all with context (3). *Medial* and, even less so, *late peaks* do not match with context (1). The *late peak* matches best with context (3), but the *medial peak* matches with both contexts (2) and (3), and the *late peak* matches fairly well with context (2). This shows a sharp functional separation of *early* and *non-early peaks*, in addition to their sharp psychophonetic distinction.

In Mandarin Chinese, the psychophonetic distinction functions at the level of lexical tones 3 versus 4. In Swedish and Norwegian, it functions at the level of early peak word accent I versus late peak word accent II (Bruce 1977; Gårding 1979, 1982). In Russian, it operates as F0 peak contour synchronisation that is either slow rising in the pre-accent syllable or fast rising late in the accent syllable for STATEMENTS versus POLARITY QUESTIONS (Khromovskikh 2003; Rathcke 2006). All these different language-specific functions are carried by a high-low versus a low-high pitch change across the accented-syllable onset. In Neapolitan Italian, a *medial* versus a *late* F0 peak synchronisation *within* the accented vowel is used to differentiate STATEMENTS with narrow focus and POLARITY QUESTIONS, with additional raising of the F0 descent in the latter (d'Imperio 2000). Pitch height in relation to accented-syllable synchronisation again plays the essential role for functional differentiation.

The importance of this psychophonetic principle of a pitch-level difference for the coding of communicative functions at all linguistic levels makes it mandatory to incorporate it as a basic component in any prosodic model and in the annotation system based on it. It is an exciting challenge for comparative linguistics to investigate the functional use of this prosodic patterning across the languages of the world and to provide a prosody-function typology. Complementary research questions concern the formal exponents of such functional categories as FINALITY versus OPENNESS in languages like Mandarin Chinese and Swedish, where high-low versus low-high pitch is already bound at the lexical level, or in languages like Russian or Neapolitan Italian, where it is bound in the STATEMENT versus QUESTION functions. It may well be that Russian and Neapolitan Italian distinguish CONCLUSIVE from OPENING ARGUMENTATION by distinctive synchronisations that are also different from the late synchronisation in questions. The experimental paradigm asking whether stimuli were statements or questions, used in these studies, was not delicate enough to elicit the FINALITY versus OPENNESS function. For Swedish, see the study of Ambrazaitis (2009).

2.8.3 Further Peak-Shift Experiments in German

In the course of experimenting with peak pattern synchronisation in German, it was observed that the perceptual categories of *early* and *medial peaks* are also determined by the internal timing of pitch rises and falls in narrow time-windows before and after the accented-vowel onset, over and above their external synchronisation with vocal-tract timing (see 2.8.1). To test this additional factor systematically, Niebuhr (2003a,b, 2007b) repeated the peak-shift discrimination and identification experiments with the German sentence 'Sie war mal Malerin' [She used to paint], and applied four peak types, using all possible combinations of narrow and broad time-windows for rises (149 ms and 296 ms) and falls (133 ms and 266 ms), in each case with peak maximum, left and right base point F0 values of 150 Hz, 105 Hz and 110 Hz, i.e. 6.3 st rises and 5.4 st falls. The short rise and fall windows generated a peak pattern comparable to the one used in Kohler (1987b), which was a little narrower (120 ms for both rise and fall) and had slightly lower maximum and base point values (140 Hz and 85 Hz), i.e. 8.5 st for the rise and the fall. Niebuhr's peak contours with one or two broad time-windows spanned 400 ms< t <565 ms, or between 40% and 60% of the total voiced sonorant utterance stretch.

The sentence was produced on a monotone by the author (which is not mentioned in Niebuhr 2003b, 2007b, but is part of the experimental description in Niebuhr 2003a). 'Malerin' was to receive a sentence accent, which, in the absence of F0 movement, had to be implemented by energy and duration. The rationale was that a neutral F0 pattern without falls and rises would provide a better basis for high auditory-quality synthesis of an F0 peak-shift series. Four stimulus series were generated by superimposing each rise-fall combination on the original utterance. The F0 maximum was synchronised with the /m/-/a:/ transition of the accented word 'Malerin', and the peak configuration was then shifted in 5 steps of 20 ms to either side. Listening to these series shows that, in addition to intonation, accentuation also changes as the peak contour is shifted through the utterance from left to right. The monotone production changed the temporal structure and the energy profile of the utterance, resulting in longer unaccented syllables and stronger accented ones than in a natural medial peak production.

The timing of the spectral energy distribution, as well as of the global energy in the original monotone utterance, displayed in Figure 2.19, indicates a prominence profile 'weak – strong – weak – very strong – weak – very weak' in the six successive syllables 'sie', 'war', 'mal', 'Ma-', '-le-', '-rin', based on the energy and duration of their vowel nuclei. This prominence profile makes the syllables 'Ma-' and, to a smaller degree, 'war' stand out, giving special weight to the word 'Malerin' and some weight to the function word 'war'. The monotone prominence pattern is strengthened when rise-fall F0 contours are added. This is especially the case when a broad rise creates a long rise that

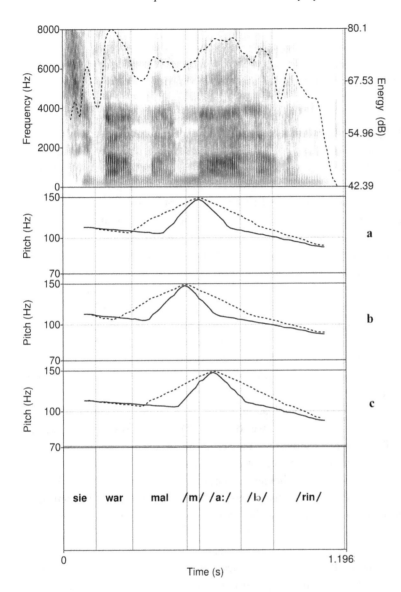

Figure 2.19. Spectrogram, energy profile, F0 traces (log scale) and phonetic segmentation of syllables, as well as segments /m/ and /a:/, in the German utterance 'Sie war mal Malerin' (Niebuhr 2003a). Each pitch panel shows the same global F0 peak patterns, with narrow and broad time-windows for rise and fall (plain and dashed lines). In **a**, the peak maximum is synchronised with the /m/-/a:/ transition of the stressed syllable of the accented word 'Malerin'. In **b** and **c**, the peak maximum is shifted 60 ms to the left and to the right, respectively. Original utterance spoken on a monotone, Standard German, male speaker (ON).

starts on 'war' and follows the rising energy (as in Figure 2.19a,b,c), or when a broad fall raises F0 at the high energy level of 'Ma-' (as in Figure 2.19a,c).

The synchronisation of the narrow rise-fall maximum with the vowel onset of 'Ma-' produces a single **&2** accent on 'Malerin' with an indecisive peak between *early* and *medial* (Figure 2.19a, plain line). Replacing the narrow by a broad *fall* (plain-line rise, dashed-line fall) adds extra prominence to the accent and changes the intonation to *medial*. On the other hand, a broad instead of a narrow *rise* (dashed-line rise, plain-line fall) gives 'war' a **&1** accent, foregrounding the past tense of the verb, and weakens the accent on 'Malerin', turning the intonation to *early*. If both narrow rise and fall are replaced (Figure 2.19a, dashed line) 'war' receives a **&1** accent, and accent **&2** on 'Malerin' is intensified, producing a strange effect because accentuating 'war' points to CONCLUSION, and intensifying 'Malerin' stresses OPENNESS OF ARGUMENTATION: the pattern hangs between the two functional interpretations.

All the rise and fall window combinations with the peak synchronisation of Figure 2.19b – 60 ms before vowel onset in 'Ma-' – are perceived as *early peaks*, but the broad fall makes the accent on 'Malerin' more prominent compared with the narrow fall. 'war' stays unaccented in this and in the other four early broad-rise synchronisations, because the total low-high F0 trajectory to the *early peak* maximum gets successively shorter in the left-shift from the position in Figure 2.19a and thus does not become a prominence-lending rise, separated from the fall and associated with 'war'.

All the rise-fall combinations with the peak synchronisation in Figure 2.19c – 60 ms after vowel onset in 'Ma-' – are perceived as *medial peaks*. The broad fall intensifies the accent on 'Malerin', and the broad rise creates a clear partial accent on 'war'. This also applies to the first two shifts after vowel onset; in post-boundary shifts 4 and 5, accent **&2** on 'Malerin' increases, but **&1** on 'war' disappears, as the rise can no longer be connected with a separate prominence-lending rise on 'war', the start of the rise being closer to the onset of accented 'Ma-'.

Thus, there was interaction of accent and intonation perception in Niebuhr's peak-shift series. It introduced two uncontrolled accent variables: (a) the influence of energy and duration patterns in monotone stimulus production, (b) the influence of F0 rise and fall time-windows that are too broad. Variable (b) hampers the investigation of intonation contrasts at constant accent positions, since the very broad windows span too many syllables in which the prominence-lending aspect of F0 may change prominence relations in combination with the energy and duration variables of (a). The paradigm is not suited to investigate the *high-low* versus *low-high* pitch-level change in peak patterns across an accented-vowel onset. This change is determined by peak maximum synchronisation and by peak-internal F0 timing around the accented-vowel onset, as discussed in 2.8.1 with reference to Figure 2.15. This is micro-timing within macro-timing, which cannot be captured by the broad time-windows used by Niebuhr. This is a conceptual problem, created by the term *contour shape* for the additional distinctive feature beside temporal peak synchronisation. Although *shape* also has a time reference, it was taken out of the domain of F0 timing, and thus the analysis lost sight of the central issue of the integration of macro- and micro-timing. There is a discrepancy between the more finely grained peak shift in steps of 20 ms, rather than 30 ms in Kohler (1991a), and the crude internal F0 timing in broad rise and fall windows.

On the strength of the findings of intonation categorisation in 2.8.1 and 2.8.2, perceptual processing of F0 peak timing can be modelled as follows. A prototypical *early peak* has a low fall into the accented vowel, following high F0 before its onset if it is preceded by sonorous segments. This strengthens the perception of *low* pitch initially in the accented syllable nucleus. The reverse holds for the prototypical *medial peak*, for which F0 rises to the peak maximum into the accented vowel, thus strengthening the perception of *high* pitch initially in the accented syllable nucleus. These *low* or *high* pitch-related percepts for an *early* or a *medial peak* can also be achieved by a later synchronisation of the F0 maximum, together with a slower rise and faster fall for *early*, or by an earlier synchronisation, together with a faster rise and a slower fall for *medial*. The essential production strategy is to create a lower or higher paradigmatic pitch contrast initially in the accented vowel, and to achieve this by a syntagmatic pitch change across the vowel boundary. The important condition is that this difference in syntagmatic change is substantial enough within a critical pre- and post-boundary time-window. The steep flanks of a narrow rising-falling peak pattern create a clear reversal from high-low to low-high when the peak is shifted through this time-window. But the flattened flanks of a broad rising-falling peak pattern reduce the syntagmatic pitch contrast in the critical pre- and post-boundary time-window and thus weaken the paradigmatic opposition between early and medial synchronisation.

Synchronisation and contour-internal timing across the consonant-vowel transition are thus not independent variables in F0 generation but work together to achieve a pitch distinction. Synchronisation will always be the primary factor, because external-internal timing compensation occurs within a relatively small time-window around the pre-accent to accent transition. That such compensation can create the same functionally triggered pitch effect introduces flexibility into the timing of F0 peak movement with vocal-tract shaping. There is a margin of variability of phonetic alignment within the same synchronisation category, adaptable to phonetic context and communicative situation. It is an issue for further research to investigate this external-internal F0 timing interaction also for the medial to late peak shift, especially in connection with the exponents of POLARITY QUESTIONS in languages like Russian or Neapolitan Italian, but it requires a procedure that separates accent from intonation effects better than the broad window combinations used in Niebuhr (2007a,b).

2.8.4   *Peak-Shift Experiments in English*

The same experimental paradigm of *discrimination in series presentation*, of *two-step paired discrimination* and of *identification* was applied to English in a study by Kleber (2006). It used the sentence 'She has gone to Malaga', produced after the context sentence 'I almost forgot', spoken by a male speaker of Standard Southern British (WJB). Both sentences were pronounced with one accent, on 'Malaga' and 'forgot', and with medial peak synchronisation. The F0 contour was stylised with five F0 points: 111 Hz at utterance voicing onset, 114 Hz and 96 Hz left and right base points of the peak contour, 140 Hz peak maximum and 76 Hz utterance voicing offset. The distances between the F0 maximum and the F0 base points were 128 ms each, and the maximum was synchronised 43 ms into the vowel. This stylised contour was then shifted in four steps of 29 ms to the left and in six to the right. Since the accent-initial [m] was 73 ms, this shift synchronised the F0 maximum of the first stimulus of the resulting eleven-step series with the onset of [m]. Thus, the peak-shift series was constructed with reference to the onset of [m], rather than the onset of the accented vowel.

The peak pattern is comparable to the one used by Kohler (1987b), as well as to the narrow one used by Niebuhr (2003a,b), but the accented vowel is phonologically short, rather than long as in the German experiments (English [æ] 100 ms, German [oː], [aː] 200 ms). Three perception tests were performed by twenty-five subjects. The results are:

- Stimulus 4, with peak-maximum synchronisation 14 ms into the accented vowel, is the first in *left-right serial discrimination* for which a melodic change is observed, and it receives the highest number of responses in the whole series. After that, serial discrimination drops, but there is a minor response peak for stimulus 9, synchronised 159 ms after accented-vowel onset. These results parallel the ones obtained for German in Kohler (1991a), cf. Table 2.1: discrimination in the left-right peak-shift series is sharpest for the first synchronisation after accented-vowel onset, then sensitivity decreases abruptly, staying low until a minor increase late after accented-vowel onset.

- Left-right *two-step paired discrimination* yields greatest sensitivity for pairs 2–4, 3–5 and 4–6 (72%, 82%, 72% different), i.e. for synchronisation distances spanning 58 ms across the accented-vowel onset, from -44 ms to +14 ms in 2–4 and from -15 ms to +43 ms in 3–5, as well as from +14 ms to +72 ms in 4–6, early in the accented vowel. Before and after, sensitivity is low but increases again a little for the late synchronisation of 8–10, 130 ms and 188 ms after accented-vowel onset in [l] and [ə] of the following syllable (picking up the serial discrimination profile). This is again in line with the German data in Kohler (1987b), cf. Figure 2.17 (in Niebuhr 2003a,b the shift did not go so far to the right). There is also a comparable order effect in the English data. These discrimination results confirm the importance of narrow time-windows before and after accented-vowel onset; across it, differentiation of *early* and *medial peak* synchronisations is sharpest. The window width seems to be independent of phonological vowel quantity.

- *Identification* increases almost linearly from 23% for stimulus 1 to 91% for stimulus 6 (58 ms into the accented vowel), stays high for stimuli 7 and 8, and then drops gradually to 61% for stimulus 11. The identification function does thus not match the discrimination functions, as it does not sharply separate *early* and *medial* peaks. Therefore, the English identification results differ from the ones obtained by Kohler (1987b), cf. Figure 2.18, and by the narrow time-window in Niebuhr (2003a,b, 2007b) for German. Late synchronisations were not included in the German identification test, as its aim was to determine the *early-to-medial peak* boundary with a context suggesting the opening of an argument. The diverging pattern in English is most probably not the result of different perceptual identification, but of non-unique contextualisation. The context sentence 'I almost forgot' can easily be part of a concluding argument. 'She's gone to Malaga' may then be constructed by the listener as old information that the speaker did not mention earlier, or as new information that the speaker is mentioning now. Consequently, responses depended on subjects' interpretation of contextualisation, introducing an uncontrolled variable into the perceptual identification task.

2.8.5   Discrimination and Identification Tests with Valley Patterns

In an *early valley*, the minimum F0 point occurs before or at the accented-vowel onset, and F0 enters the accented vowel as a rise. In a *late valley*, the rise from the minimum F0 point occurs in the vowel. The question then is whether rising or falling F0 trajectories across the consonant-vowel transition produce a categorical change in pitch perception comparable to the one found for falling versus rising trajectories in *early* or *medial peaks*. Niebuhr and Kohler (2004) investigated this question with two parallel sets of peak and valley shifts, applying the same experimental paradigm of pairwise discrimination and of identification as in 2.8.2. The sentence 'Und wie ist dein Name?' [And what's your name?] was spoken with a *medial peak* and with a *late valley* on 'Name' by a male speaker of Standard German (KJK). It was preceded by the context 'aha' [OK], with final stress, and a matching *medial peak* or *late valley*. This communicative particle provided the contextual setting for ±matching identification judgements of the stimuli in two series of peak and valley shifts. The F0 contours in the two natural productions were processed in Praat. They were stylised by linear interpolation between five points, which formed sequences of semitone steps up or down on two mirrored scales for the peak and the valley pattern:

(1)   112 Hz at voice onset
(2)   1.1st down/up (105/120 Hz)
(3)   6.2st up/down (150/84 Hz), 150 ms after (2)
(4)   1.2st down/up (140/90 Hz), 100 ms after (3)
(5)   down to 70 Hz or up to 220 Hz, at voice offset.
       The exact reversal of semitone steps down and up was not possible, because an octave rise was not sufficient to create a convincing, friendly question intonation.

Point (3) was located at the boundary between [n] and [aː] of the accented syllable, and the complete (2) to (4) pattern was shifted in four and in five equal steps of 25 ms to the left and to the right, respectively. The leftmost synchronisation occurred at the end of [aɪ] in 'dein', the rightmost about 90 ms before the offset of [aː] in both series. Figure 2.20 shows the synchronisation at vowel onset and the 50 ms left and right shifts for each pattern. The two original stimuli were resynthesised with the ten F0 patterns in the peak or valley synchronisation series for discrimination and identification tests.

For discrimination, each stimulus in each series was paired with the stimulus two steps removed in an ascending order, resulting in eight unequal pairs (1–3 up to 8–10). In addition, the odd-numbered stimuli were combined to five equal pairs (1–1 to 9–9). Subjects judged whether the stimuli in a pair sounded

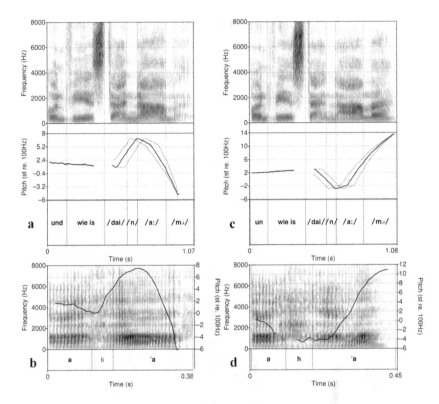

Figure 2.20. Spectrogram, stylised F0 trace (semitone) and phonetic segmentation of the original German utterances 'Und wie ist dein Name?' with **a** the peak and **c** the valley pattern, peak maximum and valley minimum synchronised at accented-vowel onset (plain line), 50 ms before and after (dotted lines): stimuli 3, 5 and 7 in each ten-point shift series. Spectrogram, original F0 trace and phonetic segmentation of the context 'ah'a': **b** in the peak and **d** the valley setting. Each original context and test stimulus spoken as a single utterance, Standard German, male speaker (KJK).

the same or different. For identification, each stimulus was preceded by the constant context phrase 'ah'a', either with a *medial peak* for the peak series or with a *late valley* for the valley series, separated by a silent interval of 250 ms. Subjects judged whether context and stimulus were a semantic match. It was assumed that with the *medial peak* in 'ah'a' the speaker conveys OPENNESS towards another person's communicative action, for example in dealing with an enquiry at a reception desk, and would continue to show this open interest in asking for the person's name in order to be able to deal with the matter. So,

Discrimination 'Name'

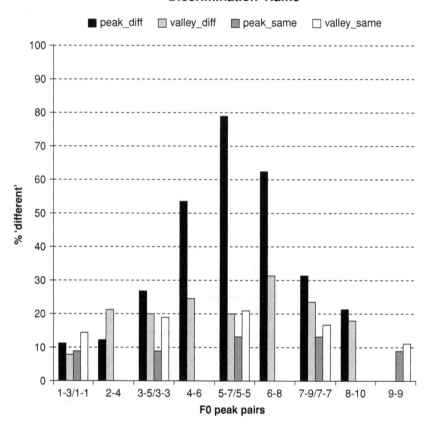

Figure 2.21. Pairwise discrimination of F0 synchronisation in the peak and valley series of 'Und wie ist dein Name?': percentage different judgements for two-step distances between stimuli in left-right ordering, and for identical pairs of uneven-numbered stimuli. Eighteen subjects; for each stimulus n = 90.

for a semantic match between context and question the *medial peak* would be expected to be carried over to 'Und wie ist dein Name?' The *early peak*, which may be paraphrased as 'So let's have your name and be finished with it!', is not compatible with this open attitude. Analogously, the *late valley* in 'ah'a' conveys a FRIENDLY CONCERN for the hearer, which sounds odd when it is followed by an *early valley*, expressing CASUALNESS. So, a *late valley* in the test stimulus is assumed to be necessary for semantic matching. The same eighteen native speakers of German did all four tests, first with the peak,

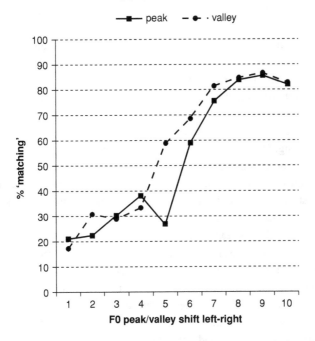

Figure 2.22. Identification functions showing percentage 'matching' judgements for ten stimuli 'Und wie ist dein Name?' in the peak and valley shift series, with the contexts of *medial-peak* and *late-valley* 'ah'a'. Eighteen subjects; for each stimulus n = 90.

then with the valley series, and discrimination came before identification. Figures 2.21 and 2.22 show the results.

The results give a clear picture of the perception of peak and valley patterns in a *sentence-accent* language like German.

- Discrimination in the peak series is strong when the F0 maximum of one stimulus in a pair is synchronised in the narrow time-window after accented-vowel onset, i.e. for pairs 4–6, 5–7 and 6–8; otherwise it is weak, approaching the response to pairs of identical stimuli.

- This discrimination response pattern replicates the one obtained in the original peak-shift experiment with the utterance 'Sie hat ja gelogen' (see 2.8.2). It also mirrors the results of the peak-shift experiments with the narrow-peak utterance 'Sie war mal Malerin' (2.8.3) and with the English utterance 'She's gone to Malaga' (2.8.4).

- Identification in the peak series produces high matching scores for stimuli 7–10, low ones for stimuli 1–5 and an indecisive one for stimulus 6.
- The identification response pattern also replicates the one in the original peak-shift experiment, but it is less sharp: stimuli 1–5 show a substantially higher percentage of matching judgements. So, there is a residue of matching the *early peak* synchronisation with the *medial-peak* context, which, on the one hand, indicates that identification between stimulus and context must have gone beyond simple pitch matching. On the other hand, it indicates that the initial hypothesis of medial peak semantics of 'ah'a', necessitating a medial peak in the stimulus, was too strong. It is conceivable that a speaker signals interest by *medial-peak* 'ah'a' and then continues 'but now I need your name', thus expressing FINALITY, rather than OPENNESS of interaction. In the context of the original German peak-shift experiment, OPENNESS was not just signalled by intonation on a communicative particle carrier but was phrased as observing something new by 'Now I understand.' This produced a much stronger contextual setting for medial-peak matching in the test stimulus.
- Identification replicates the general trend found in all the other peak-shift experiments carried out in German and English (2.8.3–2.8.4).
- Discrimination in the parallel valley-shift series is very different: it is low for all stimulus pairs and quite similar to pairs of identical stimuli.
- On the other hand, identification in the valley series parallels the one in the peak series.
- Thus, whereas the discrimination and identification patterns found in all peak-shift experiments may be interpreted as showing categorical pitch perception in the Haskins sense (Repp 1984, Kohler 1987b), this does not apply to the parallel valley-shift data. But although there is no division of the synchronisation continuum into discrete categories by sharp changes in pattern discrimination, there is category perception in relation to a meaning scale from CASUALNESS to FRIENDLY CONCERN; the functional categories are cognitively processed, without determining physical boundaries between them. Perception is continuous, but cognitive processing allocates stimuli of the continuum to two functional categories.
- Even in the peak series the boundary between *early* and *medial* is not physically fixed. It will change with speech rate, F0 range and

acoustic energy, and the same physical parameters may result in different discrimination patterns, as shown by the position effect in right-left as against left-right ordering of stimuli in pairs (see Figure 2.17). This non-determinacy of physical boundaries of perceptual categories applies to the Haskins principle of *Categorical Perception* in general. For example, the phonemic differentiation between so-called voiced and voiceless plosives in English by a physical property bundle containing VOT, intra-oral pressure, duration of pre-plosive vowel and stop-occlusion varies with lexical stress, degree of word accentuation, speech rate and F0 range.

We now need to find an answer to the question that follows on from these data: why do the peak and the valley series, which were generated in a parallel fashion on a mirrored semitone scale, trigger such different pitch-perception strategies? By relating the synchronisations of the generated stimuli to the definitions of peak and valley contours we shall propose an answer that does not support the assumption that the valley patterns used are mirror pitch images of peak patterns.

(1)   The peak pattern is defined as a summit contour that rises above a surrounding low pitch base.

(1.1) The synchronisation of this summit contour in relation to an accented-vowel onset creates functionally different types of peak pattern, from *early* to *late*.

(1.2) In this synchronisation continuum, the positioning of the summit contour in narrow windows of about 60 ms before and after the accented-vowel onset produces distinctive high-low versus low-high trajectories across the divide, which are categorically salient in perception, supported by the increase in acoustic energy as articulation opens into the vowel.

(1.3) Stimulus 5 of the present experiment has its F0 maximum synchronised with accented-vowel onset, and pitch is in a high range in narrow time-windows before and after. Pitch in the two windows of stimulus 3, synchronised 50 ms into the preceeding [n], is very similar. This differs from stimulus 7, synchronised 50 ms into the accented vowel (see Figure 2.20a). In the latter, pitch rises from the low base to the maximum across the two windows. These pattern characteristics are reflected in the discrimination score, which is high for stimuli 5–7 but low for stimuli 3–5, and in the identification score, which is low for stimuli 3 and 5 but high for stimulus 7 (see Figures 2.21 and 2.22).

(1.4) Stimulus 4, synchronised between stimuli 3 and 5, like them has high-range pitch in both windows; by contrast, stimulus 6 has a low-high pitch rise across the accented-vowel onset, but not so extended as in stimulus 7. Discrimination of stimuli 4–6 rises well above the level for the pairs at the lower and the higher end of the synchronisation scale, and identification of stimulus 6 is above 50%, and between the low and high scores for the lower- and higher-ranked stimuli, respectively.

(1.5) In the pairing of stimuli 6–8, stimulus 6 occurs in the narrow post-vowel onset window, stimulus 8 outside. Discrimination is also above the levels of early and late pairings. Stimulus 8 is identified as clearly matching.

(2) The valley pattern is defined as a low-pitch precursor to a rise whose end point, ranging from medial to high, is outside the narrow time-window after accented-vowel onset.

(2.1) The rise may start before or after the accented-vowel onset, giving different extensions of low-level pitch to functionally distinct *early* or *late* synchronisations.

(2.2) If the valley pattern were defined as the exact mirror image of the peak pattern, it would be a dip to low pitch in a high-pitch setting before and after. This clearly does not conform to the characteristics of a valley pattern.

(2.3) The consequence is that in the pattern used in valley shift, the compared stimuli for discrimination have similar low pitch ranges across the windows before and after accented-vowel onset, resulting in low discrimination scores.

(2.4) This lack of categorical discrimination between differently synchronised typical valley patterns does not preclude the categorisation of stimuli along the synchronisation continuum as *early* or *late valley* for functional distinctions.

Since the above argumentation proceeds deductively from pitch-pattern definition and pitch salience in narrow time-windows before and after an accented-vowel onset, the perception difference found for peak versus valley contours synchronised around a prominent syllable is expected to be valid in any language, especially in languages that have a sentence accent built on lexical stress, such as the Germanic, Slavonic and southern Romance languages. This is the psychophonetic principle controlling the perception of pitch peak contours in human speech, which was introduced in 2.8.1 and which can now be singled out as specific in the processing of one type of pitch movement, the summit contour rising above a surrounding low pitch base.

2.9   Concatenation of Pitch Patterns

Peak, valley, peak-valley and level pitch patterns are concatenated in prosodic phrases which may coincide with syntactic phrasing or cut across it. Several cases of different pattern concatenations have already been discussed in the sections on *Prominence, Sentence Accent, Declination, Downstep and Upstep* and *Intonation* (2.1, 2.2, 2.3, 2.4, 2.7), and in connection with the modelling of (rise-)fall-rises and falls+rises (1.4.1–1.4.4). Figure 2.1 illustrates the concatenation of *two valley* (a) and *two peak* patterns (b)

2.1a   &2]Wie &0weit &0ist &0es &0bis &, &2[H'amburg &? &PG
2.1b   &2)/(Wie &0weit &0ist &0es &0bis &2. &2^H'amburg &2. &PG

The first *peak* in 2.1b is *early* or *late*, the second *medial*. It can be turned into an *early peak* &2)H'amburg &2. if the preceding unaccented word 'bis' is raised to, or above, the level of the onset of the fall, thus shifting the peak maximum into the time-window before the accent. In the absence of unaccented syllables before the first accent, there is no pitch rise, but the characteristic high-low fall into the accented vowel is sufficient to signal the *early peak*. When both peaks are early, the question conveys the meaning that there is only a final piece of information missing for an assessment or for a decision – for example, 'we have planned our trip now, how far is it to our first stop, then?'

The first *valley* in 2.1a is *low rising* and *early*, the second *high rising* and *late*. It can be turned into an *early valley* &2]H'amburg &? if the monotonic pitch rise is broken before the unaccented word 'bis' rather than after it, thus shifting the start of the second pitch rise to a position before the accented-vowel onset. The first valley may also be *late*. When both valleys are *early*, the question is casual and detached; when both are *late* it expresses increased interest in getting the answer.

Peaks may be concatenated either as *separate rising-falling patterns*, with variable frequency drops in the intervening dip between the two maxima, or they may be fused into a double-accent rising-falling *hat pattern* with a time-expanded summit, where the rise is linked to the first accent, the fall to the second. Although undipped, it has the characteristics of a *medial* or a *late peak* in the rising part, and of a *medial* or *early peak* in the falling part. An *early peak* at the first accent and a *late peak* at the second are ruled out because the former lacks the essential early low fall, the latter the essential late low rise. The formal fusion of two accents into one *hat pattern* serves their semantic integration. The pattern groups accented meaningful elements together whereas a *dipped peak concatenation* separates them.

The English and American comedy duo of the silent-film era **&2**^L'aurel/ Stan and **&0. &2**)H'ardy/'Ollie **&2**. are known in German as **&2**^ Dick und **&0. &2**)/^Doof **&2**. **&2**^Fat and **&0. &2**)/^Dumb **&2**. If someone is described as being 'dick und doof', the two adjectives are no longer being used to refer to the joint appearance of an actor duo but to point out the physical and mental attributes of one person. They may be seen as going together, which is manifested in a *hat pattern*, or they may be seen as being separate, in which case the realisation is a *dipped peak pattern* **&2**^dick und **&1. &2**^doof **&2**. Similarly, the question 'Wie weit ist es (bis Hamburg)?' in Figure 2.2c asks for a measure of distance with a double-accent *hat pattern* spread over the qualifier 'wie' and the quantifier 'weit'. In Figure 2.2d, the two are separately intensified with a two-accent peak sequence.

The *hat pattern* is a characteristic prosodic feature of a multitude of set phrases in English and German phraseology, binding semantic elements together, usually two, but the expanded summit contour may comprise more. Examples are 'up and down', 'there and back', 'look left and right', 'search left, right and centre / high and low' (= everywhere), 'in black and white', 'with bow and arrow', 'over hill and dale'; 'rauf und runter', 'hin und zurück', 'links und rechts schauen', 'schwarz auf weiß', 'mit Pfeil und Bogen', 'über Berg und Tal'. Cockney rhyming slang uses phrases to replace a single word, e.g. 'trouble and strife' for 'wife'. On the other hand, the formally divided dipped peak pattern signals semantic separation, increasing from a shallow **&1.** to a deep **&2.** further reinforced through insertion of a phrase boundary, marked by combinations of slowing down articulation, non-modal phonation, silent interval and F0 reset at the accent after the boundary (see 2.12).

The following examples illustrate the whole range of peak and valley concatenations in the same word string, from *hat* or *tub* to *dipped* patterns with different degrees of separation between the accented words. In the QUESTION context (I), Speaker A asking 'Wann können wir uns diese Woche treffen?' [When can we meet this week?], Speaker B may reply:

(a)   Am **&2**^/(S'onnabend oder **&0. &2**)S'onntag **&2. &PG** (Figure 2.23a)
       On **&2**^/(S'aturday or **&0. &2**)S'unday **&2. &PG**

(b)   Am **&2**^/(S'onnabend oder **&1. &2**^S'onntag **&2. &PG** (Figure 2.23b)
       On **&2**^/(S'aturday or **&1. &2**^S'unday **&2. &PG**

(c)   Am **&2**^/(S'onnabend **&2. &PG** oder **&2**^S'onntag **&2. &PG** (Figure 2.23c)
       On **&2**^/(S'aturday **&2. &PG** or **&2**^ S'unday **&2. &PG**

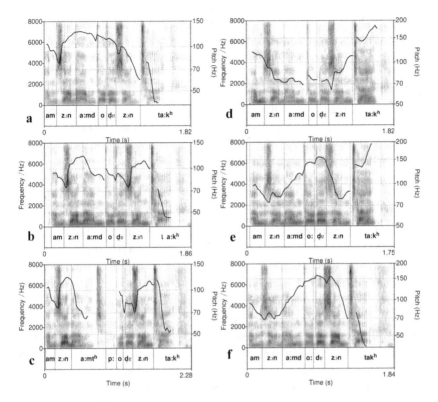

Figure 2.23. Spectrograms, F0 traces (log scale) and phonetically annotated syllabic segmentation of the German utterance 'am Sonnabend oder Sonntag' with a variety of distinctive intonation patterns: **a**, *hat pattern*; **b**, sequence of two *peaks* in one prosodic phrase; **c**, phrase boundary between two *peaks*; **d**, *tub pattern*; **e**, sequence of two *valleys* in one prosodic phrase; **f**, sequence of *valley* and *peak*. Standard German, male speaker (KJK).

(d) Am **&2[**S'onnabend oder **&0, &2]**S'onntag **&, &PG** (Figure 2.23d)
  On **&2[**S'aturday or **&0, &2]**S'unday **&, &PG**

(e) Am **&2[**S'onnabend oder **&, &2[**S'onntag **&? &PG** (Figure 2.23e)
  On**&2[**S'aturday or **&, &2[**S'unday **&? &PG**

(f) Am **&2[**S'onnabend oder **&? &2)**S'onntag **&2. &PG** (Figure 2.23f)
  On **&2[**S'aturday or **&? &2)**S'unday **&2. &PG**

In (a), the speaker offers a closed set of two weekend days as the only option; in (b) and (c), the speaker gives two separate days as possibilities, with weaker or stronger separation. Instead of the *hat pattern* in (a), Speaker B may use a double-accented *tub pattern* in (d), with F0 descending from mid-level 'am' into a low-level stretch on the first accent and the connective, and then rising through the second accent to mid-high, either *early* or *late*. The *tub pattern* may be regarded as the fusion of two *low valleys* into a new rising pattern, in parallel with the fusion of two *peaks* into a *hat pattern* (PROLAB label **&0**, analogous to **&0.** in a hat). It may be generated by folding the *hat pattern* at the 110 Hz line in (a). Like the *hat pattern*, the *tub pattern* groups the two connected accented words into a closed set but adds listener-directed appeal signals to the proposition, of the type 'if that's all right with you'. In parallel to the sequence of two peaks in (b), there is a sequence of two valleys in (e). The rise is broken and restarted at a lower level (see also Figure 2.1). The concatenated accented words are again separately selected, and the proposition is combined with a questioning appeal signal to the addressee, of the type 'Would either of these days do?'

The F0 rise in *hat patterns* is fast and reaches the contour maximum well before the F0 fall for the second accent. It differs from a rise in a *valley+peak sequence* in (f), which is slower and extends right up to the onset of the second accented syllable, where the fall for an early peak starts. There is a distinctive difference between a *double-accented hat pattern* and a *valley+peak pattern*, which is exploited functionally. In context (I), B's reply may be speaker-oriented with a *hat pattern* (a), intensified by a *late peak*, or it may be listener-oriented with the *valley+peak sequence* (f). In the context of A's QUESTION with the broad time reference 'this week', (f) is a friendly offer of the two weekend days in a STATEMENT. In the STATEMENT context (II),

> Speaker A proposing 'We need to get together this weekend to discuss the matter.'

Speaker B asks a QUESTION with the *valley+peak pattern* (f), requesting a choice between the two days. To create the QUESTION effect the *valley pattern* is essential but not sufficient. The F0 maximum must be reached before the second accented syllable, contrasting high pitch before the second accent with the low pitch of an *early peak* in the second accent. If the *valley* rise only reaches its high level in the second accent syllable, creating a *medial peak*, the two accents are contrasted, stressing the either-or structure; this pattern is not appropriate for a QUESTION. It would be a STATEMENT of contrasted weekend alternatives in the QUESTION context (I). The *medial+early peak hat pattern* in (a) lacks the QUESTIONING *valley* pattern and would thus be ruled out as a QUESTION in the STATEMENT context (II). But if the *hat pattern* starts with a *late peak*, i.e. a fast rise from a low pitch level, it becomes a QUESTION that demands, rather than requests, a response from the addressee.

2.10   Contour-internal F0 Timing in Falls and Rises

It has been noted in several places that, besides global F0 movements and the synchronisations of their maxima or minima in relation to accented-vowel onset, an adequate prosodic model also needs to incorporate contour-internal F0 timing as a further theoretical category in the production and perception of intonation for the transmission of communicative functions. In 2.8.1, 2.8.3 and 2.8.5, it was discussed how high versus low or low versus high pitch in narrow time-windows before and after accented-vowel onset contributes to the distinction of rise-fall peak patterns as *early* versus *medial*. A medial peak depends on high pitch in the narrow window after accented-vowel onset, signalled by peak maximum synchronisation or by slowing down the F0 descent in this window. This trading relation between external and internal F0 timing is also found in Neapolitan Italian, where POLARITY QUESTIONS and STATEMENTS are both coded by rising-falling peak contours, but in the former, pitch in the accented vowel is raised, either by later synchronisation, or by slower F0 descent (d'Imperio 2000; Niebuhr, D'Imperio, Gili Fivela and Cangemi 2011).

In 2.9, *fast rises of hat patterns* and *slow rises of valley+peak sequences* were differentiated in a closed-set *either-or* structure to distinguish demanding from requesting in QUESTIONS, or speaker from listener orientation in STATEMENTS of alternatives. The use of two rising patterns with either slow-fast or fast-slow internal F0 timing was investigated by Dombrowski and Niebuhr (2005) on the basis of turn yielding and turn holding in the *Kiel Corpus of Spontaneous Speech*. The curves were described qualitatively as *concave* or *convex*, bulging down or up. They were quantified by *F0 range proportion*, which is the ratio between the F0 rise to the end of the accented vowel and the total rise to the end of the utterance, both measured from rise onset before the accented vowel, followed by at least one unaccented syllable in *early valleys*. A low value of range proportion reflects a slow rise speeding up later (*concave*), a high value the opposite of a fast rise slowing down later (*convex*). Low as against high range proportion was found to be significantly different in the two functional contexts of TURN YIELDING or TURN HOLDING. Dombrowski and Niebuhr (2010) subsequently tested the functional categorisation of the two rise patterns in a perception experiment with the Semantic Differential, complementing and supporting the spontaneous production data. The authors concluded that the slow or fast rise signals an open or a restricted action channel for the addressee; therefore, the rises were called ACTIVATING versus RESTRICTING.

These terms are defined in a perception perspective from signal to addressee. When it is replaced by a speaker–addressee interaction perspective, activation and restriction are redefined. A speaker seeks to enter into a relationship with an addressee by using a rising rather than a falling pitch pattern, and in addition signals subordination in the interaction, either of the addressee by a fast rise, or of the speaker by a slow rise. In a turn-taking context, the different interaction relationship restricts or opens the action channel for the addressee. In a question context, the speaker stimulates an addressee into action or invites action from an addressee, either demanding or requesting an answer, e.g. with a *late peak hat pattern* versus a *valley+peak* pattern in 'Am Sonnabend oder Sonntag?' (see 2.9). In the opening of an interaction, for example with a greeting or by giving one's name when answering the phone, the speaker either keeps their distance from, or connects with, the addressee. This is illustrated by the following two introductions from the same speaker in the *Kiel Corpus of Spontaneous Speech* (the bracketed sections are not shown in the figures):

> File g111a001
> '(Ja, einen wunderschönen) guten Tag. (Hier ist der) Herr Doktor Müller-Lüdenscheid. (ähm. Ich ruf noch mal an wegen der zweitägigen Arbeitssitzung.) [(Well, wishing you a very) nice day. (This is) Herr Dr Müller-Lüdenscheid. (Um, I'm calling again about the second work session)] (see Figure 2.24a)

> File g113a001
> 'Guten Tag. (Hier ist) Herr Müller-Lüdenscheid. Hören Sie mich?' [Good day. (This is) Herr Müller-Lüdenscheid. Can you hear me?] (see Figure 2.24b)

In g111a001, the stand-offishness in greeting and introduction is not only expressed by the fast rises on the accented syllables 'Tag' and 'Lü-', continuing in 'den-', and levelling out in '-scheid', but also by the very formal, impersonal phrasing 'der Herr Doktor Müller-Lüdenscheid', with definite article and title. In g113a001, the accented syllables have the slow rise, the introduction is less formal, and it is followed by another slow rise in a question enquiring whether reception is good. The fast, convex and slow, concave patterns for 'Lüdenscheid' are shown in the F0 traces. The question, likewise, has the slow, concave shape. Things are less clear in the F0 traces for 'Tag', although auditorily they are quite distinct and conform to the other fast or slow patterns. 'Tag' being monosyllabic limits the fast-slow versus slow-fast exponency. The rise starts more slowly from a lower level and moves to a lower end point in **b** than in **a**, and the vowel is also longer, thus highlighting the pattern.

Monosyllables were not included in the Dombrowski and Niebuhr studies (2005, 2010) because the definition of range proportion presupposed

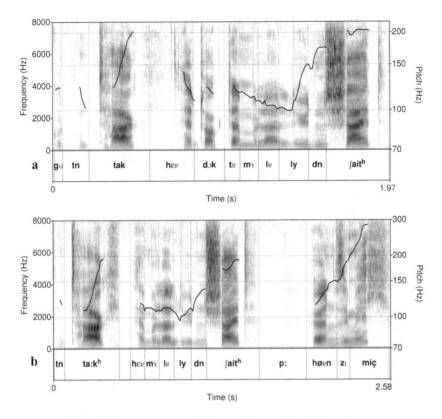

Figure 2.24. Spectrograms, F0 traces (log scale) and phonetically annotated syllabic segmentation of excerpts from German speech files (spliced together): **a**, two fast rises from g111a00l; **b**, three slow rises from g113a00l. Standard German, male speaker (JAK).

unaccented syllables after the accent, so it could not be calculated for monosyllables. The definition will have to be changed, for example by marking a point in time somewhere half-way between the onset of the rise and its offset. For instance, when F0 is raised or lowered by Praat manipulation at such a mid-point in Figure 2.25, there is a clear perceptual change between a *fast-slow* and a *slow-fast rise*, which is recognised as SUBORDINATION moving from the ADDRESSEE to the SPEAKER. This change is gradual, but opposite ends of the mid-point F0 continuum fall into separate categories, another case of category, rather than categorical perception (see 2.8.5).

Figure 2.25 shows a naturally produced *early-valley* version of the German INFORMATION QUESTION 'Und wie ist dein Name?' [And what's your name?].

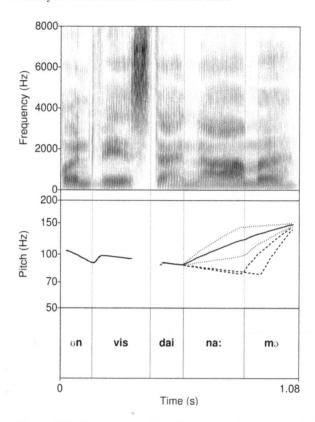

Figure 2.25. Spectrogram, rising F0 contours (log scale) and phonetically annotated syllabic segmentation in the German INFORMATION QUESTION 'Und wie ist dein Name?': neutral *early valley*, stylised and time-adjusted (plain line); F0 mid-point raised and lowered (dotted lines); *non-early valley* at mid-point and *non-early valley* shifted further to the right (dashed lines). Standard German, male speaker (KJK).

The F0 trace was stylised and adjusted in Praat with the following values: onset 108 Hz, start of rise 88 Hz, mid-point 120 Hz, end point of rise 150 Hz. This neutral rise is shown as a plain line. The mid-point was located at the end of the accented vowel [aː] of 'Name', a little more than half-way into the word. This point was raised to 140 Hz and lowered to 100 Hz. Both curves are shown as dotted lines. The mid-point was then lowered to 78 Hz, which entailed an F0 descent into the vowel, i.e. the generation of a *late valley*. This low point was shifted to the beginning of the final, unaccented vowel, generating a *later non-early valley*. The two *late valleys* are shown as dashed lines. All five patterns have distinctly different functional meanings.

As discussed in 2.8.5, rising contours change along a continuum of F0 minimum synchronisation from *early* to *late valley*. This covers the speaker's expressive range from neutral to increasing concern and feeling for the addressee and for the matter under discussion. So, rising contours are located in a two-dimensional plane of external F0-minimum synchronisation and internal F0 timing. Their primary function is for a speaker to establish contact with an addressee. The neutral contact signal is a rise starting before the accented-vowel onset and continuing to the end of the prosodic phrase, without macroprosodic deviations up or down from a linear course. By raising the F0 mid-point into a fast-slow rising pattern, the addressee is subordinated to the speaker in the communicative interaction; by lowering the mid-point into a slow-fast rising pattern, the reverse happens. All *non-early valleys* are by definition *concave slow-fast rising*, so they all subordinate the speaker to the addressee. But, in addition, they add to the speaker's expressiveness. There is a third F0 variable affecting the function of rises: the *height of the end point*. Raising it intensifies the CONTACT, SUBORDINATION and EXPRESSIVE functions. Rises are thus located in a three-dimensional space for signalling speaker–listener relationships in speech interaction. This is an empirical and theoretical expansion of the traditional one-way classification of rises into low and high in the London School analysis, e.g. Cruttenden (1995).

The question now is how these valley timing patterns can be adequately represented in a model of intonation as part of a wider prosodic model. KIM already has the contour distinction of *early* and *non-early valleys*, and separates a double-accent *slow-rise valley+peak* pattern from double-accent *hat pattern*, where a fast rise before a fall is categorised as a *medial* or *late peak*, with its fall being deferred to the fall in the second accent. This rise in the *hat pattern* is symbolised in PROLAB as a peak with zero descent: **&2^/(&0**. The *zero-descent peak* may be extrapolated from the *hat pattern* to final position. For example, parallel to the greeting 'Guten **&2**(Tag, Herr Kohler **&2. &PG**', with a *late peak*, rising on 'Tag' and falling on 'Herr', then trailing off on 'Kohler', we may get a fast, late rising peak on 'Tag' that levels out after the accent: 'Guten **&2**(Tag, Herr Kohler **&0. &PG**.' The rises are identical. This justifies categorising fast-slow rises as *zero-descent peak* contours. Further research into the three-dimensional space of rising contours will determine whether this categorisation is sufficient or needs to be supplemented by finer differentiation of rising parameters.

As regards different contour-internal F0 timings, there is a phenomenon that has become known under the name of High Rising Terminal (HRT), a relatively recent development in English prosody, which apparently had its origin in Australia, spread to New Zealand and the United States, and is now entering British English. It is characteristic of young, more particularly female speakers, and is very common in reporting and story-telling. Its phonetic feature is a fast rise that levels out at the maximum (see Fletcher and Harrington 2001). It differs from a rise in questions, although it has generally been discussed as a misuse of question intonation when no question is being asked. It is not only a clear case of a fast-slow convex rise but is also a signal sent out by the speaker to stimulate the listener into staying connected (Fletcher et al. 2002).

2.11   Prehead and Register

Unaccented syllables before the first accent in a prosodic phrase are the *prehead* of the contour. Its F0 range is adjusted either to the minimum or the maximum of a peak or a valley, resulting in a *low* or a *high prehead*. Combined with a peak contour, a low prehead is in the F0 region of the peak tail and falls; a high prehead is in the region of the peak maximum and may be level or descending slightly. Preceding a medial peak, the high prehead declines slightly at a high level to allow for the F0 rise into the accented vowel. Before a late peak, there is an F0 drop from the high prehead to the low level in the accented syllable. Combined with a valley contour, a low prehead is in the region of the valley minimum and falls; a high prehead is in the region of the valley maximum and is level or rises. Functionally, high prehead + peak and low prehead + valley correspond: in both cases, the prehead expands the total pitch range between beginning and end of the contour, i.e. the high-low or low-high contrast. Low prehead + peak and high prehead + valley also correspond: in both cases, the peak or valley is embedded in low, or high, beginning and ending, highlighting the peak or valley pitch characteristics. PROLAB marks high preheads by **&HP** prehead-initially.

In addition, deviations from a speaker's impressionistically judged mean pitch are taken into account as register changes, change to a lower pitch level **&LR**, or to a higher pitch level **&HR**. These changes within a speaker's delivery are commonly associated with prosodic boundaries, and are therefore marked at the beginning of prosodic phrases in which they take place.

In Kohler (2011b), the results of a perception and functional categorisation experiment with the Semantic Differential Technique were reported, on the basis of natural productions of the German phrases 'In Stockholm. Auf der ICPhS' [In Stockholm. At the ICPhS], produced as STATEMENTS or QUESTIONS. This data generation followed the analysis of the phrases from the appointment-making scenario of the *Kiel Corpus of Spontaneous Speech*, cf.

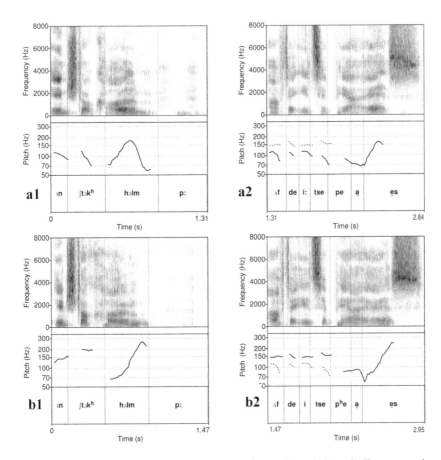

Figure 2.26. Spectrograms, F0 traces (log scale) and phonetically annotated syllabic segmentations of the original German utterance 'In Stockholm. Auf der ICPhS' in two parts as STATEMENT (**a1**+**a2**) and as QUESTION (**b1**+**b2**). Plain F0 traces = original utterances; dashed F0 traces in **a2** and **b2** = swapped *preheads* of QUESTION and STATEMENT by manipulation in Praat. Standard German, male speaker (KJK).

Kohler (2011b, Figure 2). Figure 2.26 presents the F0 traces for the two-accent phrases in two sections, the STATEMENTS in **a1** and **a2**, the QUESTIONS in **b1** and **b2**. Whereas the *late peak* and the *concave valley* contour are differentiated as *rising-falling* and *rising patterns* in fully voiced syllable rhymes of **a1** and **b1**, the F0 fall of the late peak is curtailed in the obstruent context. The difference between peak and valley, signalling STATEMENT versus QUESTION, depends on finer detail in the F0 trajectories. The *peak* pattern has a *fast F0* *rise*, the *concave valley* pattern a *slow F0 rise* and a considerably higher F0 end point. In addition, the final [s] is low-pitched in the *peak* pattern, high-pitched in the *valley* pattern, manifested by increased energy in the lower or the higher part of the spectrum, respectively. This, together with the small F0 descent after the maximum, identifies the pattern in **a2** as a clear rising-falling *late peak*, against the *valley* in **b2**. A comparison of the F0 curves in **b1** and **a2** shows that the internal timing of the valley and peak rises is crucial for pattern identification. The low and high precursors of the natural productions in **a2** and **b2** were also swapped by F0 manipulation in Praat, indicated by dashed traces in the graphs. The *peak* and *valley* patterns with the two *preheads* and the two [s] spectra in **a2** and **b2** entered test stimulus generation. For further details of experimental design and results, see Kohler (2011b).

The two preheads produced very clear results on the semantic-differential scale *gegensätzlich/einvernehmlich* [*contrary/agreeable*]. Both the *high prehead* with a *late peak* and the *low prehead* with a *concave valley* raised the contrariness scores considerably compared with the other prehead pairings, yielding a highly significant statistical difference. This result converges with the Dutch findings of Grabe et al.'s (1997) Semantic Differential investigation into the combinations of high %H or low %L preheads with immediately following H*L and L*H pitch accents, which correspond to medial peak and high-rising valley categorisations used in KIM. Judgements on *friendliness, politeness* and *irritation* scales were affected by agreement or disagreement of the prehead tone with the initial pitch-accent tone. Polar sequences of the two tones yielded more positive (*friendlier, more polite, less irritated*) judgements on the scales, non-polar sequences more negative ones. The *friendliness, politeness* and *irritation* scales refer to the relationship between speaker and hearer in communicative interaction, as does the *contrary/agreeable* scale in the German data. However, in the German data, the concatenation of a high prehead with a late peak increases *contrary* judgements in spite of a polar-tone succession. This indicates that it is not the equivalence or divergence of the initial pitch-accent tone and the preceding prehead tone that is relevant in perception and cognitive processing but the relation between the utterance-initial and the utterance-final pitch level. The extended F0 range intensifies the contrastive statement of the late peak and the surprise question of the concave high-rising valley, in both cases conveying an attitude of contrariness in the speaker–listener relationship. This semantic interpretation of a global utterance contour presupposes the recognition of a much wider processing window in speech perception than the postulate of intonational morphemes for prehead and nuclear tones in Grabe et al.'s approach allows.

2.12   Prosodic Phrasing

Accents are organised into phrasal structures whose boundaries are marked by a hierarchy of weak to strong distinctive bundles of juncture properties. This hierarchical phrasal organisation reflects ARGUMENTATION, superimposed on an external-world INFORMATION STRUCTURE. Prosodic phrases are further organised into speaker turns in communicative interchanges. Speakers exhibit varying degrees of delicacy in turn-internal prosodic phrasing according to their proficiency in expressing these structures orally in interaction. The discussion below is based on the *Kiel Corpus of Spontaneous Speech*, which provided the dialogue data for an extensive study of prosodic phrasing in German (Kohler, Kleber and Peters 2005; Peters 2001).

The phonetic properties of prosodic phrasing examined in these dialogue interchanges include (1) final syllabic lengthening, which disrupts speech fluency if it is above a threshold set by speech rate, (2) low-falling, high-rising or falling-rising pitch leading up to the boundary, (3) F0 reset after it, (4) a pause or breathing, scaled in duration, (5) interactional non-lexical sounds and (6) glottal stop, and glottalisation in sonorants. It is clear that with such multivalued feature bundles, phrase boundaries cannot be discretely present or absent but have gradient variability according to the semantic weight of phrase separation. This weight reflects the ARGUMENTATION the speaker wants to convey in speech interaction within the flexible frame of a particular language, and at the same time its phonetic exponents are an index of the speaker's rhetorical proficiency.

In the *Kiel Corpus* analysis, phrase boundaries were first determined auditorily and then related to acoustic properties, with numerical subclassification of **&PG** in PROLAB as follows:

- **&PG1** the weakest break, signalled by segmental lengthening and/or by pitch features (**±L±F**), but no pause/breath (**-P**)
- **&PG2** signalled by segmental lengthening and/or pitch features (**±L±F**) + perceptually short pause/breath (**+P-l**), whose evaluation depends on its duration in relation to overall speech rate and position in syntactic structures
- **&PG3** signalled by segmental lengthening and/or pitch features (**±L±F**) + perceptually long pause/breath (**+P+l**)
- **&PG4** signalled by segmental lengthening (**+L**) and terminal pitch features, falling very low or rising very high (**+Ft**), either at the end of a dialogue turn (**+T**) or followed by a perceptually long pause/breath (**+P+l**)

- **&PG1** and **&PG2** may need further subclassification according to the perceptual grading of different combinations of ±L and ±F; this is an open research question.

The following passage provides highly skilled prosodic phrasing for weighted information grouping in an appointment-making task (g212a07r, male speaker ANL).

> ja, **&PG2** gerne. **&PG2** ich habe also Zeit vom Donnerstag, den zweiten Juni **&PG2** bis Mittwoch, den achten, **&PG3** und von Samstag, dem achtzehnten, **&PG2** bis Donnerstag, **&PG1** den dreiundzwanzigsten, **&PG3** und dann wieder vom siebenundzwanzigsten bis zum dreißigsten. **&PG4**

> [yes, **&PG2** OK. **&PG2** I've got time from Thursday, the second of June **&PG2** till Wednesday, the eighth, **&PG3** and from Saturday, the eighteenth, **&PG2** till Thursday **&PG1** the twenty-third, **&PG3** and then again from the twenty-seventh to the thirtieth. **&PG4**]

The dialogue turn contains three blocks of dates, which are separated by **&PG3**; within the first two blocks, the speaker structures the periods of time by **&PG2** 'from ... to...'. The first block is introduced by two affirmative links to the preceding turn, marked by **&PG2**. At the end of block 2, the day of the week and the date are separated by a weaker **&PG1**. In block 3, the two dates of the period are integrated into a *hat pattern* with a low-falling early F0 peak contour and laryngealisation to signal the end of the turn.

This perfect hierarchical structuring of syntagmatic grouping, to highlight the speaker's ARGUMENTATION, contrasts with less transparent chunking in the following example from the same scenario (g072a15r, male speaker TIS).

> wo ich im Juni Zeit hätte, **&PG1** ich kann Ihnen das ja mal sagen, **&PG2** wäre **&PG3** Samstag den achtzehnten bis Donnerstag den dreiundzwanzigsten, **&PG1** und dann wieder ab **&PG2** Montag den siebenundzwanzigsten bis Ende des Monats. **&PG2** Vielleicht haben Sie da irgendwann Zeit. **&PG4**

> [when I would have time in June, **&PG1** I may tell you this, **&PG2** would be **&PG3** from Saturday the 18th to Thursday the 23rd, **&PG1** and then again from **&PG2** Monday the 27th till the end of the month. **&PG2** Perhaps you are free on any one of these dates. **&PG4**]

There is less grading of boundary strength for the mapping of the structural hierarchy in the information the speaker wants to transmit. Moreover, instances of **&PG2** and **&PG3**, and signal dysfluencies as a result of wording problems, are located inside syntagmas.

The English translations with **&PGn** markings postulate the same prosody-argumentation mapping for English. Comparable large-scale analysis of spontaneous speech will be able to provide a definitive answer. The foregoing discussion shows that data should not be analysed blindly and indiscriminately but need to be screened as to the speaker's speech proficiency before generalising to cognitive structures in the language. Such a preliminary screening takes the form of competent native observers ranking speakers or corpora collected from them on such scales as, e.g., 'acoustic clarity/intelligibility' and 'content organisation', in each case from 'bad' to 'good'. The speakers are then allocated to groups according to their screening indices, and these groups are analysed separately. Such a procedure allows us to give theoretically motivated accounts of phonetic variability across speaker proficiency within the same analytical frame of reference.

2.13   Microprosody

As Figure 2.26 in 2.11 demonstrated, macroprosodic function-oriented pitch patterns are shaped in their physical manifestation by vocal-tract articulation, resulting in widely differing F0 traces for perceptually identical patterns, such as late peaks. This microprosodic influence has three dimensions: (1) intrinsic F0 differences between low and high vowels, (2) coarticulatory F0 changes in context, especially in voiceless obstruent as against voiced sonorant environments, (3) curtailing of F0 trajectories before voicelessness. Voiceless obstruents determine the F0 course of peak contours (Gartenberg and Panzlaff-Reuter 1991, Kohler 1997a). On the one hand, they raise F0 onset, without the perceived contour class being affected. On the other hand, they mask it, e.g. after short vowels in *late peak* contours of utterance-final monosyllables, where the F0 descent is strongly curtailed, compared with the F0 fall in *early peaks*, due to time constraints (see 2.11). Grabe (1998) also found this truncation in her German data for a pattern she classified as H*+L in ToBI notation. She compared it to compression in what she noted as the same pattern H*+L in English. However, closer inspection reveals that the contexts in the data acquisition are not identical for the two languages. They are as follows:

> Anna and Peter are watching TV. A photograph of this week's National Lottery winner appears. Anna says: Look Peter! It's Mr Sheafer/Sheaf/Shift! Our new neighbour!

> Anna und Peter sehen fern. Ein Lottogewinner wird vorgestellt. Anna sagt: 'Na sowas! Das ist doch Herr Schiefer/Schief/Schiff! Unser neuer Nachbar!

The German context suggests expressively evaluated contrast with 'Na sowas!' [Well I never!], reinforced by the contrastive particle 'doch'. This connotation is absent from 'Look Peter!' in the English context. In such a context, German uses a semantically and pragmatically contrastive *late peak*. It is thus most likely that Grabe's German speakers produced a *late*, her English speakers a *medial*, *peak*, and it is therefore to be expected that alignment is later in the German than in the English data. Truncation then follows naturally from the greater time constraint in the voiceless context of monosyllables in German than in English. So, Grabe used different contextualisations to obtain her H*+L samples in the two languages, favouring CONTRAST and UNEX-PECTEDNESS in German but NEW OBSERVATION in English. This resulted in different peak contour categories, a *late peak* in German versus a *medial peak* in English, with different consequences for the manifestation of F0 across syllables ending in voiceless obstruents (Kohler 2006b). It shows that communicative function is already important at the data collection stage, and that different *phonological* synchronisations of F0 patterns with articulation need to be distinguished from variable *phonetic* alignment to avoid misinterpretation.

What Grabe interpreted as a difference of alignment strategies in the two languages relates to two functionally distinctive peak patterns that belong to both languages. This also means that the non-occurrence of truncation in the rising pattern L*+H, which Grabe found in her data of both languages, does not create a compression-truncation asymmetry for German. Rising contours have to reach their F0 targets for the listener to be able to decode the final pitch level in the highly variable upper range of a speaker's voice, whereas the final pitch level of a curtailed fall can be reconstructed from its onset in relation to the lower end of a speaker's voice range.

As discussed in 2.11, there is also the opposite influence of prosodic patterns on variable realisation of segments: relaxation or tension in low-falling peak or high-rising valley patterns produces widening/narrowing of obstruent constrictions and resonance channels behind them, resulting in low-spectrum or high-spectrum strengthening, for instance in post-vocalic [s]. This phenomenon has also been found in aspiration differences of syllable-final [t] after short [ɪ] in early versus late peak contours in German: the low-pitch or high-pitch peak patterns are heightened by the different articulatory dynamics (Niebuhr 2008).

2.14   Stepping Patterns

By the side of continuous pitch patterns at accent positions in utterances of any syntactic structure (declarative, interrogative, imperative or elliptic), English and German also use stepping between perceptually constant pitch levels, either up or down and in a variety of intervals. To differentiate this pitch sequencing terminologically from the phonological categories of *downstep* and *upstep* (see 2.4), it is referred to as *stepping, down-stepping* and *up-stepping*. Dombrowski (2013) was the first prosodist to provide a comprehensive systematic formal account of stepping intonation patterns as a parallel set beside continuous ones. He conceptualised them as derivatives from the continuous peak and valley categories of KIM by F0-stylisation, thus expanding the theoretical framework for the description of German intonation. But his categorisation of stepping patterns can also be applied to English. The rationale behind Dombrowski's postulate of an independent set of stylised F0 patterns, separate from continuous ones, was to relate pitch stepping to specific types of behaviour in speech communication, i.e. routine and situationally predictable exchanges, especially signalling initiation, continuation or conclusion of an interaction with formalised utterances, such as greeting, leave-taking or thanking. Figure 2.27 provides examples of thanking with stylisations of *early* and *late valleys* and *peaks*.

Dombrowski applied the Semantic Differential Technique in a perception experiment using the utterance 'In Andalusien', pronounced with five KIM patterns and their stylisations: *early, medial, late peaks* and *early, late valleys*. MANOVAs and Discriminant Analyses tested for weightings on twelve semantic scales between the two pitch modes and between the five patterns in each mode. The interpretation derived from the statistical results points to a semantic weakening of stepping as against continuous contours in the direction of stereotypy, but also to comparable semantic profiles between the five patterns in each pitch mode. Differences are largest between the *early peak* and the *valleys* on the scales *question-statement* and *closed-open* in both modes. This function-form approach will be integrated into the APPEAL function of Bühler's *Organon Model* in Chapter 4.1 (see also 1.2.1.2).

Stepping patterns have been discussed sporadically in the literature under a variety of terms, generally not from the point of view of their communicative function but from the formal angle, as deviations from the usual continuous pitch contrasts. The most common reference is to *call(ing) contours* (Abe 1962; Ladd 1996 (2nd edn 2008)) or *calls* (Gibbon 1976), and *vocative patterns* or *vocative contours* (Pierrehumbert 1980), The calling contour is sometimes equated with *chant* ('vocative chant': Liberman 1975; *chanted call*: Gussenhoven 1993; *spoken chant*: Pike 1945), and thus to a very narrow and specific interactive use. By referring stepping patterns in receiver-directed deixis to chant, the pointing function is lumped together with children's chant of the type '↑Susie ↓is ↑a ↓tattle ↓tale', because of the formal similarity of pitch

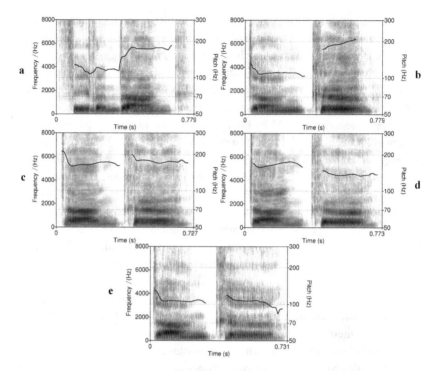

Figure 2.27. Spectrograms and F0 traces of stepping patterns in phrases of thanks in German: **a**, 'Vielen Dank', up-stepping stylisation of *early valley*; **b**, 'Danke', up-stepping stylisation of *late valley*; **c**, 'Danke', high-level stylisation of *early valley*; **d**, 'Danke', down-stepping stylisation of *medial peak*; **e**, low-level stylisation of *early peak*. Standard German, male speaker (KJK).

stepping instead of continuous pitch movement. Pike (1945, p. 71) defines it as 'CHILDHOOD TRIUMPH [which] can be gentle, a sheer effervescence of joy, or may be maliciously taunting.' So, the communicative function of chant is quite different from the use of stepping patterns in a pointing field, and the term 'chant' is therefore not appropriate for the deictic signal.

Ladd (1978, 1983) introduced the concept of *stylised intonation* into the analysis of stepping, with a functional perspective contrasting stereotyped, routine, predictable communicative acts as *stylised* as against *plain*, and associating them with stepping versus continuous pitch patterns. Ladd (1996 (2nd edn 2008)) renounced the earlier function-form approach in the wake of AM Phonology, and, concentrating on form, integrated stepping patterns into the L-H and downstep framework developed for English intonation analysis. He not only gave up the functional orientation but also covered both types of pitch generation by the same formal descriptive device. The concepts of *stereotyped patterns*, e.g. 't Hart (1998), and *intonation clichés*, e.g. Fónagy, Bérard and Fónagy (1983) and Di Cristo (1998), are other terms for the same idea of semantic stylisation.

The functional approach in this monograph treats the two types of pitch as different *formal*, continuous versus stepping, manifestations of distinct FUNCTIONS in their own right, unfolding in different communicative fields: form is stylised but meaning is not – it is independently related to types of communicative interaction. Gibbon (1998) also adopted the functional perspective in the analysis of (mainly) down-stepping patterns by expanding their field of occurrence from calling to greeting, leave-taking, thanking and discourse repairs, and proposed, as their communicative function, the signalling of 'the opening, sustaining, and closing of a channel of communication' (p. 91). Dombrowski (2013) developed his system of formal stylisation of the pitch categories of KIM within such a functional framework, leading on from the minimal two-level synthesis of German intonation by Isačenko and Schädlich (1970). Chapter 4.1 expands this theoretical and empirical frame by moving 'calling contours' from the traditionally casuistic treatment into a comprehensive systematic function-form analysis of the use of pitch in speech communication.

Stepping pitch may be expected to occur in all non-tone languages, linked to sentence accents. In those languages where accents dock at lexical stress positions in syllable chains, pitch stepping marks accented *words* for specific communicative functions, especially to control interaction with a receiver. The functional links will vary, but calling will most probably always be a function signalled by a down-stepping pattern. French differs quite considerably from English and German in the functional uses of pitch stepping. It has been reported in *istic* deixis of calls, greetings and friendly warnings, as in English and German (Di Cristo 1998; Fagyal 1997), e.g.:

A	Bon	tten
nna	jour !	tion !
		A

But Fagyal also mentions its occurrence in listings when the enumerated items are not meant to give individually new information but the total list is to refer to shared knowledge of a set relevant in the communicative situation. For example, when a speaker lists the ingredients for a recipe, every one of which is important for the dish, pitch will be rising on each item (Fagyal 1997 p. 84):

```
          œufs    beurre        rine …
il te faut                de la
      des       du              fa
['(You know...) you need eggs, butter, flour...']
```

If, instead, the speaker refers to the shared knowledge of the recipe and simply reminds the addressee of the list, down-stepping patterns are used:

```
        des        du            fa
il te        œufs       beurre    de la   rine …
    faut
        [You need eggs, butter, flour...]
```

This pitch pattern was already described beside several alternatives in French enumerations by Coustenoble and Armstrong (1934). Stepping in French is not just used as a simple control signal of interaction, it also introduces FINALITY OF ARGUMENTATION in PROPOSITIONAL REPRESENTATION (see Chapter 3), which in German and English is manifested by an *early peak*:

> Du brauchst **&2)**Eier **&2.** und **&2)**Butter **&2.** und **&2)** Mehl **&2. &PG**
> You need **&2)** eggs **&2.** and **&2**butter **&2.** and **&2)** flour **&2. &PG**

In each case, pitch is high on the unaccented syllable before the accent and then falls low into the accented syllable. The argumentative FINALITY in the *early peak* of the 'gelogen' example (see 2.8) would therefore be rendered in French by 'Elle a menti' with down-stepping pitch on 'menti', as against a high pitch fall on the final syllable to signal OPENNESS, corresponding to the German or English *medial peak*. Fagyal subsumes this use of down-stepping pitch in French under *implicature* (p. 86).

These examples show that the functions of pitch stepping in French differ in a fundamental way, compared with German and English. Besides serving the APPEAL function in interaction-controlling calls, greetings and friendly warnings, they are also integrated in the REPRESENTATION function. This seems to be due to a different formal structuring of pitch patterns. In French, accent does not mark *words*, but intonation *phrases*. An utterance is divided into a sequence of intonation phrases according to information units, and, in non-emotional speech, the last non-schwa syllable of each phrase receives an accent. (The EXPRESSION function adds *accents d'insistance* elsewhere word-initially.) Pitch moves up in a step-wise fashion through the syllable chain to the phrase-final accent. This reduces pitch movement on syllables in non-emotional speech and creates stepping pitch patterns in the REPRESENTATION function, which are then also used for certain interaction-controlling APPEAL functions. This overall stepping organisation of French neutral intonation patterns is an essential prosodic property contributing to the perception of regularity of syllable sequencing. Together with the high frequency of simple CV syllables in French utterances, it is at the root of categorising French as a typical syllable-timed language (see 3.4).

In the sub-Saharan register tone languages, the integration of pitch stepping into the REPRESENTATION function goes even further, because every syllable has a distinct level tone for lexical and morphological differentiation; and pitch movement results from tone concatenation and merging. So, it is a question for further research what other prosodic variables enter the signalling of interaction control, for example in calls, which can be assumed to exist as a general category of speech communication, and whether loudness through greater physical energy may be the prime candidate. Finally, contour tone languages like Mandarin Chinese cannot use pitch stepping as an acoustic signal of *istic* deixis. It remains an open question what other formal means are used instead, for example in calling.

In an extension of PROLAB within KIM, a symbolisation is adopted for stepping patterns that uses arrows pointing up or down, put in front of the syllable where the higher or lower pitch level starts. This pitch level stays until the next arrow or the end of the utterance. The accented syllable is underlined. If an arrow pointing up or down occurs before the first syllable of the utterance, pitch starts high or low, respectively. A graded succession of two or more steps up or down is marked by a series of ↑ or ↓, implying that each following syllable is higher or lower than the preceding one. A step up or down within a final accented syllable is marked by one arrow at the beginning and the other one at the end of the syllable (for examples and an illustration of the marking conventions, see 4.1).

2.15   Time-Windows in Speech Production

The preceding sections have dealt with various signal aspects of accentuation and intonation in speech production and perception, and have presented a network of prosodic relationships. Before relating the categories of this model to the functions of REPRESENTATION, APPEAL and EXPRESSION in speech interaction, the prosodic strand of speech needs to be integrated into an overall framework of articulated sound production.

Speech is produced by controlling and coordinating time courses of subglottal airflow, glottal phonation and pitch, and supra-glottal vocal-tract articulation for specific communicative functions in languages. On the subglottal tier, airflow is controlled in long breathing-out cycles for glottal and supra-glottal speech production by maintaining a stable macro pressure level, which is set on an effort scale by coordinated chest-muscle contractions (Draper, Ladefoged and Whitteridge 1959, 1960; Ladefoged 1960; Ladefoged, Draper and Whitteridge 1958). The force of the airflow determines the acoustic energy level of sound generation at the glottis for overall loudness. It is modulated across the glottis by phonation-type settings through laryngeal muscle control (see Catford 1964; Laver 1980) and, in the case of quasi-periodic vibration, by pitch. On the supra-glottal tier, coordinated movements, driven by muscular force, of jaw, tongue, lips and velum generate sequences of varying opening and closing vocal-tract configurations. They are excited by the glottally modulated airflow, and are, in turn, organised into a language's characteristic set of different types of acoustic syllables, comprising sonorous and asonorous parts of various duration, spectral composition and energy. The simplest syllable type combines a closing consonant with an opening vowel configuration (CV), as in English 'bow'. All languages have it, and some languages, such as Japanese, have no other, except for single V. In the Romance languages, supra-glottal articulation is predominantly organised in this simple CV way. The Germanic and the Slavonic languages have a greater variety of more complex types, such as complex opening-closing vocal-tract configurations getting integrated into a syllable, e.g. in English 'glimpse', segmentally represented as CCVCCC, or even more complex in German 'schimpfst' CVCCCCC.

The activities on the three production tiers are organised in time-windows of different extensions (Kohler 2003, 2007). The time-window on the subglottal tier is the broadest, spanning whole utterances of the type illustrated in Figures 2.9 and 2.10. The basic time-window on the supra-glottal tier is narrow, spanning the syllable. Activity on the glottal tier is either linked to the narrow time-window of the syllable by syllable phonation and syllable pitch, thus adding parameters of voice, voicelessness, breathy voice, creak, etc. and tone to its specification. Or phonation and pitch are organised in global patterns, the former in long-term voice quality for expressive functions, the latter in intonation, in a separate prosody time-window in between the syllable and the breath group. The extension of the prosody window is quite variable, depending on how the speaker chunks the message to be conveyed to a listener.

The control of utterance intonation in a variable broad prosody time-window is demonstrated for German and English by:

- F0 downstep across the speech chunk inside a time-window and by upstep to the speech chunk in the following window (2.4)

- a high prehead extending the fall of a peak contour, and a low prehead extending the rise of a high valley contour, and by both patterns
  signalling contrariness, as against the reversed prehead combinations
  (2.11)
- high versus medial register, irrespective of local ups and downs in
  pitch, coding communicative functions (2.11)
- controlling peak and valley contours as unitary intonation patterns
  associated as such with communicative functions (2.7, 2.8, 2.9).

Pitch combines with syllable duration, phonation and pausing to mark the
right edges of successive prosody time-windows on a scale of terminality, e.g.
across a dialogue turn (2.12).

The narrow-window syllables are also integrated into broader supra-glottal
articulation windows in two ways:

(a) The sequencing of vocal-tract opening and closing is shaped by
    long-term *articulatory prosodies*, of, e.g., *labialisation, palatalisa-
    tion, velarisation, nasalisation* (Firth 1948; Kohler 1999; Kohler and
    Niebuhr 2011), also including vowel harmony

    - either as a purely phonetic process, for example the look-ahead ad-
      justment of vocal-tract opening in non-final syllables to that in the
      final syllable of French phrases, e.g. 'j'étais' [ʒɛtɛ] versus 'j'ai été'
      [ʒeete] or 'phonologue' [fɔnɔlɔg] versus 'phonologie' [fonoloʒi]
    - or exploited in morphology, for example in carry-on adjustment of
      liprounding/spreading and front/back from a lexical stem vowel to
      suffix vowels in Turkish

kol-um	arm-my	my arm
göz-üm-üz	eye-my-*plural*	our eyes
kol-lar-ım- ız	arm-*plural*-my-*plural*	our arms
göz-ler-im-iz	eye-*plural*-your-*plural*	your eyes

(b) The sequencing of vocal-tract opening and closing is organised in
    fluctuating prominence patterns in conjunction with pitch generation
    in the prosody time-window on the glottal tier, and is most strongly
    regularised in specific rhythm time-windows for rhetorical or poetic
    functions (Kohler 2008, 2009a; cf. 2.1 and 3.4).

Intonation and prominence patterning in the prosody time-window, linking the glottal and supra-glottal tiers, is used, together with syntactic form, to
structure the transmission of meaning. In 2.2 and 2.3 the category of *sentence
accent* is introduced to represent the prosodic structuring found in German and

English for weighting elements of information in relation to one another. In these languages, sentence accentuation highlights lexical elements in syntactic structures. But not all languages behave like this, because languages differ in how they insert words in syntax and how they dock prosodic patterns on the lexical syllable chain. In the West Germanic and other sentence-accent languages, words have *lexical stress*, which abstractly marks a syllable in a lexical item that functions as a docking place for a sentence accent when the lexical item is to be highlighted (2.5, 2.6). Prominence-lending syllable features achieve this (2.7, 2.8). In the West Germanic languages, accentuation not only increases the prominence of the stressed syllable of the lexical item to be highlighted but also complements it by decreasing the prominences of surrounding, especially following, unstressed syllables, by reducing the timing and extension of their articulatory movements (see 2.6) and by integrating their pitch into the rising-falling peak or the falling-rising valley patterns docked at the stressed syllables (see 2.1). Reduction is strongest in English, where vowel centralisation and elision commonly occur. The combined pitch-articulation patterns in sentence accentuation can create the temporal prominence regularity characteristic of the so-called *stress-timed* languages (see 3.4). This is one more reason for categorising peak and valley patterns as unitary intonation contours (see 2.7).

Not all sentence-accent languages have complementary unstressed syllable reduction. Spanish and Italian, although lexical-stress languages, do not have it, and in view of the preponderance of CV syllables, they give the auditory impression of a very regular rhythmic syllable flow characteristic of the so-called *syllable-timed* languages (see 3.4). This is even more prominent in Spanish than in Italian because, in the latter, there is a dyadic relation of long vowel + short consonant or short vowel + long consonant in stressed syllables of disyllables, interfering with an even CV flow.

Among the Romance languages, French stands out in lacking *lexical stress*, which means that lexical items are not weighted in relation to one another by sentence accents docking at *lexical stress* positions. Lexical items are integrated into the supra-glottal articulation, the prominence pattern and the intonation of the phrase. Lexical items thus do not have a stable phonological form. Rather, syntax-based utterance phrasing determines the shape of lexical items, even the formation of lexical compounds, as is shown by constructions like 'boîte aux lettres', 'porte-manteaux', 'porte-clefs', as against English 'letter box', 'coat rack', 'key ring', or German 'Briefkasten', 'Garderobenständer', 'Schlüsselring'. In German and English, the specifying part of the compound is positioned before its general referent and receives a sentence accent docked at the lexical stress syllable of the specifying part. In French the order is reversed, and the phrase receives a prominence pattern with an increase on its final syllable to mark different phrase-boundary strengths, thus weighting phrases, rather than lexical items, in relation to one another in meaning transmission. This may be called a *phrase accent* (different from AM Phonology) as against a word-bound sentence accent. Vaissière (2006) refers to French as *une langue à frontières* (p. 100) with different degrees of boundary strength (p. 97) marking the ends of sentences and prosodic phrases within them (pp. 109ff).

The graded raising of prominence at the right edge of phrases is achieved by duration, pitch and vocal-tract control of the last syllable. Duration increases with the syntactic hierarchy from *mot phonétique* to *phrase prosodique* to utterance ending. In non-expressive speech, pitch moves up stepwise to the last or the penultimate syllable of a phrase, depending on non-final or final utterance position, and on statement or question mode. In statements, the pitch of the utterance-final syllable drops low. The combination of pitch and duration generates a prominence profile that culminates at the right edge of a prosody window, thus adding prosodic marking to syntactic phrases in utterances. This may be illustrated by the following examples of French phrasing distinctions, and compared with the equivalent English and German accentuation differences:

(a)   un acteur de cinéma I muet II [a silent actor in films]
        a **&2^**silent **&0. &2^**film actor **&2. &PG**
        ein **&2^**stummer **&0. &2** Filmschauspieler **&2. &PG**

(b)   un acteur I de cinéma muet II [an actor in silent films]
        a **&2^**silent **&1. &1^**film actor **&2. &PG**
        ein **&2^**Stummfilm **&1. &1** schauspieler **&2. &PG**

(Fónagy 2003, p. 4; I marks the weaker internal, II the stronger final boundary)

The adjectival attribute 'muet' is syntactically determined to follow the nominal head, which is either a nominal phrase in (a) or a noun inside another nominal phrase in (b). Since the syntactic and lexical forms are the same for both structures, prosodic phrasing takes over, distinguishing between them by bracketing either 'un acteur de cinéma' or 'de cinéma muet' prosodically. In (a), the last syllable of the first prosodic phrase is lengthened before a pitch drop, with greater lengthening on the adjective in the second prosodic phrase. The same duration and pitch structuring is applied to the first prosodic phrase in (b); the second prosodic phrase follows, with a renewed stepwise rise to the penultimate syllable and a fall on the lengthened final syllable.

This prosodic phrasing of syntactic structures in French contrasts with the graded accentual weighting of simplex and compound lexical items in the corresponding syntactic structures of English and German. Both these languages differentiate pre-nominal adjectival attribution, additionally inflected in German, and compound formation, which goes much further in German. French and the Germanic languages are thus diametrically opposed in the way they use the prosody window to structure glottal sound production: either for prosodic phrasing or for sentence accentuation. This casts doubt on the adequacy of adopting the AM pitch accent concept, worked out for English, in the analysis of French prosody (Jun and Fougeron 2002).

There is an accent category in French that is not used for information weighting but for the EXPRESSION function to intensify the meaning of words. This *accent d'insistance* manifests itself on the first syllable of a word that begins with a consonant, including a glottal stop initiating a word-initial vowel, by increased duration of this consonant, and raised F0 as well as energy of the vowel, for example in 'c'est é**pou**vantable!' (Grammont 1934, pp. 139ff). Consequently, the transfer of Germanic accentuation into French by speakers of German or English is perceived by the French ear as continual insistence and emphasis (Vaissière pers. comm.). A similar intensifying accent does occur in the Germanic languages as well. It is related to intensification in EXPRESSIVE HIGH KEY and is grafted onto the general sentence accentuation that marks information structure (see 5.1). On the other hand, there is, of course, also prosodic phrasing by timing, pitch, phonation and pausing/breathing in the Germanic languages (see 2.12), but it operates in a broader time frame than the prosody window on the glottal tier, including breath control and pausing to mark higher-order speech chunking in information structure, extending to dialogue turns. This prosodic phrasing belongs to human speech generally, although the prosodic manisfestations may change between languages.

Whilst the edges of the prosody time-window mark syntactic boundaries in French, lexical boundaries inside the prosodic phrase are disregarded, and bridged by historically conditioned prevocalic *liaison*. This results in the occurrence of strings of open CV syllables, which is nicely illustrated by Vaissière (2006, p. 112) with the sentences:

Cet homme ǀ est énormément bête.	[This man is enormously stupid.]
Cet homme est énorme, ǀ et m'embête.	[This man is enormous, and annoys me.]

They both contain the same sequences of vocal-tract opening and closing, which are organised as two prosodic phrases in two different ways. In both sentences, both phrases end in prominent closed syllables, and the phrase-internal syllables are open, with the exception of '-nor-' in the first sentence.

Closed syllables in the prosodically marked phrase-final position increase its prominence and thus contrast it more strongly with the even prominence flow of open syllables preceding it. This vocal-tract structuring inside the prosody window is a rich source for word play. For example, in:

> [Louis XVIII on his deathbed, addressing his doctors around him and referring to his successor to the throne, Charles X]
> Allons! Finissons-en, Charles attend!
> [Come on! Let's get it over with, Charles is waiting / charlatans!]
> 'Charles attend' and 'charlatans' become identical as [ʃaʁlatɑ̃].

The generation of an even prominence flow of syllables inside prosodic phrases is further supported by breaking up heavy consonant clustering into vocal-tract [ə] openings. This is the segmental phrase-phonetic phenomenon of *e caduc* in Standard (Parisian) French, which has been dealt with extensively in the literature for over a century from the point of view of elision or preservation of historical [ə]. The discussion was started by Grammont (1894). He formulated *la loi des trois consonnes*, which states that [ə] can be elided if it does not result in a cluster of two consonants before a syllable onset consonant. There is the word-initial consonant cluster [fn] after the definite article in 'la f(e)nêtre' [the window], but a vocal-tract opening [fən] after the indefinite article or the numeral in 'un(e) fenêtre'. Further examples are 'portefeuill(e)' [wallet], 'quatre-vingt' [eighty], 'quat(re) chevaux' [four horses, 4hp Citroën car] versus 'deux ch(e)vaux' [two horses, 2hp Citroën car]. This is paralleled by the optional deletion and obligatory preservation, respectively, of [rə] in 'arb(re) de Noël' [Christmas tree] versus 'arbre vert' [green tree].

The name *la loi des trois consonnes* does not capture the facts of *e caduc* adequately and leads to misunderstanding. The occurrence of two consonants *before* a syllable onset necessitates a vocal-tract opening into [ə]; the occurrence of only one consonant allows consonant clustering, and thus the reduction of a syllable, irrespective of the number of consonants following the juncture. Thus, 'Il n'a pas d(e) scrupules' [He has no scruples] (Grammont 1934, p. 113) is perfectly regular because [d] closes the previous syllable, and [skr] is a possible syllable- and word-initial cluster. Similarly, involving two *e caduc*, 'Tu me demand(es) c(e) que c'est? [You're asking me what this is?] (Grammont 1934, p. 113) has regular syllable coda and onset phonotactics and thus does not require a vocal-tract opening into [ə], although it is a sequence of three cononants. What determines consonant clustering or [ə] breaking is that, in the sequencing of vocal tract closing and opening, a single consonant can form a regular closing syllable before the next syllable onset, whereas two consonants cannot. (This is actually how Grammont (1934, p. 105f) describes the 'law' in his text.) This principle operates continually through the vocal-tract sequencing in an utterance, and in the case of a series of *e caduc* results in an alternation of clustering and [ə] breaking, because clustering requires subsequent breaking, which in turn allows clustering, e.g. 'Qu'est-c(e) que j(e) **te** disais?' [What did I tell you?]. Although preservation has been considered the default state from the historical perspective, breaking of consonant clusters by [ə] opening is more widespread and can be independent of an historical [ə] antecedent, as in 'ours [ə] blanc' [polar bear], or in popular speech 'Arc [ə] d(e) Triomphe' (Grammont 1934, p. 105).

Further data analysis, for example by Delattre (1948, 1949, 1951, 1966), Léon (1966) and Malécot (1976), has shown that *e caduc* is a multifaceted phrasal phenomenon that cannot be captured fully by *la loi des trois consonnes*. Speaking style has always been regarded as the overriding factor: the more formal it is, the more [ə] are preserved. Within the generally selected educated speech level, articulatory force, monotonic aperture decrease and back-to-front sequence in surrounding consonants, position in the phrase and rhythm have been adduced as phonetic factors determining elision, in addition to the number of consonants preceding a syllable juncture. For instance, if there is a non-schwa syllable before the phrase-final one, a preceding [ə] can be absent, although a cluster of two pre-juncture consonants results, as in 'port(e)-manteaux' [coat rack], but [ə] is preserved in the absence of such a non-schwa penultimate syllable, as in 'portefeuille' [wallet].

These data point the way to an insightful interpretation of *e caduc* (cf. Kohler 2002, 2007). The phenomenon should be dissociated from its historical origin and treated as an integral part of organising prosodic phrases in French. In this view, *e caduc* is no longer regarded as a segmental phoneme /ə/, which is either preserved or elided, but as a syllable juncture, linking consonants to the next syllable onset in a prosodic phrase. The articulatory exponent of this juncture is consonant clustering or vocal-tract [ə] opening, depending on speech style and prosodic variables of the phrase. Both manifestations contribute to an even prominence flow of syllables up to the final one in a prosodic phrase, which receives increased prominence to mark the right edge of the prosodic time-window. If there were no opening of [rt] into [ə] in 'portefeuille', or of [rb] into [ə] in 'arbre vert', the heavy consonant clustering [rtf] or [rbv] would increase the prominence of the penultimate syllable and would thus disturb the prominence profile in the right-bound prosody phrase.

This data assessment is further underscored by transcriptions in Passy and Rambeau (1918):

(a)   Les choses en restent là pour l'instant.
        [leʃoːz | ɑ̃ rɛstə **la** | pur lɛ̃stɑ̃. ‖] (p. 16, *ə* in italics = optional)

(b)   Le bonhomme, qui n'avait pas grande littérature, ne comprends pas et reste
        là, tout confus.
        [lə bɔnɔm:, | ki n avɛ **pa** | grɑ̃d literatyːr, | nə kɔ̃ˈprɑ̃ **pa** | e rɛstə **la**, ‖ **tu**
        kɔ̃ˈ**fy**.‖] (p.18)[1]

Bold type indicates prominent syllables, | and ‖ utterance internal and final
prosodic phrase boundaries, respectively. The strongest boundaries are at the
end of each sentence and after the fifth prosodic phrase in (b). Next in strength
are the boundaries after the first, third and fourth prosodic phrases in (b) (also
marked by final consonant lengthening), which may be further graded first,
third > fourth; the second boundary is the weakest. In the case of *reste là*
preceding such a strong boundary, [ə] is obligatory before the immediately
following final syllable. In the first sentence, however, the boundary between
'en restent là' and 'pour l'instant' is weaker, due to the greater semantic unity,
and [ə] may be absent or present depending on how strong the speaker wants to
mark the boundary. Thus, the analysis of e *caduc* has progressed from segmental exponents in narrow syllabic frames to articulatory sequencing in extended
phrasal time windows bounded by pitch and prominence profiles.

---

[1] The two French quotations may be freely translated into English as:

(a)   [Things are left at that for the time being.]
(b)   [The good man, who was not very literary, does not understand and is left all confused.]

Neither translates the crucial phrase 'reste(nt) là' literally, and therefore does not connect with
the subsequent discussion of the phonetic realisations. So, the translations do not give the reader
any additional help in understanding it. This is the reason why the translations are not provided
in the main text, with the simple assumption that the linguistic reader – even without any knowledge of French – will be guided by the phonetic transcription and will thus be able to relate the
phonetic explanation to the utterances.

3 *The REPRESENTATION Function*

This chapter picks up Bühler's notion of the two-dimensional symbolic, syn-semantic field of linguistic signs in linguistic contexts, for the function of REPRESENTATION. It is structured by morphology and syntax on the one hand and by prosodic phrasing on the other. Although it may be completely dissociated from the deictic field, and from a receiver in a communicative situation, for example in logical propositions, it does make use of deictic signs for anaphoric reference in the symbolic field. These signs are related to the ones used in the deictic field, but they are integrated into the morphology and syntax of the symbolic field. In everyday speech communication, however, linguistic signs and structures are always linked to a SENDER and a RECEIVER anchored in the communicative context to varying degrees, according to the situation dependence of speech actions. For explanatory insight into speech interaction, the analysis of syntagmatic structuring of messages needs to be put in relation to communicative functions in contexts of situation.

The reference of the REPRESENTATION function is the world of Objects and Factual Relations constructed with symbolic signs by a sender through AAA and GOV channels. The principal category of this function is the STATEMENT, by which the sender sets out aspects of the world in their own right, as seen by the sender, separate from an APPEAL to the receiver. Another type of REPRESENTATION function results from combining a STATEMENT with an APPEAL to receivers to assess their own potential actions, in their own interest, in relation to facts set out in the STATEMENT. This is the RECOMMENDATION function, which either points to harmful or beneficial effects that the facts may have on the receiver in subsequent action. The former, negative, RECOMMENDATION is a WARNING. For example, a pictorial road sign, meaning 'Beware of falling rock!', or a road sign with the written word 'Floods', warns motorists of natural dangers for their driving. The message 'Smoking kills' on cigarette packets gives a health warning, latterly intensified with a picture of rotten teeth. On a path along a river, a notice may inform walkers 'After prolonged spells of rain this path becomes impassable.' In face-to-face interaction, or in an e-mail message, a sender may say to a receiver, 'You shouldn't take the path along the river, it will be very muddy and slippy, and may even be flooded after all the rain we have had.' A WARNING leaves it to the receiver to heed it, but makes a strong case for consequences when it is ignored. This appeal to a free-will decision distinguishes a WARNING from a COMMAND, for example the message 'Stop!' of a red traffic light, or the notice 'No trespassing!' at the entrance to a field, or the written message 'Smoking is not allowed in this office' displayed on a board at the entrance.

The positive RECOMMENDATION may be a PROPOSAL in personal interaction, such as proposing a toast at a birthday party, or suggesting action to be taken, or it may be an advert in public ADVERTISING, for example on television, to get receivers to buy the products praised in STATEMENTS. It may be required by law to add a negative WARNING to the ADVERTISING of certain products, especially in the medical field. For example, German television is full of adverts for pharmaceutical products that are available without a doctor's prescription, and they are all followed by the full-screen written message 'Zu Risiken und Nebenwirkungen lesen Sie die Packungsbeilage und fragen Sie Ihren Arzt oder Apotheker' [As regards risks and side effects, you are advised to read the leaflet in the packet and ask your doctor or chemist]. This message is not only presented via the GOV but also via the AAA channel to ensure that receivers take notice of it. But in order to keep the harmful effects low in prominence, the receiver is referred to other sources of information, and the text is read at very high speed.

Another REPRESENTATION function results from an APPEAL overlay on a STATEMENT when the sender refers to past or future action that clashed or may clash with the receiver's expectation, and asks the listener to understand and forgive. This is the function of APOLOGY, which includes varying degrees of EXPRESSION of contrition, such as 'I'm terribly sorry I didn't make it to the scheduled meeting this morning. I had to go and urgently see a dentist with excruciating toothache', or 'I'm afraid we won't be able to come to your party tonight, we have to babysit our grandson. Pity, but I am sure you'll understand.'

The chapter focuses on the STATEMENT function, primarily via the AAA channel. It deals with syntagmatic organisation by syntactic structure and prosodic phrasing in German and English. The two formal devices are basically independent of each other. Prosodic phrasing may converge with, or diverge from, syntactic structure for efficient chunking of meaning transmission to a listener. A STATEMENT may be a non-sentential syntactic element ('ellipsis'), e.g. in response to a question, or a single sentence in declarative syntax, or a sentential structure of main and subsidiary clauses, or a sequence of sentences. Section 3.1 deals with syntactic structures, accentuation and prosodic phrasing.

The discussion then moves to Information Selection and Weighting and their formal manifestations along a scale from segmental *reduction* to segmental *elaboration* in 3.2, and develops a distinction between Information Structure and Argumentation in 3.3. The former refers to the factual world; the latter is the result of the speaker's view of objects and relations under the categories of Finality, Openness, Contrast and Unexpectedness. Section 3.4 supplements the grammatical account of symbolic field structures by a description of patterns of principally independent rhythmic organisation as an important Guide function in meaning transmission to a listener.

3.1   Syntagmatic Organisation of Statements

3.1.1   Declarative Syntactic Structures

Syntactic structure is not an interlevel between function and prosody, but is related to function in parallel with the prosodic level. In 1.3, functional relations between semantic constituents were distinguished from syntactic structures between formal elements:

<Action/Occurrence> <Agent> <Goal> <Recipient> <Time> <Place> <Manner>
<verb> <subject> <indirect object> <adverbial or prepositional phrases>

A German or English Statement like

Martin trifft seinen alten Kumpel heute Nachmittag in der Stadt.
Martin is meeting his old pal in town this afternoon.

contains the following semantic constituents:

<Action>   <Agent>   <Goal>   <Time>   <Place>

In German, the default syntactic order is:

<Agent>	<Action>	<Goal>	<Time>	<Place>
<subject>	*<verb>*	*<direct object>*	*<adv phrase>*	*<prep phrase>*
<Martin>	<trifft>	<seinen alten Kumpel>	<heute Nachmittag>	<in der Stadt>.

In English, it is:

<Agent>	<Action>	<Goal>	<Place>	<Time>
<subject>	*<verb>*	*<direct object>*	*<prep phrase>*	*<adv phrase>*
<Martin>	<is meeting>	<his old pal>	<in town>	<this afternoon>.

In both languages, the inflected verb or the auxiliary of a verbal phrase fills the second structural slot. In German, the *uninflected verb* of a verbal phrase, e.g. 'will treffen', 'hat getroffen' is put at the end of the sentence: 'Martin will seinen alten Kumpel heute Nachmittag in der Stadt treffen.'

Whereas in English, the STATEMENT syntax is rigid, in German, <ACTION> can be put on its <TIME> and <PLACE> coordinates by moving the <TIME> adjunct, or both adjuncts in either order, into the position immediately after the inflected verb:

> Martin <ACTION trifft>   <TIME heute Nachmittag> <GOAL seinen alten Kumpel> < PLACE in der Stadt >.
> Martin <ACTION trifft>   <TIME heute Nachmittag> < PLACE in der Stadt > <GOAL seinen alten Kumpel>.
> Martin <ACTION trifft>   <PLACE in der Stadt> < TIME heute Nachmittag> <GOAL seinen alten Kumpel>.

In the default structure, <ACTION> is propositionally bracketed with <GOAL>; in the structural derivatives, it is bracketed with the coordinates of <TIME> or <PLACE>. The propositional division after or before <GOAL> may be prosodically marked by either *upstep* on the constituent following the division, or by a weak phrase boundary **&PG1** (see 2.12), with a *low-rising valley* pattern (*continuation rise*) preceding it. This gives the constituent after the division, <TIME> in default or <GOAL> in the other structures, more prominence and more information weight. If <AGENT> and <GOAL> are filled by pronouns (e.g. 'er' [he], 'ihn' [him] in the above examples), they must be proclitic or enclitic to the verb, because pronouns are by default unaccented function words.

> <AGENT Er> <ACTION trifft>   <GOAL ihn>   <TIME heute Nachmittag> <PLACE in der Stadt>.

The fourth possibility of ordering <PLACE> closely before <GOAL> and <TIME>

> *Martin trifft <PLACE in der Stadt> seinen alten Kumpel < TIME heute Nachmittag>.

sounds disorganised when <TIME> is accented, as it violates default structure. However, when <TIME> is unaccented, with a low-falling peak contour preceding, it is marked as a given coordinate for the <ACTION> in the communicative situation and therefore makes a well-formed sentence. This is also true when <MANNER> 'zum Kaffee' [for coffee] is appended, with a *hat pattern* spanning the final three accents of <GOAL> <TIME> <MANNER>.

The only flexibility of structural ordering in English STATEMENTS occurs when a <TIME> or <PLACE> coordinate for an <ACTION> is picked up from a preceding interchange as the theme for a new proposition

> <TIME This afternoon>, Martin is meeting his old pal in town.

and with anaphoric pointing

> <Martin is taking the 2.30 bus into town.
> <Place There>, he will be meeting his old pal for coffee.

The initial position of <Time> or <Place> stays outside the Statement structure. It is also marked prosodically by a peak-valley pattern and a strong phrase boundary **&PG>1** (see 2.12), setting the theme to which the sentence then provides the rheme.

Either <Time> or <Place> can also be put initially in a German Statement:

> <Time Heute Nachmittag> trifft Martin seinen alten Kumpel zum Kaffee in der Stadt.
> Martin fährt mit dem Bus um 14 Uhr 30 in die Stadt. <Place Dort> trifft er seinen alten Kumpel zum Kaffee.

It requires prosodic intensification, for example by a *late peak* **&2**(Nachmittag. Again, this fronting creates a theme-rheme structure, but, different from English, the theme <Time> or <Place> is integrated in the syntactic structure of the Statement, with the effect that the obligatory verb-second position necessitates the post-verb placement of *subject*, and that the theme cannot be set apart by a strong phrase boundary.

The exposition of Statement in German and English has so far focused on propositions that relate <Agent> and <Goal> to <Action>, with <Time> and <Place> coordinates as secondary attributes, manifested by various orderings of *subject, object, verbal, adverbial* and *prepositional phrases* in syntactic structures. Let us now take a look at propositions of <Event Occurrence>, such as 'X ereignet sich' [X occurs], 'X findet statt' [X takes place], 'X tritt auf' [X happens], 'es gibt X' [there is/are X], for which <Time> and <Place> coordinates are primary. In general, <Event Occurrence> is separated into <Event *subject*> and <Occurrence *verb*> in both languages, and the syntactic pattern parallels the one found for <Action>. In German, the basic Statement structure is, e.g.:

< Event *subject*>	<Occurrence *verb infl*>	<Time>
<Der jährliche Bauernmarkt>	<findet>	<am Wochenende>
<Place>	<Occurrence *verbal adjunct*>	
< auf Gut Emkendorf>	<statt>.	

In English:

> < EVENT *subject*>   <OCCURRENCE *verbal phrase*>
> <The annual farmers' market>   <will take place>
> <PLACE>>   <TIME >
> <on the Emkendorf Estate>   <this weekend>.

The definite article and the adjectival attribute of the <EVENT> specify a particular type of 'market' that recurs. It is the theme for a proposition that provides <TIME> and <PLACE> for the upcoming occasion. On the other hand, if <EVENT> is left indefinite, 'ein Bauernmarkt' [a farmers' market], the <EVENT> theme structure is not used, but is replaced by a structure that specifies <TIME> and <PLACE> and associates an <EVENT> with them. In German we get:

> <OCCURRENCE *verb infl impers*>   <TIME>   <PLACE>
> <Es findet>   <am Wochenende>   <auf Gut Emkendorf>
> <EVENT *subject*>   <OCCURRENCE *verbal adjunct*>
> <ein Bauernmarkt>   <statt>.

In English:

> < OCCURRENCE *verbal phrase*> <EVENT *subject*>   <PLACE>
> <There will be>   <a farmers' market>   <on the Emkendorf Estate>
> <TIME>
> <this weekend>.

Whereas English introduces <OCCURRENCE *verbal phrase*> and <EVENT *subject*> and then adds <PLACE> and <TIME> to it, in this fixed order, German locates <OCCURRENCE *verb*> in <TIME> and <PLACE> and relates <EVENT *subject*> to them. Since <*verb*> must be in second structural position in a STATEMENT, the dummy subject placeholder 'es' is put initially in an impersonal verb construction. The order of <TIME> and <PLACE> is again free, and may be sentence-initial, making the dummy placeholder superfluous:

> <PLACE Auf Gut Emkendorf> <OCCURRENCE *infl* findet> < TIME am Wochenende>
> <EVENT *subject* ein Bauernmarkt> <OCCURRENCE *uninfl* statt>.
>
> <TIME Am Wochenende> <OCCURRENCE *infl* findet> <PLACE auf Gut Emkendorf>
> <EVENT *subject* ein Bauernmarkt> <OCCURRENCE *uninfl* statt>.

There is a class of compound verbs in German that follow the sentence structure of *verb + prepositional phrase* in their morphology. 'heimfahren' follows 'nach Hause fahren' [drive home]:

er fährt nach Hause   er fährt heim
er wird nach Hause fahren   er wird heimfahren
er ist nach Hause gefahren   er ist heimgefahren

When the verbal part of the compound verb is inflected, it is in the second structural position in the *declarative syntax* of a STATEMENT; when it is uninflected – infinitive or past participle – it is put sentence-final. The adjunct part is in the same syntactic slot as a prepositional or adverbial phrase. Other verbs in this class that can no longer be considered to model the semantic constituents <ACTION/OCCURRENCE> + <PLACE> by *verb + prepositional phrase* in their *verb + adjunct* morphology still behave in the same way, e.g. 'es findet statt' – 'es wird stattfinden' – 'es hat stattgefunden'. Here phrase-structure syntax has been completely morphologised. The verbal adjunct in these compound verbs receives the *lexical stress*, and a sentence accent docks at this stress position when the compound verb is to be made semantically prominent.

3.1.2 Accent Patterns

In both German and English STATEMENTS, the syntactic form of each semantic constituent has the potential for receiving an *accent*, depending on how the speaker wants to weight their mutual semantic relevance in the communicative situation. If all the semantic constituents of STATEMENT are given equal weight, they all receive accent **&2**. Grading may be introduced by *upstep* and *downstep*. *Upstep* produces phrasing through increased prominence of the upstepped accented element, complemented by subsequent *downstep* in *peak* patterns; it may occur at any point (see 2.4). If a propositional constituent is coded by a syntactic phrase, the head receives the accent **&2** or **&1**. Depending on the weighting given to the qualifiers, they may also be accented as **&2** or **&1**, or may be downgraded to **&1** or **&0**. When an <ACTION/OCCURRENCE> is specified for several semantic attributes, especially <PLACE> and <TIME>, its verbal form may be backgrounded to **&1** or even to **&0**. Typical phrasings are (with unaccented function words unmarked):

<&2Martin> <&1trifft> <seinen &1alten &2Kumpel> <&1heute &l2Nachmittag>
<in der &2Stadt>.
<&2Martin> <will>   <seinen &1alten &2Kumpel> <&1heute &l2Nachmittag>
<in der &2Stadt> <&1treffen>.
<&2Martin> <is &1meeting> <his &1old &2pal> <in &2town> <this &l2aftern'oon>.
<&2Martin> <will &1meet> <his &1old &2pal> <in &2town> <this &l2aftern'oon>.

<Der &1jährliche &2Bauernnmarkt><&0findet><am &2Wochenende>
‿auf &1Gut &2Emkendorf> <&1statt>.
<Der &1jährliche &2Bauernnmarkt><wird>   <am &2Wochenende>
‿auf &1Gut &2Emkendorf> <&1stattfinden>.
<The &1annual &0farmers' &2market> <will &0take &1place>
<on the &2Emkendorf &2Estate> <this &1week&2end>.

In the above examples, **&1** subordinates <ACTION/OCCURRENCE> to its semantic attributes of <PLACE>, <TIME>, <GOAL> and <EVENT>; **&0** makes it
semantically irrelevant for the STATEMENT. Complete deaccentuation **&0** of
German sentence-final verbal adjuncts or uninflected verb forms concomitantly increases the weighting of the preceding constituent, highlighting one token of <PLACE> etc. against others. **&2** sets <ACTION/OCCURRENCE> against
non-<ACTION/OCCURRENCE>. For **&0** the associated pitch trails a preceding
peak or *valley* pattern; for **&1** the preceding *peak fall* or *valley rise* is broken
to add a minor pattern; for **&2** a separate peak or valley is created (see 2.1).
Default accentuation **&2** may also be combined with upstep.

Any part of the syntactic structure, representing a semantic constituent of the
proposition, may be put in focus by deaccenting all other structural elements; in
addition, the focus may be reinforced to accent **&3**. In communicative interaction, a speaker decides on how many of these backgrounded constituents may
be formally omitted because they can be inferred by the listener, for example:

> A: Has our farmers' market been advertised yet?
> B: Yes, as usual, on the Emkendorf Estate next weekend.

3.1.3   Prosodic Phrasing
The discussion of prosodic phrasing in 2.12 showed that finely graded prosodic
properties are essential for a highly skilled syntagmatic semantic organisation
of STATEMENTS. On the other hand, prosodic structuring may bridge syntactic
boundaries between sentences:

> Er **&1**^sagt, er hat **&2**^kein **&0**. **&2**^Geld mehr **&2**. **&PG4**
> He **&1**^says he has **&2**^no **&0**. **&2**^money left **&2**. **&PG4**

Inside weakly graded sentences, syntactic structures are also bridged prosodically by the use of *hat patterns* and *peak downstep*. These prosodic devices
may bind the syntactic units representing the semantic constituents <ACTION>
<AGENT> <GOAL> on the one hand and <TIME> <PLACE> on the other. The
division between these two complexes is only weakly marked by a *peak dip*
&1. between the two *hat patterns*.

> **&2**^Martin **&0**trifft seinen **&0**alten **&0**. **&2**^Kumpel **&0**heute **&1**.
> **&2**^Nachmittag in der **&0**. **&2**)Stadt **&2**. **&PG4**

> **&2**^Martin's **&0**meeting his **&0**old **&0**. **&2**^pal in **&1**. **&2**^town this **&0**.
> **&1**-after**&2**)noon **&2**. **&PG4**

But more finely structured delivery introduces *prosodic boundaries* between
syntactic units. Thus, the two syntactic groups for the <ACTION> complex

and for the <Time> and <Place> coordinates may be separated by a phrase boundary **&PG1** and by a continuation rise leading up to it.

> **&2**^Martin **&0**trifft seinen **&0**alten **&2**. **&2**]Kumpel **&**, **&PG1** **&0**heute
> **&2**^Nachmittag in der **&0**. **&2**)Stadt **&2**. **&PG4**
> **&2**^Martin's **&0**meeting his **&0**old **&2**. **&2**[pal **&**, **&PG1** in **&2**^town this
> **&0**. **&1**-after**&2**)noon **&2**. **&PG4**

The more deliberate or even insistent a speaker becomes, the more syntactic units will be marked by phrase boundaries. Other possibilities of marking sentence-internal syntactic structures prosodically are *upstep* (see examples in 3.1.2) or a combination of upstep with phrasing boundaries.

Different prosodic grouping of syntactic units may change the meaning of a Statement, as in the following example.

In March 1983, two parliamentary elections took place in Schleswig-Holstein. There was first the general election to the federal parliament, and a week later the election to the Schleswig-Holstein parliament. At the federal election, the Green Party had gained a substantial number of votes at the expense of the Social Democrats. In order to avoid this happening again and ruining their chances of winning the election, the leader of the Social Democrats published a large advert in a local Kiel newspaper on the day before the election. It contained the following passage:

> Ich bitte alle Wähler, die am letzten Sonntag grün gewählt haben, ihre Stimme morgen nicht zu verschenken und SPD zu wählen.
> [I ask all the voters who voted for the Green Party last Sunday not to waste their votes tomorrow, by voting SPD.]

The advert addressed two requests to those who had voted for the Green Party:

> Don't waste your votes. Vote SPD.

When spoken, the meaning of these two requests would be transmitted by two prosodic phrases:

> ihre **&2**^Stimme morgen nicht zu **&1**. **&2**^verschenken **&2**. **&PG2** und
> **&2**^SP'D zu wählen **&2**. **&PG4**
> not to **&2**^waste their **&2**^votes tomorrow **&2**. **&PG2** by **&2**^voting
> **&2**^SP'D **&2**. **&PG4**

With one prosodic phrase for a single request, we get:

> ihre **&2**^Stimme morgen nicht zu **&1**. **&2**^verschenken und **&1**. **&2**(SP'D
> zu wählen **&2**. **&PG4**
> not to **&2**^waste their **&2**^votes tomorrow **&1**. by **&2**^voting **&1**. **&2**^SP'D
> **&2**., **&PG4**

This prosodic phrasing of the same sequence of syntactic elements transmits exactly the opposite meaning: 'Don't vote SPD – that would be a waste of votes.' Here 'und SPD zu wählen' or 'by voting SPD' qualifies 'waste', whereas in the two-request version there are two independent phrases with separate actions: 'not wasting votes' and 'voting SPD'. This difference can be indicated in English writing by the presence or absence of a comma before 'by'. German punctuation rules do not allow this differentiation. Of course, the context of situation made it quite clear which meaning was intended by the advert, and it is very unlikely that anybody else apart from a phonetic nitpicker noticed the potential ambiguity in the written text. But on many occasions when I presented this example orally in talks to large German audiences it was immediately understood and received with laughter. This confirms listeners' awareness of syntagmatic prosodic organisation imposed on syntactic structure in the coding of communicative meaning.

A continuation rise inside single-sentence or multi-sentence STATEMENTS signals to the listener that the speaker has not finished talking. If this signal is combined with the APPEAL to the listener to stay connected, the stimulating high-rising valley is used in some types of English (High-Rising Terminal (HRT), see 2.10). In the types of German and English this monograph is based on, pitch tends to end low or falling in fact- and speaker-oriented terminal STATEMENTS. Concern for the listener intervenes as the speaker qualifies the validity of a STATEMENT by phrases of the type *I think*, *I suppose*, *may be*, *question tags*, by final low-rising pitch and by voice quality (breathy voice). It has been reported for some Irish, Scottish and Northern English accents (Urban North British, UNB) that pitch in terminal STATEMENTS is also rising (cf. Ladd 1978, pp. 123ff and 143ff). This topic will not be discussed here because in order to assess it faithfully it would be necessary to describe the whole function-form systems that are used in each of these varieties, and this is largely unknown territory.

3.1.4   *Look-ahead Prosodic Phrasing: The Classified Football Results on BBC Radio*

Since there are dependencies between prosodic sections in syntagmatic parsing, it must be possible, in certain constellations, for a listener to detect early on how a pattern will develop. Such phrase-internal cues to the continuation of the next phrase can be illustrated by the classified football results on BBC radio. The ritual of listening to them at teatime on a Saturday was, in the days of coming into big money through the pools, an exciting game to guess, after the first club and score had been read, whether the match was a draw, or a home or an away win. In the 1950s–60s they were read by John Webster, who set the pattern; in 1974 James Alexander Gordon (JAG) took over and continued it with modifications until 2013. Their patterns of prosodic phrasing were so transparent that the whole nation was able to decide correctly, e.g. in 'Manchester United 2, (Arsenal 2/Arsenal 3/Arsenal 1)'. In the case of a draw, there is only one high-rising accent on the first name, and the pitch of the score levels out. In the other two cases, there are two accents, on the name and the score; they may both be rising, or falling(-rising), but for an away win, they are less extensive, or the whole pattern is in a lower register than for a home win (see Figure 3.1). As JAG worded it in a BBC video 'James Alexander Gordon to retire as football results reader' (www.bbc.com/sport/0/football/23434092): 'If Arsenal have lost, I am sorry for them, if Manchester United have won, I am happy for them.' In his weekly readings on radio, he put these expressions in his voice as low or high pitch, and in the video he accompanied the voice inflection by a sombre or a smiling face as well as head lowering or raising. Cruttenden (1974) ran a perception experiment, but did not use original speech samples: he produced contour sequences himself, which he cut off after the second name. So his test results with children do not reflect what listeners to the classified football results up and down the country were able to do with great accuracy every week. Charlotte Green, who took over from JAG, has changed the pattern: with her it is now necessary to hear the second name. In Figure 3.1 there are F0 traces of JAG reading the three result types.

What listeners relied on in their highly successful guessing cannot have been different types of pitch accents and boundary tones, because they are not uniquely associated with any one of the three result types. The F0 traces in Figure 3.1 show clearly differentiated global patterns, which must be the basis for their perceptual distinctiveness in the recognition process. For a home win, the speaker produces a pitch pattern in the high region of his voice range, for an away win in the low region, and for a draw in the central region, with a levelling for the stressed syllable of the team name and the following score, which produces just one accent on the former.

3.2 Information Selection and Weighting

In verbal interaction, communicators select information points to which they give weight in relation to one another in the communicative situation. The languages of the world use a great variety of formal means to achieve this, e.g. structural devices, such as deviation from default declarative word order,

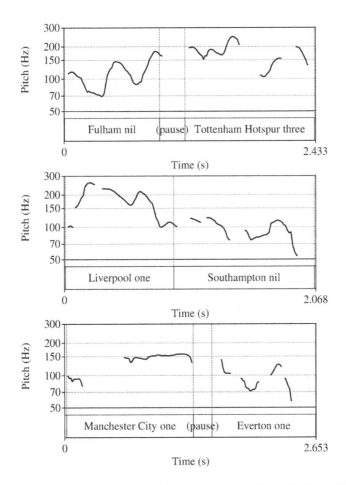

Figure 3.1. F0 traces (log scale) and annotations of classified football results read by James Alexander Gordon (JAG): away win (top), home win (centre), draw (bottom).

cleft sentence constructions and lexical intensifiers, but also graded sentence accentuation based on pitch and energy patterns and segmental duration (of vowel nuclei and/or initial consonants). Accentuation creates prominence profiles across utterances and makes specific syllables more salient for information highlighting of words and syntactic units. Traditionally the study of INFORMATION SELECTION AND WEIGHTING has centred on referential meaning in STATEMENTS, but the same function-form link applies to QUESTIONS,

COMMANDS/REQUESTS and EXCLAMATIONS in the APPEAL and EXPRESSION functions. For this semantic scaling, the categories of *focus* and *presupposition* or *new* and *given* have been proposed in a framework of INFORMATION STRUCTURE. Focus came to be studied in just one formal feature, namely F0 patterns of pitch accents. It was initiated in the analysis of English (Liberman and Pierrehumbert 1984), but has also been applied to German (Baumann 2006; Féry and Kügler 2008) and to a number of other languages. In the West Germanic languages, focus can be freely marked by sentence accentuation, whereas in French, for example, syntactic means intervene. The accentual manifestations of INFORMATION SELECTION AND WEIGHTING have been set out within the framework of the Kiel Intonation Model (KIM) for German, and in comparison with English, in 2.2, 2.3, 2.4 and 3.1.1, 3.1.2. In addition to graded accentuation of words and syntactic units, there is grading of the timing and the extension of articulatory opening-closing gestures inside these linguistic elements, along a scale from *reduced* to *elaborated*. Both formal scales converge in coding variation of INFORMATION SELECTION AND WEIGHTING along a functional scale from backgrounding to foregrounding, for which I propose the term REFERENTIAL LOW-TO-HIGH KEY. It is supplemented by the EXPRESSIVE LOW-TO-HIGH KEY scale in the EXPRESSION function, discussed in Chapter 5.

The relationship between the formal *reduced-to-elaborated* scale and the functional LOW-TO-HIGH KEY scale was already clearly formulated by Passy in his published PhD thesis *Étude sur les changements phonétiques et leurs caractères généraux* (1890):

> des tendances phonétiques que nous avons constatées, se dégagent bien nettement deux principes fondamentaux:
> 1° Le langage tend constamment à se débarasser de ce qui est superflu.
> 2° Le langage tend constamment à mettre en relief ce qui est nécessaire.
> ... tous les changements ... ont pour résultat une économie dans l'activité des organes
> ... On parle pour être compris ... Tout ce qui est nécessaire pour être compris et bien compris, on le conserve soigneusement, on l'accentue, on l'exagère; le reste, on le néglige, on le laisse aller, on l'omet. (Passy 1890, pp. 227–9)

This is the position on which Lindblom (1990) built his hyper-hypo (H&H) theory, and which I developed into a theory of phrase-level articulatory dynamics (Kohler 1979, 1990b, 2001a), combined with a programme of empirical investigation in German (Kohler 2001b,c). This phrase-level phonetics results from the interaction of five factors:

- the speaker's tendency to reduce effort
- the listener's demands on distinctivity
- variable distinctivity requirements in different communicative situations
- linguistic units
- social conventions.

So the theory of phrase-level phonetics is part of a theory of speech communication. The effect of the five conditioning factors on phrase-level phonetic output cannot be deterministic, but leads to statistically variable reduction patterns, some of which have very high, others quite low frequencies. In the LOW section of the LOW-TO-HIGH KEY functional scale, the space-time dynamics of opening-closing gestures are reduced in relation to a neutral setting when the gestures are unstressed syllables or unaccented words. Different linguistic units set different reduction ranges. Function words, such as pronouns, definite and indefinite articles, auxiliary verbs, prepositions, conjunctions, modal particles, all of which are unaccented by default, have a broader reduction range than content words. For instance, for preposition + definite article in the German phrase '(ich fahr) mit dem Auto (zur Arbeit)' [(I go to work) by car] there is the following graded scale of increasingly weakened bundles of articulatory-acoustic properties, represented in segmental phonetic transcription as:

[mɪɟəm ʔˈaʊtʰoˑ], [mɪpm ʔˈaʊtʰoˑ], [mɪʔm ʔˈaʊtʰoˑ], [mɪbm ʔˈaʊtʰoˑ], [mɪm ʔˈaʊtʰoˑ]

In this example, the extreme reduction [mɪm ʔˈaʊtʰoˑ] means 'by car' and has a generic reference, in the same class as 'mit dem Bus' [by bus], 'mit dem Fahrrad' [by bike], 'mit dem Zug' [by train]. If this utterance is continued with 'und zwar *mit dem* BMW meiner Frau' [actually in my wife's BMW], the specific reference makes the full reduction of 'mit dem' less likely – the deictic indicator in the form of the initial stop of the definite article (compare the whole deictic family 'dieser, der, da, dort, dann') must be present. Thus, any of the other forms that have some reflex of this stop, even if assimilated in place of articulation to [m] or glottalised, are preferred in this specific context. This suggests that in LOW-KEY, the generic phrase is activated in its completely reduced phonetic form from the mental lexicon, rather than being generated from a canonical phonological representation. But at the same time, [mɪm] is not fully lexicalised, because it is still part of the whole reduced scale of 'mit dem'. This differs from 'zum' versus 'zu dem', 'zur' versus 'zu der', 'ins' versus 'in das', 'im' versus 'in dem', 'ans' versus 'an das' 'am' versus 'an dem', for example in:

(1)   (a)   damit komme ich *zum Schluss* meines Vortrags [this brings me to the end of my talk]

        (b)   ich bin *zu dem Schluss* gekommen, dass ... [I have come to the conclusion that ...]

(2)   (a)   er geht noch *zur Schule* [he still goes to school]

        (b)   er geht *zu der Schule*, die sein Vater besucht hat [he goes to the school that his father went to]

(3)   (a)   er geht regelmäßig *ins Konzert* [he regularly goes to concerts]

        (b)   wir gehen heute Abend *in das Galakonzert der Berliner Philharmoniker* [we are going to the gala concert of the Berlin Philharmonic Orchestra tonight]

(4)   (a)   er ist *im Konzert* [he is at the concert]

        (b)   *in dem Konzert* heute abend wird Yehudi Menuhin spielen [Yehudi Menuhin will be playing in the concert tonight]

(5)   (a)   er fährt dieses Jahr zum Urlaub *ans Meer* [he is going to the seaside for his holiday this year]

        (b)   er fährt dieses Jahr zum Urlaub *an das französische Mittelmeer* [he is going to the French Mediterranean for a holiday this year]

(6)   (a)   wir treffen uns *am Bahnhof* [we are meeting at the station]

        (b)   wir treffen uns *an dem kleinen Brunnen neben der Kirche* [we are meeting at the small fountain beside the church]

In all (a) examples the contracted form refers to a generic action ('zum Schluss kommen', 'zur Schule gehen' = being at school age), or a generic place ('ins Konzert', 'ins Kino', 'ins Theater'; 'im Konzert', 'im Kino', 'im Theater'; 'ans Meer', 'ins Gebirge' [to the mountains]; 'am Meer', 'im Gebirge'), or a particular place that needs no further specification ('am Bahnhof', 'am Marktplatz' [in the market square]). In these cases the contracted forms are obligatory. When a specification is added in the (b) examples, the speaker may use the deictic form of the definite article to *point* to a more narrowly defined action or place for the listener to understand. If this pointing is absent because the speaker assumes that the listener does not need it, the contracted forms are also possible in (b). The contracted forms in (a) have been taken out of the preposition + definite article reduction scale and are lexicalised, which is also shown by the fact that they are treated as words in their own right in codified orthography.

Different types of function words may have different degrees of reduction, and it may be higher in post-accent than in pre-accent position and inside a phrase than phrase-final. In German, personal pronouns are reduced further than possessive pronouns. The personal pronoun 2nd pers pl 'ihr' may be reduced to [ɐ] in enclitic position to the verb ('*habt ihr* das gemacht?' [have you done it?]), but only to [ɪɐ] in proclitic position ('*ihr habt* es geschafft' [you have made it]), and the proclitic possessive pronoun 3rd pers sg fem 'ihr' only goes as far as [iɐ] ('sie hat *ihr Kleid* in die Reinigung gebracht' [she took her dress to the cleaners]). In English, prenominal prepositions get reduced, but in phrase-final position they do not, in spite of being unaccented: 'I am doing this *for* [ə] you', 'who are you doing that *for* [ɔː]?'

In content words, reduction of opening-closing movements is typically linked to syllables that do not receive an accent, and that in the lexical-stress languages German or English are unstressed. The syllable that is particularly affected in both languages is [ə] after consonants, which is extremely common in German because of its regular occurrence in verbal and nominal inflection, but which is also quite frequent in English words. German examples are (a) verb, infinitive or 1st, 3rd pers pl: 'retten' [save], 'reden' [talk], 'stoppen' [stop], 'loben' [praise], 'packen' [grab, pack], 'sagen' [say], 'stehlen' [steal]; (b) noun pl: 'Affen' [monkeys, apes], 'Löwen' [lions], 'Rassen' [races], 'Rosen' [roses], 'Flaschen' [bottles], 'die Beamten' [the civil servants]; (c) adjective, inflected: 'die grünen' [the green ones], 'die lahmen' [the lame ones], 'die langen' [the long ones], 'die bunten' [the coloured ones]. English examples are 'button', 'rotten', 'written', 'ridden', 'happen', 'ribbon', 'bacon', 'waggon', 'London', 'mountain', 'orphan', 'even', 'lesson', 'brazen', 'fashion', 'stolen', 'lemon', 'Shannon'.

The opening into the central vowel is quite generally eliminated in all preceding segmental contexts in German, and the spatial position at the initiation of this curtailed gesture commonly determines where it ends. This is the dynamic process interpretation of what in traditional static descriptive terminology is called progressive place assimilation, for example 'lo<u>ben</u>' [bm], 'pac<u>ken</u>' [kŋ], 'la<u>ngen</u>' [ŋŋ]. In English Received Pronunciation (RP), elimination of the opening and the spatial adjustment of the gesture are far more restricted, but are more widespread in other varieties of British English, including Standard Southern British, and particularly in American English. When there is nasality preceding stop + [ən], as in 'London', 'mountain', the opening gesture is usually maintained in British English, but strong cohesion in compounds, such as 'mou<u>ntain b</u>ike' may favour curtailing the gesture, and having its spatial position controlled by the initiation of the next gesture: [mpmb]. This is fully comparable to German 'mit bu<u>nten</u> Papierschlangen' [with coloured paper streamers] [mpmp]. Both examples show that spatial adjustment of articulatory movement is not juxtapositionally conditioned but is a controlled closing-opening trajectory across nasal-oral-nasal-oral alternation. For more descriptive data from German related to a dynamic reduction-elaboration model, see Kohler (2001a,b,c).

This phonetic variability is generally conceptualised as formal reduction from underlying canonical forms along a *reduced-to-elaborated* scale, and models of word perception relate the recognition of reduced signals to canonical forms in the mental lexicon. So, in the above example 'mit dem Auto', all the phonetic forms are linked to the one postulated underlying canonical phonological form /mɪt deːm aʊto/. Such canonical reference is certainly very useful for organising pronunciation dictionaries, and for systematising the reduction processes that occur in different speaking styles, dialects and languages, and historical stages of languages, but it cannot reflect the articulatory processes that are implemented in Low-Key speech communication. And as regards the perception of utterances containing reduced forms, it is worth reminding ourselves that the goal of communication is the transmission of meaning, and that speech recognition means understanding utterances and content words in them, not recognising phonemes and canonical forms. Thus, speech recognition is to be placed in the functional diversity of communicative situations, and the mental lexicon may be conceived of as reflecting such a functional structure, and as containing set phrases represented as exemplars besides words.

Since reduction has been related to reduction from a canonical form, and since canonical forms are associated with word citation forms derived from orthographic lexicon entries, elaboration in High Key has largely been ignored. The concept of 'reduction from canonical form' represents a *descriptive model* of Low-Key exponency. In such a model, phonetic variance of words and phrases, linked to invariant phonological form, is 'explained' in terms of articulatory adaptation in segmental and prosodic context, and of progressive reduction of effort, and is captured by reduction rules. This physical link shows up speech production patterns that occur over and over again in the speaking styles of the world's languages and in historical sound change, but they cannot be mapped onto speech production in communicative acts. It does not make sense to assume that a speaker goes through the succession of reduction rules from the canonical form to arrive at the specific phonetic variant in a particular speech situation. To gain insight into speech communication we need a *process model* from speech function to phonetic form in production and perception.

The degrees of freedom in gestural control may be set at different values by different (groups of) speakers, and there may even be different coexistent 'canonical' forms for the same lexical items within a speech community.

Thus, for a small number of German speakers (e.g. elocutionists) the canonical form of 'haben' [have] may still be [haːbən] (getting elaborated to [haːbɛn]), whereas for the majority it is [haːbm], with [haːbən] being an elaborated form; yet for some speakers it may even be [haːm], with both other forms being elaborated. These (groups of) speakers then start their contextual and situational adjustments from different canonical bases in the mental lexicon. What these different settings are we do not know, because we have pooled the variation across the whole speaker population. We would need to get sufficient data of phonetic variation in the same lexical items from individual speakers and then to compare their ranges of phonetic manifestation. This is certainly a task for the future. But irrespective of this, there is no denying the fact that we have to work with phrase-level adjustment rules beside phonetic lexical representations, no matter whether we deal with individual speakers or groups of speakers. The discussion of a reduction-to-elaboration scale will be picked up again in connection with EXPRESSIVE LOW-TO-HIGH KEY in Chapter 5.

3.3   ARGUMENTATION

Speakers select and weight information points for an utterance by syntax and sentence accentuation and develop them into an ARGUMENTATION by adding pitch patterns to the accents. It was shown in 2.8 that when an F0 peak maximum is shifted from a pre-accent position to an accented vowel, the change from a high-low to a low-high F0 movement into the vowel results in a sharp pitch discrimination maximum, which separates an *early* from a *medial peak* pattern. It has been described as a psychophonetic principle of pitch perception in human speech, and is assumed to be a language universal exploited in identifying communicative functions in individual languages. It has been demonstrated for German and for English that the pitch discrimination maximum coincides with an abrupt change in the identification of either a CONCLUDING or an OPENING ARGUMENTATION. This is a clear case of categorical pitch perception. The further shift of the F0 peak maximum through the accented vowel and into a following unaccented syllable does not change the general direction of the low-high F0 trajectory in the accented vowel and therefore does not trigger similarly sharp discrimination maxima. A minor maximum was found near the end of the accented vowel in the German experiments, obviously due to the long low F0 precursor before the rise. Irrespective of this lack of sharp discrimination inside the accented vowel, further communicative categories are identified: progressively later peak positions add increasing CONTRAST to OPENNESS, and the very late positions add EXPRESSIVE EVALUATION to

Contrast. There is category perception, but the category boundaries are not as clearly defined as they are for Concluding versus Opening Argumentation. These areas of the peak-shift scale have been labelled *medial-to-late* and *late peaks*.

The validity of the functional system of four peak categories for Argumentation in German was confirmed by a perception experiment (Kohler 2005) using the Semantic Differential Technique on data that were obtained in the peak-shift paradigm with the sentence 'Er war mal mager' [He used to be thin]. The stimuli were contextualised in a situation where two people are looking at old photos and come across one of an old friend. Based on the results of the earlier experiments (cf. 2.8), the following four-category function-form system was projected onto the stimulus set of 'Er war mal mager' (cf. also Kohler 2009b):

> Finality
> In a concluding argument, the speaker sums up his/her own apperception of a communicative outcome as being obvious, final and no longer debatable: *early peak*.
> 'That's it, he's no longer the thin guy he used to be.'
>
> Openness
> In an opening argument, the speaker indicates that s/he has observed, and become aware of, something for further (inter)action: *medial peak*.
> 'I see, he used to be thin.'
>
> Contrast
> In an opening argument, the speaker indicates with an overlay of contrast that observation contradicts expectation: *medial-to-late peak*.
> 'Ah, that's new for the books, he used to be thin.'
>
> Unexpectedness
> In an opening argument with an overlay of contrast, the speaker adds expressive evaluation to an unexpected observation: *late peak*.
> 'Oh well I never, he used to be thin.'

Descriptive and inferential statistics confirmed that there is semantic category formation corresponding to the ranges of *early* versus *medial* versus *medial-to-late* versus *late peak* positions by semantic feature bundles of the scales *concluding–continuing, accepted–contrastive, known–unexpected, matter-of-fact–surprised*, which represent the semantic content of the four argumentative functions.

These functions are set by the partners engaging in communication and are not identical with an external information structure of 'given' and 'new'. The photo provides the externally given fact 'he was once thin'. The speaker decides on the argumentative weight of this fact and puts it into the frame of 'this is what it is' or 'this is how I see it' by different synchronisations of F0 and energy trajectories associated with the accented vowel. Thus, INFORMATION STRUCTURE and ARGUMENTATION are differentiated conceptually. *Given/New* of information structure and FINALITY/OPENNESS of ARGUMENTATION may even go against each other, as the following examples show:

- After a long discussion at the beginning of term about finding a suitable alternative time and day for the weekly colloquium to accommodate all those who want to attend, the tutor says, 'We are going to move the colloquium to Thursday.' He says it with an *early peak* on the last word to indicate to the audience that this is final and the discussion is now closed, although this is *New* information.
- The session then continues to discuss other course matters, and, at the end, before departing, the tutor reminds the audience, 'Please remember. We have moved the colloquium to Thursday.' He says it with a *medial peak*, although the information is now *Given*.

To signal modes of ARGUMENTATION speakers also use valley patterns at selected and weighted information points in STATEMENTS, marking continuation and establishing contact with the listener. They may be either *low rising* or *high rising*, and they may have *early* or *late* synchronisation with the accented vowel (see 2.7). The perception experiment in 2.8.5 showed that *early* synchronisation is associated with CASUALNESS, *late* synchronisation with FRIENDLY CONCERN for the listener. Like the functional categories associated with post-medial peak synchronisations, these valley-related ARGUMENTATION categories do not have clearly defined boundaries on the shift scale. The semantic-differential experiment in Kohler (2005) included *low-rising* and *high-rising valleys* in *early* and *late* synchronisation. The high-rising stimuli received high ratings on the *question* differential; the low-rising ones did not. The combination of declarative syntax with a high-rising valley pattern codes a CONFIRMATION QUESTION (see 4.2.2.4). The details of the system of ARGUMENTATION with *valley* and *peak-valley* patterns are still to be worked out. This is the field of intonation where German and SSB English, and different varieties of English, diverge considerably. The use of F(all)+R(ise) or

F(all)R(ise) patterns to make an associative or a dissociative reference to alternatives (cf. 1.4.1) is very characteristic of SSBE, but how these two patterns enter into a system of ARGUMENTATION by the side of *early* and *late valleys* still has to be worked out.

Here is an example I came across recently when I tried to phone my daughter in London but got the BT automated answering service (another female voice):

&2[hell'o &, &PG we are not &2^av'ailable &2. &1[now &, &PG
F(all)+R(ise)
'we're out, try again later.'

After a pause, this message was followed by: 'Please leave your name and phone number after the beep, we *will* return your call.' In this customer-friendly service context, the F(all)R(ise) would sound abrupt:

&2[hell'o &, &PG we are not &2^av'ailable now &., &PG
'why are you phoning now, we're out'

And so would an *early* or a *late valley*:

&2[hell'o &, &PG we are not &2]/[av'ailable now &, &PG

The former is too casual in this context. The latter is customer-friendly but, due to unaccented 'now', does not lead up to the added alternative of phoning back later. The German translation with the same listener-oriented ARGUMENTATION would be:

&2[hall'o &, &PG wir sind zur &2^Zeit nicht &2. &2[da &, &PG

followed quickly by 'Bitte hinterlassen Sie Name und Telefonnummer nach dem Ton, wir rufen dann zurück.' Accented 'zur Zeit' prepares for pointing to the alternative. The F(all)R(ise) pattern

&2[hall'o &, &PG wir sind zur &2^Zeit nicht &1. &2da &., &PG

would signal an explanatory apology without offering to phone back: 'Sorry, you can't reach us, we are out.' Finally, the *early valley* in

&2[hall'o &, &PG wir sind zur &2^Zeit nicht &2. &2]da &, &PG

would be too casual, as in English.

3.4   Syntagmatic Rhythmic Organisation of Utterances: The GUIDE Function of Prosody

In parallel with the semantic organisation through the formal devices of morphosyntax, lexicon, accentuation and intonation, utterances are also given a rhythmic structure, i.e. a regularity of recurring waxing and waning prominence patterns across syllable chains, produced by a speaker for a listener to assist the transmission of meaning. Its physical variables are patterns of syllabic timing, of spectral variation, of fundamental frequency and of energy. The semantic strand interferes with perfect rhythmic regularity, on the one hand through accentual intensification at the phrase level, and on the other hand through articulatory complexity at the lexical level. Especially the last two variables in the above list define temporal chunks that are long enough to allow for a good deal of variability, caused by more local accentual and segmental constraints, without disrupting a percept of regularity for a listener. In spontaneous speech interaction, hesitations, break-offs and interruptions also disturb rhythmical patterning, and there are good and bad rhythmical speakers. It is the competent orator who optimally combines the rhythmic with the semantic strand in speech performance. The rhythmic principle is further stylised in verse, which is built on a regular number of beats per line in the Germanic languages, but on a regular number of syllables in the Romance languages.

Irrespective of being disturbed in language use, the rhythmic principle comes to the fore in idioms and popular phrases, such as combinations of a monosyllable and a disyllable, linked by 'and', that are felt to be more rhythmical than the reverse order because of the greater regularity of rhythmic feet, e.g. English 'with bow and arrow' and the German semantic reversal but rhythmical equivalent 'mit Pfeil und Bogen'. Titles of novels and films point in the same direction, e.g. Jane Austen's *Pride and Prejudice* and *Sense and Sensibility*, where the rhythmic beats are additionally heightened by alliteration. The German translations *Stolz und Vorurteil* and *Gefühl und Verstand* lose the alliteration but keep the rhythm, the latter with a different semantic ordering. The film version is marketed with the semantically wrong but rhythmically much closer title *Sinn und Sinnlichkeit*. In other cases, the ordering of binominals is clearly governed by meaning, for example 'father and son', 'mother and child', 'husband and wife', where the first element may be seen as being closer to a prototypical orientation in society – adult, male. In 'sons and daughters', both principles coincide.

But spectral patterning as a result of vocal-tract dynamics is also a contributing factor to rhythmicity: 'tit for tat', 'tick-tock', 'sing-song', 'ding-dong', 'ping-pong', 'zigzag', 'flip-flop' and 'wishy-washy' in English, and 'ticktack'; 'Singsang', 'dingdong', 'Pingpong', 'Zickzack', 'Hickhack', 'klippklapp', 'Mischmasch', 'Wirrwarr', 'Krimskrams', 'wischiwaschi', 'Tingeltangel' and 'lirumlarum' in German, with a close-open sequence of vocal-tract shaping. They are more rhythmical than their reverse orders. The explanation may be sought in the energy dispersion in the high-frequency spectrum for highish front vowels as against its concentration in the lower-frequency spectrum for low and back vowels, coupled with higher versus lower intrinsic fundamental frequency. The sequencing of high-low spectral pitch may be perceived as being more appropriately linked to the progression from the beginning to the end of a word or short phrase, just as, at the intonation level, high-low marks conclusion in phrasal utterances. Furthermore, since citation-form utterances of these words and short phrases in English or German get accentual patterns that favour high-low progression of fundamental frequency, there is coincidence of high-low spectral pitch and tonal pitch in one vowel sequencing but not in the other. There is also the concomitant intrinsic shorter-longer duration, all converging on a perception of moving from the beginning to the end of a linguistic unit. This preference of vowel sequencing has nothing to do with lexical stress, because some of the English examples have double, some single, stress; nor is it causally linked to sentence accent, but instead reflects rhythmic patterning for a listener that exploits the vocal-tract acoustics of speech production.

Languages differ in their rhythmic patterning. Pike (1945) divided the languages of the world into two classes. In *stress-timed* languages, prototypically English and German, beat syllables tend to recur at regular time intervals, whereas in *syllable-timed* languages, prototypically French and Spanish, it is syllables in general. Extensive experimental research into this rhythmic difference has concentrated on foot and syllable durations. It has already been pointed out that perceived foot regularity in English or German depends on spectral variation, fundamental frequency and energy as well. Spectral change is particularly relevant in the reduction of unstressed syllables and unaccented function words, to squeeze them into a regular foot pattern. But the three additional factors besides syllable timing also apply to French, where in non-expressive accentuation the sequence of predominantly open syllables forms an ascending pitch scale to the penultimate syllable of a phrase, followed, in a statement, by an abrupt pitch drop, with equal accentual weight of all syllables up to the somewhat more prominent ultimate syllable. All these factors contribute to the perception of French as the *syllable-timed* language *par excellence*.

To advance the analysis of rhythm in language and speech it needs to be extended to more variables than just the duration of feet or syllables. What is essential for the production of rhythm in speech of whatever type and in any language is the global temporal bracketing of the speech signal into chunks that have recurring phonetic characteristics over and above the syntactic and semantic organisation, to guide the listener and assist understanding. This approach to rhythm in speech and language introduces rhythmic structuring as

a GUIDE function in meaning transmission and defines rhythmicity in speech
and language as follows:

> Constrained by the phonetic structures of the languages of the world, speech
> rhythm is the production, for a listener, of a regular recurrence of waxing
> and waning prominence profiles across syllable chains over time, with the
> communicative function of making speech understanding in various speaking
> styles more efficient.

This new rhythmic paradigm was presented in Kohler (2008, 2009a), together
with an overview of seventy years of research into speech rhythm (see details
there).

4   *The* APPEAL *Function*

In an APPEAL, speakers use speech to solicit verbal or non-verbal actions from listeners. In the simplest case, acoustic pointing signals in a sympractical field control verbal interaction with receivers or induce them to act in response to this pointing. This *Istic* DEIXIS APPEAL is discussed in 4.1.

In another type of APPEAL, the speaker solicits a *communicative response*, commonly *verbal*, to a proposition with an unknown, which the speaker constructs with linguistic signs in a synsemantic field, and addresses to the listener to solve the unknown. The unknown is either the truth value or a semantic constituent of the proposition, such as AGENT, GOAL, PLACE, TIME, MANNER. The response may be gestural rather than verbal, such as nodding or shaking one's head for 'Yes' or 'No', or shrugging one's shoulders for 'I don't know', but the response is still a communicative action. The APPEAL may take place in a sympractical instead of a synsemantic field, when gesture and facial expression are essential accompaniments of verbal communication, as in the examples quoted in 1.2.1.3, or when they replace it altogether, as in the following constructed communicative interaction.

> Father and son are working in the garden. The father says to the boy, 'Go and get me a flower-pot from the far end.' The boy goes and finds two different sizes. As there is visual contact across a large distance, the boy does not shout but lifts one pot up with one hand and points to it with the index finger of the other hand. The father sees this and nods. The boy sends a sympractical visual APPEAL signal that conveys the meaning of the synsemantic verbal message 'Do you want this size?', and the father responds with a sympractical visual signal meaning 'Yes.'

These types of communicative interaction are instances of the QUESTION APPEAL. Its synsemantic manifestations are discussed in 4.2.

In a third type of APPEAL, speakers also perform speech actions with linguistic signs in a synsemantic field, directed to receivers, yet they solicit *actions of body and mind*, rather than a communicative response to an unknown in REFERENTIAL REPRESENTATION. There are two subtypes, depending on the speaker's attitude towards the listener. It may be considerate or dominant. The Appeal may again be accompanied by gesture, for example ordering a person to leave by shouting 'Out!' and pointing to the door at the same time. These Request or Command Appeals are discussed in 4.3.

The three types of Appeal are defined as different communicative functions. By the side of these functions, there are different syntactic forms – *declarative, interrogative, imperative, vocative* and *non-sentential* ('*elliptic*') structures. There is no strict correlation between any particular function and any one of the syntactic structures. In German and English, each of the three Appeal functions can be coded in different syntactic structures, and, together with specific intonation patterns, they yield subcategories in each function. The links of communicative functions with syntactic and prosodic forms are outlined under the headings of each Appeal function. In Kohler (2013b), declarative and interrogative structures were differentiated from declarative and interrogative functions. The conceptual distinction is maintained, but now Interrogativity is placed in a network of Appeal functions, and the function-form distinction is given a more stringent terminology: Deixis Appeal, Question – Command – Request Appeals, Statement (Asserting Representation) versus *vocative, non-sentential* ('*elliptic*'), *interrogative, imperative, declarative* and *exclamatory structures*, in conjunction with distinctive prosody patterns.

4.1   The Deixis Appeal

4.1.1   Types of Formal Patterns

While there are special linguistic signs for *hic* and *illic* deixis in German and English, as in other languages ('hier', 'dieser' – 'dort', 'der'; 'here', 'this' – 'there', 'that'), *istic* deixis relies on attention-getting signals, like 'he', 'hallo' / 'hey', 'hello', or naming vocatives, to point to the receiver and prepare them for the sender's message. For example, the speaker addresses the listener with a personal name to rouse attention to an upcoming Statement, Question, Request/Command:

> **&2^**Angela **&2. &PG1** das können wir so nicht **&2^**machen **&2. &PG4**
> **&2^**Angela **&2. &PG1** we can't **&2^**do it like this **&2. &PG4**

> **&2^**Robert **&2. &PG1** wie sollen wir das denn **&2^**machen **&2. &PG4**
> **&2^**Robert **&2. &PG1** how shall we **&2^**do it then **&2. &PG4**

> **&2^**Sarah **&2. &PG1 &2^**gib mir bitte mal das **&0. &2^**Salz rüber **&2. &PG4**
> **&2^**Sarah **&2. &PG1 &2^**pass me the **&0. &2^**salt **&2. &1]**please **&, &PG4**

In German, the 2nd person personal pronouns, informal 'du' or formal 'Sie', may also be used to address the receiver in this way, either by themselves or preceding a personal name to reinforce the deixis.

> &2^du/Sie **&2. &PG1** das können wir so nicht **&2**^machen **&2. &PG4**
> **&1** du **&2.&2**^Peter/**&PG1** Sie **&2.&2**^Herr Schmidt **&2. &PG1** das können wir so nicht **&2**^machen **&2. &PG4**
> **&2**^Peter/Mr Smith **&2. &PG1** we can't **&2**^do it like this **&2. &PG4**

Since the personal name is the deictic trigger, it has to be accented. Being tightly linked to the following message the prosodic phrase boundary after it is weak (see 2.12) but will be more strongly marked in reinforced deixis. The vocative can also be appended to the speaker's message but can then no longer be accented, because it does not direct the listener to an upcoming message. It becomes a deictic suffix in a STATEMENT, a QUESTION or a REQUEST/COMMAND:

> **&2X &0**Angela/Robert **&2. &PG4**

German pronouns, either on their own or together with vocative naming, cannot be post-positioned because their forms would have to be elaborated, which runs counter to suffixation.

Instead of by a naming vocative, the DEIXIS APPEAL may be signalled by such phrases as 'hör/hören Sie mal (zu)', 'listen', to point to the listener's ear for attention, or 'sag/sagen Sie mal', 'tell me', to point to the listener's mouth for verbal response. They are signals controlling interaction, linked to a following STATEMENT or QUESTION. They are not self-sufficient REQUEST APPEALS, in spite of their *imperative* form. For example:

> **&2**^Hör/Hören Sie mal **&2. &PG1** das **&2**^geht so nicht **&2. &PG4**
> **&2**^Listen **&2. &PG1** this won't **&2**^do **&2. &PG4**
>
> **&2**^Sag/Sagen Sie mal **&2. &PG1** ist das dein/Ihr **&2**^Ernst **&2. &PG4**
> **&2**^tell me **&2. &PG1** are you being **&2**^serious **&2. &PG4**

The accentual and phrasing features are the same as for naming vocatives. In German, 'hör/hören Sie mal' may be reinforced to **&2**^Hör/Hören Sie mal **&2**^zu **&2. &PG1**, and both 'hör/hören Sie mal' and 'sag/sagen Sie mal' may be prefixed by an accented naming vocative, and/or by informal 'du' or formal 'Sie', either unaccented as part of the deixis, or accented as a separate, reinforced address; this introduces an offensive note, which in the case of the formal address violates a social code and sounds rude. The ear- and the mouth-directed deictic signals may also be appended to the STATEMENT or QUESTION as unaccented suffixes:

> **&2X &0**hör mal/sag mal **&2. &PG4**

This is not possible with reinforced 'hör/hören Sie mal zu'. In English, the equivalent deictic signal cannot be integrated as an unaccented deictic suffix in the message. Its occurrence in German seems to be linked to the use of the modal particle 'mal', which gives the verbs 'hör' and 'sag' the meaning of the general faculty of 'hearing' or 'speaking', and thus removes the function of a specific REQUEST or COMMAND from the *imperative* form. The English translation lacks a corresponding modal particle.

If the general German verbs for 'hearing' and 'speaking' are replaced by more specific ones, such as 'pass mal auf' [pay attention] and 'erzähl mal' [let's have the story], the function of REQUEST or COMMAND stays, and the phrase does not become a DEIXIS APPEAL. This means that the phrase can precede or follow in accented form, and suffixation is excluded. For example:

> &2^erzähl mal &2. &PG4 was ist denn &2^gestern &0. &2^pass'iert &2.
> &PG4
> &2^tell me &2. &PG4 what &2^happened &0. &2^yesterday &2. &PG4
>
> was ist denn &2^gestern &0. &2^pass'ier̲t &2. &PG4 &2^erzähl mal &2.
> &PG4
> what &2^happened &0. &2^yesterday &2. &PG4 &2^tell me &2. &PG4

A QUESTION with an unknown object can be integrated into a REQUEST, resulting in what is traditionally termed an *indirect question*:

> &2^erzähl mal was &0. &2-gestern &0. &2^pass'iert ist &2. &PG4
> &2^tell me what &0. &2-happened &0. &2^yesterday &2. &PG4

Besides these lexical *istic* pointers, communicators use stepping, instead of continuous, pitch patterns as acoustic interaction control signals (see 1.2.1.2 and 2.14). In such exchanges, social and personal attitudes between acting partners, emotional expressiveness of speakers, and propositions about the world and the communicative setting play a minor role. This results in stepping patterns becoming less forceful than their continuous counterparts. Thus, compared with '↓good ↑mor↓ning, Anna', the same sentence with a high-low *medial peak* contour on 'morning' is more categorical and superior sounding, and may even be taken as a reproach when the person comes to the breakfast table rather late, whereas the down-stepping pattern would not, least so with a small step-down interval of a minor third. Similarly, 'your tickets, please' with a high-low *medial peak* contour on 'tickets' has a commanding tone, compared with the down-stepping pattern '↓your ↑tick↓ets, please'.

The discussion in the following sections develops a functional network of distinct types of interaction control by stepping as the most elementary

APPEAL function. The primary division is between *controlling connection with a receiver* and *inducing action in a receiver*.

4.1.2 *Controlling Connection with a Receiver*

A sender signals the wish or the readiness to connect with a receiver. This may be done in three different ways: (1) calling someone to connect, or giving one's position in response; (2) initiating, sustaining and closing an interaction; (3) re-establishing connection. Whenever a sender considers it necessary to control sender-receiver channel connection for these communicative acts, stepping pitch patterns are used.

(1)   Calling

This 'calling contour', usually across a spatial distance between speaker and listener, is a stepping pattern going down from high pitch by a variety of intervals – the larger the interval, the more dominant the summoning appeal. Duration and energy are further variables that distinguish different types, depending, for example, on distance or indoors/outdoors. The pattern may be a mother's call to a child to stop playing or watching television, or anything else the child may be doing, because it is dinner-time or bedtime, or just time to come home, e.g. '↑John↓. ↑Lunch↓', with high-mid stylised *medial peaks*, turning the words into disyllables. If the child does not respond, the mother will repeat her call more loudly and eventually revert to continuous pitch with increased loudness, pitch excursion and non-modal phonation, adding strong expression and commanding appeal to the call. Down-stepping may also be used to call someone to disclose their whereabouts and thus to enter the speaker's action field, e.g. '↑Ro↓bert. ↓Where ↑are ↓you?' Likewise, in the example quoted in 1.2.1.1 (1), Speaker A may use a down-stepping pattern on both '↑An↓na' and '↓where ↑are ↓you?' to get the addressee to establish contact. Disyllabic '↑Here↓' in the answer, over and above signalling *hic* deixis, also signals *istic* deixis with a stepping pattern, to connect with the caller. The same applies to '↓It's ↑me↓' in 1.2.1.1(2).

A special case of this calling contour is its use to rouse the attention of someone who has fallen asleep, or is otherwise occupied, or just does not take part in a communicative interchange, e.g. '↑John↓, ↑wake ↓up' (with down-stepping on 'John' and on 'wake up'). This sounds more friendly than the use of a continuous falling contour. The latter is a COMMAND to act, the former is a receiver-directed control signal to enter communicative interaction.

A receptionist in a doctor's surgery calling the next patient in the waiting-room to come forward to see the doctor is another instance of *istic* deixis:

'↓Mister ↑Mil↓ler'/'↑Next one, ↓please.' In this case, up-stepping is also possible: '↓Mister ↑Miller'/ '↑Next one, please.' The difference between down-stepping and up-stepping in calls is one of Summoning versus Inviting, reflecting the distinction between Command and Request in synsemantic speech. With downward pitch movement, a speaker signals terminality in a speech action and authority towards the listener, the more so the larger the interval; upward pitch movement signals continuation and compliance. This applies to both continuous and stepping pitch patterns. Due to this function-form link, mothers calling their children will be more likely to use down-stepping, whereas receptionists will prefer up-stepping.

(2)   Initiating, Sustaining, Concluding Interactions

Stepping patterns in greetings, or in leave-taking, or in answering the telephone, or in routine selling–buying interactions have the function of controlling the communicative connection. At the check-out in supermarkets, the cashier may open, sustain and conclude a selling–buying interaction in this fashion, as in the following example observed in a German supermarket:: 'Hal↑lo. – ↑Vierzehn Euro ↓dreißig. – ↑Siebzig Cent zu↓rück, ↑und der ↓Bon. ↑Schönen ↓Tag noch' [with the English equivalent ↓Hel↑lo. – ↑Fourteen pounds thirty ↓pence. – ↑Seventy pence ↓change, ↑and the re↓ceipt. ↑Have a nice ↓day]. Answering the telephone will usually be up-stepping '↓Hel↑lo' to signal 'Who's calling? Identify yourself!', but it may also be '↑Hel↓lo', very short, and with a very small interval to convey, 'I'm busy, what do you want, whoever you are?' If, after an opening '↓Hel↑lo', there is no response, the sender tries to establish connection with down-stepping '↑Hul↓lo.'

The completion of an interaction may be signalled with 'Thank you', either high-level, up-stepping or down-stepping, for example to a clerk, bank teller or waiter. Ladd (1978, p. 524) points out that these stepping patterns would be totally inappropriate 'to someone who had just returned our lost wallet to us', because it lacks an expressive component, which is inherent in continuous contours. A special case are perfunctory answers to polarity-question calls, e.g. ('↓are you coming ↑with us?') '↑Yes (↓)/↑No (↓)' or '↓Per↑haps (↓), ↓don't ↑know (↓)yet.'

(3)   Re-connecting with a Receiver

Re-establishing connection may be illustrated by the following example:

> At a barbecue in the garden, the husband is having a bit of trouble getting the fire going. After some time, he calls out to his wife, who has gone into the house: '↓It's ↑bur↓ning' with a down-stepping pattern on 'burning'. In this

way, he signals to his wife that she can now bring the steaks, the burgers and the sausages for grilling.

If, on the other hand, the husband suddenly discovers that his garden shed is ablaze, he will not call to his wife in the same way but will use a continuous falling contour, with pressed phonation and intensified loudness and pitch excursion.

Another case of re-connecting with a receiver is the use of a stepping pattern as a reaction to being reminded, or reprimanded, for having contravened a social code. Wichmann (2004, p. 1540) provides the following example of a parent–child interaction in a British middle-class family:

A   Robert doesn't want any yet
Z: Yes (I do ? unclear). I'd like some of that and some strawberry ice cream.
D: What
A: Please (loudly on fall-rise tone)
Z: Please (quietly on level tone)

The parent admonishes the child for not observing the code of saying 'please' after a request. The child knows the code and re-connects with the parent by giving an extracommunicative citation of the code word on mid-level pitch.

An example of the same genre comes from a German conversation I once overheard in the departure lounge of Hamburg airport between a father and his approximately 5-year-old daughter, who was wrapped up in playing games on a small computer. (I am translating the conversation into English since the patterns can be exactly the same.) The father was going to buy something to drink for himself and asked the daughter whether she would like some water. The daughter said 'yes', and a few minutes later the father put the glass in front of her, saying 'Here's your water.' This was greeted with silence. The father asked, 'What does one say?' – '↑<u>Thank</u> you' on mid-level pitch was the answer.

Niebuhr (2013) quotes the example of a teenager having his hi-fi on full blast, so the neighbours complain about the noise, and his mother tells him to turn it down. The teenager complies with the code of neighbourly behaviour: '↓mach ich eben ↑<u>lei</u>ser', [OK. I'll turn it ↑<u>down</u> then]. Here the up-stepping pattern conveys irritation at being reminded, due to the strengthening of high pitch in a stylisation of an *early valley*. Complying with the code might also be signalled by '↓mach ich eben ↑<u>lei</u>↓ser' or '↑mach ich eben ↓<u>lei</u>ser', with the stylisations of a *medial* or an *early peak* respectively (see 2.7, 2.8). In these cases, the irritation is absent, and the early high-mid drop into the accented syllable signals Finality and thus adds a connotation of resignation.

In all these examples of a speaker re-connecting with a receiver in order to correct previous behaviour, e.g. the infringement of a social code, the speaker does not express concern for the recipient, but verbalises the required action as a citation removed from the symbolic field of communication. They all have the connotation of 'reluctantly giving in', especially the third example. This is not due to the formal feature of pitch stylisation *per se*. Social demands enforce behavioural codes on the speaker, who re-connects with the listener, using receiver-directed acoustic pointing. The use of the particle 'eben' (which may be rendered in English by prefixed 'OK' and suffixed 'then') in the third example expresses reluctance lexically. The meaning of the utterance keeps this connotation even when a continuous pattern replaces stepping. Niebuhr takes the surface meaning of the utterance, which is the result of lexical as well as prosodic coding, as the meaning of the stepping pattern, and calls it 'resistance is futile', barring prosodic research from semasiological understanding.

4.1.3   *Inducing Action in a Receiver*
In this set of *Istic* Deixis, receiver-directed pointing is meant to stimulate receivers into action. They may be (1) specific proximate or distant receivers or (2) anonymous receivers.

(1)   Specific Proximate or Distant Receivers
Ladd (1978, p. 123) quotes an example from Bolinger:

>   A.   Where's the phone book
>   B.   ↓on the ↑tab↓le (… right where it belongs)

Here the response to a question for place information contains an acoustic pointing signal telling the receiver to look for the thing in the place where it always is.

In the following example, Ladd (1978, p. 523) illustrates the use of stepping to induce action in a pointing field, and contrasts it with the use of a continuous pattern in a symbolic field to transmit information:

>   A.   [from a distance, pointing to the car from which B has just emerged]
>   Y' ↑left your lights ↓on.
>   B.   [who had been jangling keys getting ready to lock the car]
>   What?
>   A.   [louder, and with a rising intonation pattern up to the final accent, which is followed by an abrupt low fall on the last syllable]
>   You left your lights on.

'When an utterance is called with stylised intonation and the addressee does not understand, the speaker will repeat with normal intonation' (p. 523).

In this case, A's interactive trigger signal was not successful in inducing B to act appropriately. So, B asks for referential information, which A provides with a continuous pitch pattern. But, contrary to Ladd's interpretation of the use of stepping, I believe that his example does not demonstrate a stylisation of the *meaning* of a plain contour; rather, stepping patterns have a different function of their own, i.e. controlling interaction and getting dialogue partners to act in stereotypical ways. This contrasts with continuous patterns, which provide referential information, speaker attitudes and emotional expression.

Another example from Ladd (1978, p. 524) illustrates the lack, in an action-triggering stepping pattern, of attitudinal and expressive meaning, which would have to be transmitted by a continuous pattern:

> we can squeeze past people in a crowd, with either ↑Xcuse ↓me, or ↑'Xcuse ↘ me, [high on the first syllable, falling on the second] But when we bump into people in the supermarket causing them to drop a dozen eggs all over the floor, it will not do to say ↑'Xcuse ↓me.

In this situation, an attitude of being sorry and an apology are asked for, which the interactive trigger signal cannot give. If this pattern were used nevertheless, it would be a downright rude remark, signalling to the other person, 'Look where you are going – be more careful next time.'

Ticket collectors on trains commonly ask passengers with stepping patterns to show their tickets, signalling that this is a formal act, not the initiation of a conversation with the traveller. The use of continuous falling contours turns the ticket collector's matter-of-fact ticket-checking into a communicative act, i.e. into a Command, and therefore sounds less customer-friendly.

(2)   Anonymous Receivers

In public announcements, a stepping pattern draws anonymous receivers' attention to certain constellations in the environment and points to actions they should take. For example, at Schiphol Airport in Amsterdam, passengers are reminded with high-mid down-stepping '↑Mind your ↓step' from a female voice that they should pay attention on the travellators. This is stylisation of an *early peak* contour. Its function is to give general advice to all passengers, the passenger in the abstract, to adapt their walking to the demands of the circumstances in the action field: the meaning of Finality of an *early peak* (see 2.7, 2.8). If the downward step were to occur on the vowel of 'step', breaking it up into two syllables, the function changes to an admonition of the individual passenger who may not be walking cautiously: the meaning of Openness of a *medial peak* (see examples in 4.1.4).

By such a stylised pattern the speaker gives a friendly warning, which is neither a Command nor a Request, and which it is in the passenger's interest to follow. A high-falling *medial peak* pattern on 'step' would signal a Command 'watch where you are going', a *low-rising early valley* a Request 'please comply with my wish'. The latter would be out of place in this situational context. Since the Schiphol announcement does not address a particular passenger in a speaker–listener communicative interaction, the speaker detaches the information from speaker-oriented expressiveness and from listener-oriented attitudes, apart from getting listeners' attention. Rather than being an act in communicative interchange, the prime purpose of the message is to point to aspects in an action field considered relevant for the receiver, and to control the addressee's actions in it.

A different example is provided by announcements in London Underground stations that have curved platforms. When a train stops, a gap forms between the carriage and the platform. Passengers' attention is drawn to this hazard so that they may act to avoid it. 'Mind the gap' is announced when the doors open. At some stations, the announcement is made in synsemantic form with continuous pitch movement: 'Please, mind the gap between the train and the platform.' It becomes a Request to pay attention to a hazardous constellation of objects, which is described with linguistic form. At other stations, the announcement is in sympractical form, with rising and falling pitch on 'mind' and 'gap' respectively, pointing to an object in a deictic field the anonymous passenger is expected to be part of. Understanding the announcement presupposes that the passenger knows what 'gap' points to. It is a Warning, appealing to the passenger to be careful. This is more than simply drawing their attention to their action in a deictic action field, as is the case at Schiphol Airport. The announcement could, of course, be reduced to simple pointing, and would then also be realised as a stepping pattern. But none of the male and female voices that have recorded the announcement use it. London Transport opted for addressing the potential passenger with a personal appeal in addition to pointing.

A third example refers to market criers offering their goods with stepping patterns to attract anonymous listeners' attention and induce them to buy: '↓fresh ↑ve̲getables', '↓tasty ↑sa̲usages'. The typical pattern is up-stepping to raise the pitch level for a heightened stimulating effect. Down-stepping weakens the stimulatory force of the speaker's appeal to the listener. It turns an interaction inducement into an interaction offer by supplementing the appeal with information about the content of the interaction, i.e. it becomes more speaker- and fact-oriented. This gets the more prominent the larger the down-step. The high-mid stepping in a market crier's call '↓tasty ↑sau↓sages', in-stead of '↓tasty ↑<u>sausages</u>', is not confined to controlling an interaction by attracting attention and stimulating the receiver into buying, but also puts more weight on the produce offered.

4.1.4   *Naming and Pointing in Sympractical Fields*

Stepping is also used when synsemantic naming is added to sympractical pointing, for instance in reminder calls:

> ↑Don't forget your ↓<u>lunch</u>. [with a step down to 'lunch']
>
> or   ↓Don't forget your ↑<u>lunch</u>↓. [with a high-mid step on 'lunch'] (Ladd 1978, p. 520)

The former points to the packed lunch that has been prepared as usual, whereas the latter points to the packed lunch that is waiting to be taken, e.g. sitting visibly on the kitchen table. This is again the difference between *early peak* FINALITY and *medial-peak* OPENNESS (see 3.3), now with stepping pat-terns pointing to the generally given or the specifically selected in the action field, respectively. If the continuous contours

> Don't forget your **&2)/^**lunch **&2. &PG**

are used instead, the utterances lose their pointing and become synsemantic references to a packed lunch, with an appeal to the receiver not to forget it. The *early peak* may be contextualised as 'and before you go, pick up your packed lunch', the *medial peak* as 'you've packed everything else'.

The example

> ↑Daddy forgot his <u>brief</u>↓case. (Ladd 1978, p. 521)

with high-mid stylised *medial peak* down-stepping on 'briefcase' also belongs to this category. The speaker observes an item in the pointing field which the person it belongs to forgot to take with him, and verbalises this observation in a structured sentence addressed to some listener in the action field. However, the main goal of the utterance is not the transmission of information but drawing attention to an action field, and to trigger the same observation in the listener by a stimulating signal. If down-stepping occurs early

> ↑Daddy forgot his ↓briefcase.

the stimulating signal is absent: the speaker simply points to the established fact in the field, possibly also suggesting that Daddy is generally forgetful. If, on the other hand, the speaker wants to pass on important information to a nearby listener, also expressing concern and appealing to the listener to see that Daddy gets his briefcase, pitch is continuous in a raised *medial peak*:

    &HP Daddy forgot his **&3**^briefcase **&2. &PG**

Ladd illustrates the use of such a continuous contour with the example (in PROLAB notation)

    &HP Daddy fell **&3**^down<u>stairs</u> **&2. &PG** (Ladd 1978, p. 521).

It shows a raised *medial peak* on 'stairs' (together with other acoustic properties for intensification) in a naming field, transmitting factual information, expressive concern and an appeal to the addressee(s) to come and help. If 'downstairs' were to have low-high-mid stepping

    ↓Daddy fell down↑<u>stairs</u>↓. [a stylised *medial peak*]

the speaker would point to a quite common event: 'Not the first time it has happened, we were only talking about the problem the other day, and we now have to do some serious thinking.' If there is stepping from high 'down' to mid 'stairs'

    ↓Daddy fell ↑down↓stairs. [a stylised *early peak*]

the soliciting signal to the addressee(s) is absent, and the utterance only refers to the common occurrence in the pointing field.

Ladd (1978, p. 526f) links the early down-stepping pattern to a stylisation of the continuous low rise. He contrasts the meanings of the two patterns as follows: 'in statements [the low rise] often conveys belligerence or defensiveness, or some special involvement of the speaker … In many cases the stylized connotation emerges as tiredness, resignation, or "I-been-there-before"'. He quotes 'I'm coming' with both patterns in a Bolinger-type annotation, marking 'I'm' high level in both cases, and 'coming' either as a low rise or as low down-stepping. As to their meanings, the former 'in answer to a parent's call could come out as belligerent or insolent', the latter 'puts up only broken (= stylized?) resistance to parental authority, and conveys resignation to the inexorable approach of bedtime or dinnertime'. Apart from having some feature of low pitch in common, the two patterns are formally very different: one rises, the other falls. On the other hand, the down-stepping pattern has early, pre-accentual synchronisation of high pitch, and low pitch on the accented vowel, in common with continuous *early peak* patterns. This gives early down-stepping the function of FINALITY, which is different from the function of a *low rise*. Thus, neither the formal nor the functional aspect justifies a stylisation relationship between the two patterns. Dombrowski (2013) demonstrated conclusively in his semantic-differential experiment that the early downstep pattern is the stylisation of the continuous *early peak*. A continuous *early valley* establishes a rapport with a caller, a continuous *late valley* includes friendliness in the reaction to being called. To sound 'belligerent or insolent' other acoustic properties must be added, especially greater pitch range in the drop from a high prehead to the start of a rise that is accompanied by non-modal phonation.

Down-stepping may also be pointing to a hazard in the action field of which the individual receivers should be aware in order to adapt their behaviour in their own interests. Ladd (1978, p. 520f) gives two examples:

↑Look out for the broken ↑step↓.

with a stylised *medial peak* on 'step' is directed towards the individual listener, possibly as a reminder to the listener's previous experience of the hazard, also referring to the step having been broken for some time. This meaning is absent when the downward step occurs in a stylised *early peak* from high-level 'broken' to 'step'. As in the Schiphol announcement (see 4.1.3(2)), the speaker just points to the hazard. If the utterance is meant as a warning, with the speaker's expressive concern added, it would have continuous pitch movement and a *medial peak* on 'step':

&2^Look out for the **&0. &2**-broken **&0. &3**^step **&2. &PG**

The same applies to Ladd's second example in a mountaineering scenario.

&2^Look out for the **&0. &3**^crev'asse **&2. &PG**

However, if the two mountaineers have done their climb before, the one behind may shout to the one ahead with *early peak* down-stepping to 'v'asse'

↑Look out for the cre↓v'asse.

telling him that he must be close to the previously encountered hazard. Or the one ahead may shout to the one behind with *medial-peak* high-mid down-stepping on disyllabic 'v'asse':

↑Look out for the cre↑v'asse↓.

and the meaning 'this is where the hazard is'.

Naming and pointing in a sympractical field of calls may be illustrated by the following constructed communicative exchanges.

A couple have discussed a family outing with their children. Some time later, the father calls to Jeannette, who is out of sight, either somewhere else in the house or outside:

↓Jean↑n'ette, ↓we're ↑going now, ↓are you ↑coming?

There is high-level up-stepping on each of the three accented syllables, stylising *early valleys*. The high levels in the father's calls (*vocative – declarative – interrogative structures*) signal the father's openness to Jeannette's response. If he expects the answer to be 'I'm coming', in full agreement with the previous discussion, he will use high-mid stylised *medial peaks* in all three calls:

↓Jean↑nette↓, ↓we're ↑go↓ing now, ↓are you ↑com↓ing?

In both cases, Jeannette may answer

↑<u>Yes</u>, ↓I'm ↑<u>com</u>↓ing.

with high-level pitch on the first accent, a stylised *early valley* and high-mid down-stepping on the second accent, a stylised *medial peak*, signalling an open-action response: 'OK. I'll get on my way.' Synchronisation of high pitch with the accented vowel conveys argumentative OPENNESS in stepping as well as in continuous contours.

But Jeannette may also answer

↑I'm ↓<u>com</u>ing.

with high-level 'I'm' followed by mid-level 'coming', a stylised *early peak*, signalling a forced-action response and an undertone of resignation: 'OK, I'll get on my way then.' Here synchronisation of lowered pitch with the accented vowel conveys argumentative FINALITY, as in continuous contours.

A third possibility for Jeannette's answer is

↓I'm ↑<u>com</u>ing.

a stylised *early valley*, signalling readiness to comply with the action call. It may be called the 'compliance function in the sympractical field'.

In these cases, acoustic pointing to the receiver (Jeannette or the father) occurs with reference to the discussion among the family, and the communicative exchanges take place within this frame of *phaniasma deixis* (cf. 1.2.2). The father picks up information available to all family members from the previous discussion, and Jeannette answers accordingly. If the information exchange does not precede, the father's speech action with Jeannette may run like this:

↓Jean↑<u>nette</u>. **&2^**Mum and I are **&1. &2^**going down to the **&1. &2^**beach **&2. &PG** Are you **&2]**coming **&? &PG**

starting with high-level pitch, a stylised *early valley*, on the vocative to get Jeannette's attention from a distance, followed by a sequence of three *medial peak* contours with terminal falls on the next three accents, and finally a high-rising *early valley*, expecting an open response. Jeannette may respond

&2^Yes, I'm &1. &2^coming &2. &PG

with *medial peaks* and terminal falls at both accents. The absence of a mutual information base prevents a pointing field from being set up for an interaction in relation to this base. The exchanges between the father and Jeannette are still distance calls, and will be marked as such by increased loudness, but they are no longer *istic* deixis calls. They are now exchanges of new information, for which stepping patterns are no longer adequate: continuous contours take their place.

4.1.5   *Explaining the Use of Stepping Pitch Patterns for* DEIXIS APPEAL

The typical explanation of the use of stepping pitch in calling contours, the originally analysed data set, referred to a greater distance from the receiver requiring greater acoustic energy which can be better generated on sustained pitch (Abe 1962). Apart from the fact that calls are adjusted to the distance estimated, which may be quite small, the occurrence in, e.g. greetings, cannot be explained by a need to raise the energy of the transmitted signal. Rather, for a successful control of connection with a receiver, the sender wants to ensure a high degree of signal intelligibility by reducing its acoustic variability. Therefore the stability of key prosodic properties – syllable nucleus sonority, rhythmic structure and pitch – is heightened. Pike (1945, p. 71) mentions durational restructuring of syllable timing in speech chant, under which he subsumes calling. Syllable nuclei as pitch carriers are lengthened, and pitch is levelled to transmit two basic patterns, (higher-)lower or (lower-)higher, depending on whether the sender signals readiness or expectation to connect, or whether the sender stimulates connection. If the higher-lower readiness/expectation signal is transmitted on a final accented syllable, the nucleus is lengthened irrespective of the vowel quantity ('↑Jane↓', '↑Jen↓') and perceptually splits into two syllables to accommodate the two level pitches (cf. also Gussenhoven 1993).

The low-high step-up presupposes an unaccented syllable before the accented one, e.g. '↓Ni↑cole, ↓come ↑here', but in '↑Jane/Jenny, ↓come ↑here' the corresponding pattern is high. When in a step-up pattern the unaccented syllable precedes an accent initiated by a voiceless obstruent, as in 'Okay', the whole syllable may lose its periodicity and therefore its periodic pitch level, but low aperiodic pitch perception persists. The articulatory movement for the unaccented syllable may, in turn, be eliminated altogether, resulting, e.g., in '↑kay', with possible reinforcement (lengthening) of the initial obstruent.

When the word 'Danke' or the phrase 'Thank you' occurs with this step-up pattern it may become an unaccented-accented syllable sequence, although the first syllable is lexically stressed. It can then follow the same path as 'Okay', resulting in '↑ke', or '↑kyou'. This will not happen in the high-mid step-down on these phrases. It leads to increased distinctiveness between the two step patterns. The perceptual separation, by pitch as well as duration and syllabification, of the stepped level-pitch sequences in, e.g., '↑<u>Jane</u>↓' and '↑<u>Jane</u>' is also more clearly marked than the one between the continuous contours of, e.g., falling '\<u>Jane</u>' and rising '/<u>Jane</u>?' Stepping patterns are thus more adequate signals for interaction control. Furthermore, as pitch stylisation reduces APPEAL and EXPRESSION features, stepping becomes a specific signal for the pointing, as against the symbolic, function of speech communication.

The difference between appeal signals in the deictic and the symbolic field may be illustrated by the following interchange between a driver and a passenger as the car is approaching a red traffic light rather fast. At a fair distance away, the passenger may point to the light being red and draw the driver's attention to its meaning 'Stop!' by issuing the gentle appeal '↑Red↓', or '↑Red' with greater stimulatory force to act. But if the car is already dangerously close to the lights, suggesting that the driver might not have seen it, this pointing reminder is not strong enough: the passenger issues a high-key COMMAND APPEAL with an expression of fear by using an expanded continuous pitch fall, pressed phonation and intensified loudness to get the driver to stop in time. The linguistic sign 'red' is no longer simply a pointer to the traffic signal and the Highway Code, and to the need to act, but it has become a *symbol* of DANGER with a *signal* of WARNING and a *symptom* of FEAR.

4.1.6 Stepping Patterns in Ritual, Liturgy, Children's Chant and Nursery Rhymes

The use of level pitch in religious ritual, such as the Lord's prayer in the Christian church or the liturgy of Holy Mass, is another manifestation of descaling the linguistic sign of Bühler's *Organon Model* for routine interaction. Communication with Spirits and God(s) isolates the speaker from human communication; the speaker bows to the superior forces and tones down all features that mark interaction between speakers and listeners. In the Catholic church, the use of Latin texts removes a substantial part of referential meaning. Here again, the use of stepping is the obvious choice for this special type of communicative situation. But being a calling scenario, the worshipper only uses the down-stepping pattern, with different intervals, the largest to mark the end of the spiritual interaction, for example in '↑Amen↓.' Children's chant (see 2.14) and nursery rhymes are further examples of the use of stepping pitch patterns for specific interactive functions. They use a greater number and a greater variety of stepping levels than the more monotonous routines in prayers and liturgy. All these uses differ from stepping in *istic* deixis as they feature in entire spoken texts, whilst stepping in DEIXIS APPEAL is pointing interspersed in sympractical and synsemantic communication.

4.2   The QUESTION APPEAL

4.2.1 Overview
Whilst the function of the *ISTIC* DEIXIS APPEAL is to attract a listener's attention and to control interaction, the QUESTION APPEAL solicits a *communicative response* to an unknown in a proposition, which the speaker constructs with linguistic signs and addresses to the listener in a synsemantic speaker–listener action field. There are two types of unknowns (with illustrations from German and English):

(a)	*the truth value of the proposition,* for example

    Kannst du Spanisch?   Can you speak Spanish?
    <TRUTHX>: Du kannst Spanisch.   <TRUTHX>: You can speak Spanish.

(b)   *a semantic constituent*<SEMCON>*of the proposition –* <AGENT> <GOAL> <PLACE>
    < TIME> <MANNER>, for example
    Wer kann Spanisch?   Who can speak Spanish?
    <AGENTX>: kann Spanisch   <AGENTX>: can speak Spanish

The speaker constructs the proposition, with the unknown inserted, in two different ways:

(_1)   *making the proposition without reference to one already available in the interaction*

(_2)   *picking up a proposition made by a dialogue partner, or deducing it from the speaker–listener common ground in their action field,* for example

    A: Alex hat ein Haus gekauft.
          Alex has bought a house.
    B: **&HR &2^**Alex hat ein **&0. &2^**Haus gekauft**&2. &PG**
          &HR &2^Alex has bought a **&0. &2^**house **&2. &PG**

    A: Wir treffen uns morgen früh um sieben im Labor.
          We are meeting in the lab at seven tomorrow morning.
    B: Um **&2[**wieviel Uhr treffen wir uns im Labor **&? &PG**
          At **&2[**what time are we meeting in the lab **&? &PG**

    B: Wir treffen uns um **&2[**wieviel Uhr im Labor **&? &PG**
          We are meeting in the lab at **&2[**what time **&? &PG**

The constellations (a_1) and (b_1) are POLARITY QUESTION and INFORMATION QUESTION with propositional structures '<TRUTHX>: proposition' and '<SEMCONX>: in proposition', respectively; the constellations (a_2) and (b_2) are CONFIRMATION QUESTIONS about the validity of a proposition already available, or about semantic constituents of information already provided in it, with propositional structures '<CTRUTHX>: proposition' and '<CSEMCONX>: in proposition'. In Kohler (2013b) these questions were called Repeat Questions (see also Cruttenden 1986), with reference to questioning a proposition by repeating it. Since this term leads to misunderstanding, it has now been replaced by CONFIRMATION QUESTIONS. Another commonly used term is 'echo question' (Ladd 1996), which is not clearly separated from an interrogative-form echo of a preceding question (QUESTION QUOTE, see 4.2.2.7).

If the proposition that is picked up is itself contained in a QUESTION asked previously by the speaker or by the dialogue partner, we are dealing with a QUESTION QUOTE of the propositional content of the preceding POLARITY or INFORMATION QUESTION; for details in German and English, see 4.2.2.7. In the literature, POLARITY QUESTIONS are commonly referred to as 'yes'–'no' questions, which is a misnomer, because they may be responded to in a great variety of ways. The lexical items 'yes' and 'no' may even be excluded in alternative questions, such as 'Do you want the white bowl or the brown bowl?' But they are still POLARITY QUESTIONS, because they enquire as to whether X or Y is true, and, if one is true, the other is not.

The coding of POLARITY QUESTIONS in the languages of the world relies on a variety of formal means, including syntactic structure (initial verb position in the West Germanic languages), question particles, e.g. *ma* in Mandarin Chinese (Liu 2009; Liu and Xu 2005), *li* in literary Russian, *kya* in Hindi, or prosodic patterns on declarative syntax, e.g. in spoken Russian (Bryzgunova 1977, 1980, 1984; Khromovskikh 2003), or in Neapolitan Italian (d'Imperio 2000). But irrespective of the coding of the polarity function by syntactic or lexical means in a language, prosody always intervenes and codes subcategorisations. This prosody effect also applies to INFORMATION QUESTIONS. In CONFIRMATION QUESTIONS, prosodic patterns are of prime importance, in combination with a variety of formal structures, ranging from question-word to declarative syntax to non-sentential phrases.

INFORMATION QUESTIONS are coded uniformly across the languages of the world by lexical interrogative elements, e.g. English *who, what, where, when, at what time, why, for what reason, how, what for*, German *wer, wen, was, wo, wann, um wieviel Uhr, warum, aus welchem Grund, wie, wozu*. Languages differ as to the position of the lexical question marker in syntactic structure (Dryer 2013). In European languages, they have a sentence-initial position by default, for example in German and English

| Wer hat das gemacht? | Who did that? |
| Wann/Wo/Wie ist es passiert? | When/where/how did it happen? |

Other languages, such as Mandarin Chinese, Japanese or sub-Saharan African, do not have this default initial-position rule. For example, Chinese sentences have the basic semantic frame <AGENT> <ACTION> <GOAL>. <TIME> and <PLACE> can either precede or follow <AGENT>, together or separately, but cannot occur before or after <GOAL>. The sequencing of <TIME> and <PLACE> is such that <TIME> always comes first. This semantic frame applies both to STATEMENTS and INFORMATION QUESTIONS. In the QUESTION, the respective STATEMENT slot is filled by the <TIME>, <PLACE>, <AGENT> or <GOAL> interrogative word. The interrogative stays in the corresponding structural place of the STATEMENT, which may vary according to accentuation, communicative contextualisation and speaking style. Here are some examples showing the principle (I thank Wentao Gu, Nanjing, for providing them):

<Wang2Fang1>	<jin1tian1 xia4wu3>	<zai4 cheng2li3>	<yu4dao4 le0>
<WangFang>	<this afternoon>	<in the town>	<meet>
<ta1 de0 lao3peng2you3>			
<his old pal>			

<Wang2Fang1>	<jin1tian1 xia4wu3>	< PLACEX *zai4 nar3*>	<yu4dao4 le0>
<WangFang>	<this afternoon>	< PLACEX *where*>	<meet>
<ta1 de0 lao3peng2you3>			
<his old pal>			

<Wang2Fang1>	< TIMEX *shen2me0 shi2hou4*>	<zai4 cheng2li3>	<yu4dao4 le0>
<WangFang>	<TIMEX *when*>	<in the town>	<ymeet>
<ta1 de0 lao3peng2you3>			
<his old pal>			

<Wang2Fang1>	<jin1tian1 xia4wu3>	<zai4 cheng2li3>	<yu4dao4 le0:
<WangFang>	<this afternoon>	<in the town>	<meet<
< GOALX *shui2*>			
< GOALX *whom*>			

Deviation from default initial position is possible in German or English for specific communicative functions, especially turn sequencing in dialogue. The principle is the same as in Mandarin Chinese: a question-word phrase is inserted in the appropriate slot of declarative syntax. In German declaratives, the ordering of propositional constituents is

<AGENT> <ACTION> < GOAL> <TIME> <MANNER> <PLACE>,

whereas in English it is

<AGENT> <ACTION> <GOAL> <PLACE> <MANNER> <TIME>.

The following examples illustrate the interrogative insertion into declarative structure:

<Martin> <trifft> <seinen alten Kumpel><TIMEX *wann*><zum Kaffee><in der Stadt>
<Martin> <is meeting> <his old pal>   <in town>   <for coffee> <TIMEX *when*>

(For further details, see 4.2.2.3)

The QUESTION APPEAL in human communication across languages is conceptualised as a proposition with semantic unknowns sent to a receiver to be verbally resolved. STATEMENTS and QUESTIONS are thus postulated in parallel as either ASSERTING or ENQUIRING REPRESENTATION.

In a POLARITY QUESTION, the unknown truth value is formally realised by:

- a particle, initial or final in the sentence, or before the focused element
- sentence-initial position of the inflected verb
- a paraphrase, e.g. French 'est-ce que'
- pitch patterns that boost high frequency, e.g. in colloquial Russian, Neapolitan Italian, colloquial French (beside word order and paraphrase).

Initial particle or verb placement identifies an utterance immediately as a POLARITY QUESTION against a STATEMENT. A later position in the sentence, such as the final *ma* in Mandarin Chinese, is usually coupled with raising pitch level early on. Alongside sentence-initial verb position, there are also post-statement *question tags* in English ('He's in Rome, is he/isn't he?'), or post-statement particles in German ('Er ist in Rom, ja/nicht (wahr)?'), see 4.2.2.6. This reverses the semantic structure from a unitary '<TRUTHX>: proposition' to a theme-rheme sequence 'proposition: <TRUTHX>' and moves the utterance more in the direction of a STATEMENT.

In an INFORMATION QUESTION, the unknown semantic constituent is formally realised by an interrogative pronoun or adverb referring to the corresponding structural element of the declarative syntax, and is either put in sentence-initial position by default or is inserted in the appropriate slot of the declarative syntax.

In a CONFIRMATION QUESTION, an already available proposition is queried with regard to its truth value or with regard to a semantic component in the proposition by raising pitch in one form or another in all languages.

4.2.2   Question *Functions and Interrogative Forms in German and English*

4.2.2.1   *Interrogative Structures* and *Prosodies* in Polarity and Information Questions

Over and above *word order* and *lexical interrogatives*, there are also prosodic differentiators between Polarity and Information Questions in German and English. Textbooks on these languages have been proposing a tight correspondence between syntactic form and prosodic patterning for a long time: *word-order interrogatives* have final rising, *lexical interrogatives* final falling intonation (Armstrong and Ward 1931; von Essen 1964). Von Essen codified this postulated syntax–prosody link terminologically by coining the term *question intonation* to refer to a high-rising pitch pattern, which he associated with *word-order interrogatives*. The London School of Phonetics described deviations from these patterns as attitudinal overlays on basic form determined by sentence type (Halliday 1967, 1970; O'Connor and Arnold 1961). Even as recently as 2012, Xu and Liu (p. 16) maintain that the 'pitch target of a stressed syllable is [rise] in a yes/no question' – in the opening paper of a collection under the title 'Understanding prosody', which the editor (Niebuhr 2012) praises as 'incredible progress in our understanding of prosodic patterns' (p. vii).

Fries (1964) questioned this tight syntax–prosody link of *word-order interrogatives* and tested it with the analysis of an extensive American English corpus of thirty-nine television–radio programmes in which a panel of four persons, using, in turn, only yes-no questions, attempted to identify the precise vocation, occupation or special activity of each of several 'contestants'. He found, across all speakers, 61.7% of examples with falling and 38.3% with rising intonation. This result was contrary to the textbook statement. He comments on it as follows:

> The circumstances in which the programmes were carried on made the speech forms used by these panellists the actual live conversation of language actively fulfilling its communicative function. The speed and spontaneity of the language activity of these panellists reduced to practical zero the chance that the intonation forms of that language activity could have been premeditated or deliberately chosen. (Fries 1964, p. 247)

In the structuralist tradition, Fries only provides the empirical data, without attempting to explain them. He concludes:

> The facts seem to support the conclusion that in English (at least in American English) there is no question intonation pattern as such ... when one compares the intonation patterns of all yes-no questions with the intonation patterns of all other types of questions, he will find that, even with the ratio 3 to 2 in favour of falling intonation patterns for yes-no questions, which the

evidence here supports, there will be a higher proportion of rising intonation patterns on yes-no questions than on other questions. But there seem to be no intonation sequences on questions as a whole that are not also found on other types of utterances, and no intonation sequences on other types of utterances that are not found on questions. (Fries 1964, p. 250f)

Fries leaves unexplained

(a)   why his data show the opposite trend to what the textbooks say

(b)   why yes-no questions still have more rising contours.

As regards (a), the key lies in the communicative situation. Panellists word their questions in a way to get the highest possible number of 'yes' responses in order to win the game: they expect the answer 'yes' and indicate prosodically that they prejudge the contestant's decision. It is a typical case of fact and speaker orientation, which is associated with falling pitch. This does not, of course, mean listener orientation does not occur; it is quite common in Fries's corpus when questions are repeated immediately by the same panellist because they were not heard clearly or not understood. The repetition is listener-directed after the factual question has been asked, i.e. rising pitch is very likely. There are also cases where a first repetition has rising intonation, signalling listener orientation, and a second repetition has falling pitch turning factual.

As regards (b), the explanation points to a default link between question functions and formal exponents. Fries is right in rejecting a question intonation as such, determined solely by syntactic form. However, the probability of listener orientation, coded by rising pitch, is higher in *word-order* than in *lexical interrogatives* because commonly the speaker does not prejudge the listener's polarity decision, or, contrariwise, because the speaker generally enquires about facts, without concern for the listener. The actual pitch manifestation in dialogue depends on the interaction of the basic functions of POLARITY and INFORMATION QUESTIONS and their pragmatic placing in the communicative situation.

Kohler (2004) investigated the use of falling and rising pitch in both *word-order* and *lexical interrogatives* in the *Kiel Corpus of Spontaneous Speech, Appointment Scenario* (IPDS 1995–7). Table 4.1 gives the distribution of absolute and relative frequencies of falling (f), high-rising (hr), low-rising (lr) and other (o) pitch patterns in word-order and question-word interrogatives. It may be summarised in three statements:

- *Falling* and *rising* patterns occur with both *interrogatives.*
- *Word-order interrogatives* have predominantly *rising* patterns, *lexical interrogatives* predominantly *falling* ones.

Table 4.1. *Distribution of pitch patterns across word-order and lexical interrogatives in the Kiel Corpus of Spontaneous Speech*

	f	hr	lr	o	total
word-order	25 (21%)	47 (39%)	37 (30%)	12 (10%)	121 (100%)
lexical	98 (57%)	17 (10%)	42 (24%)	15 (9%)	172 (100%)

- There is a negligible proportion of high-rising contours in *lexical interrogatives*, whereas this pattern dominates in *word-order interrogatives*.

Among the corpus data there are examples of all four syntax–prosody combinations spoken by one and the same female speaker (ANS) in appointment-making dialogue session g09a. They are presented graphically in Figure 4.1. Below they are given in orthographic form with PROLAB prosodic annotation and interpreted semantically in their contextual settings. In a complementary step, they were resynthesised, changing the pitch pattern from falling to rising or vice versa in each case, using Praat. They will be interpreted in the same naturally produced context with regard to contextual compatibility and pragmatic and attitudinal change of meaning.

Aa word order + final rising intonation – g091a13l
&1[Würde Ihnen das &, &2[passen &? &PG
[Would that suit you?]

Two turns back; ANS asked about the possibility of arranging a two-day workshop meeting in December. Dialogue partner FRS replies that it may be arranged from the 14th onwards. ANS picks this up with the suggestion 'vierzehnter und fünfzehnter Dezember' [14 and 15 of December], followed by her question. In this dialogue context, ANS stimulates FRS to give an answer whether she really can fit these two dates into her calendar. The stimulation signal is a final &? *high rise.* By using a *low dip* into a *high rise* in a *late valley*, the speaker signals personal concern to find a suitable date, and thereby makes the stimulation more demanding. An *early valley*, without a low dip, on the other hand, signals detached matter-of-fact stimulation. When the dip into the accented vowel is increased, the personal concern becomes more prominent.

Resynthesised with a final *fall*, the utterance suggests that the speaker prejudges the answer 'yes'. This effect is strongest with an *early peak*, by which the speaker concludes that the two dates she has mentioned are settled, because

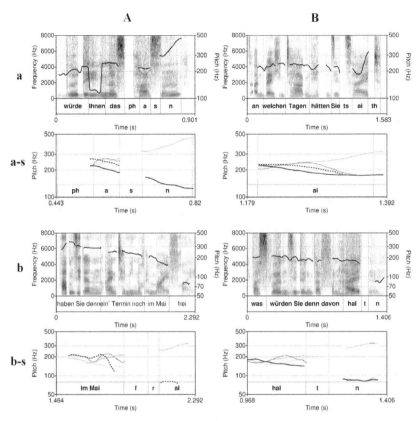

Figure 4.1. 2x2 syntax–prosody display of four QUESTIONS from one speaker in the *Kiel Corpus of Spontaneous Speech*. **A** *word order* **B** *lexical* **a** *rising* **b** *falling* F0. Spectrograms with F0 traces (log scale) of complete original utterances: **Aa** *late-valley* 'Würde Ihnen das passen?' **Ba** *late-valley* 'An welchen Tagen hätten Sie Zeit?' **Ab** *early peak* 'Haben Sie denn ein' Termin noch im Mai frei?' **Bb** *medial peak* 'Was würden Sie denn davon halten?' More clearly marked F0 dip into the accented vowel of **Ba** also transferred to **Aa** (dotted line). Four synthetic changes of F0 in the final accent section: in panel **a–s** reversal to three *falling* patterns (*early*, *medial*, *medial-to-late peaks*) and *early valley*; in panel **b–s** reversal to two *rising* patterns (*early*, *late valleys*) and two *falling* patterns (**Ab–s** *medial*, *medial-to-late* **Bb–s** *early*, *medial-to-late*); *valleys* thin lines (*early* plain, *late* dotted), *peaks* thick lines (*early* plain, *medial* dashed, *medial-to-late* dotted). Standard German, female speaker (ANS).

they agree with the boundary date already established by the dialogue partner. The *early peak* interrogative may be paraphrased as 'I'm sure you will agree.' In a *medial-peak* resynthesis, the speaker asks for a decision on her proposal and expects it to be 'yes'. This may be paraphrased as 'What about these two dates?'

Finally, *a medial-to-late peak* resynthesis adds irritation to prejudging the answer: 'I hope you are not going to turn this offer down!' This is in keeping with the semantics of the *medial-to-late peak*, i.e. 'pointing to some contrast to one's expectation'. It is out of place in the context created here by the dialogue partners.

Ab word order + final falling intonation – g092a00l
&2^-(Haben Sie denn einen &1. &2)Term'in noch im &0. &2)Mai frei &2. &PG
[Have you still got a free date for an appointment in May?]

This question is preceded by ANS thanking FRS for the invitation to meet. With the final *early peak fall*, she concludes with confidence that the dialogue partner will be able to offer a date in May.

The resynthesis with a final &? *high rise* stimulates the listener to suggest a date. A *late-valley rise* signals personal concern and makes the stimulation more demanding; an *early-valley rise* is detached matter-of-fact. The resynthesis with a *medial peak* also prejudges the answer 'yes', but gives 'May' greater weight, singling it out as the month when ANS would like to have the meeting. Resynthesis with a *medial-to-late peak* puts the speaker's expectation in contrast to what the listener might propose, and thus introduces a note of 'irritation'. This is inappropriate in a cooperative appointment-making context.

Ba question word + final rising intonation – g095a02l
An &2^-(welchen &0. &1-Tagen hätten Sie &1. &2[Zeit &, &PG [On which days are you free?]

This turn was preceded by two turns in which an appointment was discussed in general terms and where the dialogue partner mentioned that her timetable was very tight. ANS refers back to this with 'Das heißt' [That means] and then asks the question with a *late-valley*. The final rise ends considerably lower than in g091a13l, and at the same time has a larger F0 dip into the accented vowel. These features signal request rather than stimulation, categorised as &, *low rise*, rather than &? *high rise*. The speaker expresses personal concern for the listener's scheduling problems and requests her to give more specific information. This personal concern makes the utterance more subdued, polite and friendly. A final *early-valley rise* turns the question into a routine request without personal concern.

The resynthesis with a final *fall* lacks the effects of stimulation and consideration; it becomes entirely factual. The *early peak* conveys the meaning of restricting the discussion to a closed set of dates available to the dialogue partner: 'Let me have your free dates then, and we will see what we can do.' The *medial peak* conveys the meaning of opening a discussion of mutually suitable dates: 'Let's discuss how your free dates fit in with mine.' The *medial-to-late peak* adds a note of irritation, expressing opposition to the dialogue partner's vagueness and limitation in the appointment-making: 'When, after all, WOULD you be free?'

The *valley* patterns are the best fit in the cooperative context the dialogue partners create in three turns. The *medial-to-late peak* is not contextually compatible with cooperative appointment-scheduling. The *medial peak* would be more appropriate in an opening turn, when the speaker expresses the wish to arrange a meeting and then asks for a suggestion of dates. The *early peak* can occur in the setting of g095a021 because it refers back to pre-established facts, in this case to the limited availability previously mentioned by the dialogue partner. But it would be incompatible with an opening turn, because there is no pre-established reference, unless the speaker offers a restricted list and then asks which of these dates are suitable. For example: 'Wir müssen uns zu einer Besprechung treffen. Ich kann nächste Woche anbieten. An welchen Tagen hätten Sie Zeit?' [We need to meet for a discussion. I can offer next week...]

Bb question word + final falling intonation – g094a001
Was &2^würden Sie denn davon &1. &2^halten &2. &PG
[What do you think of that?]

The question ends in a *medial-peak fall* and concludes the opening dialogue turn, in which the speaker proposes a meeting to prepare a trip they will have to do together. The speaker's intention is not to sound out the other person's attitude towards such an arrangement but to hand over the turn for a concrete statement about a date for a preparatory meeting.

The resynthesis with final **&?** *high-rising* pitch stimulates the addressee to convey how she feels about a preparatory meeting. The effect is stronger with a *late valley*, which adds the expression of personal concern. An *early peak* resynthesis supports turn conclusion. A *medial-to-late peak* resynthesis adds contrast, suggesting that the dialogue partner might not be in favour. This is not contextually compatible with cooperative appointment-scheduling.

The context-rooted discussion of the data from speaker ANS in dialogue g09a of the Kiel *Corpus* and of the systematic synthetic derivations, presented graphically in Figure 4.1, leads to the following statements about intonation in German QUESTIONS.

- All four combinations of *word-order* versus *lexical interrogative*, and *rising* versus *falling pitch* on the final accent, differentiate types of POLARITY and INFORMATION QUESTIONS.
- The basic semantics of POLARITY QUESTIONS is listener-oriented, and in this function they use *word-order interrogative* syntax with final **&?** *high-rising pitch*, stimulating the listener to make a polarity decision.
- The basic semantics of INFORMATION QUESTIONS is fact- and speaker-oriented, and in this function they are *lexical interrogative* with *falling pitch*.
- *Falling pitch* in *word-order interrogatives* moves the orientation to the facts and to the speaker, as it focuses on the speaker's expectation that the answer to the question will occur at one pole, 'yes' in the case of positive, 'no' in the case of negative phrasing.
- Final **&?** *high-rising pitch* in *lexical interrogatives* moves the orientation to the listener, as it stimulates the listener to provide information.
- The *falling pitch* in both question functions may be an *early*, a *medial* or a *medial-to-late peak*. With an *early peak*, the speaker signals that a final judgement or a piece of information is required from the receiver to conclude the preceding interaction: this is the FINALITY function. With a *medial peak*, the speaker signals that the question opens a new interaction: this is the OPENNESS function. The *medial-to-late peak* introduces CONTRAST into OPENNESS. These functions of the different peak synchronisations are discussed for STATEMENTS in 3.3. The *late peak* for EXPRESSIVE UNEXPECTEDNESS, superimposed on CONTRAST, is also part of the STATEMENT pattern set, but was not found in the QUESTION data of the corpus, because the EXPRESSIVE FUNCTION is alien to more matter-of-fact appointment-scheduling. Its occurrence in QUESTIONS is discussed in 4.2.2.2/3.
- The final **&?** *high-rising pitch* in both question functions may be an *early* or a *late valley*. Both pitch patterns function as RESPONSE STIMULATION signals to the listener, either to make a polarity decision or to provide information. With an *early valley*, RESPONSE STIMULATION is MATTER-OF-FACT; with a *late valley*, the speaker adds

EXPRESSION OF PERSONAL CONCERN to STIMULATION, making it more demanding.

- In the corpus data, there are also final **&**, *low rises*, with which the speaker signals RESPONSE REQUEST, i.e. SUBORDINATION to, rather than STIMULATION of, the listener, thus swapping the active and passive roles in the interaction between sender and receiver, compared with the *high rise*. The question becomes a polite enquiry, which is MATTER-OF-FACT with an *early valley*; a *late valley* adds EXPRESSION OF PERSONAL CONCERN to REQUEST, making it more subdued, polite and friendly. This type of QUESTION comes under Ohala's *Frequency Code* (1983, 1984); see 6.2.

- There is a considerable proportion of final *low rises*, but only very few final *high rises*, in *lexical interrogatives* in the corpus. But if the speaker stimulates the listener with a CONFIRMATION QUESTION, i.e. the repetition of what the addressee has already said, a *high rise* on the interrogative word is obligatory. On the other hand, if the speaker makes a polite enquiry for more specific information than the addressee has given, this additional INFORMATION QUESTION has a *low rise* on the interrogative word; see 4.2.2.3.

The re-interpretation of Fries's English data under a functional perspective shows that, given the appropriate communicative context, *falling pitch* is the accompaniment of *interrogative syntax* in American English POLARITY QUESTIONS. It may be assumed that this pattern is widespread across varieties of L1 English (but see 3.1.3 for Urban North British). Furthermore, it may be hypothesised that the patterning found in the German corpus data and in their resynthesised derivatives can also be postulated for the network of *interrogatives* and *prosodies* in POLARITY and INFORMATION QUESTION functions in English. Corresponding data need to be collected and analysed equally systematically.

The German data demonstrate that corpus analyses that are approached only from a descriptive statistical point of view, like Fries's, miss important explanatory aspects, which come into focus when the data are investigated in their contextual setting. This is considered the key to the understanding of the use of pitch patterns in speech communication. But prosody also needs to be modelled theoretically as an independent constitutive determinant of meaning that goes beyond the concrete environment found *hic et nunc* in a corpus. This approach thus follows Selting (1995) as far as focus on the communicative setting is concerned, but goes beyond the individual corpus data to arrive at generalisations about REPRESENTATION, APPEAL and EXPRESSION in Bühler's communication triangle. The following sections develop a comprehensive framework of functions and forms of QUESTIONS for German and English.

4.2.2.2 POLARITY QUESTIONS

To enquire about the unknown truth value of a proposition, POLARITY QUESTIONS, with LISTENER or FACT AND SPEAKER ORIENTATION, combine *interrogative word-order* syntax with accentuation and intonation patterns.

(1) Syntactic Structures

A German or English POLARITY QUESTION like

> Trifft Martin seinen alten Kumpel heute Nachmittag in der Stadt?
> Is Martin meeting his old pal in town this afternoon?

enquires about the truth value of a proposition that contains the following semantic constituents:

<TRUTH x>: <ACTION>   <AGENT>   <GOAL>   <TIME>   <PLACE>

With the default syntactic structures for the semantic constituents of propositions in STATEMENTS (see 3.1), we get

in German

<TRUTH x>:
<AGENT>   <ACTION> <GOAL>   <TIME>   <PLACE>
<Martin>   <trifft>   <seinen alten Kumpel> <heute Nachmittag> <in der Stadt>.

in English

<TRUTH x>:
<AGENT> <ACTION>   <GOAL>   <PLACE>   <TIME>
<Martin> <is meeting> <his old pal> <in town>   <this afternoon>.

In a POLARITY QUESTION in German, the inflected auxiliary or finite verb changes places with the constituent in the first structural slot; the syntactic order of the remaining constituents stays the same for QUESTION and STATEMENT, including the sentence-final position of the uninflected verb of the verbal phrase. In English, the auxiliary part of a verb form, or the placeholder 'do' in case the verbal phrase does not contain an auxiliary, is assigned to the new initial position, and the verb representing the <ACTION> fills the same slot as in the STATEMENT:

<ACTION Trifft>   <AGENT Martin>   <GOAL seinen alten Kumpel>
< TIME heute Nachmittag> <PLACE in der Stadt>?

<ACTION *auxiliary* Will> <AGENT Martin>   <GOAL seinen alten Kumpel>
< TIME heute Nachmittag> <PLACE in der Stadt> <ACTION *verb uninfl* treffen>?

<ACTION *auxiliary* Is>   <AGENT Martin>   <ACTION *verb* meeting>
<GOAL his old pal>   <PLACE in town>   < TIME this afternoon>?

If, in German, <AGENT>and <GOAL>are filled by pronouns (e.g. 'er' [he],
'ihn' [him] in the above examples), they are enclitic to the verb:

<ACTION Trifft> <AGENT er>   <GOAL ihn>   < TIME heute Nachmittag>
<PLACE in der   Stadt>?

The German flexibility of syntactic ordering in STATEMENTS is replicated
when the verb is fronted for POLARITY QUESTIONS:

<ACTION Trifft> Martin <TIME heute Nachmittag> <GOAL seinen alten Kumpel>
< PLACE in der Stadt >?

<ACTION Trifft> Martin <TIME heute Nachmittag> < PLACE in der Stadt >
<GOAL seinen alten Kumpel>?

<ACTION Trifft> Martin <PLACE in der Stadt> < TIME heute Nachmittag>
<GOAL seinen alten Kumpel>?

The only flexibility of structural ordering in English STATEMENTS occurs
when the <TIME> or <PLACE> coordinates for an <ACTION> are set as the
theme for the proposition. A POLARITY QUESTION cannot have such a theme-
rheme structure because it enquires about the truth value of the whole proposition (but see 4.2.2.6 for *question tags*). Therefore, <TIME> or <PLACE> have to
stay in their propositional structural slots, unless they form a separate CONFIR-
MATION QUESTION (see 4.2.2.4) and are picked up by unaccented anaphoric
deixis in the POLARITY QUESTION following it, as in:

A: &2What are &2Martin's &2plans for this &2afternoon?
     Has he got anything &2on in &2town this &0afternoon?
B: This &3afternoon? Isn't he &2meeting his old &2pal in &2town for
     &2coffee &1then?
     In &3town? Isn't he &2meeting his old &2pal &1there for
     &2coffee?

Either <TIME> or <PLACE> can also be put initially in a German STATE-
MENT, but, as in English, the theme-rheme structure is excluded from a
POLARITY QUESTION, except when a tightly linked preceding CONFIRMATION
QUESTION functions as the theme:

A: Was für **&2**Pläne hat **&2**Martin für heute **&2**Nachmittag?
      Hat er irgend was **&2**vor in der **&2**Stadt heute **&0**Nachmittag?
B: Heute **&3**Nachmittag? **&2**Trifft er **&1**dann nicht seinen alten
      &2Kumpel in der **&2**Stadt zum **&2**Kaffee?
      In der **&3**Stadt? **&2**Trifft er **&1**da nicht seinen alten **&2**Kumpel zum
      &2Kaffee?

In both languages, POLARITY QUESTION structures are derived in the same way from any STATEMENT structure when the proposition is based on <EVENT OCCURRENCE>. The inflected verb is put in first position, which removes the need for a *<subject>* placeholder 'es' in German. For example:

<OCCURRENCE *infl* Findet> <EVENT *subject* der jährliche Bauernmarkt>
<TIME am Wochenende> < PLACE auf Gut Emkendorf> <OCCURRENCE *uninfl* statt>?

<OCURRENCE *infl* Will> <EVENT *subject* the annual farmers' market>
<OCURRENCE *uninfl* take place><PLACE on the Emkendorf Estate>
<TIME this weekend>?

<OCCURRENCE *infl* Findet> <TIME am Wochenende> <PLACE auf Gut Emkendorf>
<<EVENT *subject* ein Bauernmarkt> <OCCURRENCE *uninfl* statt>?

<OCCURRENCE Will there be> < EVENT *subject* a farmers' market>
< PLACE on the Emkendorf Estate> < TIME this weekend>?

In certain contexts of situation, a POLARITY QUESTION may be limited to asking for the truth value of the predicate of a proposition, or of one of the semantic predicate components. In that case, declarative structure is reduced to various elliptic forms, with a declarative intermediary in English, moving meaning from linguistic to situational context. For example, at a business meeting, assistants may go round serving coffee, asking:

'Would you like some coffee?' or
'D'you like some coffee?' or
'(You) like some coffee?' or
'(Some) coffee?'
with *high-rising valleys.*

All these forms are POLARITY QUESTIONS, enquiring as to the truth value of 'coffee wanted'.

In German, the options are more restricted:

'Möchten Sie 'ne Tasse Kaffee?' or
'(('ne) Tasse) Kaffee?',
with *high-rising valleys.*

The *declarative* form

> 'Sie möchten Kaffee?'

is not possible because the content verb swaps structural positions with the subject. It is thus not a step in a linear curtailing of *interrogative* form, as it can be in English. It becomes a CONFIRMATION QUESTION, enquiring the truth value of the speaker's presupposition of common ground in the speaker–listener action field (see 4.2.2.4):

> 'You've seen me serving coffee, and from your looking towards me I assume that you might like some. Confirm.'

Another instance of ellipsis in POLARITY QUESTIONS is addressing someone by their name without being absolutely certain. 'Michael Smith?' means 'Are you Michael Smith?' The intonation may be either a *high-rising valley*, or a *medial peak in high register* when the speaker is fairly confident of being right.

(2) Accent Patterns

In both German and English POLARITY QUESTIONS, the same accentuation patterns hold as in STATEMENTS (see 3.1).

> <&1trifft> <&2Martin>   <seinen &1alten &2Kumpel> <&1heute &I2Nachmittag> <in der &2Stadt>?
> <&0Will> <&2Martin> <seinen &1alten &2Kumpel> <&1heute &I2Nachmittag> <in der &2Stadt> <&1treffen>?
>
> <&0Is> <&2Martin> <&1meeting> <his &1old &2pal> <in &I2town> <this &2aftern'oon>?
> <&0Will> <&2Martin> <&1meet> <his &1old &2pal> <in &I2town> <this &2aftern'oon>?
>
> <&0Findet><der &1jährliche &2Bauernmarkt><am &2Wochenende> <auf &1Gut &2Emkendorf> <&1statt>?
> <&0Wird><der &1jährliche &2Bauernmarkt><am &2Wochenende> <auf &1Gut &2Emkendorf> <&1stattfinden>?
> <&0Will> <the &1annual &0farmers' &2market> <&0take &1place> <on the &2Emkendorf &2Est'ate> <this &1week&2end>?

Any part of the syntactic structure representing a semantic constituent of the proposition may be put in focus by deaccenting all other structural elements; in addition, the focus may be reinforced to accent **&3**. In communicative interaction, a speaker decides on how many of these backgrounded elements may be omitted because their semantic referents can be inferred by the listener. In a POLARITY QUESTION, the unknown truth value of an <EVENT> may be put in focus by reinforcing either the uninflected non-initial part of the verbal phrase, as in

> <&0Findet> <der &1jährliche &1Bauernmarkt><am &1Wochenende>
> <auf &1Gut &1Emkendorf> <&3statt>?
> <&0Will> <&1the annual &0farmers' &1market> <&0take &3place>
> <on the &1Enkendorf &1Est'ate> <this &0week&1end>?

or the initial inflected part, as in

> <&3Findet> <der &1jährliche &1Bauernmarkt><am &1Wochenende>
> <auf &1Gut &1Emkendorf> <&0statt>?
> <&3Will> <the &1annual &0farmers' &1market> <&0take &1place>
> <on the &1Enkendorf &1Est'ate> <this &0week&1end>?

The former enquires in an intensified fact-oriented way as to whether the 'annual market' specified for <TIME> and <PLACE> will actually be on; the latter adds the expression of doubt about the <EVENT OCCURRENCE> being true.

(3) Intonation Patterns

In addition to the accentual scalings, various peak and valley pitch patterns may be linked to the accents, producing a great variety of prosodic realisations with fine semantic differentiation. The pitch pattern at the last full accent = >&2 in the prosodic phrase, the *nucleus*, determines the question subcategory. The system of POLARITY QUESTIONS comprises the following terms:

PQ-1	FACT AND SPEAKER ORIENTATION: prejudging a uni-polar decision
PQ-1a	FINALITY
PQ-1b	OPENNESS
PQ-1c	CONTRAST
PQ-1d	EXPRESSION OF UNEXPECTEDNESS
PQ-2	LISTENER ORIENTATION: soliciting a bi-polar decision
PQ-2.1	RESPONSE REQUEST
PQ-2(.1)a	MATTER-OF-FACT
PQ-2(.1)b	EXPRESSIVE
PQ-2.2	RESPONSE STIMULATION
PQ-2(.2)c	MATTER-OF-FACT
PQ-2(.2)d	EXPRESSIVE

The pitch patterns associated with these question categories are illustrated by the displays of the possible intonations in the German sentence 'Ist er in Rom?' in Figure 4.2. The utterance is contextualised in the following dialogue, with English function and form equivalents, followed by the functional descriptions of the *peak* and *valley* patterns at '&2Rom'.

A1:	Wo ist er denn eigentlich?	Where is he, I wonder?
B:	Er ist nach Italien gefahren.	He's gone to Italy.
A2:	Ist er in **&2**Rom?	Is he in **&2**Rome?

PQ-1a   With an *early peak*, A wants more information about the person's whereabouts and suggests a place, expecting the answer to be 'yes' and signalling that the preceding interchange will thus be concluded: FINALITY 'where he always goes'
Ist er in **&2**)Rom **&2. &PG**

PQ-1b   With a *medial peak*, A wants more information and suggests a place, expecting the answer to be 'yes' – as in **PQ-1a** – but opens a new interchange: OPENNESS
Ist er in **&2^**Rom **&2. &PG**

PQ-1c   With a *medial-to-late peak*, A wants more information, as in **PQ-1b**, but singles out a place and suggests it contrastively as the most likely one. This superimposes CONTRAST on OPENNESS.
Ist er in **&2^-(**Rom **&2. &PG**

PQ-1d   With a *late peak*, A signals the need for more information, as in **PQ-1c**, but adds EXPRESSION OF UNEXPECTEDNESS. This superimposes the EXPRESSION OF UNEXPECTEDNESS on OPENNESS and CONTRAST
Ist er in **&2(**Rom **&2. &PG**

PQ-2a   With an *early low-rising valley*, A does not prejudge the answer but *requests* an open polarity decision from the listener. The sender is the passive, the receiver the active, partner in this interaction of MATTER-OF-FACT RESPONSE REQUEST.
Ist er in **&2]**Rom **&, &PG**

PQ-2b   With a *late low-rising valley*, A still requests an open polarity decision from the listener, but adds EXPRESSION OF PERSONAL CONCERN, which makes the request more subdued, polite and friendly.
Ist er in **&2[**Rom **&, &PG**

PQ-2c   With an *early high-rising valley*, A does not prejudge the answer but *stimulates* the listener to make an open polarity decision. The sender is the active, the receiver the passive partner in this interaction of MATTER-OF-FACT RESPONSE STIMULATION.
Ist er in **&2]**Rom **&? &PG**

PQ-2d   With a *late high-rising valley*, A still stimulates the listener to make an open polarity decision, but adds EXPRESSION OF PERSONAL CONCERN, which in this context is SURPRISE at 'the person perhaps being in Rome'.
Ist er in **&2[**Rom **&? &PG**

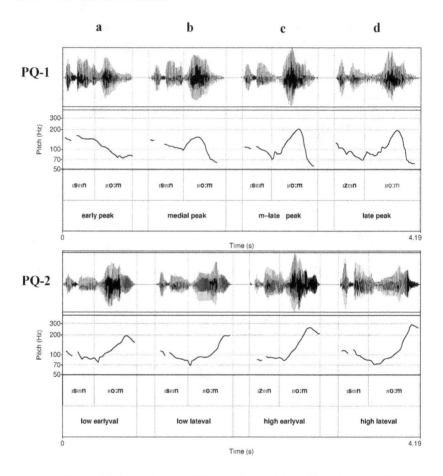

Figure 4.2. Speech waves, F0 traces (log scale), segmental transcriptions, grouped into prehead and nucleus, and nucleus classifications in the German Polarity Questions of 'Ist er in Rom?' **PQ-1** Speaker Orientation **a** Finality **b** Openness **c** Contrast **d** Unexpectedness; **PQ-2** Listener Orientation **a** Response Request, Matter-of-fact **b** Response Request, Expressive **c** Response Stimulation, Matter-of-fact **d** Response Stimulation, Expressive. Standard German, male speaker (KJK).

4.2.2.3 Information Questions

For enquiring about an unknown semantic constituent of a proposition, Information Questions, with Fact or Listener Orientation, combine *lexical interrogative* structures with accent and intonation patterns.

(1) Syntactic Structures and Accent Patterns

Taking the German and English STATEMENTS

<AGENT> <ACTION> <GOAL>	<TIME>	<MANNER>	<PLACE>
<Martin> <trifft> <seinen alten Kumpel>	<heute Nachmittag>	<zum Kaffee>	<in der Stadt>.

<AGENT> <ACTION> <GOAL>	<PLACE>	<MANNER>	<TIME>
<Martin> <is meeting> <his old pal>	<in town>	<for coffee>	<this afternoon>.

as points of departure, any one of the propositional constituents may become an unknown, coded by the corresponding interrogative pronominal or adverbial in an INFORMATION QUESTION:

<AGENTX>	<GOALX>	<TIMEX>	<MANNERX>	<PLACEX>
<wer,was/who,what><wen/who(m)>	*<wann/when>*	*<wozu/what for>*	*<wo/where>*

The interrogative is put in sentence-initial position, and, for other than <AGENTX> (or <EVENT X>), *subject>* and *<infl verb>* (which in English is an auxiliary or the placeholder 'do') are inverted, but the syntactic ordering of the other constituents is retained, for example

<TIMEX *wann*> <trifft> <Martin>   <seinen alten Kumpel> <in der Stadt>?
<TIMEX *when*> <is>   <Martin> <meeting> <his old pal>   <in town> ?

When <ACTION> or <EVENT OCCURRENCE> is the unknown, the question is whether the action takes place or the event occurs, i.e. whether they are true, which is coded by a POLARITY QUESTION.

It follows from the structural parallelism of INFORMATION QUESTIONS and STATEMENTS that the default accent pattern is the same for both: each propositional constituent, including the unknown, receives an accent, which is **&1** associated with <ACTION/EVENT OCCURRENCE>, **&2** in all other cases. Any constituent, including the unknown, may be put in focus with a default **&2** or a reinforced **&3** accent, and deaccentuation of all the others. As in STATEMENTS and POLARITY QUESTIONS, the speaker decides what can be inferred from the communicative situation and may thus be omitted. Backgrounding is also achieved by unaccented pronominal reference. In the following dialogue, Speaker A leaves out the <TIME> information, which Speaker B then enquires about, with a peak accent on the interrogative word and at least partial deaccentuation of all the other propositional constituents, and with pronominal anaphoric <AGENT> and <GOAL> references.

A: <Martin> <trifft>   <seinen alten Kumpel> <zum Kaffee> <in der Stadt>.
    <Martin> < is meeting><his old pal>   <in town>   <for coffee>.

B: <**&2**TIMEX *wann*> <**&0**trifft er ihn>   <zum **&0**Kaffee> <in der **&0**Stadt?
    <**&2**TIMEX *when*> <is he **&0**meeting him><in **&0**town>   <for**&0** coffee>?

This lexical interrogative structure is commonly curtailed by leaving out the non-pronominal referents, and, in a second step, also the pronominal ones, retaining only the interrogative word, successively replacing linguistic context by situational context.

It was mentioned in 4.2.1 that INFORMATION QUESTIONS formed with interrogative words in declarative slots in e.g. Mandarin Chinese are also found in German and English as a deviant structure from sentence-initial position for specific semantic purposes. An unknown propositional constituent is singled out for information retrieval and is put, in its lexical interrogative form, in the appropriate declarative slot. This type of INFORMATION QUESTION asks for more information than has already been given, for instance to supply <TIME> or <PLACE> when only one, or neither, was provided by a dialogue partner in a preceding statement. The focused internal interrogative word receives a peak accent **&2^** or **&3^**, followed by at least partial deaccentuation of all subsequent propositional constituents in the utterance and by pronominal anaphoric reference, as in the case of the initial lexical interrogative. Thus, Speaker B may produce the following turn in the above statement-question dialogue frame:

> B: <er **&0**trifft ihn> <**&2**TIMEX *wann*><zum **&0**Kaffee>   <in der **&0**Stadt>?
> <he is **&0**meeting him><in **&0**town> <for **&0** coffee>   <**&2**TIMEX *when*>?

This internal lexical interrogative differs functionally from its initial counterpart; it sets a theme for the question by introducing it with an explicit reference to the proposition of the preceding statement. Deaccentuation of all the propositional constituents after the interrogative word continue the question theme and embed the question rheme in it. The theme-rheme structure in an internal lexical interrogative is also the reason the German question is still regular when <**&2^**TIMEX *wann*> is moved from its default declarative slot to the end of the utterance. With this theme-rheme structure the speaker signals that s/he not only wants more specific information but also has to ask for it specially because the dialogue partner did not provide it. This insistence on missing information is absent from the initial lexical interrogative since it does not set a theme that explicitly links the question to the preceding statement. The internal lexical interrogative can also be curtailed, but the theme part before the focused interrogative word stays to maintain coding of this type of INFORMATION QUESTION.

If the <TIME> or <PLACE> information that Speaker A gives is not considered precise enough by Speaker B, s/he may ask for more detail by putting the known broad <TIME> or <PLACE> frame in its declarative slot, and the unknown narrow <TIMEX> or <PLACEX> before it or initially in the utterance:

B: <**&2**TIMEX *wann*><**&0**trifft er ihn><heute **&0**Nachmittag> <zum **&0**Kaffee>?
<er **&0**trifft ihn><**&2**XTIME *wann*><heute **&0**Nachmittag> <zum **&0**Kaffee>?
<**&2**PLACEX *wo*> <**&0**trifft er ihn> <zum **&0**Kaffee> <in der **&0**Stadt>?
<er **&0**trifft ihn> <zum **&0**Kaffee> <**&2**XPLACE *wo*> <in der **&0**Stadt>?

<**&2**^TIMEX *when*><is he **&0**meeting him><for**&0**coffee><this **&0**afternoon>?
<he's **&0**meeting him><for **&0**coffee><**&2**XTIME *when*><this **&0**afternoon>?
<**&2**PLACEX *where*> <is he **&0**meeting him> <in **&0**town> <for**&0**coffee>?
<he's **&0**meeting him> <**&2**PLACE *where*>   <in **&0**town> <for**&0**coffee>?

Speaker B may also eliminate thematic information from the question and reduce the enquiry to the narrow <TIME>or <PLACE> frame, with or without the broad one, thus moving thematic information from the linguistic context to the context of situation set by Speaker A:

<**&2**TIMEX *wann*> (<heute **&0**Nachmittag>)?
<**&2**PLACEX *wo*> (<in der **&0**Stadt>)?

<**&2**TIMEX *when*> (<this **&0**afternoon>)?
<**&2**PLACEX *where*> (<in **&0**town>)?

(2) Intonation Patterns

The system of INFORMATION QUESTION categories and of the peak and valley pitch patterns associated with them at the last full accent = >**&2** in the prosodic phrase parallels the one outlined for POLARITY QUESTIONS:

IQ-1	FACT ORIENTATION: obtaining information about a propositional constituent
IQ-1a	FINALITY
IQ-1b	OPENNESS
IQ-1c	CONTRAST
IQ-1d	EXPRESSION OF UNEXPECTEDNESS
IQ-2	LISTENER ORIENTATION: adding appeal to information enquiry
IQ-2.1	RESPONSE REQUEST
IQ-2(.1)a	MATTER-OF-FACT
IQ-2(.1)b	EXPRESSIVE
IQ-2.2	RESPONSE STIMULATION
IQ-2(.2)c	MATTER-OF-FACT
IQ-2(.2)d	EXPRESSIVE

The pitch patterns associated with these question categories are illustrated by the displays of the possible intonations in the German sentence 'Wo?' in Figure 4.3. The utterance is contextualised in the dialogues below, with

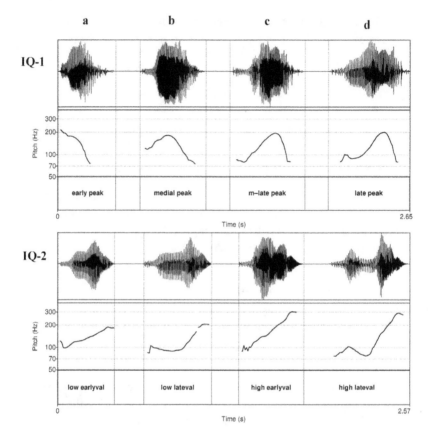

Figure 4.3. Speech waves, F0 traces (log scale), word segmentations and pitch classifications in the German INFORMATION QUESTIONS 'Wo?' **IQ-1** SPEAKER ORIENTATION **a** FINALITY **b** OPENNESS **c** CONTRAST **d** UNEXPECTEDNESS; **IQ-2** LISTENER ORIENTATION **a** RESPONSE REQUEST, MATTER-OF-FACT **b** RESPONSE REQUEST, EXPRESSIVE **c** RESPONSE STIMULATION, MATTER-OF-FACT **d** RESPONSE STIMULATION, EXPRESSIVE. Standard German, male speaker (KJK).

English function and form equivalents, followed by the functional descriptions of the *peak* and *valley* patterns at '**&2**wo'.

(I)   A: Martin trifft seinen alten Kumpel heute Nachmittag zum Kaffee.
              Martin is meeting his old pal for coffee this afternoon.
       B: **&2**Wo?
              &2Where?

(II)   A: Martin trifft seinen alten Kumpel zum Kaffee in der Stadt.
              Martin is meeting his old pal in town for coffee.

B: **&2**Wo in der **&0**Stadt?
    &2Where in **&0**town?

(III) A: Martin trifft seinen alten Kumpel zum Kaffee in der Stadt.
           Martin is meeting his old pal in town for coffee.
       B: **&2**Wo?
           &2Where?

In (I), Speaker A does not give any <PLACE> information, so Speaker B asks for it. In (II), Speaker A provides a <PLACE> frame that Speaker B does not consider sufficiently detailed, so Speaker B asks for a more specific narrow frame explicitly by adding Speaker A's broad frame to the unknown. In (III), Speaker A gives the same information as in (II), but Speaker B refers to a single <PLACE> frame. Speaker B's intention may be either to obtain information in a narrow <PLACE> frame, against the broad frame set by Speaker A, or to appeal to Speaker A to confirm the given <PLACE> information, (CONFIRMATION QUESTION – see 4.2.2.4). Syntactic structure and accentuation cannot distinguish between these two possibilities in (III): intonation solves the ambiguity.

In all three dialogues, 'wo/where' receives one of the *peak* or *valley* patterns of Figure 4.3. In (II), the fall of a peak trails off on low pitch, or the rise of a valley continues monotonically across 'in der Stadt/in town'. Since the single accent on an initial or an internal interrogative word puts the <PLACE> enquired about in focus, the question appeals to the receiver for <PLACE> information. In dialogue (I), the question solicits altogether new information, because there is no preceding <PLACE> reference; in dialogue (II), it solicits more specific information with explicit reference to the broad <PLACE> frame given in the preceding statement. In dialogue (III), the question does not solicit altogether new <PLACE> information because the statement context provided a frame. What it does solicit depends on the intonation pattern used on the focused constituent. With *peak* patterns and with RESPONSE REQUESTING *low-rising valley* patterns, the question solicits more specific information in a narrower <PLACE> frame. But RESPONSE STIMULATING *high-rising valley* patterns add insistence to the enquiry, appealing to Speaker A to confirm the given <PLACE> information. Below are the detailed functional descriptions of the eight formal patterns.

IQ-1a   With an *early peak*, B asks for (more detailed) <PLACE > information, which is missing but needed to complete the information exchange: FINALITY – 'That's all I still need to know.'
            &2)Wo **&2.** **&PG**

IQ-1b   With a *medial peak*, B asks for (more detailed) <PLACE> information
– as in **IQ-1a** – but without indicating that this will complete the
information exchange: OPENNESS – 'I need to know more.'
&2^Wo &2. &PG

IQ-1c   With a *medial-to-late peak*, B asks for (more detailed) <PLACE>
information – as in **IQ-1b** – but with a note of annoyance,
superimposing CONTRAST on OPENNESS – 'I need to know, but you did
not tell me.'
&2^-(Wo &2. &PG

IQ-1d   With a *late peak*, B asks for (more detailed) <PLACE> information – as
in **IQ- 1c** – but adds EXPRESSION OF UNEXPECTEDNESS to OPENNESS
and CONTRAST – 'Where on earth are they meeting?'
&2(Wo &2. &PG

IQ-2(.1)a   With an *early low-rising valley*, B requests <PLACE> information from
A which is either missing in dialogue (I), or not detailed enough in
dialogues (II) and (III). The low F0 end point precludes interpretation
as a CONFIRMATION QUESTION in dialogue (II). This is a MATTER-OF-
FACT RESPONSE REQUEST.
&2]Wo &, &PG

IQ-2(.1)b   With a *late low-rising valley*, B still requests <PLACE> information from
A as in **IQ-2a**, but adds EXPRESSION OF PERSONAL CONCERN, which
makes the request more subdued, polite and friendly.
&2[Wo &, &PG

IQ-2(.2)c   With an *early high-rising valley*, B sends MATTER-OF-FACT RESPONSE
STIMULATION to A, to provide the missing <PLACE> information in
dialogue (I), or to fill a narrow <PLACE> frame within A's broad frame
in (II). But since in dialogue (III) B's <PLACE> frame is not formally
marked as narrow, versus a broad frame from A, the *early high-rising
valley* stimulates A to CONFIRM the <PLACE> INFORMATION already
given: CONFIRMATION QUESTION (see 4.2.2.4).
&2]Wo &? &PG

IQ-2(.2)d   With a *late high-rising valley*, B stimulates A to provide <PLACE>
information in the same three different ways as in **IQ-2c**, but adds
EXPRESSION OF PERSONAL CONCERN, which in dialogues (I) and (II)
may be impatience to get the information; in dialogue (III), it may be
disbelieving the information received, therefore needing confirmation:
CONFIRMATION QUESTION (see 4.2.2.4)
&2[Wo &? &PG

To round off this section on INFORMATION QUESTIONS, here are some se-
lective original data from English, illustrated in Figure 4.4 and functionally
interpreted in the context:

A: We'll meet in Auchterarder tomorrow.

B: **&2**Where?

IQ-1a   With a *medial peak*, B asks for more information about the location of
the venue in the town.
&2^Where &2. &PG

IQ-1b   With a *medial-to-late peak*, B stresses the need for more information
about the venue against the insufficiency of the information so far given
by A. The utterance has a tone of irritation and impatience: 'But where?
Your information is rather imprecise.'
&2^-(Where &2. &PG

IQ-2b   With a *late low (falling-)rising valley*, where the rise starts in the accented
vowel, B still asks for more information about the venue, but makes a
request appeal to the listener. The fall adds contrast, but the utterance
sounds less categorical and more friendly than with a peak pattern.
&2^Where &,. &PG   **&2[Where &, &PG**

IQ-2c   With an *early high-rising valley*, B stimulates confirmation of the
<PLACE> information A has already given, because B disbelieves what
s/he has perceived due to the strangeness of the name and the unfamiliarity
with the small Scottish town: CONFIRMATION QUESTION (see 4.2.2.4)
&2] Where &? &PG

4.2.2.4 CONFIRMATION QUESTIONS

Two types of CONFIRMATION QUESTION were distinguished in 4.2.1, depending on whether a semantic component, or the truth value of a proposition, already available in the interaction, is questioned for confirmation. This makes it
necessary to relate CONFIRMATION QUESTIONS to INFORMATION QUESTIONS
on the one hand, and to STATEMENTS and POLARITY QUESTIONS on the other.

(1) Lexical Interrogative Structure in INFORMATION *versus* CONFIRMA-
TION QUESTIONS

Lexical interrogative structures do not just code one type of INFORMATION
QUESTION. There is a fourfold functional opposition among *lexical interrogative
structures*, cutting across the categories of INFORMATION QUESTIONS and CON-
FIRMATION QUESTIONS, and subcategorising them. The functional reference is
determined by context of situation and is manifested by prosodic patterns of
accent and intonation. The function-form system is organised as follows:

(a)   INFORMATION QUESTION *with the propositional relation* '<SEMCOMX>: *in
proposition*' *and lexical interrogative structure, which may be reduced to
the interrogative word*

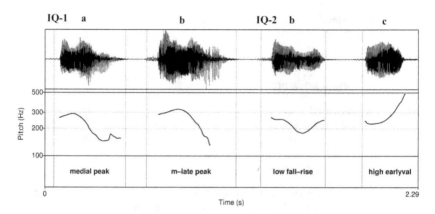

Figure 4.4. Speech waves, F0 traces (log scale), word segmentations and pitch classifications in the English INFORMATION QUESTIONS 'Where?' **IQ-1** SPEAKER ORIENTATION **a** OPENNESS **b** CONTRAST; **IQ-2** LISTENER ORIENTATION **b** RESPONSE REQUEST, EXPRESSIVE **c** RESPONSE STIMULATION. Standard Southern British English, female speaker (RMB).

(a1)   *asking about a propositional constituent that is missing from the preceding interchange*

The lexical interrogative is in *structure-initial position* and there are accents on constituents that are to be foregrounded, with either a *peak* or a *low-rising valley* pattern at the last accent, depending on whether the sender just enquires about facts or requests them (see 4.2.2.3). The interrogative word may be accented in addition to other accents; in elliptic form, it receives accent and intonation patterns.

(a2)   *asking for more detail of a propositional constituent that has already been provided*

The lexical interrogative is in the *appropriate slot of declarative syntax*, which receives the last default accent in the utterance, and, like (a1), is combined with either a *peak* or a *low-rising valley*. In the case of an elliptic interrogative, (a2) is distinguished from (a1) by context of situation, and (b2) from (a2) by a *high-rising valley* in addition to context of situation.

(b)   CONFIRMATION QUESTION *with the propositional relation* '<CSEMCOMX>: in proposition' *and lexical interrogative structure, which may be reduced to the interrogative word, eliminating the formal distinction between (b1) and (b2)*

It stimulates repetition and confirmation of a propositional constituent when the sender wants to make sure that s/he has perceived the message correctly, for example in poor transmission, or when the sender cannot believe what s/he has heard or understood.

(b1)   *with initial-lexical interrogative structure*

The lexical interrogative gets a single focus accent, and *high-rising* intonation starting there, either as an *early valley* for MATTER-OF-FACT (**CQ-1**), or as a *late valley* for EXPRESSIVE (**CQ-2**), RESPONSE STIMULATION (see below).

(b2)   *with internal-lexical interrogative structure, picking up a previous theme for the receiver to provide the confirmation rheme.*

The interrogative has a single focus accent with a *high-rising valley* as for (b1).

The following two sets of dialogues between a wife and a husband illustrate the association of *lexical interrogative* structure with INFORMATION QUESTIONS and CONFIRMATION QUESTIONS, respectively, and another two sub-categorisations within each. The two sets differ in that in (I) the wife does not specify the length of time her mother wants to stay, but does so in (II), and the husband asks for information to be expanded upon or confirmed, respectively.

(I)   Wife: &2Mutti hat angerufen, sie will uns wieder &2besuchen.
                          &2Mother phoned, she wants to &2visit us again.

INFORMATION QUESTIONS
(Ia1) Husband: **IQ-1b** &2^Wie lange will sie &1. &2^diesmal &0. &2^bleiben &2. &PG
                          &2^How long will she &1. &2^stay &0. &2^this time &2. &PG

                IQ-2b &2^Wie lange will sie &1. &2^diesmal &1. &2[bleiben &, &PG
                          &2^How long will she &1. &2^stay &1. &2[this time &, &PG

(Ia2)   **IQ-1b** Sie will &1^diesmal &1. &2^wie lange &1. &1^bleiben &2. &PG
                          She will &1^stay &1. &2^how long &1. &1^this time &2. &PG

                IQ-2b Sie will &1^diesmal &1. &2^wie lange &1. &1[bleiben &, &PG
                          She will &1^stay &1. &2^how long &1. &1[this time &, &PG
(II)   Wife: &2Mutti hat angerufen, sie will uns wieder &2^besuchen,
                          &2diesmal für &2zwei &2Wochen.
                          &2Mother phoned, she wants to &2visit us again, &2this time for
                          &2two &2weeks.

CONFIRMATION QUESTIONS
(IIb1)Husband: **CQ-1** &2]Wie lange will sie diesmal bleiben &? &PG
                          &2]How long does she want to stay this time &? &PG

                CQ-2 &2[Wie lange will sie diesmal bleiben &? &PG
                          &2[How long does she want to stay for this time &? &PG

(IIb2)   **CQ-1** Sie will diesmal &2]wie lange bleiben &? &PG
                          She wants to stay &2]how long this time &? &PG

                CQ-2 Sie will diesmal &2[wie lange bleiben &? &PG
                          She wants to stay &2[how long this time &? &PG

In dialogue (I), the husband simply enquires as to how long his mother-in-law wants to stay. In (a2), as against (a1), he picks up the theme of 'Mother wanting to come and stay again', and focuses the precise length in the question rheme. In dialogue (II), he is taken aback by the extended length mentioned by his wife, compared with previous occasions, and hesitates to believe what he has understood her to say. Therefore, he stimulates a confirmation response.

If he wants to add EXPRESSIVE personal concern over having his mother-in-law around the house for an extended period because her previous, shorter visits were already taxing, he uses a *late valley* and may add NEGATIVE IN-TENSIFICATION (see 5.1.2). In version (b2), 'Mother wants to visit us again' is taken up as the theme of the question. Instead of commenting on it, the husband questions the expected length of the stay in an internal rheme with a *high-rising valley* from the rheme accent to the end of the question.

(2) Declarative Structure in STATEMENT *versus* CONFIRMATION QUESTION
Declarative form is to be distinguished from the functions of STATEMENT and CONFIRMATION QUESTION, which state the truth value of a proposition, or stimulate a receiver to confirm it. In German and English, there is a four-fold opposition among *declarative structures*, cutting across the functions of STATEMENT and CONFIRMATION QUESTION, and subcategorising them. The functional reference is determined by context of situation and manifested by prosodic patterns of accent and intonation. The function-form system is organised as follows:

(a)   STATEMENT *in declarative or non-sentential ('elliptic') syntax*

It is a proposition about <ACTIONS>, <EVENTS> and <STATES> in the world of objects and relations. In its non-sentential form, for example in answer to an INFORMATION QUESTION, individual propositional constituents are selected.

(a1)   *In speaker- and fact-oriented* ARGUMENTATION (**FactOri**)

It states a general truth, such as 'two times two is four', or a scientific or historical fact, such as 'Bernoulli's principle is the basis of vocal cord vibration', or 'The Roman Emperor Hadrianus built Hadrian's Wall to protect the northern limit of Britannia', or it makes a proposition in a communicative situation, such as answering a QUESTION asked by another communicator, or stating facts, also following social rituals in *phatic communion* (Malinowski 1923). The exponents are accents on propositional constituents that are to be foregrounded, and *peak* patterns at accents, at least at the last one.

(a2)   *In listener-oriented ARGUMENTATION* (**LISTORI**)

It makes a proposition, called for in a communicative situation, such as answering a QUESTION asked by another communicator. This is achieved with accents on constituents that are to be foregrounded, and with a *low-rising valley* pattern at the last accent to express a subdued attitude towards the receiver. On the other hand, *high pitch* is used to stimulate the receiver to pay attention to the facts and accept them. High pitch is manifested as a *high-rising valley* pattern at the last accent to express SURPRISE (**STIMSUR**), or as a *falling* pattern *in high register* to express IRRITATION (**STIMIRR**).

(b)   CONFIRMATION QUESTION *with the propositional relation* '<CTRUTHX>: proposition' *in declarative or elliptic syntax*

It is an appeal to the dialogue partner for confirmation: it picks up a proposition from a preceding STATEMENT, or deduces it from the common ground in the speaker–listener action field, and stimulates the dialogue partner to confirm its truth value.

(b1)   *asking for confirmation of the truth value*

With a *high-rising valley* pattern at the last accent and *early* synchronisation the speaker makes a MATTER-OF-FACT enquiry, but expresses SURPRISE with *late* synchronisation.

(b2)   *expecting confirmation of the truth value*

With a *peak* pattern *in high register*, the speaker expresses SURPRISE on a scale from listener-directed CONFIRMATION QUESTION to speaker-centred EXCLAMATION; a response is optional. Depending on the dialogue context, QUESTION or EXCLAMATION may be more prominent. To strengthen the QUESTION function the speaker may use *interrogative*, instead of *declarative*, syntax with a *peak* pattern *in high register*

The following two sets of dialogue turns illustrate the association of *declarative* structure with STATEMENTS and CONFIRMATION QUESTIONS, respectively, and further subcategorisations within each. The two sets differ in that, in turn (I), Speaker B answers Speaker A's question in a number of possible distinctive ways, but, in turn (II), Speaker A asks for confirmation of Speaker B's answer to Speaker A's initial question.

A/1:		Wo **&2**ist er denn eigentlich?	
		Where **&2**is he, I wonder?	
(I)	B:		STATEMENT
(Ia1)	**FACTORI**	(Er ist) in **&2^**Rom **&2. &PG**	
		(He is) in **&2^**Rome **&2. &PG**	
	LISTORI	(Er ist) in **&2]/**[Rom **&, &PG**	
		(He is) in **&2]/**[Rome **&, &PG**	

(Ia2)	StimSur	(Er ist) in **&2[**Rom **&? &PG**
		(He is) in **&2[**Rome **&? &PG**
	StimIrr	**&HR** (Er ist) in **&2^**Rom **&2. &PG**
		&HR (He is) in **&2^**Rome **&2. &PG**
(II) A/2:		Confirmation Question
(IIb1)	CQ-2.1a	(Er ist) in **&2]**Rom **&? &PG**
		(He is) in **&2]**Rome **&? &PG**
	CQ-2.1b	(Er ist) in **&2[**Rom **&? &PG**
		(He is) in **&2[**Rome **&? &PG**
(IIb2)	CQ-2.2c	**&HR** (Er ist) in **&2^**Rom **&2. &PG**
		&HR (He is) in **&2^**Rome **&2. &PG**

In turn (Ia1), Speaker B provides the <Place> information fact-oriented with a *peak* pattern (**FactOri**); or listener-oriented with *low-rising valley* patterns (**ListOri**), either *early* to express a casual, or *late* to express a friendly, attitude towards the listener.

In turn (Ia2), Speaker B gives the <Place> information in a stimulating listener-oriented way with high pitch. This high pitch stimulates attention and introduces the expression of Surprise or Irritation at Speaker A asking or not knowing. It is a *late high-rising valley* pattern at the last accent to express Surprise (**StimSur**), e.g. to remind Speaker A: 'Have you forgotten that he told us some time ago?' Or the whole utterance, with a *peak* pattern at the last accent, is in *high register* to express Irritation (**StimIrr**), e.g. telling Speaker A pointedly: 'Everybody knows that and so should you!'

In turn (IIb1), Speaker A signals being open to receiving confirmation or correction (**CQ-2.1**), but, in turn (IIb2), confirmation is taken for granted (**CQ-2.2**), if it is solicited at all in an Exclamation (see 4.2.2.5). StimSur in turn (I) of Speaker B and **CQ-2.1b** in turn (II) of Speaker A coalesce phonetically (see 4.2.2.5).

(3) The System of Confirmation Questions

After delimiting the Question Appeal function of the Confirmation Question in its own right, against the functions of Information Question and Statement, we can now draw up its systemic organisation, and illustrate some of its categories with displays of signal data from German and English. With a Confirmation Question, a speaker picks up the verbalised or deduced theme of a preceding interaction and stimulates the dialogue partner to confirm a propositional constituent in it or its truth value. There are various subtypes, which form the following system:

CQ-1	STIMULATING CONFIRMATION OF PROPOSITIONAL CONSTITUENT
CQ-1a	MATTER-OF-FACT
CQ-1b	EXPRESSION OF SURPRISE
CQ-2	STIMULATING CONFIRMATION OF TRUTH VALUE
CQ-2.1	CONFIRMATION OPEN
CQ-2(.1)a	MATTER-OF-FACT
CQ-2(.1)b	EXPRESSION OF SURPRISE
CQ-2(.2)c	CONFIRMATION EXPECTED

CONFIRMATION QUESTIONS **CQ-1** have already been introduced in the discussion of **IQ-2(.2)c** in 4.2.2.3(2), with reference to German 'Wo?' in Figure 4.3 and to English 'Where?' in Figure 4.4. Figure 4.5 displays additional data for German and English, contrasting MATTER-OF-FACT and EXPRESSION OF SURPRISE in **CQ-1a** and **CQ-1b**.

CQ-1a   *lexical interrogative structure* and *high-rising valley* pattern, starting on the interrogative word with *early* synchronisation for MATTER-OF-FACT STIMULATION
&2]Wo **&? &PG**
&2]Where **&? &PG**

CQ-1b   *late* synchronisation adds the EXPRESSION OF SURPRISE; it may be further heightened by pressed phonation, increased duration, increased F0 rise and increased energy for NEGATIVE INTENSIFICATION (**NI** – see 5.1.2)
(**&NI**) **&2**[Wo **&? &PG**
(**&NI**) **&2**[Where **&? &PG**

CONFIRMATION QUESTIONS **CQ-2** in German and English are illustrated by the following dialogue (adapted from the one discussed in 4.2.2.4(2), and displayed in Figure 4.6:

(I)	B:	Er ist nach **&2**Rom gefahren.
		He has gone to **&2**Rome.
(II)	A/2:	Er ist in **&2**Rom? / Nach **&2**Rom?
		He is in **&2**Rome? / To **&2**Rome?

CQ-2(.1)a   *declarative* or *elliptic syntax* and a *high-rising valley* pattern with *early* synchronisation on the last accent, asking for confirmation of a queried truth value and soliciting an answer

Er ist in **&2**]Rom **&? &PG**   Nach **&2**]Rom **&? &PG**
He is in **&2**]Rome **&? &PG**   To **&2**]Rome **&? &PG**

CQ-2(.1)b   *late* synchronisation for the additional EXPRESSION OF SURPRISE; it may be further heightened for NEGATIVE INTENSIFICATION (**NI**, see 5.1.2)

CQ-1a   NI_CQ-1b

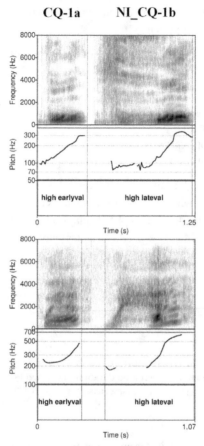

Figure 4.5. Spectrograms, F0 traces (log scale), word segmentations and pitch classifications of German 'Wo?' (upper panel, Standard German, male speaker (KJK)) and English 'Where?' (lower panel, Standard Southern British English, female speaker (RMB)) in CONFIRMATION QUESTIONS **CQ-1a** and **NI_CQ-1a**.

(**&NI**) Er ist in **&2**[Rom **&? &PG**	(**&NI**) Nach **&2**[Rom **&? &PG**
(**&NI**) He is in **&2**[Rome **&? &PG**	(**&NI**) To **&2**[Rome **&? &PG**

CQ-2(.2)c   *peak* pattern *in high register*: the high register signals the question, and the peak pattern in declarative syntax points to the expected confirmation; the

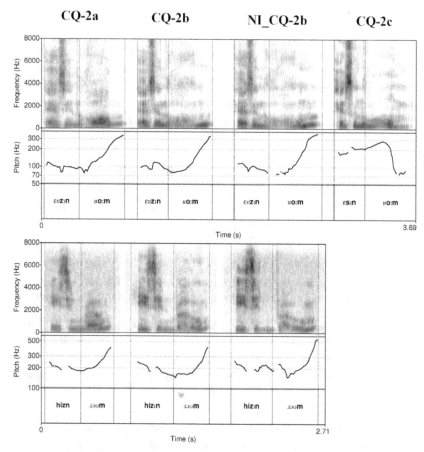

Figure 4.6. Spectrograms, F0 traces (log scale) and segmental transcriptions, grouped into prehead and nucleus of German 'Er ist in Rom?' (upper panel, Standard German, male speaker (KJK)) and English 'He is in Rome?' (lower panel, Standard Southern British English, female speaker (RMB)) in CONFIRMATION QUESTIONS CQ-2a, CQ-2b, NI_ CQ-2b and CQ-2c.

formal devices signal that confirmation of the truth value of what was said previously is taken for granted, and that an answer is optional

&HR Er ist in &2^Rom &2. &PG   &HR Nach &2^Rom &2. &. &PG
&HR He is in &2^Rome &2. &PG   &HR To &2^Rome &2. &. &PG

4.2.2.5   Communicative Function and Linguistic Form in Context of Situation

It can be concluded from the preceding discussion of German and English data that the communicative functions of POLARITY, INFORMATION and CONFIRMATION QUESTIONS, and of STATEMENT and EXCLAMATION are categories of speech interaction that are manifested by overlapping syntactic structures and prosodic patterns. This, in turn, means that the interaction context contributes to the interpretation of an occurring linguistic form as the exponent of a particular function.

In the dialogue of 4.2.2.4(2), utterances **STIMSUR** of Speaker B in turn (I) and **CQ-2.1b** of Speaker A in turn (II) coalesce phonetically, but the former is a STATEMENT in the context after a QUESTION, the latter a CONFIRMATION QUESTION in the context after a STATEMENT. The same applies to utterances **STIMIRR** of Speaker B in turn (I) and **CQ-2.2** of Speaker A in turn (II). When a dialogue is opened by a STATEMENT such as

Ich hab heute **&2^**Post von **&2^**Peter bekommen **&2. &PG** er ist in **&2^**Rom **&2. &PG**
I've received a **&2^**letter from **&2^**Peter today **&2. &PG** he's in **&2^**Rome **&2. &PG**

the response in the form of **CQ-2.2c** is more likely to be intended and interpreted as a SURPRISE EXCLAMATION. However, when *declarative* structure in *high-register* **CQ-2.2c** is replaced by *high-register interrogative* word order the questioning function is strengthened, signalling a SURPRISE CONFIRMATION QUESTION. This applies even more when Speaker A asks back in this form after the original question A/1.

Since **CQ-2** CONFIRMATION QUESTIONS take up a dialogue partner's STATEMENT as a whole and enquire about its truth value, 'He is in Rome?' would only follow the STATEMENT 'He has gone to Italy' if the speaker assumes high probability or even certainty that the person would be in Rome when in Italy. If the speaker wants to get the truth value of more specific <PLACE> information, s/he asks a POLARITY QUESTION 'Is he in Rome?', e.g. **PQ-1b**, **PQ-1c**. Contrariwise, since the LISTENER-ORIENTED POLARITY QUESTION **PQ-2c** stimulates a yes-no decision, it is unlikely to be used when the answer is already in a dialogue partner's previous assertion. So, 'Is he in Rome?' with an *early high-rising valley* may not be expected to follow 'He has gone to Rome.'

But a *late high-rising valley* is quite possible in this context for the EXPRESSION OF SURPRISE, also with NEGATIVE INTENSIFICATION. This is a SURPRISE CONFIRMATION QUESTION in the same form as a POLARITY QUESTION **PQ-2d**. It differs functionally from a *late high-rising valley* with *declarative* *syntax* **CQ-2(.1)b** by strengthening the QUESTION function, whereas the latter strengthens the EXCLAMATION function. *Interrogative syntax* can also occur in the same context with a *peak* pattern *in high register*, asking for CONFIRMA-TION of 'Are you really saying he is in Rome?' (see **CQ-2.2c** above). A *late peak* pattern with *neutral register* in this context is a POLARITY QUESTION **PQ-1d**, in which Speaker A constructs a new proposition 'he is elsewhere' and enquires about the truth value of Speaker B's proposition with UNEXPECTED-NESS and CONTRAST to the new one.

The strengthening of *high pitch* by *raised register* in *peak* patterns or by *high-rising* F0 in *valley* patterns is crucial for signalling CONFIRMATION QUESTIONS. If 'He is in Rome' has a *peak* pattern in a *non-high register* it can no longer be a CONFIRMATION QUESTION and therefore is unlikely to follow a dialogue partner's STATEMENT 'He has gone to Rome', because restating what has already been stated by a dialogue partner is no longer listener-ori-ented but self-reflecting, and is usually reinforced by some such introduction as 'Aha', 'I see'. In English, the CONFIRMATION function may be taken up again by a *constant-polarity question tag* with a *low rise* on the *tag* after a *fall* on the *declarative* 'He is in Rome, is he?' (see 4.2.2.6). Similarly, 'He is in Rome' with an *early* or *late low-rising valley* pattern is a STATEMENT with listener orientation and does not become a CONFIRMATION QUESTION, and so is excluded from the STATEMENT context 'He has gone to Rome', unless a *constant-polarity question tag* follows ('He is in Rome, is he?'), continuing the *rise* of the *declarative* (see 4.2.2.6). Both types of *question tag* add an AP-PEAL to confirm the STATEMENT that the speaker picked up from the dialogue partner.

The use of the same prosodic forms for different functions – QUESTION and STATEMENT, QUESTION and EXCLAMATION – in different verbal and situa-tional contexts, and the exclusion of interrogative forms that violate function in communicative interaction, show that QUESTION, STATEMENT and EXCLAMA-TION cannot be defined by form but need to be referred to functional-semantic categories, which, together with the communicative setting of REPRESENTA-TION, APPEAL and EXPRESSION, determine their phonetic (prosodic and seg-mental) as well as gestural exponency. Bolinger (1978, p. 503f) highlights this function-form relationship and situation dependency:

> It is not by any means certain that 'question' is a grammatical category at all to the extent that it is marked only by intonation. And if it is not, then we need to ask what the intonations mean, independently of any grammatical type. An utterance such as

And ^{he} bel_i*e*_v*es* that.

can be a question, a statement, or an exclamation, depending on context and gesture. But the intonation is just as conclusive one way or another. As a question the sentence is incurious, it probably calls for confirmation of what is already assumed. With fuller descriptions, we may find the same variety prevailing everywhere. (Cf. also Bolinger (1989), chapter 5, questions, 6. Nonquestions.)

In this communicative function-form frame, QUESTION and STATEMENT are defined as semantic propositions in the speaker–listener interaction. They are either made as propositions about objects and factual relations in STATE-MENTS, or their truth value or a propositional component is enquired about in QUESTIONS. In the case of a QUESTION, the speaker may either make a new proposition or refer to one already introduced as valid in the communicative interaction, asking for confirmation. The former is a POLARITY or an INFOR-MATION QUESTION, the latter a CONFIRMATION QUESTION. Instead of refer-ring to a proposition made by a communicative partner in the interaction, the speaker may refer to a presupposition of common ground for both speaker and listener. For example, in a long discussion on prosodic matters between Speak-ers A and B, A may feel like having a break: he looks at his watch, realises that it is coffee time, and assumes that B feels the same way and also knows that it is coffee time. A may then ask the CONFIRMATION QUESTION, 'We'll have a coffee break now (, shall we)?' [Wir machen jetzt 'ne Kaffeepause (,ja)?] with a *high-rising early valley.* Or, B looks at his watch, and A interprets it as B wanting a break and so, assuming that they both know it is coffee time, asks the same CONFIRMATION QUESTION. On the other hand, when A is paying no attention to common ground and feels concentration is flagging, s/he may set a new proposition by asking the POLARITY QUESTION, 'Shall we have a coffee break?' [Machen wir mal 'ne Kaffeepause?] with either a *high-rising early valley* for an open decision, or with a *medial peak* expecting agreement.

This shows that a CONFIRMATION QUESTION is not just triggered by the availability of a proposition made by another person or implied in the common ground of the communicative situation, but also by the speaker's decision to pick it up and have it confirmed. There is the possibility of the speaker just using the proposition as a trigger not to have it confirmed but to enquire about its *independent* truth value. Thus, the speaker may ask a POLARITY QUESTION in a situation that looks like a CONFIRMATION QUESTION context when the speaker's decision-taking is excluded. The speaker is free to *passively* refer to observed signals in common ground for a communicative act, or to *actively* construct a new proposition, i.e. to ask either a CONFIRMATION QUESTION ('Is that so? Please confirm') or a POLARITY QUESTION ('Is that so? Think about it again!') in the same context of situation. The latter is dissociated from the other person's action and may therefore be regarded as less polite. So it may be inappropriate because the speaker either accidentally or deliberately infringes a social code. This view takes degrees of freedom in interaction into account for the shaping of linguistic form by communicative function.

A nice example illustrating the speaker's passive or active role in the two types of question comes from Wes Anderson's film *The Grand Budapest Hotel*. In a breakfast-table scene between Madame D., one of the elderly, female, very rich and upper-class but insecure clientele, and M. Gustave, the hotel's concierge, the original English screenplay gives the following dialogue:

> M. GUSTAVE: Dear God. What've you done to your fingernails?
> This diabolical varnish. The color's completely wrong.
> MADAME D: Really? You don't like it?

The two successive CONFIRMATION QUESTIONS are realised as 'You really don't like it?' with high-register falling intonation by English actress Tilda Swinton in the original English version, accompanied by her examining her hands. The English sound version on DVD is also supplied with English subtitles, which render the question as 'Don't you like it?' It would have to be sounded either as falling pitch in high register or as high-rising pitch to fit the situation. It is no longer a passive CONFIRMATION but an active POLARITY QUESTION, which is out of keeping with the subdued-dominant relationship that the film wants to depict between the woman and the man.

Freedom of interrogative form selection is exemplified by the following dialogue interchanges in English and German (cf. the data collection of Mandarin Chinese in 6.1.2):

A:	He &1^wants to go to the &1. &2^beach &2. &PG
	Er &1^will zum &1. &2^Strand &2. &PG
B/1:	He &1^wants to go to the &1. &2]beach &? &PG
	Er &1^will zum &1. &2]Strand &2? &PG
continued with	B/2a:	(Does) &2^not (want to go) to the &2. &2]zoo &? &PG
		(Will) &2^nicht zum &2. &2] Zoo &? &PG
or followed by	B/2b:	&2^Doesn't he want to go the &1. &2(zoo &2. &PG
		&2^Will er nicht zum &1. &2(Zoo &2. &PG

The two *declarative* forms with *high-rising early valley* in B/1 and B/2a combine to one CONFIRMATION QUESTION, querying A's proposition and asking to confirm its negation. But when *interrogative* B/2b follows *declarative* B/1, there are two utterances. The first is an exclamatory Surprise Confirmation Question referring to A's proposition; the second changes this proposition to B's own new one 'He wants to go to the zoo' and, in a *late peak* pattern, asks about its truth value with Unexpectedness of, and Contrast to, A's proposition. So it is a Polarity Question. B/1 and B/2a most probably follow each other without a pause, or with just a short one, whereas some pausing is highly likely between B/1 and B/2b.

After A's Statement, the *interrogative* form

> B/1'   Does he **&2**^want to go to the **&1. &2**^beach **&2. &PG**
> **&2**^Will er zum **&1. &2**^Strand **&2. &PG**

with accents on both 'want' [will] and 'beach' [Strand] would be situationally inappropriate because it has just been stated by A 'He wants to go to the beach.' So only the *declarative* Confirmation Question is possible. But if B changes A's proposition from 'He wants to go to the beach' to the new proposition 'He doesn't want to go to the beach', B may enquire about its truth value in the Polarity Question

> B/2c: **&2**[does he (really) want to go to beach **&? &PG**
> **&2**[Will er (wirklich) zum Strand **&? &PG**

with focus accent on the first word, and no further accent.

Thus, both Question functions can occur in the same context of situation, depending on how the speaker constructs the communicative interaction in this context. In speech communication, speakers mould the interchange by introducing their perspectives at any point, either making a new proposition or referring to someone else's proposition or to a presupposition in the speaker–listener common ground. Reference to propositions and presuppositions in Confirmation Questions is by default made in the syntactic structure of Statements, thus expressing what is set as valid. Deviations from *declarative* to *interrogative* structure in Confirmation Questions strengthens the Question over the Exclamation function under Surprise conditions with specific prosodic patterns.

It has already been pointed out in 4.2.2.2(1) that *elliptic interrogatives* are another formal device to be considered in the discussion of Question functions by leading to the formal coincidence of Polarity with Confirmation Questions in different situational settings. This may be illustrated by the following two examples from English, which have exact German equivalents:

(I)   (a)   At a business meeting, an assistant goes round with a coffee jug asking '(Cup of) coffee?' *high rising* with *early valley*. This is a POLARITY QUESTION ellipsis of 'Would you like a cup of coffee?'

        (b)   In a café, a customer who has already had a cup of coffee takes his empty cup to the counter to get a refill. The person behind the counter, realising that the customer wants another cup of coffee says 'Cup of coffee?' with *high-rising early valley*. This is now a CONFIRMATION QUESTION ellipsis of 'You want a cup of coffee?'

(a) and (b) may be formally identical. However, each will be properly understood as one or the other functionally in their respective situational contexts. In (b) an alternative is possible – falling pitch in high register, which is excluded from (a).

(II)   A1:   'It must have been an insider who passed the information on to the press.'

        B: '[Could it be] Ronald Smith?' – *late valley high-rising* POLARITY QUESTION ellipsis

        A2:   'Ronald Smith?' – *late valley high-rising* SURPRISE CONFIRMATION QUESTION

The two forms may be identical, but their functions are different and are decoded as such in the different contexts. CONFIRMATION QUESTION A2 may also be falling in high register, expecting agreement; this form is impossible in POLARITY QUESTION B.

For successful communication the listener has to take all the syntactic, lexical, prosodic and gestural forms in their situational setting into account, since there is no one-to-one correspondence singly between any of these and communicative functions. POLARITY QUESTIONS commonly have *interrogative syntax*, and *interrogative syntax* commonly codes POLARITY QUESTIONS; CONFIRMATION QUESTIONS commonly have *declarative syntax*, and *declarative syntax* commonly codes CONFIRMATION QUESTIONS. But, due to ellipsis, *non-interrogative* form can also code POLARITY QUESTIONS, and in order to strengthen the QUESTION over the EXCLAMATION function *interrogative* form can also code CONFIRMATION QUESTIONS. Since, in addition, both question functions can occur in the same context of situation if speakers construct one or the other in it, listeners need to globally assess the total formal and situational embedding to decide which function is communicatively relevant at any moment, and they generally tune in very acutely.

4.2.2.6   Theme-Rheme Questions: *Tag Questions* in English and *Modal Particles* in German

It was pointed out in the discussion of English Confirmation Questions in 4.2.2.5 that the request of confirmation may be strengthened by the addition of a *constant-polarity question tag* in the rising pitch movement of the repeated assertion: 'He is in Rome, is he?' The tag 'reinforces verbally the questioning intonation' (O'Connor 1955, p. 102). Neither a peak pattern on the tag nor a reversed polarity of the tag would be possible in this Confirmation Question context. 'The [constant-polarity] tag question refers back to a fact already and recently established *by the listener*, whereas it is precisely the listener's view the reversed tag question seeks to elicit ... This difference of background explains why it is impossible with the [constant-polarity] tag question to have the pitch pattern of fall plus fall except with a violent disjunction' (p. 102); 'a falling tone would demand agreement from the listener, but demanding agreement when the listener has already himself presented the information is pragmatically inappropriate' (Cruttenden 1997, p. 98). The *reversed-polarity question tag* 'He is in Rome, isn't he?' does not refer back to a dialogue partner's proposition; rather, the speaker makes a new one of his/her own, and asks for its truth value with a tag. This Polarity Question either prejudges agreement, with falls on both the declarative structure and the tag (O'Connor 1955, p. 98), or expresses increasing doubt as to the truth value of the declarative, with a low or high rise on the tag (p. 99), thus leaving the answer open in 'a normal conducive question' (Bolinger 1986, p. 389).

The functions of Questions *with declarative syntax + tag* differ from those of the Confirmation Question ('He is in Rome?') and of the Polarity Question ('Is he in Rome?') discussed so far, in that they set a proposition in a Statement Theme and then either ask for confirmation or enquire about the truth value of the Theme in a Question Rheme. English *tag questions* are an ordered formal system of *constant versus reversed-polarity* syntactic structures and a set of *falling* or *rising pitch* patterns as the exponents of a fine-grained set of communicative functions in speech interaction. This function-form system is particularly characteristic of spontaneous English dialogue in England. With constant polarity (I), the speaker makes a proposition referring to the receiver's previous speech action (the Statement Theme) and asks the receiver for Confirmation (the Question Rheme). This is the Theme-Rheme Confirmation Question. Its proposition may be of two different kinds, (a) or (b):

(I)   (a)   The speaker picks up a preceding proposition from the receiver:

         (1)   'He's gone to Rome.'
              'He's in Rome, is he?' *(falling or rising declarative, rising tag)*

      (b)   The speaker deduces a proposition from the receiver's preceding actions, including gestures and facial expression:

         (2)   The receiver looks washed out on returning from jogging.
              'You've overdone it again, have you?' *(falling or rising declarative, rising tag)*

         (3)   Father and 10-year-old son are working in the garden. The son picks up a bag of garden refuse and says 'Oof.'
              Father: 'It's heavy, is it?' *(falling or rising declarative, rising tag)*
              Father did not know that the bag was heavy.

         (4)   Speaker A: 'We have not heard anything from Claudia for some time. I wonder how she's getting on. We should get in touch with her.'
              Speaker B: 'I'll send her an e-mail, shall I?' *(falling or rising declarative, rising tag)*

Speaker B makes a proposition to act in response to Speaker A's proposition, either as a categorical STATEMENT with *falling intonation* or as a receiver-oriented one with *rising intonation*. With the *constant-polarity question tag*, the proposition becomes a CONFIRMATION QUESTION APPEAL: 'Do you agree with my proposition?'

With reversed polarity (II), the sender makes a new proposition in a sender-receiver action field and asks for a POLARITY DECISION. This is the THEME-RHEME POLARITY QUESTION:

(II)   (5)   'He's gone to Italy.'
              'He's in Rome, isn't he?' *(falling declarative, falling tag)*
              The speaker is certain that the proposition 'He is in Rome' is true.

         (6)   'He's gone to Italy.'
              'He isn't in Rome, is he?' *(falling declarative, rising tag)*
              The speaker assumes that the proposition 'He is not in Rome' may be true but is not sure.

         (7)   The jogger looks worse for wear.
              'You've overdone it, haven't you?' *(falling declarative, falling tag)*
              The speaker expects the reply 'Yes, I have.'

         (8)   Son lifting the bag: 'Oof.'
              Father: 'It's heavy, isn't it?' *(falling declarative, falling tag)*
              The father knew that the bag was heavy, and he is certain that his interpretation of his son's expression is true.

In a THEME-RHEME QUESTION the speaker turns a listener-related propositional theme into an explicit STATEMENT for truth evaluation in a QUESTION rheme. THEME-RHEME QUESTIONS are integrated, as ENQUIRING STATEMENTS, into a system of <TRUTH> propositions beside STATEMENTS, POLARITY QUESTIONS and CONFIRMATION QUESTIONS.

The POLARITY QUESTIONS 'Is he in Rome?' / 'Have you overdone it again?' / 'Is it heavy?' / 'Shall I send her an e-mail?' have the propositional representation:

> <TRUTHX>: proposition (p)
> He's in Rome. / You have overdone it again. / It's heavy. / I shall send her an e-mail.

The speaker solicits a POLARITY DECISION <TRUTHX> on the proposition (p).

The CONFIRMATION QUESTIONS 'He's in Rome?' / 'You have overdone it again?' / 'It's heavy?' / 'I shall send her an e-mail?' (*high-rising*) have the propositional representation:

> <CTRUTHX>: proposition (p)
> He's in Rome. / You have overdone it again. / It's heavy. / I shall send her an e-mail.

The speaker asks for CONFIRMATION <CTRUTHX> of the proposition (p) picked up from the receiver. This introduces an element of STATEMENT into the QUESTION.

The THEME-RHEME CONFIRMATION QUESTIONS (1), (2), (3), (4) have the propositional representation:

> proposition (p): <CTRUTHX>
> (1) / (2) / (3) / (4)

The recipient has signalled a proposition (p), which the speaker presents as a STATEMENT for CONFIRMATION <CTRUTHX>. The QUESTION function is weakened further in comparison with the CONFIRMATION QUESTION, resulting in an ENQUIRING STATEMENT.

The THEME-RHEME POLARITY QUESTIONS (5), (6), (7), (8) have the propositional representation:

> proposition (p): <TRUTHX>
> (5) / (6) / (7) / (8)

The speaker makes a proposition (p) as a STATEMENT THEME and solicits a POLARITY DECISION <TRUTHX> on it in a QUESTION RHEME, expecting agreement with the truth value of the STATEMENT in the *falling-falling* pattern, but expressing doubt in the *falling-rising* pattern. These are ENQUIRING

STATEMENTS. With the *falling-falling* pattern the THEME-RHEME POLARITY QUESTION comes closest to a STATEMENT.

In German, a very complex system of *modal particles* with intonation patterns is used to cover some of the functions of English *question tags*. The particles establish the link to the preceding dialogue turn and signal the communicative transition from PROPOSITIONAL REPRESENTATION to QUESTION APPEAL derived from it. Without the particles, the utterances are either STATEMENTS or CONFIRMATION QUESTIONS, depending on intonation. The division into STATEMENT theme and QUESTION rheme is not systematically and sequentially organised as it is in English, but it is still there. The *modal particles* take over the QUESTION RHEME function. Here are possible equivalents of the eight English examples discussed above:

(1) 'Er ist in Rom, **ja**?' *(falling declarative, rising modal particle)*

(2) 'Du hast dich **wohl** wieder übernommen (, ja)?' *(falling declarative, including modal particle (+ rising modal particle))*

(3) 'Der Sack ist schwer, **ja**?' *(falling declarative, rising modal particle)*
     'Ist der Sack **etwa** schwer?' *(falling or rising interrogative, including modal particle)*

     'The sack is not heavy, is it?' *(falling declarative, rising modal particle)* may be rendered by 'Der Sack ist **doch** nicht (**etwa**) schwer (,**oder**)?' *(falling declarative, including modal particles (+ rising modal particle))*

(4) 'Ich schick ihr **dann mal** 'ne Email (, ja)?' *(falling or rising declarative, including modal particles (+ separate or continuing rising modal particle))*

(5) 'Er ist in Rom, **nicht (wahr)**?' *(falling declarative, rising modal particle)*

(6) 'Er ist **doch** nicht **etwa** in Rom (, **oder**)?' *(falling or rising declarative, including modal particles (+ rising modal particle))*

(7) 'Du hast dich übernommen, **nicht (wahr)**?' *(falling declarative, rising modal particle)*

(8) 'Der Sack ist schwer, **nicht (wahr)**?' *(falling declarative, rising modal particle)*

The correspondences between the systems of English *question tags* and German *modal particles* are only approximate because the *modal particles* introduce further interaction aspects that are absent from *tag questions*. For further detail, see Kohler (1978).

The account of *tag questions* given here relates their formal system to their communicative functions in speech interaction, a perspective that is absent from a recent corpus analysis (Dehé and Braun 2013). The factors tested in this study were:

> polarity, position in the sentence and the turn as well as verb type. Generally, prosodic phrasing and intonational realization were highly correlated: separate QTs were mostly realized with a falling contour, while integrated QTs were mostly rising. Results from regression models showed a strong effect of polarity: QTs with an opposite polarity were more often phrased separately compared to QTs with constant polarity, but the phrasing of opposite polarity QTs was further dependent on whether the QT was negative or positive (more separate phrasing in negative QTs). Furthermore, prosodic separation was more frequent at the end of syntactic phrases and clauses compared to phrase-medial QTs. At the end of a turn, speakers realized more rising contours compared to QTs within a speaker's turn. Verb type also had an effect on the phrasing of the tag. Taken together, our results confirm some of the claims previously held for QTs, while others are modified and new findings are added. (Dehé and Braun 2013, p. 129)

It may be of some interest to learn something about the distribution of these formal patterns in a fairly limited corpus, but they do not tell us anything about the functional conditions of their occurrence in dialogue interaction, and the authors do not even cite O'Connor's (1955) seminal paper on the subject, which gives all the basics on the strength of acute phonetic and semantic observation. The 2013 investigation simply follows the mainstream paradigm of doing linguistic and prosodic corpus research: it is fixed on form and frequency without semantic anchoring in speech communication.

4.2.2.7   QUESTION QUOTES

With a (THEME-RHEME) CONFIRMATION QUESTION a speaker repeats a proposition or a semantic constituent of a proposition which has been established through communicative interaction and wants to have it confirmed. This differs from another type of interrogativity: the repetition of an immediately preceding question that was asked either (1) by the same speaker or (2) by another speaker. In (1), the speaker's *own* original enquiry is not answered, due to transmission problems or because of incredulity; the other speaker asks for repetition instead; in (2), the speaker repeats the *other* speaker's original enquiry as a theme for a rheme comment. These are QUESTION QUOTES, which pick up any type of QUESTION APPEAL – POLARITY, INFORMATION, CONFIRMATION QUESTION – and report its propositional content. They are no longer QUESTIONS, as defined here, because they lack the APPEAL function. In (1), they transmit the content of the original enquiry and may be paraphrased by introducing them with 'I'm asking ...' or 'I asked ...'. In (2), they set the theme for a reflective or an exclamatory STATEMENT from the speaker; they may be paraphrased by introducing them with 'You're asking ...'

In German QUESTION QUOTES of both contextual types, a special interrogative form of an indirect question is used, with the inflected verb in final position in subsidiary clause structure that is introduced either by the subordinate conjunction 'ob' to report on a proposition enquiry or by a lexical interrogative in the case of a propositional constituent. These stand-alone interrogative forms are derived from the syntactic structures introduced by 'Du fragst / Ich fragte, ob / wo, wann...'. Since word order is identical in main and subsidiary clauses in English, QUESTION QUOTES cannot have a special interrogative form in the same way, but fall back on word order or lexical interrogative syntax, as in POLARITY or INFORMATION QUESTIONS, unless the speaker introduces type (2) with 'You're asking ... '. But there are also prosodic features that can mark QUESTION QUOTES in both languages. For a start, stimulating rising intonation patterns of preceding questions are replaced by fact-oriented falling ones in the content-reporting repeats in both types (1) and (2) and in both languages (cf. the discussion of Fries 1964 in 4.2.2.1). This is the formal exponent that distinguishes a QUESTION QUOTE from a QUESTION APPEAL. It represents a communicative act that is centred reflexively on the speaker: type (1) is a repetition of what the speaker has said, type (2) sets the theme for the speaker's comment. This differs from the listener-directed APPEAL. The listener knows from context that the speaker is repeating question content and is not sending a QUESTION APPEAL.

In type (1), the speaker may want to make sure that the content of the question, which was missed, gets across to the dialogue partner the second time: high register and increased loudness serve this communicative function. In type (2), on the other hand, the repeat either becomes a reflective STATEMENT to oneself, spoken in low register and with reduced loudness, because the speaker is uncertain and verbalises it by adding a phrase such as 'I have not decided yet.' Or the repeat becomes an EXCLAMATION in high register and with increased loudness, because the speaker is absolutely certain and expresses it emphatically by adding a phrase such as 'Of course!', 'On no account!'

The following examples illustrate the use of QUESTION QUOTES in German and English, picking up POLARITY, INFORMATION or CONFIRMATION QUESTIONS in the situational contexts (1) and (2). Since a QUESTION QUOTE only reports content it does not preserve the characteristic communicative reference of a CONFIRMATION QUESTION to a preceding STATEMENT, for example in dialogue type (1) B/1-B/2 below:

(1)   A telephone conversation between an employee and his boss.

A/1a: Das müssen wir noch eingehend besprechen. Kommen Sie doch morgen früh um 8 in mein Büro.
We need to discuss this more thoroughly. Would you like to come to my office at 8 tomorrow morning.

A/1b: Das müssen wir noch eingehend besprechen. Kommen Sie doch morgen früh in mein Büro.
We need to discuss this more thoroughly. Would you like to come to my office tomorrow morning.

B/1a: POLARITY QUESTION
&2^Könnte es ein &1. &2^ bisschen &2. &2]später sein &? &PG
&2^Could it be a &1. &2^ little &2. &2]later &? &PG

CONFIRMATION QUESTION
&2[Welche Zeit schlagen Sie vor &? &PG
&2[What time are you suggesting &?&PG

B/1b: INFORMATION QUESTION
Welche &2^Zeit schlagen Sie vor &2. &PG
What &2^time are you suggesting &2. &PG

A/2:   (noise disturbance)
POLARITY QUESTION
&2^Was meinten Sie &., &PG
&2^What did you say &., &PG

B/2:   QUESTION QUOTES
of B/1a POLARITY QUESTION
&HR Ob es ein &2^ bisschen &0. &2^später sein könnte &2. &PG
(I'm &2^asking &1. &PG) &HR Could it be a &2^ little &0. &2^later &2. &PG
of B/1a CONFIRMATION QUESTION or B/1b POLARITY QUESTION
&HR welche &2^Zeit Sie vorschlagen &2. &PG
(I'm &2^asking &1. &PG) &HR what &2^time are you suggesting &2. &PG

(2)   A: POLARITY QUESTION
Machst du &2^dieses Jahr wieder &1. &2^Urlaub in &1. &2^It'alien &2. &PG
Will you be spending your &2^holiday in &1. &2^Italy again &2. &1^this year &2. &PG

INFORMATION QUESTION

&2^Wo machst du **&1. &2**^dieses Jahr **&1. &2**^Urlaub **&2. &PG**
&2^Where will you be going for your **&1. &2**^holiday this year
&2. &PG

B: QUESTION QUOTES

&LR Ob ich **&2**^dieses Jahr wieder **&0. &2**-Urlaub in **&0.**
&2^It'alien mache **&2. &PG** Das **&2**^weiß ich noch nicht **&2. &PG**
&LR Will I be spending my **&2**^holiday in **&0. &2**^Italy again this
year **&2. &PG** I don't **&2**^know yet **&2. &PG**

&HR Ob ich **&2**^dieses Jahr wieder **&0. &2**-Urlaub in **&0.**
&2^It'alien mache **&2. &HR &3**^Natürlich **&2. &PG** / **&HR** Auf
&3^keinen **&0. &2**^Fall **&2. &PG**
&HR Will I be spending my **&2**^holiday in **&0. &2**^Italy again
this year **&2. &PG &HR** Of **&3**^course I will **&2. &PG** / **&HR**
&3^Certainly **&0. &2**^not **&2. &PG**

&LR &2^Wo ich **&0. &2**-dieses Jahr **&0. &2**^Urlaub mache **&2.**
&PG Mal **&2**^sehen **&2. &PG**
&LR &2^Where will I be going for my **&0. &2**^holiday this year
&2. &PG We'll **&2**^see **&2. &PG**

&HR &2^Wo ich **&0. &2**-dieses Jahr **&0. &2**^Urlaub mache **&2.**
&PG &HR &3^Keine **&0. &2**^Ahnung **&2. &PG**
&LR &2^Where will I be going for my **&0. &2**^holiday this year
&2. &PG &3^No **&0. &2**^idea **&2. &PG**

Speaker B's long QUESTION QUOTE 'Ob ...' and affirmative comment in
(2) may be reduced to the short reinforced affirmative EXCLAMATION 'Und
&3^ob **&2. &PG**'. This shows the relationship between type (2) QUESTION
QUOTES and EXCLAMATIONS. Since 'ob' repeats are reflexively centred on the
speaker, the syntactic structure may also be used for stand-alone deliberative
STATEMENTS of the type 'I wonder if ...'. For example:

Ob **&2**^Helga darüber wohl **&1. &2**^Besch'eid weiß **&2. &PG**
I **&2**^wonder if **&1. &2**^Helga **&0. &2**^knows about this **&2. &PG**

Ob ich **&2**^diesmal vielleicht **&1. &2**^mehr Glück habe **&2. &PG**
I **&2**^wonder if I'll have **&1. &2**^better luck **&0. &2**^this time **&2. &PG**

With utterances like these, the speaker does not send an APPEAL to a listener
for a verbal response concerning their <TRUTH> value. Therefore, they are not
QUESTIONS, as defined here.

4.3   The Request and Command Appeals

When, instead of soliciting a communicative response to a Question, a speaker appeals to a listener to carry out some action, this Appeal varies along a scale from Request to Command, depending on the speaker's considerate or dominant attitude towards the listener. The scale is continuous rather than discrete, ranging from a very polite, subdued Request to a forceful, expressively heightened Command. The recipient may or may not perform the requested or ordered action, and may accompany or replace it by a communicative response, in an apology for having failed to act, or in a rude refusal to act. Both Appeals use *interrogative, imperative,* or even *declarative,* syntax, with the addition of *positive* or *negative lexical intensifiers, question tags* or *modal particles, rising* or *falling pitch,* and *modal/breathy-voice* or *pressed phonation. Interrogative* syntax, *rising pitch* and *breathy-voice phonation* are indices of Request; *imperative* and *declarative* syntax, *falling pitch, overaccentuation* on every syntactic component or even word and *pressed phonation* are indices of Command. The more of the features in each group are bundled in an utterance, the more the Request or Command Appeal gets strengthened. High-rising pitch has greater stimulatory force than low-rising pitch in the Request Appeal, and an early peak as against a medial one strengthens the Command Appeal. The combination of an *imperative* with a *question tag* in English may have a *single rise* starting in the *imperative* phrase, or a *fall* ending the *imperative* phrase and a *partially deaccented rise* in the question tag. The single rise is more requesting than the fall + rise (see O'Connor 1955).

The following examples from German and English illustrate the functional scale and the use of the syntactic, lexical and prosodic means:

Request with decreasing semantic strength

interrogative
> Wärst du (bitte) so gut, die **&2**[Tür zuzumachen **&?/, &PG**
> Wärst du (bitte) so gut, die **&2^/)**Tür zuzumachen **&2. &PG**
> Would you mind shutting the **&2**[door (, please) **&?/, &PG**
> Would you mind shutting the **&2^/)**door (, please) **&?/, &PG**

> Würdest du (bitte) / Könntest/Kannst du (bitte) die **&2**[Tür zumachen **&?/, &PG**
> Würdest du (bitte) / Könntest/Kannst du (bitte) die **&2^/)**Tür zumachen **&2. &PG**
> Would/Could/Can you shut the **&2**[door (please) **&?/, &PG**
> Would Could/Can you shut the **&2^/)**door (please) **&?/, &PG**

imperative
> Sei so gut und mach die **&2**[Tür zu **&?/, &PG**
> Sei so gut und mach die **&2^/)**Tür zu **&2. &PG**

Be so good and shut the **&2**[door will you **&**, **&PG**
Be so good and shut the **&2^/**)door **&2**. **&1**[will you **&**, **&PG**

Mach bitte die **&2**[Tür zu **&?/**, **&PG**
Mach bitte die **&2^/**)Tür zu **&2**. **&PG**
Shut the **&2**[door please **&**, **&PG**
Shut the **&2^/**)door please **&2**. **&PG**

COMMAND with increasing semantic strength
imperative
Mach die **&2^/**)Tür zu **&2**. **&PG**
Shut the **&2^/**)door **&2**. **&PG**

Mach **&2^**endlich die **&0**. **&2^**Tür zu **&2**. **&PG**
&2^Do **&1**. **&2^**shut that **&0**. **&2^**door **&2**. **&PG**

interrogative
Machst du **&2^**endlich die **&0**. **&2^**Tür zu **&2**. **&PG**
&2^Will you **&1**. **&2^**shut that **&0**. **&2^**door **&2**. **&PG**

Bist du **&2^**endlich **&0**. **&2^**fertig **&2**. **&PG**
Are you **&2^**going to be much **&0**. **&2^**longer **&2**. **&PG**

imperative with lexical and accentual intensification
&2^Mach **&1**. **&2^**die **&1**. **&2^**Tür **&2**. **&1^**zu' **&2**. **&PG**
&2^Will **&1**. **&2^**you **&1**. **&2^**shut **&2**. **&2^**that **&1**. **&2^**door **&2**. **&PG**

&2^verflucht noch mal **&2**. **&PG** **&2^**mach die **&0**. **&2^**Tür zu **&2**. **&PG**
&2^damn it **&2**. **&PG** **&2^**shut the **&0**. **&2^**door **&2**. **&PG**

declarative with accentual intensification
&2^Du **&2**. **&2^**machst **&2**. **&2^**jetzt die **&2**. **&2^**Tür **&2**. **&1^**zu **&2**. **&PG**
&2^You 2. **&2^**are 2. **&2^**going to 2. **&2^**shut that 2. **&2^**door 2. **&2^**now 2.
&PG

On the basis of this preliminary function-form data classification, future research can devise experiments to investigate the semantic scaling of REQUEST and COMMAND in relation to formal bundles of syntax, lexicon and prosody, using the Semantic Differential Technique, for example.

5 The EXPRESSION Function

The EXPRESSION function was introduced as overlay on the REPRESENTATION and APPEAL functions in Chapters 3 and 4. This chapter develops it further in two directions, by introducing the concepts of (1) the speaker's EXPRESSIVE EVALUATION of communicative action, graded along a LOW-TO-HIGH KEY scale, and (2) SPEAKER ATTITUDES TOWARDS THE LISTENER along a scale from AUTHORITY to SUBORDINATION.

EXPRESSIVE EVALUATION is distinguished from INFORMATION WEIGHTING in the REPRESENTATION function, i.e. the REFERENTIAL LOW-TO-HIGH KEY (see 3.2). The upper end of the EXPRESSIVE LOW-TO-HIGH KEY scale is usually referred to as 'emphasis', with a broad spectrum of different meanings given to the term, in many cases suggesting a binary opposition 'emphatic – non-emphatic'. The scale character may be illustrated with the grading of 'I do not know' from a highly reduced mumbled aside to an insisting proposition with an accent on each word. The LOW KEY end is the expression of the speaker's detachment from the communicative situation; the HIGH KEY end is the expressive reinforcement of points of ARGUMENTATION referring to the factual world. This ARGUMENTATIVE HIGH KEY for ARGUMENTATIVE REINFORCEMENT differs from the EMOTIVE HIGH KEY for EMOTIVE INTENSIFICATION. EMOTIVE HIGH KEY may be NEGATIVE, for example when 'I do not know' expresses exasperation at a person's persistent asking. In addition to overaccentuation, it has greatly increased overall acoustic energy, as well as pressed phonation associated with each accent, i.e. tense laryngeal action oscillating between breathiness, creak and tense voice (see Catford 1964). EMOTIVE HIGH KEY may also be POSITIVE, for example in an exuberantly apologising 'I don't know' with two accents, on 'don't' and 'know', modal voice and expanded as well as slowly falling pitch spanning the two accents.

Besides being an overlay on the REPRESENTATION function, EXPRESSIVE EVALUATION is also typically used as an overlay on the APPEAL function, for NEGATIVE INTENSIFICATION in COMMANDS or in SURPRISE CONFIRMATION QUESTIONS, and for POSITIVE INTENSIFICATION in REQUESTS. An exasperated

'Shut the door!', with F0 peak accents, increased acoustic energy and pressed phonation on each word, or an indignant query 'Where?!', with considerable lengthening of a high-rise valley accent and pressed phonation, which starts tense-breathy and then changes into tense voicing, illustrate the former (cf. 4.3; 4.2.2.4 (3)). An exuberantly polite 'Would you mind shutting the door, please?' with modal voice, and time and frequency expansion of a falling-rising pitch pattern across the utterance, illustrates the latter (cf. 4.3).

The distinction between INFORMATION WEIGHTING and EXPRESSIVE EVALUATION was already recognised by Armstrong and Ward (1931) and Coustenoble and Armstrong (1934). They differentiated two main categories of 'emphasis': (1) special prominence which a speaker gives to certain words for rational focus and contrast to what has been said; (2) special prominence to amplify the meaning of words and to express a particularly great degree of what they imply. The former was called *emphasis for contrast*, the latter *emphasis for intensity*, picking up a distinction made previously by Coleman (1914). The difference was illustrated with the example 'There's an enormous improvement.' Contrasting the word 'enormous', for example to a preceding utterance 'There was very little improvement', results in a focus on the word, with a high pitch fall on the only accented syllable '-nor-'. *Contrast* is scaled by different ranges of the fall. *Intensity* on the same word produces an upward pitch glide with levelling out on '-nor-', followed by a gradual descent on the subsequent syllables and a nuclear accent on '-prove-'; there is also greater acoustic energy and lengthening of the accented-syllable onset. However, the two types of 'emphasis' do not take the difference between ARGUMENTATIVE and EMOTIVE HIGH KEY, or between NEGATIVE and POSITIVE INTENSIFICA-TION, into account, and the concept of 'emphasis' cuts off the low end of a LOW-TO-HIGH KEY scale altogether. An 'emphasis' framework was first presented by Kohler (2006a) , experimentally supported by Kohler and Niebuhr (2007) and expanded by Niebuhr (2010). The semantically multifarious and opaque term 'emphasis' has now been replaced by a systematic terminology of INFORMATION WEIGHTING and EXPRESSIVE EVALUATION subcategorised into ARGUMENTATIVE REINFORCEMENT and EMOTIVE NEGATIVE or POSITIVE INTENSIFICATION for a functional network within the *Organon Model*.

The functions of EXPRESSIVE EVALUATION are manifested by formal bundles of graded prosodic features – pitch, acoustic energy, phonation – as well as graded articulatory space-time trajectories in sequences of opening-closing gestures. A formal scale from *reduced* to *elaborated* has already been introduced as one of the exponents of INFORMATION WEIGHTING (see 3.2), but its range is greatly extended at both ends in EXPRESSIVE EVALUATION. A comprehensive investigation of the prosodic and segmental manifestations in EXPRESSIVE LOW-to-HIGH KEY, even just for German and English, is still waiting to be done. The following sections focus on representative examples for the different functions of EXPRESSIVE EVALUATION from these two languages. Section 5.1 deals with EXPRESSIVE HIGH KEY in ARGUMENTATIVE REINFORCEMENT and in NEGATIVE as well as POSITIVE INTENSIFICATION; Section 5.2 relates the *reduced-elaborated* articulation scale to the EXPRESSIVE LOW-TO-HIGH scale; Section 5.3 proposes some postulates for research into EXPRESSIVE EVALUATION in human language; Section 5.4 says a few words about SPEAKER ATTITUDES TOWARDS THE LISTENER.

5.1   From NEUTRAL to EXPRESSIVE HIGH KEY

HIGH-KEY EXPRESSIVE EVALUATION is coded by an array of syntactic, lexical and prosodic means. ARGUMENTATIVE REINFORCEMENT and EMOTIVE INTENSIFICATION have some exponents in common, such as repeating words and increasing the number of **&3** accents, but they differ in lexical choice, phonation, intonation and acoustic energy. Some patterns of acoustic energy control and phonation in the two types of HIGH KEY may be universal in human language, others just characteristic of specific languages or language groups.

5.1.1   *ARGUMENTATIVE HIGH KEY for ARGUMENTATIVE REINFORCEMENT*
The simplest device in ARGUMENTATIVE REINFORCEMENT is the repetition of the word or phrase to be reinforced, with an increased accent level **&3** and peak patterns on each repetition, as in the old VW beetle advert of the 1960s, 'er läuft und läuft und läuft'. Greater intensification uses lexical intensifiers and their repetition, as in 'very, very good'; 'it's absolutely meaningless', each with an accent raised to **&3**; accents are also docked at secondary stresses, as in **&3**absol**&3**utely, or even at unstressed syllables as well, for example in **&3**abs**&3**ol**&3**utel**&3**y.

President Clinton's pronouncement at the famous press conference

I did **&3**[not **&**, [pause] **&3**-have **&0**. [pause] **&3**-sexual **&0**. [pause] **&3**-rel'ations with that **&0**. **&2**[woman **&**, [long pause] Miss **&2**[Lew'insky **&**, **&PG**

is another example of ARGUMENTATIVE REINFORCEMENT, highlighting four essential semantic elements 'not', 'have', 'sexual', 'rel'ations' in a defence against a public accusation. This is achieved by accenting each word, lengthening and strengthening the stressed syllable-initial consonant, by pausing before accents and by accompanying the AAA production by downward movements of the arm and pointed index finger, banging the lectern. There is also an element of Appeal to the receiving audience, particularly by the attention-triggering pauses before each accent.

Accented swear words may be used as lexical intensifiers in Argumentative Reinforcement of a following accented word. An interesting example comes from Stephen Fry's BBC broadcasts *Fry's English Delight* (series 6), where the story is told of two navvies digging a hole in the road around the time universal suffrage came to Britain, when there were posters everywhere that read 'One Man One Vote'. One of the navvies asked the other, 'What does that mean?' – 'It means one man, one vote.' – 'Oh, but what is that supposed to signify?' – 'It signifies one man, one vote.' – 'Oh, I am sorry, I don't understand.' – 'It means one fucking man, one fucking vote.' (pronounced with increased acoustic energy) – 'Ah, I see.' The extreme reinforcement clarified the syntactic-semantic structure of the phrase.

5.1.2   Emotive High Key for Negative or Positive Intensification

Accented swear words are commonly used in Negative Intensification: in English 'bloody hell!', 'what the fuck (WTF) do you think you are doing?'; in German 'verfluchte Scheiße!', 'das ist zum Kotzen!' In English, they may even occur before the accented syllable inside a word, as in 'abso-bloody-lutely'. It has been pointed out (Francis Nolan, pers. comm.) that for this to sound right 'one needs a word-internal foot, preferably with more than one syllable, before the insertion point; so 'over-fucking-confident' is better than 'un-fucking-confident'. 'Macna-fucking-mara' is a good Irish surname, but 'Mc-fucking-Kenzie' is a bad Scottish one. This would certainly apply to the word citation forms, but this kind of swear-word intensification occurs in utterance context, and across word boundaries the rhythmic foot structure would be perfectly regular in 'Macnamara might be quite a good choice for the job but **&3**not Mc-**&3**fucking-**&3**Kenzie!' When the names are swapped, a remiss syllable needs to be inserted to maintain a good trochee pattern: 'McKenzie might be quite a good choice for the job but **&3**not that **&3**Macna-**&3**fucking-**&3**mara!'

The same patterning is shown by the example of the British Army sergeant-major saying to the private who wants to get leave over the weekend to see his girlfriend:

All right. But remember, sonny, you'll be back by 8 on Monday morning, and **&3**don't for-**&3**fucking-**&3**get.

This was reported as a genuine incident in the discussion after a talk on 'What is a word?' given by Charles Bazell in the joint phonetics-linguistics seminar at Edinburgh University in the early 1960s. It exemplifies NEGATIVE INTEN-SIFICATION superimposed on an APPEAL, which is signalled by inserting the swear word before the accented syllable inside the essential message element 'forget', and the whole command gets raised in acoustic energy and may have been accompanied by a clenched fist hammering in the APPEAL. There may also have been a change to pressed phonation, accompanied by a furrowed brow.

Swear words are also selected for intensification according to their phonetic energy (Hughes 1998). 'Swive' existed beside 'fuck' in Chaucer's time, with the same original sexual meaning, but did not make it to the swear-word level, no doubt because it is phonetically much softer, with its mostly voiced, sono-rous articulation in the front of the mouth and with a long syllable nucleus. It is therefore less aggressive-sounding than 'fuck' with its short back vowel, its back plosive and its voiceless, asonorous consonants initially and finally. The Irish generally use 'feck(ing)' as a swear word, and revert to 'fuck(ing)' for greater intensification and aggressiveness, exchanging the back vowel for the front one. In addition to choosing swear words that support NEGATIVE INTENSIFICATION by their asonorous and posterior vocal-tract properties, the negativity is further intensified by lengthening and strengthening asonorous onsets of accented syllables, by pressed phonation and by increased overall acoustic energy.

These prosodic features are also applied to accented words outside the swear-word class for NEGATIVE INTENSIFICATION. An example is Edith Evans's rendering of Lady Bracknell's question 'A handbag?!' in Oscar Wilde's *The Importance of Being Earnest*. It is the EMOTIVE HIGH-KEY EXPRESSION of indignation and horror at a socially unacceptable origin, applying extreme lengthening, including a strengthened initial [h], and powerful pressed pho-nation, which starts with strong breathiness and then changes to high-rising tense voice. It also contains a HIGH-KEY APPEAL: the high pitch stimulates the addressee to provide a satisfactory answer to resolve the speaker's incredulity (cf. Kohler 2011a for graphic signal displays and further discussion). The same NEGATIVE INTENSIFICATION could be expressed with the same prosodic fea-tures in the corresponding German utterance 'In einer Handtasche?!'

The *imperative* structure 'Shut the door!', with accents on 'shut' and 'door' and a pitch fall on the latter, is a neutral APPEAL to act. The command gets expressively intensified by increased loudness and pitch range, and addition-ally by accentuating 'the'. It may be further heightened by lexical insertion 'b-door' or even stronger 'bloody door'. With pressed phonation the expres-sion is one of exasperation.

On the other hand, the COMMAND may be softened to a REQUEST by adding 'will you' and/or 'please' on rising pitch to the neutral APPEAL form. The request nature of the APPEAL is increased by starting the pitch rise on 'door' and expanding the pitch range of the whole utterance. The request is strengthened further when *imperative* structure is replaced by *interrogative* syntax, 'Would you shut the door, please', or even 'Would you mind shutting the door, please', in both cases with rising pitch starting on 'door' and expanded pitch range. If this is combined with modal voice, the speaker makes a polite but firm APPEAL to act, a signal of social stature. However, if it is combined with breathy-voice phonation, the sender signals submission to the receiver for compliance. This example illustrates the fine gradation of EMOTIVE HIGH KEY in the APPEAL function, from NEUTRAL to either NEGATIVE or POSITIVE INTENSIFICATION along the semantic functions of COMMAND or REQUEST and AGGRESSIVE or POLITE, signalled by varying bundles of prosodic properties and linguistic structures. These function-form relations also apply to German (see 4.3 for further details).

Typical examples of NEGATIVE or POSITIVE INTENSIFICATION occur in exclamatory utterances. They combine negative or positive lexical semantics with prosodic features that function as exponents of NEGATIVE or POSITIVE EMOTIVE HIGH KEY in peak patterns:

- *negative prosody*
  time-energy strengthening of accented-syllable onset asonority at the expense of nucleus sonority, pressed phonation, fast-falling F0 contours, increased overall acoustic energy
- *positive prosody*
  time-energy strengthening of accented-syllable nucleus sonority, modal or breathy-voice phonation, expanded plateau-like and slowly falling F0 contours.

Instances of NEGATIVE INTENSIFICATION from English and German are listed in (a), corresponding to instances of POSITIVE INTENSIFICATION in (c) (cf. Kohler 2006a, 2009b; Kohler and Niebuhr 2007; Niebuhr 2010):

(a)	It *stinks*.	Das *stinkt*.
	It's *disgusting*.	Das ist *widerlich*.
	It's *terrible*.	Das ist *schrecklich*.
	He's an absolute *bastard*.	Er ist ein absolutes *Schwein*.
(b)	You did that *beautifully*.	Das hast du *toll* gemacht.

(c)	It *smells*.	Das *riecht*.
	It's *delicious*.	Das ist *köstlich*.
	It's *lovely*.	Das ist *reizend*.
	She's a *gem*.	Sie ist eine *Perle*.
	You did that *beautifully*.	Das hast du *toll* gemacht.

| (d) | It *stinks*. | Das *stinkt*. |

The initial English lenis stops in (a) lose their voice completely and have strong releases; the initial labiodental fricative in German 'widerlich' has increased devoiced fricative noise. In (b) positive lexical semantics is combined with negative prosodic intensification properties. This semantic positive-negative clash between the two levels results in sarcasm: the negative prosodic meaning overrides the positive lexical meaning. The examples in (d) have negative lexical semantics together with positive prosodic intensification properties. The semantic clash between the two levels may signal irony, or it may be a cheese-lover's appreciation of 'a deliciously smelly Münster'. In either case, positive prosodic meaning overrides negative lexical meaning. Furthermore, in these examples NEGATIVE INTENSIFICATION may be accompanied by a furrowed brow, head-lowering and possibly a clenched fist, POSITIVE INTENSIFICATION by raising eyebrows, head and possibly arms and hands.

In exclamatory utterances, F0 peak contours may be compressed into a low F0 range, as against the expanded F0 falls typically found in aggressive commands. The prosodic exponents depend on social codes. If it is frowned upon to show one's NEGATIVE EMOTIVE EXPRESSION or to be loud in public, as it is in English middle-class society, F0 falls and acoustic energy are compressed. On the other hand, F0 expansion for POSITIVE EMOTIVE EXPRESSION, especially in female voices, is quite acceptable. Armstrong and Ward mention the lowering and narrowing of the whole range of intonation in 'emphasis for intensity' (Armstrong and Ward 1931, p. 46). They do not distinguish between POSITIVE and NEGATIVE INTENSIFICATION, but most of the examples they quote for this narrowing definitely refer to the latter: 'It's perfectly absurd'; 'He won't listen to reason'; 'I won't stand it any longer'; 'What in the name of fortune are you doing?' The example 'How very ingenious' may be ironic.

The examples in (a)–(d), although in declarative sentence mode, have only rudimentary referential meaning. They are predominantly expressive and as such are one form of EXCLAMATIONS, which may also be given negative-polarity interrogative syntax without becoming QUESTION APPEALS, as in:

| Isn't it terrible! | Ist das nicht furchtbar! |
| Isn't it wonderful! | Ist das nicht wunderbar! |

In their simplest form, EXCLAMATIONS are non-sentential utterances that serve only the EXPRESSION function. Speakers may mutter 'Oh, my God!' or 'Oh, mein Gott!' under their breath in English or German, or they may intensify the EXCLAMATION with accents on each word, pressed phonation and considerable lengthening in NEGATIVE EMOTIVE HIGH KEY, which may be further strengthened lexically in English 'Damn it all!' or in German 'Verflucht noch mal!' On the other hand, there is POSITIVE EMOTIVE HIGH KEY in exuberant exclamations like 'Wonderful!', 'How that smells!', or German 'Wunderbar!', 'Wie das riecht!', with modal voice and expanded as well as slowly falling pitch across the utterance. NEGATIVE and POSITIVE INTENSIFICATION in EXCLAMATIONS are short-time expressions of the emotions ANGER and JOY.

5.2   *Reduced-to-Elaborated Articulation* in LOW-TO-HIGH EXPRESSIVE KEY

In the realisation of the English utterance 'I do not know', a wide spectrum of accentuation, intonation, acoustic energy, phonation and articulation converge to convey specific meanings beyond the propositional meaning of lack of knowledge (Hawkins 2003). The weakly contracted form [aɪ dəʊn̩ nˈəʊ], with a *medial F0 peak* contour as well as an energy peak in the only accented syllable 'know', provides the listener with new, neutral information that the speaker cannot give the requested answer. More strongly *elaborated* or *reduced* forms add expressive and attitudinal connotations.

Prosody and articulation can be *elaborated* together in several degrees to insist on 'not knowing'. The number of accents and the F0 range are increased, and the articulatory movements are expanded in time and space (cf. also Lindblom's 1990 H&H theory). In a first step, 'don't' is given a second accent, with concomitant raising of the F0 peak in 'know', and there is considerable lengthening of the complete vocal-tract opening-closing movement in 'don't', as well as a plosive realisation at its end: [aɪ dˈəʊnt(ʰ) nˈəʊ]. An overarticulated expansion [aɪ dˈuː nˈɒtʰ nˈəʊ] of the function words 'do not', entailing additional accents on both, reinforces the truth value of the statement of 'not knowing'. This may be heightened still further by giving 'I' yet another accent and by inserting pauses between the words, and even by accompanying each accent with a downward movement of the arm and pointing index finger, and of the hand banging a table or a lectern (cf. the

pronouncement by President Clinton in 5.1.1). These are scaled ARGUMENTA-
TIVE REINFORCEMENTS.

But in the elaboration of the statement 'I do not know' the speaker may
also introduce an expressive rejection of a listener's repeated questioning. The
utterance is then no longer an ARGUMENTATIVE REINFORCEMENT of propositional components but EMOTIVE INTENSIFICATION of a negative contrastive
attitude towards the listener. This is signalled by *late peak* contours on the
accented syllables, by pressed, instead of modal, phonation throughout the
utterance and by considerable lengthening of all vocal-tract opening-closing
movements, thus expressing degrees of exasperation. Such NEGATIVE INTEN-
SIFICATION is dependent on socio-cultural conventions and is most probably
accompanied by body movements that differ from the ones used in ARGUMEN-
TATIVE REINFORCEMENT, i.e. furrowed brow and clenched fist.

Moving in the other direction on the elaboration-*reduction* scale, the opening-
closing movements of the vocal tract may be levelled, and F0 narrowed and
synchronised differently with articulation. This leads to [(aɪ) də nˈəʊ], which
is casual and informal, and conveys to the listener that the speaker does not
care about not being able to provide an answer. If the accent is marked by an
early peak contour, the speaker signals FINALITY – the closure of a communicative turn: there is no more to be said. If used in a formal situation this may
be received as insolence.

Reduction may go further to the maximally contracted form [ə̃ə̃ə̃], with very
weak segmental articulation. It may be uttered in a relaxed communicative situation between family members. For example, A asks B, who is busy reading
a book and does not want to be disturbed, where the newspaper is, and B's
response is made as a sideline to her main activity at the time. Its function is
to signal to A in an aside way not to expect help in looking for the newspaper
because she is otherwise occupied. This communicative function determines
the phonetic output. The three opening-closing gestures of the weakly reduced
form 'I don't know' in the neutral message remain in a rudimentary fashion as
a movement from a more open and fronted, through a central, to a more closed
and retracted vocoid shape of the vocal tract, reflecting the progression of the
open phases in the fuller gestures, with superimposed nasality representing the
negation. This progression could not be reversed, nor could nasality be embod-
ied in a nasal contoid, e.g. [n̩n̩n̩], but it must not be absent either. The rhythmic
timing also reflects the fuller form, with the central section being shortest, the
final one longest. A possible intonation pattern is falling on the first section and
low rising on the last, conveying a friendly rebuttal 'Don't ask me' in the situational setting described above. The open-close progression of the vocoid quality,

the nasalisation throughout and the rhythmic timing of the vocoid sections together with the falling-rising F0 pattern form the phonetic essence (Niebuhr and Kohler 2011) of this utterance in its situational speech function. If the F0 contour is resynthesised on an otherwise constant schwa hum it becomes noise and is no longer decodable as reduced speech.

The German equivalent of English 'I do not know', in its various formal manifestations reflecting the semantic and pragmatic functions, is 'keine Ahnung'. Neutral [kʰa̤ënë ˈa̰ːnɵ̃ŋ] compares with *elaborated* [kʰˈaĩːnë ʔˈa̰ːnɵ̃ŋ], and with maximally *reduced* [hä̤ë̤ ˈa̰ãõ̃]. The neutral version has four clearly demarcated opening-closing vocal-tract movements, with glottalisation marking the opening phase in the third, and an *early peak* pattern is associated with the prominent third gesture for the function of argumentative FINALITY. A *medial peak* is also possible in the neutral version to signal argumentative OPENNESS. In the *elaborated* version, articulation and prosody are intensified, a glottal closure marks the juncture between the closing of the second and the opening of the third gesture, and both 'kei(ne)' and 'Ah(nung)' are accented. If, in addition, pressed phonation with breathiness takes the place of modal phonation throughout the utterance, and *late* instead of *medial peak* contours occur with the accents, the effect of NEGATIVE INTENSIFICATION is introduced, expressing exasperation (see graphic displays in Kohler 2011b).

In the *reduced* version, the clear demarcation disappears, but the progression of closing-opening-closing front-back vocoid shaping of the vocal tract remains, and nasalisation marks the final two gestures instead of a nasal contoid separator, while the initial opening movement retains breathy phonation. The timing of the gestures is also kept, and an *early peak* pattern is again associated with the prominent third gesture to fit the conclusiveness of the communicative exchange. The vocoid modulation, its rhythmic timing, the superimposed nasalisation, together with the *early peak* synchronisation, and the initial breathiness form the phonetic essence of this reduced German utterance; reduction does not go any further if it is to stay speech.

The discussion of the form and function of corresponding English and German sets of utterances containing the same strings of words suggests that a speech-functional scale can be set up that extends from a neutral propositional pivot in two directions, to EXPRESSIVE HIGH-KEY with segmental and prosodic expansion on the one side, and EXPRESSIVE LOW-KEY with segmental and prosodic levelling on the other. Both HIGH-KEY strengthening and LOW-KEY weakening introduce the speaker's expressiveness towards the listener and the communicative situation. EXPRESSIVE HIGH-KEY may be REINFORCEMENT of the truth value of propositional meaning to drive home an

ARGUMENTATION point to the listener, or NEGATIVE or POSITIVE INTENSIFI-
CATION of expressive meaning. LOW-KEY playing-down may be a parentheti-
cal aside, or it may signal indifference to the listener and disinterest in what is
going on in the communicative situation. Different locations on this functional
scale activate distinctive bundlings of segmental and prosodic properties in
speakers' speech production. Listeners decode the received phonetically rich
signals by relating them to speech functions along the functional scale, thus
understanding the propositional, attitudinal and expressive aspects of meaning
conveyed by speakers in specific communicative situations.

5.3   Some Postulates for Research into EXPRESSIVE EVALUATION in Human Language

The principles of EXPRESSIVE EVALUATION, set out for German and English,
may be expected to have a communicative function in human speech interaction generally, with varying formal manifestations across languages. This
formal variability, along the *reduced-to-elaborated* scale among others, provides a new field of phonetic investigation into typological groupings that go
well beyond traditional segmental or prosodic typologies in the phonologies
of the world's languages. NEGATIVE INTENSIFICATION may be postulated
as a universal function expressing anything from dislike to disgust, and as
such may be considered an adaptation of the biological function of vomiting
(Trojan, Tembrock and Schendl 1975) to human speech communication. Like
its vegetative root, this communicative stylisation is characterised by vocal-
tract, especially pharyngeal, narrowing, and by raising of the larynx. The
phonetic processes of increasing non-sonority by strengthening initial voiceless consonants and by fricativising syllabic nuclei through pressed phonation
would result naturally from such a production basis. POSITIVE INTENSIFICA-
TION has the opposite articulation basis, i.e. vocal-tract widening, with the
observed phonetic properties following from it, and, of course, the differences
go together with different facial expressions of contortion versus elation.

The discussion of EXPRESSIVE weighting of messages may now be summed
up in five research postulates:

- EXPRESSIVE EVALUATION is not only manifested in prosodic
  parameters, but cuts across all linguistic levels – segmental as well as
  prosodic, lexical, morphological, syntactic.
- Manifestations differ with communicative functions and their combinations.

- This means that a communicatively insightful analysis needs to proceed from the communicative functions to their linguistic forms.
- Since the speaker's EXPRESSION is an integral part of speech communication, it needs to be included beside the traditional linguistic levels in the speech scientist's study of communicative processes in the world's languages, rather than being exiled to a field of paralinguistics.
- Long-time settings for the EXPRESSION OF THE EMOTIONS and short-time settings in EXPRESSIVE LOW-TO-HIGH KEY are future core research areas in *Communicative Phonetic Science* that go beyond the space and scope of this monograph.

5.4 Speaker Attitudes towards the Listener: From AUTHORITY to SUBORDINATION

The communicative function that plays a central role in human interaction is the expression of authority and dominance versus subordination and compliance. It has been suggested by Ohala (1983, 1984) that a speaker's general pitch level is one of the signal properties that code this speaker–listener relationship. Thus, to sound more authoritative, Queen Elizabeth II lowered her pitch level in public addresses, e.g. in the more recent Christmas Broadcasts compared with the early ones; British Prime Minister Margaret Thatcher took elocution lessons to achieve the same goal; radio and television newsreaders used to be chosen and trained with regard to a low pitch level, for example Fiona Bruce on the BBC, or Dagmar Berghoff on the German ARD television channel. When television news programmes changed from authoritative reading to interactive infotainment, for instance on BBC breakfast television, or on BBC World News, low-pitch voices no longer fitted the new way of giving information, and consequently speakers are selected more with regard to their interactive abilities and their youthfulness, both aspects favouring higher, rather than lower, pitch. But this does not remove signalling authority or subordination from the functional core of human interaction, nor does it negate a link with pitch level, at least in European languages.

Although the expression of speaker–listener attitudes is a universal communicative function across the world's languages, cultural and linguistic societies differ in the use of its formal manifestations. In Japanese, for example, the expression of social relationships is formalised at the lexical and morphological levels. How far this is combined with differences in pitch level is a question of empirical research. The use of formal means beside or instead of pitch level in sub-Saharan register and Asian contour tone languages also needs thorough investigation. Even in European languages, which Ohala took as the point of departure for his proposal of the *Frequency Code*, the exponents of this attitudinal function are not limited to F0, but include different types of phonation as further essential ingredients.

The expression of authority with low pitch and added creakiness has assumed an additional dimension of demonstrating powerful position in the public appearance of female speakers, for example US businesswomen. But this association is by no means fixed. The former CEO of Newton Investment Management (a subsidiary of the Bank of New York Mellon in the City of London), British-born and -bred Helena Morrissey, the founder of the 30% Club for women's representation on company boards in the UK, and a mother of nine children, sounds authoritative not by demonstrating her powerful position in a low and creaky voice, but by supporting her ARGUMENTATION with frequent reinforced accents for INFORMATION WEIGHTING and ARGUMENTATIVE REINFORCEMENT. In an interview on *Woman's Hour* on BBC Radio 4, 11 April 2013 (www.bbc.co.uk/programmes/b01rr7r9), her very feminine voice is in striking contrast with the deep and creaky voice of the presenter Jenni Murray. This example demonstrates that speakers may adapt the formal exponents of a specific function to their own individuality within a set cultural code.

6 Linguistic Form of Communicative Functions in Language Comparison

The framework of core communicative functions developed in this monograph is a theoretical construct of human interaction, based on observation in European languages and on the *a priori* postulate that there are functions of speech communication as part of human behaviour that are common to all language communities but have language-specific formal exponents. The constant inter-language communicative functions determine the transmission of meaning between speakers and listeners and trigger the variable intra-language forms. In this sense, function precedes form. This postulate offers a powerful methodological frame for the comparative study of formal across-language manifestations. Among such postulated interlanguage communicative functions are the following: ARGUMENTATION, QUESTION versus STATEMENT, INFORMATION SELECTION AND WEIGHTING, HIGH-KEY INTENSIFICATION. It is the speech scientist's task to investigate how the functions are formally manifested in the languages of the world, thus giving comparative prosodic research new direction.

6.1   Application to Mandarin Chinese

In a first step, some preliminary Mandarin Chinese data have been collected and analysed within this communicative framework. The discussion will focus on ARGUMENTATION in 6.1.1, and on QUESTION/STATEMENT in 6.1.2. In both cases, manifestations are set against those in German and English. Since tonal features are tied up in the lexical tones of a tone language, it is a prime question how speakers implement the categories of the functional framework as overlays of the lexical tone distinctions.

6.1.1   ARGUMENTATION
Watching Stephen Frears's film *The Queen*, with Helen Mirren in the role of Queen Elizabeth II, shortly after its release in 2006 I became aware of the actors' control of prosody in communicative ARGUMENTATION. In the opening

scene, the film shows the Queen in full regal robes in a portrait-painting session, watching a television report on the final stage of Tony Blair's 1997 General Election campaign and talking to the portrait artist, played by the Jamaican Earl Cameron. She regrets that she does not have a vote. Then the following dialogue develops:

> Q. The sheer joy of being partial.
> A. [*late peak*]Yes. Of course one forgets that, as sovereign, you are not [*late peak*]entitled to vote.
> Q. [*early peak*]No.

followed, a little later, by

> A. But it [*late peak*]is your government.
> Q. [*early peak*]Yes. S'ppose that's some consolation.

In two later telephone conversations between the Queen and Prime Minister Tony Blair, played by Michael Sheen, there are the following exchanges:

> P. Is it your intention to make some kind of appearance or statement?
> Q. [*late peak*]No. [*late peak*]No. [*late peak*]Certainly not.
> [*The Queen hurriedly rejects the Prime Minister's suggestion right at the beginning of his telephone call.*]
>
> P. Let's keep in touch.
> Q. [*medial peak*]Yes, [*medial peak*]let's.
> [*The Queen wants to end the telephone call quickly, therefore the words are spoken fast and sound clipped.*]

With the three different prosodies on 'yes', the female RP speaker and the male speaker of Jamaican English convey distinctive communicative functions of ARGUMENTATION. The auditory differences and their functional distinctions were immediately obvious to me when I was watching the film in a London cinema. On 'yes', the Queen's *early peak* signals resigned acceptance of a political fact, her *medial peak* authoritative consent, and the artist's *late peak* personally evaluated contrast to the monarch's pronouncement, spelt out by a 'But...'. With an *early peak* on 'No', the actress expresses the queen's resigned acceptance of the constitutional ruling; with a *late peak* and much higher pitch, going up in the repetition, she expresses her personally evaluated contradiction of the other speaker's question, underscored by 'Certainly not'.

Later I obtained an excerpt of the soundtrack and analysed the data in Praat. This analysis confirmed the auditory observation of *early*, *medial* and *late* peaks (see 2.7, 2.8). The female speaker's data are shown in Figure 6.1Aa/Ab. The *early peak* enters the accented vowel nucleus on descending F0 and

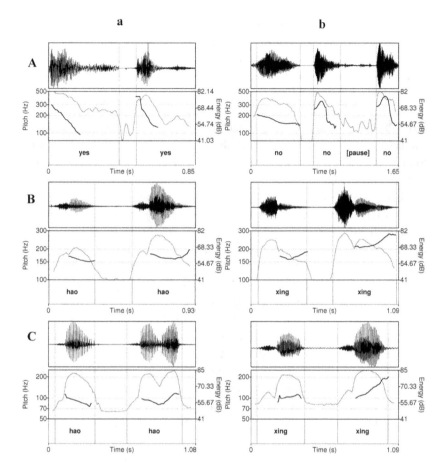

Figure 6.1. Speech waves, F0 (log scale) and acoustic energy traces (plain and dotted lines) and word-segmented annotations of affirmation/negation in RP English: **A** female, Helen Mirren; and of two affirmations in Mandarin Chinese: **B** female, Aoju Chen, **C** male, Yi Xu: **a** English 'yes', Mandarin 'hao-3' *low tone* [OK] **b** English 'no', Mandarin 'xing-2' *rising tone* [OK]. In each panel, the F0 and acoustic energy traces on the left signal FINALITY, the ones on the right OPENNESS.

strengthens low pitch in the falling pattern. The *medial peak* enters it on raised F0 and strengthens high pitch; the shortening in clipped speech prevents a slow descent, but the raised F0 maximum and the initial high level provide the high-pitch ingredients. The *late peak* shows a shift of the F0 maximum to a later point in the accented-vowel nucleus with an extensive rise-fall. In addition, the energy trace follows the more gradual descent of F0 in the longer *early peak* vowel in both 'yes' and 'no', but is more sharply peaked in the much shorter *medial peak* vowel; in the *late peak* it follows the F0 rise and fall. The three peak patterns with their different focusing on low or high pitch in different parts of the accented-vowel nucleus express FINALITY, or OPENNESS, or CONTRAST with superimposed personal evaluation, respectively.

After seeing the film, I thought that on the hypothesis of ARGUMENTATION functions being basic in human communication, words of affirmation and negation must be combined with them in any language, and that we need to find out how it is done the world over. It may be further hypothesised that higher versus lower pitch for OPENNESS versus FINALITY would play a role in all languages, because raised pitch stimulates the human receiver, whereas lowered pitch signals speaker-orientation. Raising or lowering pitch can be achieved in different ways, and it is particularly interesting to see what speakers of tone languages do, where pitch is coded at the word level and therefore more restricted in interactional coding at the utterance level. As I had arranged a meeting with Yi Xu at UCL to discuss editorial matters the day after seeing the film, I decided to broach the subject with him. He agreed that 'hao-3' and 'xing-2', both meaning 'OK', would have the F0 of their lexical tones adjusted to OPENNESS versus FINALITY contextualisation in speech communication. He recorded the words in the two different settings (shown in Figure 6.1Ca/Cb). To get a recording from a female speaker as well, I approached Aoju Chen, MPI Nijmegen at the time, who recorded the words as illustrated in Figure 6.1Ba/Bb. I am very grateful to both colleagues for providing the data. Aoju Chen also paraphrased situational contexts in English for the two functions.

FINALITY: the speaker closes the argument and may express reluctance and even resignation

> Your boss asks you to hand in a project proposal soon. You explain that this is not feasible for various reasons. But your boss insists that your company needs the proposal quickly.
>
> Your boss: Will you then hand in the proposal in two weeks?
> You: hao3, xing2 (traces on the left in panels Ba/Bb, Ca/Cb of Figure 6.1)

OPENNESS: the speaker is open to the argument and may express willingness to comply

> Your boss asks you to hand in a project proposal soon. Because it is a very short proposal and you have a clear idea of what it should be like, you think it can be done quite easily.
>
> Your boss: Will you hand in the proposal in two weeks?
> You: hao3, xing2 (traces on the right in panels Ba/Bb, Ca/Cb of Figure 6.1)

For FINALITY, the low tone ends low, and concomitantly acoustic energy is low or decreases, whereas for OPENNESS, pitch rises, and energy is high or increases. Similarly, the high tone ends lower or higher, and concomitantly the time course of acoustic energy is on a lower or higher level. FINALITY strengthens low pitch, OPENNESS high pitch in the accented syllable within the constraints of the lexical tones. So, in Mandarin Chinese pitch lowering or raising is at work in order to code FINALITY and OPENNESS, as it is in English and German, simply adapted to the conditions set by the tone language. I reported these data in a talk (Kohler 2009b) at the International Symposium on Frontiers in Phonetics and Speech Science held by the Institute of Linguistics, Chinese Academy, Beijing, in conjunction with the celebration of the 100th birthday of Professor Zongji Wu, in April 2008. Members of the audience confirmed a perceptual link between F0 lowering or raising and the ARGUMENTATION functions of FINALITY or OPENNESS for native Mandarin speakers.

The pilot study presented here needs to be extended in three ways: (1) to all four lexical tones, (2) to more words, utterance types and speakers, and (3) to systematic experimental designs in speech production and perception, to provide a statistically evaluated measurement base for the theory-driven hypothesis. This is a long-term and quite complex project, which I hope Chinese speech scientists will tackle in the near future. ARGUMENTATION functions have so far not been studied in Mandarin Chinese, although there is extensive data analysis of focus in declarative and interrogative structures in isolated sentences (Jia 2012; Liu 2009; Liu and Xu 2005; Xu 1999). But this research is not sufficient to gain an insight into communicative functions because it deals only with information structure in propositional meaning and is thus disconnected from ARGUMENTATION in speech interaction.

In this communicative approach, the possibility will also have to be considered that functions of ARGUMENTATION are not primarily signalled by prosody but by lexical and syntactic means. Here is an example from German and English to illustrate the divergence between languages. In the dialogues

> A: Kommst du nicht mit? Aren't you coming with us?
> B: Nein. / Doch. No. / Yes (I am).

A refers to a proposition 'You are coming with us', previously established or taken for granted, negates its truth value and asks whether B agrees. In case of agreement, Speaker B also negates the truth value of the proposition with 'Nein' or 'No.' This negation may be spoken with one of the four F0 peak synchronisations for one of the ARGUMENTATION functions (see the *early peak* in the Queen's 'No' above). In case of disagreement, the German speaker rejects A's negation of the truth value with 'Doch' and a *non-early peak*, its synchronisation depending on the grading of CONTRAST and EXPRESSIVE EVALUATION. The English speaker reverts to the use of 'Yes', as in a reply to a *positive* POLARITY QUESTION, but signals affirmation of the propositional truth value against A's negation with a contrastive *high-rising fall-rise* pattern **&2^yes &2.? PG** (Halliday's broken tone 2, cf. 1.4.2), which may be repeated on added 'I am', or 'Yes' may receive the fall, 'am' the rise, for degrees of HIGH-KEY INTENSIFICATION. Rejection of a negation may also be rendered lexically in English by 'Of course I am', but with greater INTENSIFICATION than German 'Doch'.

In Early Modern English until the late sixteenth century, 'yes' was used alongside 'yea', with distinctive communicative functions between the two affirmations: 'yea' is the affirmative reply to a *positive* POLARITY QUESTION, 'yes' the affirmative reply to a proposition that was negated in a *negative* POLARITY QUESTION. Early Modern English usage of 'yes', which Shakespeare still adhered to, is thus the same as that of German 'doch'. There are different opinions about the etymology of 'yes', but the syntagma 'yea so' seems to be communicatively most plausible because 'so' emphasises the affirmation by pointing to the proposition (for more details about the system of affirmation and negation in the history of English, see Kohler 1970). These data show very nicely that ARGUMENTATION may have primary lexical coding, no doubt with a prosodic subsidiary, at some language stage, but may, at a later stage, move to primary prosodic coding, whereas another language keeps the lexical marker. Research should keep this in mind.

6.1.2   *QUESTION versus STATEMENT*

Following on from the general postulate of the universality of the QUESTION-function, the three sub-functions of INFORMATION QUESTIONS, POLARITY QUESTIONS, CONFIRMATION QUESTIONS are also postulated to apply across all languages. The formal principles of INFORMATION QUESTIONS in Mandarin Chinese have been discussed in 4.2.1.

6.1.2.1   Pilot Study

Questions in Mandarin Chinese have been studied extensively, but always from the angle of linguistic form. Even the detailed analysis of parallel encoding of interrogative meaning, focus and lexical tone in Mandarin Chinese (Liu 2009; Liu and Xu 2005) starts from formal question types, graphically marked, among others, as a statement by a period, or as *ma* particle question, or as a so-called yes-no question, i.e. in declarative syntax, with a question mark. This leaves out the situational embedding of different types of QUESTION functions in speech communication. It is essential to investigate their formal realisations, superimposed on lexical tone, in a communicative framework. Kohler (2013b) collected and analysed some preliminary data from one female speaker, with dialogue texts constructed in a scenario of husband and wife wondering how to occupy their boy. The contextualisation gave a high probability of eliciting POLARITY and CONFIRMATION QUESTIONS, with and without SURPRISE, as well as STATEMENTS including CONTRAST. In the following listing of some of the dialogues, the target utterances are underlined.

> **Husband**
> *wǒmen jīntiān dài érzi qù nǎr wán ne? ní zěnme xiǎng?*
> 'What shall we do with the boy today? What do you think?'
>
> POLARITY QUESTION
> **A** *tā xǐhuan qù dòngwùyuán/hǎitān ma?*
> 'Does he want to go to the zoo/beach?'
>
> **Wife**
> STATEMENT with potential CONTRAST
> *wó xiǎng tā bú yuànyi qù.*
> 'I don't think so.'
> **B** *Tā xǐhuan qù hǎitān/dòngwùyuán.*
> 'He wants to go to the beach/zoo.'
>
> **Husband**
> CONFIRMATION QUESTIONS
> either MATTER-OF-FACT
>
> **C1** *tā xǐhuan qù hǎitān/dòngwùyuán?*
> 'He wants to go to the beach/zoo?'
> **C2** *tā búshì gèng xǐhuan qù dòngwùyuán/hǎitān ma?*
> 'He does not prefer the zoo/beach?'
> or disbelieving EXPRESSION OF SURPRISE
> **D** *tā xǐhuan qù hǎitān/dòngwùyuán? zhēn nányǐxiāngxìn!*
> 'He wants to go to the beach/zoo? I can hardly believe that.'

The dialogues were read by the speaker in the roles of both wife and husband. In the dialogue embedding, **A** is a POLARITY QUESTION of the open, listener-oriented type (cf. **PQ-2** in Germanic languages in 4.2.2.2). **B** is a STATEMENT that may also be contrastive; **C1** is a MATTER-OF-FACT CONFIRMATION QUESTION (cf. **CQ-2.1a** in Germanic languages in 4.2.2.4), followed by a REINFORCED *ma* POLARITY QUESTION **C2**; **D** is a CONFIRMATION QUESTION with EXPRESSION OF SURPRISE (cf. **CQ-2.1b** in Germanic languages in 4.2.2.4).

Although the syllable tones are shifted upwards in the *ma* POLARITY QUESTION **A**, compared with the STATEMENT **B**, the difference is concentrated more on the utterance-final word *hǎitān* or *dòngwùyuán* than being distributed over the whole sentence. When CONTRAST enters a REINFORCED *ma* Polarity Question in **C2**, the F0 maximum of the high tone in *hǎitān* is raised considerably, and the following neutral tone on *ma* does not just level out but falls to the level of the high-tone onset, producing a dome-shaped F0 contour around the high-tone level. In *dòngwùyuán*, the minimum F0 of the falling tone is lowered and the maximum F0 of the rising tone is raised, resulting in an increased F0 range into which *ma* is integrated, continuing the rise.

The Matter-of-Fact Confirmation Question **C1** differs from Statement **B** by having the entire tone sequences shifted upwards. Moreover, final high-tone *tān* rises instead of being level, and final rising-tone *yuán* rises continuously very high. In the Surprise Confirmation Question **D**, the falling-rising F0 contour of low+high-tone *hǎitān* is raised, and the F0 contour of falling+rising-tone *dòngwùyuán* is expanded in its low turning and its high end point, compared with Matter-of-fact Confirmation Question **C1**. In addition, the final syllable in both cases of **D** ends in breathiness.

The results of this pilot test indicate that a *raised register* feature superimposed on the lexical tone sequence of a *declarative* structure signals a Confirmation Question. Expanding the F0 contour of the focused word and overlaying it with breathiness adds the semantic component of disbelieving Expression of Surprise. In the *ma particle* Polarity Question, the syllable tones are also raised, especially on the final word + particle, where the F0 range is further expanded in a Reinforced Polarity Question. For further detail and graphic displays, see Kohler (2013b).

6.1.2.2   Elaborated Experimental Design

Although the data in 6.1.2.1 point to clear function-form relations in Mandarin Chinese, it is obvious that systematic data collection has to record proper dialogues with pairs of a male and a female speaker, also swapping the texts in the two roles so that complete data sets are obtained from all male and female speakers. In extensive discussion with Wentao Gu, Nanjing, the following new set of dialogues was devised for systematic data collection with several speaker pairs.

Husband/Wife Turn 1

Polarity Question   *wǒmen jīntiān dài érzi qù nǎr wán ne?*
      'Where shall we go with the boy today?'
A   *tā xiǎng qù dòngwùyuán ma/hǎitān ma?*
     'Does he want to go to the zoo/beach?'

Wife/Husband Turn 2

STATEMENT with OPENNESS

B   *wǒ juéde ba, kěnéng... <u>tā xiǎng qù hǎitān/dòngwùyuán.</u>*
'I think, perhaps, <u>he wants to go to the beach/zoo.</u>'

Husband/Wife Turn 3

CONFIRMATION QUESTIONS

either MATTER-OF-FACT, continued by STATEMENT with CONTRAST

C   *<u>tā xiǎng qù hǎitān/dòngwùyuán?</u>*
<u>wǒ hái yǐwéi, tā xiǎng qù dòngwùyuán/hǎitān.</u>
'<u>He wants to go to the beach/zoo?</u>'
'<u>I thought he wanted to go to the zoo/beach.</u>'

or disbelieving EXPRESSION OF SURPRISE

D   *<u>tā xiǎng qù hǎitān/dòngwùyuán?</u> zhēn nányǐxiāngxìn!*
'<u>He wants to go to the beach/zoo?</u> I can hardly believe that.'

Wife/Husband Turn 4

STATEMENT with FINALITY

E   *shìde, wó gán kěndìng, <u>tā xiǎng qù hǎitān/dòngwùyuán.</u>*
'I am quite sure. <u>He wants to go to the beach/zoo.</u>'

Husband/Wife Turn 5

CONCLUSION

either with FINALITY, taking final decision (in the same dialogues as **C**)

G   *nà wǒmen zhǔnbèi hǎo, <u>zhè jiù dài tā qù hǎitān/dòngwùyuán.</u>*
'OK. Then let's get ready. <u>We'll take him to the beach/zoo right now.</u>'

or with OPENNESS, proposing final agreement (in the same dialogues as **D**)

H   *nà wǒmen jiù shuōhǎo, <u>jīntiān dài tā qù hǎitān/dòngwùyuán.</u>*
'OK. That's agreed then. <u>We take him to the beach/zoo today.</u>'

Two turns were added to the three taken over from the pilot study. A dialogue conclusion is necessary, and from the same speaker who opens a dialogue. The concluding turn is G after A-B-C, and H after A-B-D. With G, the speaker takes a final decision, signalling FINALITY; with H, s/he proposes final agreement, signalling OPENNESS. In E, inserted as the fourth turn between C/D and G/H, the same speaker as in the second turn changes the previous OPEN to a FINAL STATEMENT.

The dialogues systematically vary (1) the lexical tones with the key words *hǎitān* or *dòngwùyuán*, (2) POLARITY versus CONFIRMATION QUESTION versus STATEMENT, (3) presence versus absence of SURPRISE in CONFIRMATION QUESTIONS, (4) OPENNESS versus FINALITY in STATEMENTS, resulting in 4 different dialogue texts. Two blocks are formed by the turn sequences A-B-C-E-G and A-B-D-E-H. Within each block, the turns contain either *hǎitān* or *dòngwùyuán*, and the dialogues are repeated with male/female text swapping. This yields $2 \times 2 \times 2 = 8$ dialogues. Since A, B, E are combined both with C, G and with D, H, there are two A, B, E *hǎitān* and *dòngwùyuán* tokens from each speaker. For the recording, the eight dialogue texts are put in Chinese script on separate sheets, which are presented to speakers in an ordered sequence such that the turn allocations alternate between husband–wife and wife–husband from dialogue to dialogue. This distracts speakers from text repetition and strengthens the dialogue nature.

Wentao Gu recruited nine male–female speaker pairs who were first- or second-year students of Broadcasting and Hosting Arts at Nanjing Normal University, and who all had first-class second-level Mandarin competence. They were recorded under studio conditions. In each dialogue session, both speakers were given the same ordered pack of eight dialogue sheets which they were instructed to read out, enacting eight dialogues between each other in the given dialogue sequence, as well as with the given male–female and female–male alternation. For each pair of speakers I compiled four spliced files: two for the male and two for the female speaker, containing all the eleven (underlined) *dòngwùyuán* or *hǎitān* target utterances of one speaker. Listening to the spliced files showed up to my non-native but trained ear a fair amount of variation between speakers. For adequate data interpretation, auditory assessment together with a native expert was mandatory before any signal analysis.

In a four-day working session in Kiel, Wentao Gu and I analysed the spliced data files in Praat auditorily with reference to spectrogram and F0 displays, considering two questions: (a) did the speakers produce the test stimuli in accordance with the intended contextualisation (or perhaps introduce further distinctions)?; and (b) are the speakers suitable subjects for experimental study of prosody in speech interaction? On a rating scale 'good–medium–bad' of convincing dialogue generation, two speaker pairs had to be excluded from further processing. Due to the variability between speakers in their realisations of the postulated functions, the database was neither sufficiently homogeneous nor large enough for numerical signal analysis and statistical testing. Therefore, the analysis had to be limited to auditory data description with reference to signal patterns. The results are discussed in 6.1.2.3, and the spectrogram and F0 displays in Figure 6.2 illustrate some representative signal manifestations of the functional categories for one speaker pair, GG.

6.1.2.3   Results of the Expanded Experiment

The scripted dialogues determine distinctive categorisations of the two lexical items *dòngwùyuán* and *hǎitān* as POLARITY QUESTIONS in **A**, CONFIRMATION

a male speaker GCC, Anqing, Jianghuai Mandarin

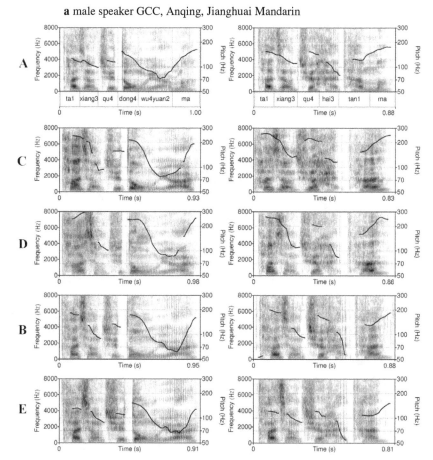

Figure 6.2. Spectrograms and F0 traces (log scale) of QUESTIONS (**A, C, D**) and STATEMENTS (**B, E**) in *dòngwùyuán* and *hǎitān* utterances (left and right columns) of Mandarin Chinese. *ma* POLARITY QUESTIONS with syllabic segmentation, same syllabic sequence without final question particle *ma* in the other utterances.

QUESTIONS in **C/D** and STATEMENTS in **B/E**. Despite variation between speakers within these categories, distinctive prosodic coding is maintained. However, the texts give the individual speakers freedom of interpretation as to FINALITY versus OPENNESS in the STATEMENTS, as to the scaling of MATTER-OF-FACT versus SURPRISE in the CONFIRMATION QUESTIONS, and as to the presence versus the absence of CONTRAST between the two localities. Through this freedom of text interpretation, speakers introduced variability in the prosodic patterning

b female speaker GCM, Wuhu, Jianghuai Mandarin.

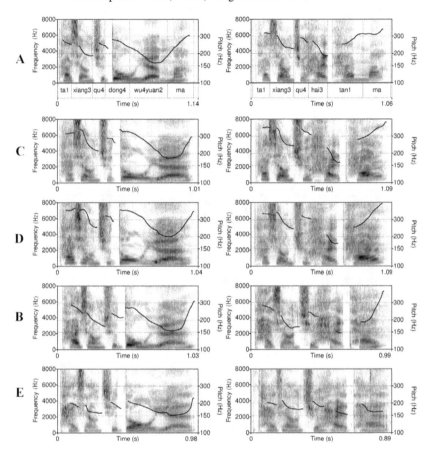

Figure 6.2. (Cont.)

of the three interactive functions. Auditory signal- and meaning-related analysis can disentangle the distinctive prosodic features of the basic functions from those of the additional ones; numerical measurement, removed from the semantic interpretation of each utterance in dialogue context, cannot achieve this on such a limited database.

POLARITY QUESTIONS in A

Although this QUESTION function is marked by the particle *ma*, *F0 raising* is an additional feature in comparison with the FINALITY STATEMENT **E**. It either spreads over the whole utterance, or it is concentrated on the word enquired about by F0 range expansion. The former pattern is found in both speakers' *hǎitān* as well as in the female speaker's *dòngwùyuán* question in Figure 6.2, and in one token of the male speaker's *dòngwùyuán* question. But the repetition, shown in Figure 6.2, has the other pattern, a lower fall and a higher rise for its falling and rising tones; this pattern was also found in the pilot study. Both patterns occur across the whole group of subjects, with pitch height varying from lower to higher to signal increasing listener-orientation: pitch height is correlated with question strength, ranging from expecting a particular answer to strongly soliciting a polarity decision. Furthermore, pitch expansion gives more weight to the word enquired about.

In addition to global and local raising of pitch, lexical tones interact with question prosody. After the *rising tone*, all the speakers integrate *ma* into a *continuous rising F0* pattern, which may become flatter towards the end. But after the *high tone*, speakers handle F0 across *ma* in two ways. Some also have a *rising* pattern throughout; others produce a *dome-shaped* pattern, rising from the high-tone syllable to *ma* and then dropping back to the rise-onset level, or further to the speaker's bottom pitch range. The *continuous rising F0* pattern generates the highest pitch level and consequently is the strongest QUESTION APPEAL; for the listener to take a POLARITY decision, the low-falling pattern is the weakest.

CONFIRMATION QUESTIONS in C/D

In this QUESTION function, all the speakers *raise pitch level* considerably, compared with the other speech functions. The differentiation between **C** and **D** is less homogeneous and sometimes less clearly marked. In the *dòngwùyuán* utterances of Figure 6.2 both speakers raise the global F0 level of **D** beyond that in **C**. On the other hand, both speakers strengthen high pitch at the end of *hǎitān*, the woman by expanded F0 range in the final syllable, starting a little lower and ending a little higher, the man by lengthened high F0 in the nasal. In both cases, the difference is small. There is breathy voice in both **C** and **D** of the male speaker, whereas it is a differentiating feature in **D** of other speakers. Subjects obviously found it more difficult to differentiate CONFIRMATION QUESTIONS with and without the expression of SURPRISE, and there may be interference from lexical tone, the gliding rising tone lending itself better to EMOTIVE HIGH-KEY raising than the high-level tone.

STATEMENTS in B/E

All the speakers realise FINALITY STATEMENTS **E** at the *lowest global pitch level* of the three speech functions, and raise OPENNESS STATEMENTS **B** to a higher level that may be similar to that in POLARITY QUESTIONS or even above it, depending on how strongly the speaker involves the listener in the decision-making (see the representative data in Figure 6.2).

Dialogue Conclusion in G/H

All the speakers conclude the dialogues with both **G** and **H** lowering the global F0 level of *tā qù hǎitān/dòngwùyuán*, but for the majority of speakers the final syllable of both words *rises higher* in **H** than in **G**. With **G**, the speaker signals Finality, concluding the dialogue with a final decision; with **H**, s/he signals Openness, concluding the dialogue with a proposal of a final agreement. These are the same prosodic Argumentation patterns favouring *low* or *high* pitch, respectively, as in the examples discussed in 6.1.1.

6.1.2.4   Communicative Function and Linguistic Form in Context of Situation

The results of the expanded experimental paradigm converge with, and complement, those of the pilot study. Confirmation Questions in the Mandarin Chinese data are coded by *intonation interrogatives* with raised pitch in declarative syntax. Pitch register is raised across the entire question, compared with the Statement. The same combination of raised register with declarative syntax occurs in English and German Confirmation Questions, besides nuclear *valley* patterns (cf. 4.2.2.4).

Polarity Questions in the Mandarin Chinese data are coded by *ma particle interrogatives*, as against the English and German *word-order interrogatives*, which combine with either a nuclear *peak* or *valley* pattern, depending on whether the speaker expects the answer to be at one pole or solicits an open polarity decision from the listener (cf. 4.2.2.2). This functional distinction between greater speaker or listener orientation was not captured systematically in the collection of the Mandarin database, but the data analysis suggests that it exists as a correlation of lower to higher global pitch levels with Question strength. Thus, with a low pitch level, a speaker signals a weak Question Appeal, being quite confident of receiving a specific polarity decision, but signals increasing uncertainty as to what the addressee's polarity decision may be with increasing pitch-level height.

The auditory signal-related descriptive analysis procedure applied to the constructed Mandarin Chinese dialogues made it possible to gain some insight into the function-form categorisations of Questions, which would have been blurred if a pure measurement approach had been adopted for the highly variable data. Intensive discussion with Wentao Gu followed the auditory analysis in a long series of e-mail exchanges. He provided further, introspective data on aspects of Mandarin Questions, which I gratefully acknowledge. Here is a systematic summary in relation to the function-form framework presented for English and German.

(1) *ba* Particle in ENQUIRING STATEMENT

If Mandarin Chinese speakers want to signal that they are certain of the listener's decision, they use the *ba* particle instead of *ma*. The equivalents in English and German are *declarative syntax* with a *reversed-polarity question tag*, and *declarative syntax* with a *modal particle*, respectively (cf. 4.2.2.6). These specific devices in the three languages serve the same function of making a statement with an appeal to comment upon and confirm an ENQUIRING STATEMENT. Here are some examples to illustrate the functional distinction between POLARITY QUESTION and ENQUIRING STATEMENT:

> POLARITY QUESTION
> *nǐ xǐ huān zhè yàng ma?* English 'Do you like it?' German 'Gefällt dir das?'

> (a)   with *high pitch* on *ma*, corresponding to English and German *valley* patterns, the higher the pitch, the greater the APPEAL for a POLARITY decision
>
> (b)   with *low pitch* on *ma*, corresponding to English and German *peak* patterns, WEAK APPEAL because the speaker is confident of an affirmative answer

> ENQUIRING STATEMENT
> *nǐ xǐ huān zhè yàng ba?* with *low pitch* on *ba*, English 'You like this, don't you?' German 'Das gefällt dir, nicht? (cf. THEME-RHEME POLARITY QUESTION in 4.2.2.6)

> (c)   the speaker takes the affirmative answer for granted

(2) Particle and Intonation Interrogative with Different Functions in Same Context

It has also become clear that both *ma particle* and *intonation interrogatives* can occur in the same situational context, for example in an adapted pilot-study dialogue:

> A: Tā xǐhuan qù hǎitān.
>   [He wants to go to the beach.]
> B/1:   tā xǐhuan qù hǎitān?
>   [He wants to go to the beach?]
> B/2a: bù xǐhuan qù dòngwùyuán ma?
>   [Doesn't he want to go to the zoo?]
> B/1:   tā xǐhuan qù hǎitān?
>   [He wants to go to the beach?]
> B/2b: bù xǐhuan qù dòngwùyuán? (with raised pitch)
>   [Doesn't want to go to the zoo?]

At first sight, this looks as if the two interrogative forms can be exchanged for the same function. But closer examination shows that this is not the case. B/1 and B/2b are *intonation interrogatives*, and, as in English and German (see 4.2.2.5), B/1 is a CONFIRMATION QUESTION, either continued by another CONFIRMATION QUESTION B/2b, or followed by a POLARITY QUESTION B/2a in *ma particle* form.

Likewise, in the situational context of enquiring about a coffee break, illustrated for English and German in 4.2.2.5, the *intonation interrogative* with *raised pitch*

> wǒmen hē diǎn kāfēi?
> [We'll have some coffee?]

functions as a CONFIRMATION QUESTION, where the speaker refers to a proposition signalled in the speaker–listener common ground, asking for confirmation. On the other hand, the *ma particle interrogative*

> wǒmen hē diǎn kāfēi ma?
> [Shall we have some coffee?]

functions as a POLARITY QUESTION, where the speaker sets a new proposition, enquiring as to its truth value.

These Mandarin data demonstrate again that both QUESTION functions can occur in the same context of situation, depending on the degrees of freedom with which the speaker constructs the communicative interaction in this context.

(3) Raised *ma* Particle as a Marker of QUESTION Strength

The data of both experimental studies point to an additional raised pitch feature in the coding of POLARITY QUESTIONS by *ma particle interrogatives*. The higher the ending pitch on *ma*, the more the QUESTION APPEAL is strengthened. Thus, the *ma* particle has become a marker of QUESTION strength and may be added to *intonation interrogative* form in CONFIRMATION QUESTIONS to raise their QUESTION APPEAL as well. This is parallel to the use of *interrogative syntax* in *high register* to code a more querying CONFIRMATION QUESTION in English and German (cf. 4.2.2.5).

(4) Ellipsis in POLARITY QUESTIONS

The *ma* particle may be left out in POLARITY QUESTION ellipsis, resulting in the *formal* coalescence of the POLARITY and CONFIRMATION *functions* in different *situational settings*, as illustrated for English (with German equivalents) in 4.2.2.5 (cf. the settings there):

(I) (a)   Lai2 bei1 ka1fei1? [Have cup of coffee?]
           elliptic derivation from *particle interrogative*
           Lai2 Bei1 ka1fei1 ma?
     Both forms are POLARITY QUESTIONS.

     (b)   Lai2 Bei1 ka1fei1?
           with *high pitch intonation interrogative*
     This is a CONFIRMATION QUESTION; it may be formally identical with the *ellipsis* in
     (a). However, unlike English, an alternative with high register falling pitch is not
     possible.

(II) (a)   B: Wang2 Fang1?
                elliptic derivation from *particle interrogative*
                Hui4 shi4 Wang2 Fang1 ma? [Can it be Wang Fang?]
     Both forms are POLARITY QUESTIONS.

     (b)   A2: Wang2 Fang1?
           with *high pitch intonation interrogative*
     This is a CONFIRMATION QUESTION. The same applies as in (I)(b).

In (I)(a), *ellipsis* cannot go as far as simple 'ka1fei1?' But this is possible in
the following scenario.

At a restaurant, A and B are reading the menu.
A1:   Xian1 kan4kan he1 dian3 shen3me. [First let's see what to drink.]
B: Ka1fei1?
This is a POLARITY QUESTION, asking A's opinion on B's suggestion.
A2:   Ka1fei1?'
This is a CONFIRMATION QUESTION, usually with surprise because A might have thought
of ordering alcoholic drinks.

There is a third possibility in (II):

     (c)   A2: Ni3 shi4 shuo1 Wang2 Fang1 ma? [Did you mean Wang Fang?]

A2 does not ask for CONFIRMATION of B's proposition but enquires about a
new proposition 'Do you really mean that it was Wang Fang?' This is a new
enquiry about the real truth value of 'Wang Fang passed on the information.'
In English, it could for example be rendered by 'Do you really MEAN Wang
Fang?' in this context. It is not a citation of the proposition for CONFIRMATION,
but a POLARITY enquiry as to whether the proposition *is* true.

(5) *Future Research*

Before any further experimental data are collected for numerical analysis,
the whole functional network of POLARITY, INFORMATION and CONFIR-
MATION QUESTIONS, and ENQUIRING STATEMENTS, using *particle* and/or
intonation interrogatives in Mandarin Chinese, requires more detailed study
through impressionistic knowledge acquisition by native-speaker linguistic
experts. This is Bertrand Russell's Knowledge by Acquaintance (see the

Introduction), which can then be set in relation to a general theory of APPEAL functions, as has been attempted for English and German in this monograph. This network will establish the default function-form relationships between POLARITY QUESTION and *particle interrogative*, on the one hand, as well as CONFIRMATION QUESTION and *intonation interrogative*, on the other. It will then provide a theoretically motivated account of the function-form overlaps deviating from these default links, as a basis for hypothesis-driven experimental measurement.

6.2   Universal Prosody Code and Prosodic Typology

Since *higher pitch*, either *higher register* or *rising*, has been found to differentiate certain types of QUESTIONS from STATEMENTS in many languages, it is legitimate to ask whether we are dealing here with a universal, iconic sound-meaning feature in all languages. Ohala (1983, 1984) answered in the affirmative by proposing the *Frequency Code*, which means that in asking a question a speaker becomes subordinate to a listener, and subordination is coded by a universal mechanism of raising pitch in speech (cf. also the three biological codes in Gussenhoven 2002, 2004). It can certainly be regarded as an ingredient in coding and decoding questions. But when the subcategorisation of questions is taken into account it becomes doubtful whether Ohala's *Frequency Code* can provide a general explanation for all types of questioning.

The function of CONFIRMATION QUESTIONS, with or without surprise, is to attract attention and to stimulate a dialogue partner into action, rather than being passive subordination to the partner's response. And POLARITY QUESTIONS in which the speaker prejudges the answer tend to have falling pitch or low pitch level in West Germanic languages or Mandarin Chinese, respectively. Furthermore, closer inspection of the QUESTION function in speech communication has demonstrated that it is impossible to subsume the subtle differentiation of many situationally determined types of question under the same code of prosody generation.

It was moreover shown for German (see 2.11 and Kohler 2011b) that the precursor to an accentual high rise may also be raised to a higher level. Listeners judged CONFIRMATION QUESTIONS with high precursors as expressing a more agreeable attitude towards the addressee (on a *contrary–agreeable* scale) than with low precursors. The same may be expected for English. As the *high rise* has an activation function, this stimulation is intensified if the difference in pitch between the utterance beginning and the end of the rise is increased, i.e. by a low precursor, whereas the high precursor softens the repeat activation in a CONFIRMATION QUESTION, making it more accommodating. In German and English, CONFIRMATION QUESTIONS may also have falling pitch patterns in declarative syntax transposed to a *higher register* to solicit confirmation that what is enquired about *is* true. This differs from a *high-rising* CONFIRMATION QUESTION, which enquires about the truth value one way or the other.

These subtle differentiations of communicative QUESTION functions need a more sophisticated *Question Code*, which goes beyond, but of course incorporates, the *Frequency Code*, to try to explain more than a broad linguistic dichotomy of *interrogative* and *declarative*. The *Question Code* encapsulates the multifarious relations in communicative interaction between speaker and listener where the listener-oriented APPEAL function is central, but gets adjusted in various ways by the speaker's attitudes and expressiveness. There is overwhelming evidence that the APPEAL function is coupled with high pitch (Bolinger 1978; Hermann 1942), but the coexistence of both high-rising and high register in the same language to code different question types makes it advisable to develop a universally valid *Question Code* cautiously within a framework of communicative functions.

The *Question Code* may be investigated across the languages of the world from a typological, rather than a universal, perspective of formal manifestations. What is universal is the QUESTION APPEAL function, and its subcategories of POLARITY, INFORMATION, CONFIRMATION QUESTIONS; ENQUIRING STATEMENTS may also be assumed to have universal functional status. All languages have INFORMATION QUESTIONS with lexical interrogatives, but they differ as to where these items are positioned in the utterance, and they may also differ as to the use of prosodic features to differentiate between fact- and listener-orientation. POLARITY QUESTIONS, too, occur in all languages. But languages differ in the use of particles and where they are put, or by interrogative syntactic structure. If they are marked by particles, there may be just one, as in Mandarin Chinese, forming a system with the ENQUIRING STATEMENT particle. Or there may be several for different expected polarity decisions, as in Latin:

> *ne* added to the focused word for open polarity
> *nonne* for expected affirmation
> *num* for expected negation

Pitch height is very common in coding the strength of the QUESTION APPEAL in POLARITY QUESTIONS, but by no means universal; other prosodic features may be combined with low pitch to generate the effect, as in African tone languages (Rialland 2007). If QUESTION APPEAL is marked by pitch height, it may be by *valley* as against *peak* patterns, as in the West Germanic languages, or by pitch register, as in Mandarin Chinese. It may also be based on high pitch in *late peak* synchronisation, as against low pitch in *early peaks* of STATEMENTS, as in Russian or Neapolitan Italian (d'Imperio 2000; Khromovskich 2003; Rathcke 2006).

The formal means of CONFIRMATION QUESTIONS in the languages of the world are less well known because they have not been clearly separated from POLARITY QUESTIONS. They differ from all the other question functions by a QUESTION APPEAL for CONFIRMATION of a PROPOSITION that was made in a previous STATEMENT by another person, or that is deduced from the communicative context. Such structurally diverging languages as European languages and Mandarin Chinese converge in coding this question function by higher register. It may be hypothesised that this prosodic form is widespread, perhaps universal, because it is the stimulating function *par excellence*, which would use high pitch to get the listener's attention to respond and confirm.

Under the *Question Code*, the function-form framework of speech communication can be further elaborated and extended to a greater variety of languages. This cross-linguistic function-form analysis may, first of all, include those European and Asian languages where such categories as *Focus* and *Sentence Mode* have been studied quite extensively, e.g. Danish, French, Italian, Spanish, Swedish, Japanese and Korean, albeit only formally and mainly in isolated read sentences (but see the functional approach to Swedish intonation by Ambrazaitis (2009)). These data need to be supplemented by data obtained with new, standardised acquisition techniques that generate tightly contextualised utterances in plausible texts anchored in communicative situations, to capture the functions under investigation. For example, there are so far no data available as to how the coding of CONFIRMATION QUESTIONS differs from the pitch markers of POLARITY QUESTIONS in Russian and Neapolitan Italian, and how CONCLUSIVE and OPEN ARGUMENTATION (cf. 2.8.2, 3.3) are further differentiated in STATEMENTS. Future research will be able to provide a comprehensive account of the whole function-form network of QUESTIONS and STATEMENTS for these languages.

The comparative study must also include the register tone languages of Africa, where question coding has been reported to be quite different. According to Rialland (2007), languages of the Sudanic region do not show a high-pitch link in QUESTIONS. Across these languages, various combinations of an open-vowel question marker, sonorant segment lengthening, delayed falling intonation and breathy termination occur to signal a QUESTION on the same syntactic structure as a STATEMENT. The author refers to these property bundles as a 'lax prosody'. However, it is not clear what position these questions have in the framework of QUESTION functions. From their English translations, most examples appear to be CONFIRMATION QUESTIONS as opposed to STATEMENTS, e.g. *beans. beans?, a slave. a slave?* It is to be expected that these languages also distinguish the functional categories of POLARITY and CONFIRMATION QUESTIONS, and use different prosodic or other means to signal them. It is still an open question as to what types of QUESTION function show the divergence from a high-pitch link, and how the different types are manifested. Furthermore, the coding of the QUESTION function in these African tone languages shows the importance of analysing acoustic energy, articulatory timing and phonation, besides fundamental frequency in the implementation of communicative functions by speakers, and in their auditory-cognitive processing by listeners.

The cross-linguistic function-form approach will lead to a new, communicatively insightful prosodic typology of the world's languages, and to a reassessment of postulates of prosodic universals. The theoretical framework of communicative functions is an important step towards the goal that Hermann (1942, p. 390) formulated over seventy years ago for an 'integral linguistic investigation of the world's languages' ('ganzheitliche Sprachforschung'), i.e. to assess 'the distribution of different rhythmic-melodic properties across the various speech functions and their summation in one and the same function' ('die Verteilung der verschiedenen rhythmisch-melodischen Mittel auf die verschiedenen Funktionen und ihre Summierung bei ein- und denselben Funktionen'). This is an enormously complex and never-ending task which requires continual contributions from many speech scientists committed to advancing the theoretical and empirical foundations of the study of speech and language. It takes the analysis of prosody a long way beyond the trodden paths of phonetic transcription and numerical measurement, and complements individually, often randomly, selected and frequently unconnected data-driven research questions with global, systemic and theory-driven investigation of speech interaction. It remains for the interdisciplinary speech research community to unite their efforts and converge on continuing progress in *Communicative Phonetic Science*.

References

Abe, I. (1962). Call contours. *Proceedings of the 4th International Congress of Phonetic Sciences (ICPhS)*, The Hague, pp. 519–23.

Abercrombie, D. (1964). Syllable quantity and enclitics in English. In D. Abercrombie, D. B. Fry, P. A. D. MacCarthy, N. C. Scott and J. L. M. Trim, eds., *In Honour of Daniel Jones*, London: Longmans, pp. 216–22.

Abraham, W. (2011). Preface: Traces of Karl Bühler's semiotic legacy in modern linguistics. In D. F. Goodwin, transl. of Bühler 1934, new edn 2011, Amsterdam: Benjamins, pp. xiii–xlvii.

Adriaens, L. M. H. (1991). Ein Modell deutscher Intonation, PhD thesis, Eindhoven.

Allen, W. S. (1954). *Living English speech*, London: Longman.

Ambrazaitis, G. (2005). Between fall and fall-rise: Substance-function relations in German phrase-final intonation contours. *Phonetica*, 62, 196–214.

(2009). Nuclear intonation in Swedish, PhD thesis, Lund University, Travaux de l'Institut de Linguistique de Lund 49.

Armstrong, L. E. and Ward, I. C. (1931). *A handbook of English intonation*, 2nd edn, Cambridge: W. Heffer.

Austin, J. L. (1962). *How to do things with words*, Oxford University Press.

Barry, W. J. (1981). Prosodic functions revisited again! *Phonetica*, 38, 320–40.

Baumann, S. (2006). *The intonation of givenness: Evidence from German*, Linguistische Arbeiten 508, Tübingen: Niemeyer.

Bolinger, D. (1978). Intonation across languages. In J. Greenberg (ed.), *Universals of human language*, Stanford University Press, pp. 371–425.

(1986). *Intonation and its parts: Melody in spoken English*, London: Edward Arnold.

(1989). *Intonation and its uses: Melody in grammar and discourse*, London: Edward Arnold.

Brazil, D. (1975). *Discourse intonation*, Discourse Analysis Monographs No. 1, ELR, Birmingham University.

(1978). *Discourse intonation II*, Discourse Analysis Monographs No. 2, ELR, Birmingham University.

Bruce, G. (1977). *Swedish word accents in sentence perspective*, Travaux de l'Institut de Linguistique de Lund XIII, Greerup: CWK.

Bryzgunova, E. A. (1977). *Zvuki i intonatsija russkoj retshi* [Sounds and intonation of the Russian language], Moscow: Russkij jazyk.

(1980). Intonatsija [Intonation]. In N. J. Shviedova, ed., *Russkaja grammatika*, vol. I, Moscow: Akademiia Nauka SSSR, pp. 96–122.

(1984). *Emotsionaljno-stilistitsheskije razlitshija russkoj zvutshashjej retshi* [Emotional and stylistic differences in Russian spontaneous speech] Moscow.

Bühler, K. (1931). Phonetik und Phonologie. *Travaux du Cercle Linguistique de Prague*, 4, 22–53.

(1934). *Sprachtheorie: Die Darstellungsfunktion der Sprache*, Jena: Gustav Fischer. English transl. by D. F. Goodwin (1990). *Theory of language: The representational function of language*, Amsterdam: Benjamins. New edn 2011, including Abraham (2011).

Catford, J. (1964). Phonation types: The classification of some laryngeal components of speech production. In D. Abercrombie, D. B. Fry, P. A. D. MacCarthy, N. C. Scott and J. L. M. Trim, eds., *In honour of Daniel Jones*, London: Longman, pp. 26–37.

Chomsky, N. (1957). *Syntactic structures*, The Hague: Mouton.

(1965). *Aspects of the theory of syntax*, Cambridge, Mass.: MIT Press.

Chomsky, N. and Halle, M. (1968). *The sound pattern of English*, New York, Evanston, London: Harper and Row.

Clark, H. (1996). *Using language*, Cambridge University Press.

Cohen, A. and 't Hart, J. (1967). On the anatomy of intonation. *Lingua*, 19, 177–92.

Coleman, H. O. (1914). Intonation and emphasis. *Miscellanea Phonetica*, 1, 7–26.

Coustenoble, H. N. and Armstrong, L. E. (1934). *Studies in French intonation*, Cambridge: W. Heffer.

Cruttenden, A. (1974). An experiment involving comprehension of intonation in children from 7 to 10. *Journal of Child Language*, 1, 221–32.

(1986, 2nd edn, 1997). *Intonation*, Cambridge Textbooks in Linguistics, Cambridge University Press.

(1995). Rises in English. In J. Windsor Lewis, ed., *Studies in general and English phonetics: Essays in honour of Professor J. D. O'Connor*, Albingdon: Routledge, pp. 155–73.

(1997). *Intonation*, Cambridge Textbooks in Linguistics, 2nd edn, Cambridge University Press.

Crystal, D. (1969a). *Prosodic systems and intonation in English*, Cambridge Studies in Linguistics, Cambridge University Press.

(1969b). Review of Halliday (1967). *Language*, 45, 378–93.

Dehé, N. and Braun, B. (2013). The prosody of question tags in English. *English Language and Linguistics*, 17, 129–56.

Delattre, P. (1948). Le Jeu de l'e instable de monosyllabe initiale en français. I. *The French Review*, 22, 455–9.

(1949). Le Jeu de l'e instable de monosyllabe initiale en français. II. *The French Review*, 23, 43–7.

(1951). Le jeu de l'e instable intérieur en français. *The French Review*, 24, 341–51.

(1966). *Studies in French and comparative phonetics*, The Hague: Mouton.

Di Cristo, A. (1998). Intonation in French. In D. Hirst, A. Di Cristo, eds., *Intonation systems: A survey of twenty languages*, Cambridge University Press, pp. 195–218.

d'Imperio, M. (2000). The role of perception in defining tonal targets and their alignment, PhD thesis, Ohio State University.

Dombrowski, E. (2003). Semantic features of accent contours: Effects of F0 peak position and F0 time shape. *Proceedings of the 15th International Congress of Phonetic Sciences (ICPhS)*, Barcelona, pp. 1217–20.

(2013). Semantic features of 'stepped' versus 'continuous' contours in German intonation. *Phonetica*, 70:4, 247–73.

Dombrowski, E. and Niebuhr, O. (2005). Acoustic patterns and communicative functions of phrase-final rises in German: Activating and restricting contours. *Phonetica*, 62, 176–95.

(2010). Shaping phrase-final rising intonation in German. *Proceedings of the 5th International Conference on Speech Prosody*, Chicago, pp. 1–4.

Draper, M., Ladefoged, P. and Whitteridge, D. (1959). Respiratory muscles in speech. *Journal of Speech and Hearing Research*, 2, 16–27.

(1960). Expiratory pressures and airflow during speech. *British Medical Journal*, 1837–43.

Dryer, M. S. (2013). Position of interrogative phrases in content questions. In M. Haspelmath, M. S. Dryer, D. Gil and B. Comrie, eds., *The world atlas of language structures online*, Leipzig: Max Planck Institute for Evolutionary Anthropology. (Available online at http://wals.info/chapter/93)

Essen, O. von (1964). *Grundzüge der hochdeutschen Satzintonation*, Ratingen: A. Hen-n Verlag.

Fagyal, Z. (1997). Chanting intonation in French. *University of Pennsylvania Working Papers in Linguistics*, 47, 77–90.

Fant, G. and Kruckenberg, A. (1989). Preliminaries to the study of Swedish prose reading and reading style. *STL-QPSR*, 2, 1–80.

(1999). Prominence correlates in Swedish prosody. *Proceedings of the 14th International Congress of Phonetic Sciences (ICPhS)*, San Francisco, pp. 1749–52.

Féry, C. and Kügler, F. (2008). Pitch accent scaling on given, new and focused constituents in German. *Journal of Phonetics*, 36, 680–703.

Firth, J. R. (1948). Sounds and prosodies. *Transactions of the Philological Society*, 127–52.

(1957). *Papers in Linguistics 1934–1951*, Oxford University Press.

Fletcher, J. and Harrington, J. (2001). High rising terminals and fall-rise tunes in Australian English. *Phonetica*, 58, 215–29.

Fletcher, J., Stirling, L., Mushin, I. and Wales, R. (2002). Intonational rises and dialog acts in the Australian English map task. *Language and Speech*, 45, 229–53.

Fónagy, I. (2003). Des Fonctions de l'intonation: Essai de synthèse. *Flambeau, Revue Annuelle de la Section Française*, Université des Langues Étrangères de Tokyo, 29, 1–20.

Fónagy, I., Bérard, E. and Fónagy, J. (1983). Les Clichés mélodiques du français parisien. *Folia Linguistica*, 17, 153–85.

Fries, C. C. (1964). On the intonation of 'yes-no', questions in English. In D. Abercrombie, D. B. Fry, P. A. D. MacCarthy, N. C. Scott and J. L. M. Trim, eds., *In Honour of Daniel Jones*, London: Longman, pp. 242–54.

Fry, D. B. (1955). Duration and intensity as physical correlates of linguistic stress. *Journal of the Acoustical Society of America*, 27, 765–8.

(1958). Experiments in the perception of stress. *Language and Speech*, 1, 126–52.

(1965). The dependence of stress judgments on vowel formant structure. In E. Zwirner and W. Bethge, *Proceedings of the 6th International Congress of Phonetic Sciences (ICPhS)*, Basle, pp. 306–11.

Gardiner, A. (1932). *The theory of speech and language*, Oxford University Press.

Gårding, E. (1979). Sentence intonation in Swedish. *Phonetica*, 36, 207–15.

(1982). Swedish prosody: Summary of a project. *Phonetica*, 39, 288–301.

Gårding, E., Kratochvil, P., Svantesson, J.-O. and Zhang, Z. (1985). Tone 4 and tone 3 discrimination in Modern Standard Chinese. *Working Papers, Department of Linguistics*, Lund University, 28, 53–67.

Gartenberg, R. and Panzlaff-Reuter, C. (1991). Production and perception of F0 peak patterns in German. *Arbeitsberichte des Instituts für Phonetik der Universität Kiel (AIPUK)*, 25, 29–113.

Garvin, P. L. (1994). Karl Bühler's field theory in the light of the current interest in pragmatics. In S. Čmejrková and F. Štícha, eds., *The syntax of sentence and text: A Festschrift for František Daneš*, Amsterdam: John Benjamins, pp. 59–66.

Gibbon, D. (1976). *Perspectives of intonation analysis*, Frankfurt a. M.: Peter Lang.

(1998). Intonation in German. In D. Hirst and A. Di Cristo, eds., *Intonation systems: A survey of twenty languages*, Cambridge University Press, pp. 78–95.

Ginzburg, J. (2012). *The interactive stance: Meaning for conversation*, Oxford University Press.

Grabe, E. (1998). Comparative intonational phonology: English and German, PhD thesis, University of Nijmegen.

Grabe, E., Gussenhoven, C., Haan, J., Marsi, E. and Post B. (1997). Preaccentual pitch and speaker attitude in Dutch. *Language and Speech*, 41, 63–85.

Grammont, M. (1894). La Loi des trois consonnes. *Bulletin de la Société de Linguistique de Paris*, 8, 53–90.

(1934). *La Prononciation française*, 8th edn, Paris: Librairie Delagrave.

Gregoromichelaki, E. (2013). Review of Ginzburg (2012). The interactive stance. *Folia Linguistica*, 47, 293–306.

Grice, H. P. (1957). Meaning. *Philosophical Review*, 66, 377–88.

(1995). Leading tones and downstep in English. *Phonology*, 12, 183–233.

Grice, M. and Baumann, S. (2002). Deutsche Intonation und GToBI. *Linguistische Berichte*, 191, 267–98.

Grice, M., Baumann, S. and Benzmüller, R. (2005). German intonation in autosegmental-metrical phonology. In S.-A. Jun, ed., *Prosodic typology: The phonology of intonation and phrasing*, Oxford University Press, pp. 55–83.

Gussenhoven, C. (1993). The Dutch foot and the chanted call. *Journal of Linguistics*, 29, 37–63.

(2002). Intonation and interpretation: Phonetics and phonology. *Proceedings of the First International Conference on Speech Prosody*, Aix-en-Provence, 47–57.

(2004). *The phonology of tone and intonation*, Research Surveys in Linguistics, Cambridge University Press.

Halliday, M. A. K. (1961). Categories of the theory of grammar. *Word*, 17, 241–92.

(1963a). The tones of English. *Archivum Linguisticum*, 15, 1–28.

(1963b). Intonation in English grammar. *Transactions of the Philological Society*, pp. 143–69.

(1967). *Intonation and grammar in British English*, The Hague: Mouton.

(1970). *A course in spoken English: Intonation*, Oxford University Press.

Halliday, M. A. K. and Greaves, W. S. (2008). *Intonation in the grammar of English*, London, Oakville, Conn.: Equinox.

Harris, Z. S. (1951). *Methods in structural linguistics*, University of Chicago Press (repr. as *Structural Linguistics*, University of Chicago Press, 1960).

Hasan, R. (2009). Wanted: A theory of integrated sociolinguistics. In J. J. Webster, ed., *Collected Works of Ruqaiya Hasan*, vol. II, Sheffield: Equinox, pp. 5–40.

Hawkins, S. (2003). Roles and representations of systematic fine phonetic detail in speech understanding. *Journal of Phonetics*, 31, 373–405.

Hermann, E. (1942). Probleme der Frage. *Nachrichten der Akademie der Wissenschaften in Göttingen, Philologisch-Historische Klasse*, 2–4, 121–408.

Hertrich, I. (1991). The interaction of intonation and accent at the sentence level: Potential perceptual ambiguities. *Arbeitsberichte des Instituts für Phonetik der Universität Kiel (AIPUK)*, 25, 187–218.

Hirschberg, J. and Ward, G. (1992). The influence of pitch range, duration, amplitude and spectral features on the interpretation of the rise-fall-rise intonation contour in English. *Journal of Phonetics*, 20, 241–51.

Hughes. G. (1998). *Swearing: A social history of foul language, oaths and profanity in English*, Harmondsworth: Penguin Books Ltd.

IPDS (1994). *The Kiel corpus of read speech*, vol. I, CD-ROM#1, Kiel: IPDS.

(1995). *The Kiel corpus of spontaneous speech*, vol. I, CDROM#2, Kiel: IPDS.

(1996). *The Kiel corpus of spontaneous speech*, vol. II, CDROM#3, Kiel: IPDS.

(1997). *The Kiel corpus of spontaneous speech*, vol. III, CDROM#4, Kiel: IPDS.

(2006). *The Kiel corpus of spontaneous speech*, vol. IV, Video Task Scenario: Lindenstrasse, DVD#1. Kiel: IPDS.

Isačenko, A. V. (1966). On the conative function of language. In J. Vachek, ed., *A Prague School reader in linguistics*, Bloomington, London: Indiana University Press, pp. 88–97.

Isačenko, A. V. and Schädlich, H. J. (1970). *A model of standard German intonation*, The Hague: Mouton.

Jakobson, R. (1960). Linguistics and poetics. In T. A. Sebeok, ed., *Styles in language*, Cambridge, Mass.: MIT Press, pp. 350–77.

Jia, Y. (2012). *Phonetic realization and phonological analysis of focus in Standard Chinese*, Beijing: China Social Sciences Press.

Jones, D. (1956). *An outline of English phonetics*, 8th edn, Cambridge: W. Heffer.

Jun, S.-A. and Fougeron, C. (2002). The realizations of the accentual phrase in French intonation. In J. I. Hualde, ed., Special issue on intonation in the Romance languages, *Probus*, 14: 147–72.

Kamp, H. and Reyle, U. (1993). *From discourse to logic*, vol. I, Dordrecht: Kluwer.

Kamp, H., Genabith, J. van and Reyle, U. (2011). Discourse representation theory: An updated survey. In D. Gabbay, ed., *Handbook of Philosophical Logic*, 2nd edn, vol. XV, pp. 125–394.

Khromovskikh, T. (2003). Perzeptorische Untersuchungen zur Intonation der Frage im Russischen [A perceptual study of question intonation in Russian], MA dissertation, University of Kiel.

Kingdon, R. (1958). *The groundwork of English intonation*, London: Longman.

(1965). *The groundwork of English stress*, 3rd edn, London: Longman.

Kleber, F. (2005). Experimentalphonetische Untersuchungen zu Form und Funktion fallender Intonationskonturen im Englischen [Form and function of falling intonation contours in English: An experimental phonetic study], MA dissertation, University of Kiel.

(2006). Form and function of falling pitch contours in English. *Proceedings of Speech Prosody*, Dresden, 61–4. (English summary of Kleber 2005.)

Kohler, K. J. (1970). Etymologie und strukturelle Sprachbetrachtung. *Indogermanische Forschungen*, 75, 16–31.

(1977, 2nd edn 1995). *Einführung in die Phonetik des Deutschen*, Berlin: Erich Schmidt Verlag.

(1978). Englische 'Question Tags' und ihre deutschen Entsprechungen. *Arbeitsberichte des Instituts für Phonetik der Universität Kiel (AIPUK)*, 10, 60–77.

(1979). Kommunikative Aspekte satzphonetischer Prozesse im Deutschen. In H. Vater, ed., *Phonologische Probleme des Deutschen*, Tübingen: G. Narr, pp. 13–39.

(1987a). The linguistic functions of F0 peaks. *Proceedings of the 11th International Congress of Phonetic Sciences (ICPhS)*, Tallinn, vol. III, pp. 149–62.

(1987b). Categorical pitch perception. *Proceedings of the 11th International Congress of Phonetic Sciences (ICPhS)*, Tallinn, vol. V, pp. 331–3.

(1990a). Macro and micro F0 in the synthesis of intonation. In J. Kingston and M. E. Beckman, eds., *Papers in Laboratory Phonology I*. Cambridge University Press, pp. 115–38.

(1990b). Segmental reduction in connected speech in German: Phonological facts and phonetic explanations. In W. J. Hardcastle and A. Marchal (eds.), *Speech Production and Speech Modelling*, Dordrecht, Boston, London: Kluwer Academic Publishers, pp. 69–92.

(1991a). Terminal intonation patterns in single-accent utterances of German: Phonetics, phonology and semantics. *Arbeitsberichte des Instituts für Phonetik der Universität Kiel (AIPUK)*, 25, 115–85.

(1991b). A model of German intonation. *Arbeitsberichte des Instituts für Phonetik der Universität Kiel (AIPUK)*, 25, 295–360.

ed. (1991c). Studies in German intonation. *Arbeitsberichte des Instituts für Phonetik der Universität Kiel (AIPUK)*, 25, 1–368.

(1995). The Kiel Intonation Model (KIM), its implementation in TTS synthesis and its application to the study of spontaneous speech. www.ipds.uni-kiel.de/kjk/forschung/kim.en.html

(1997a). Parametric control of prosodic variables by symbolic input in TTS synthesis. In J. P. H. van Santen, R. W. Sproat, J. P. Olive and J. Hirschberg, eds., *Progress in Speech Synthesis*, New York: Springer, pp. 459–75.

(1997b). Modelling prosody in spontaneous speech. In Y. Sagisaka, N. Campbell and N. Higuchi, eds., *Computing prosody: Computational models for processing spontaneous speech*, New York: Springer, pp. 187–210.

(1999). Articulatory prosodies in German reduced speech. *Proceedings of the 14th International Congress of Phonetic Sciences (ICPhS)*, San Francisco, vol. I, pp. 89–92.

(2001a). The investigation of connected speech processes: Theory, method, hypotheses and empirical data. *Arbeitsberichte des Instituts für Phonetik der Universität Kiel (AIPUK)*, 35, 1–32.

(2001b). Variability of closing and opening gestures in speech communication. *Arbeitsberichte des Instituts für Phonetik der Universität Kiel (AIPUK)*, 35, 33–96.

(2001c). Articulatory dynamics of vowels and consonants in speech communication. *Journal of the International Phonetic Association*, 31, 1–16.

(2002). Phrase-level sound structures in French. In W. J. Barry and M. Pützer, eds., *Festschrift für Max Mangold zum 80. Geburtstag*, Reports in Phonetics, University of the Saarland (PHONUS), No. 6, University of the Saarland, pp. 129–57.

(2003). Domains of temporal control in speech and language: From utterance to segment. *Proceedings of the 15th International Congress of Phonetic Sciences (ICPhS)*, Barcelona, vol. I, pp. 7–10.

(2004). Pragmatic and attitudinal meanings of pitch patterns in German syntactically marked questions. In G. Fant, H. Fujisaki, J. Cao and Y. Xu, eds., *From traditional phonology to modern speech processing: Festschrift for Professor Wu Zongji's 95th birthday*, Beijing: Foreign Language Teaching and Research Press, pp. 205–14.

(2005). Timing and communicative functions of pitch contours. *Phonetica*, 62, 88–105.

(2006a). What is emphasis and how is it coded? In R. Hoffmann and H. Mixdorff, eds., *Proceedings of Speech Prosody*, Dresden: TUD Press, pp. 748–51. ppt presentation www.ipds.uni-kiel.de/kjk/pub_exx/kk2006_2/sp2006.zip; audio files www.ipds.uni-kiel.de/kjk/pub_exx/kk2006_2/sp2006.html

(2006b). Paradigms in experimental prosodic analysis: From measurement to function. In S. Sudhoff, D. Lenertová, R. Meyer, S. Pappert, P. Augurzky, I. Mleinek, N. Richter and J. Schließer, eds., *Methods in empirical prosody research*, Berlin, New York: de Gruyter, pp. 123–52.

(2007). Review of A. Dufter, Typen sprachrhythmischer Konturbildung. Tübingen: Max Niemeyer Verlag. *Studies in Language*, 7, 873–84.

(2008). The perception of prominence patterns. *Phonetica*, 65, 257–69.

(2009a). Rhythm in speech and language. *Phonetica*, 66, 29–45.

(2009b). Patterns of prosody in the expression of the speaker and the appeal to the listener. In G. Fant, H. Fujisaki and J. Shen, eds., *Frontiers in phonetics and speech science*, Beijing: The Commercial Press, pp. 287–302.

(2010). The transmission of meaning by prosodic phrasing: A comparison of French with English and German, using no Ls and Hs. *Phonetica*, 67, 100–24.

(2011a). On the interdependence of sounds and prosodies in communicative functions. *Proceedings of the 17th International Congress of Phonetic Sciences (ICPhS)*, Hong Kong, pp. 19–27.

(2011b). Communicative functions integrate segments in prosodies and prosodies in segments. *Phonetica*, 68, 25–56.

(2012). The perception of lexical stress in German: Effects of segmental duration and vowel quality in different prosodic patterns. *Phonetica*, 69, 68–93.

(2013a). Review of Ladd (2011), From phonetics to phonology and back again. *Phonetica*, 69, 254–73.

(2013b). From communicative functions to prosodic forms. *Phonetica*, 70, 1–23.

(2011). On the role of articulatory prosodies in German message decoding. *Phonetica*, 68, 57–87.

Kohler, K. J., Kleber, F. and Peters, B., eds. (2005). Prosodic structures in German spontaneous speech. *Arbeitsberichte des Instituts für Phonetik der Universität Kiel (AIPUK)*, 35a, 1–345.

Kohler, K. J. and Niebuhr, O. (2007). The phonetics of emphasis. *Proceedings of the 16th International Congress of Phonetic Sciences (ICPhS)*, Saarbrücken, pp. 2145–8.

Kohler, K. J, Pätzold, M. and Simpson, A. (1995). From scenario to segment: The controlled elicitation, transcription, segmentation and labeling of spontaneous speech. *Arbeitsberichte des Instituts für Phonetik der Universität Kiel (AIPUK)*, 29, 1–141.

Kohler, K. J., Peters, B. and Scheffers, M. (2017a). *The Kiel corpus of spoken German – read and spontaneous speech*. New edn, revised and enlarged. Data. Kiel: Christian-Albrechts-Universität. www.isfas.uni-kiel.de/de/linguistik/forschung/kiel-corpus

(2017b). *The Kiel corpus of spoken German – read and spontaneous speech*. New edn, revised and enlarged. Documentation. Kiel: Christian-Albrechts-Universität. www.isfas.uni-kiel.de/de/linguistik/forschung/kiel-corpus/docs/Info_KielCorp_2017.pdf

Ladd. D. R. (1978). Stylized intonation. *Language*, 54, 517–38.

(1983). Phonological features of intonational peaks. *Language*, 59, 721–59.

(1996, 2nd edn 2008). *Intonational phonology*, Cambridge University Press.

(2011). Phonetics in phonology. In J. Goldsmith, J. Riggle and A. C. L. Yu, eds., *The handbook of phonological theory*, 2nd edn, Wiley-Blackwell: Chichester, pp. 348–73.

Ladefoged, P. (1960). The regulation of subglottal pressure. *Folia Phoniatrica*, 12, 169–75.

Ladefoged, P., Draper, M. and Whitteridge, D. (1958). Syllables and stress. *Miscellanea Phonetica*, 3, 1–14, London: International Phonetic Association.

Laver, J. (1980). *The phonetic description of voice quality*, Cambridge University Press.

Lee, W. R. (1956). Fall-rise intonations in English. *English Studies*, 37, 62–72.

Lees, R.B. (1961). *The phonology of Modern Standard Turkish*, Bloomington: Indiana University Press.

Léon, P. (1966). Apparition, maintien et chute du 'e' caduc. *La Linguistique*, 2, 111–22.

Liberman, M. (1975). *The intonational system of English*, PhD thesis, MIT, Indiana University Linguistic Club, Bloomington.

Liberman, M. and Pierrehumbert, J. (1984). Intonational invariance under changes in pitch range and length. In M. Aronoff and R. Oehrle, eds., *Language sound structure*, Cambridge, Mass.: MIT Press, pp. 157–233.

Liberman, M. and Prince, A. (1977). On stress and linguistic rhythm. *Linguistic Inquiry*, 8, 249–336.

Lindblom, B. (1990). Explaining phonetic variation: A sketch of the H&H theory. In W. J. Hardcastle and A. Marchal, eds., *Speech production and speech modelling*, Dordrecht, Boston, London: Kluwer Academic Publishers, pp. 403–39.

Liu, F. (2009). Intonation systems of Mandarin and English: A functional approach, PhD thesis, University of Chicago.

Liu, F. and Xu, Y. (2005). Parallel encoding of focus and interrogative meaning in Mandarin. *Phonetica*, 62, 70–87.

Local, J. and Walker, G. (2005). Methodological imperatives for investigating the phonetic organization and phonological structures of spontaneous speech. *Phonetica*, 62, 120–30.

Lyons, J. (1968). *Introduction to theoretical linguistics*, Cambridge University Press.

Malécot, A.(1976). The effect of linguistic and paralinguistic variables on the elision of the French mute-e. *Phonetica*, 33, 93–112.

Malinowski, B. (1923). The problem of meaning in primitive languages. In C. K. Ogden and I. A. Richards, eds., *The meaning of meaning*, London: Routledge, pp. 146–52.

Mathesius, V. (1966). Verstärkung und Emphase. In J. Vachek, *A Prague School reader in linguistics*, Bloomington, London: Indiana University Press, pp. 426–32.

Niebuhr, O. (2003a). Perzeptorische Untersuchungen zu Zeitvariablen in Grundfrequenzgipfeln [Perceptual investigations of timing variables in pitch peak contours], MA dissertation, University of Kiel.

(2003b). Perceptual study of timing variables in F0 peaks. *Proceedings of the 15th International Congress of Phonetic Sciences (ICPhS)*, Barcelona, pp. 1225–8. (English summary of Niebuhr 2003a.)

(2007a). Perzeption und kognitive Verarbeitung der Sprechmelodie: Theoretische Grundlagen und empirische Untersuchungen [Perception and cognitive processing of speech melody: Theoretical foundations and empirical investigations]. In A. Steube, ed., *Language, Context, and Cognition*, vol. VII, Berlin: de Gruyter.

(2007b). The signalling of German rising-falling intonation categories: The interplay of synchronization, shape, and height. *Phonetica*, 64, 174–91. (English summary of Niebuhr 2003a, 2007a.)

(2008). Coding of intonational meanings beyond F0: Evidence from utterance-final /t/ aspiration in German. *Journal of the Acoustical Society of America*, 124, 1252–63.

(2010). On the phonetics of intensifying emphasis in German. *Phonetica*, 67, 170–98.

ed. (2012). *Understanding prosody: The role of context, function and communication*, Berlin, Boston: de Gruyter.

(2013). Resistance is futile: The intonation between continuation rise and calling contour in German. *Proceedings of the 14th Interspeech Conference*, Lyons, 225–9.

Niebuhr, O. and Kohler, K. J. (2004). Perception and cognitive processing of tonal alignment in German. *Proceedings of the International Symposium on Tonal Aspects of Languages. Emphasis on Tone Languages*, Beijing: The Institute of Linguistics, Chinese Academy of Social Sciences, 155–8.

(2011). Perception of phonetic detail in the identification of highly reduced words. *Journal of Phonetics*, 39, 319–29.

Niebuhr, O., d'Imperio, M., Gili Fivela, B. and Cangemi, F. (2011). Are there 'shapers' and 'aligners'? Individual differences in signalling pitch accent category. *Proceedings of the 17th International Congress of Phonetic Sciences (ICPhS)*, Hong Kong, pp. 120–3.

O'Connor, J. D. (1955). The intonation of tag questions in English. *English Studies*, 36, 97–105.

O'Connor, J. D. and Arnold, G. F. (1961). *Intonation of colloquial English*, London: Longman.

Ogden, C. K. and Richards, I. A. (1956). *The meaning of meaning*, International Library of Psychology Philosophy and Scientific Method, London: Routledge and Kegan Paul.

Ogden, R. (2012). Making sense of outliers. *Phonetica*, 69, 48–67.

Ohala, J. (1983). Cross-language use of pitch: An ethological view. *Phonetica*, 40, 1–18.

(1984). An ethological perspective on common cross-language utilization of F0 of voice. *Phonetica*, 41, 1–16.

Osgood, C. E., Suci, G. J. and Tannenbaum, P. H. (1957). *The measurement of meaning*, Urbana, Chicago, London: University of Illinois Press.

Palmer, H. E. (1924). *English intonation with systematic exercises*, 2nd edn, Cambridge: W. Heffer.

Palmer, H. E. and Blandford, F. G. (1939). *A grammar of spoken English*, 2nd edn, Cambridge: W. Heffer.

Panconcelli-Calzia, G. (1948). *Phonetik als Naturwissenschaft*, Berlin: Wissenschaftliche Buchgesellschaft.

Passy, P. (1890). *Étude sur les changements phonétiques et leurs caractères généraux*, Paris: Firmin-Didot.

Passy, J. and Rambeau, A. (1918). *Chrestomathie française*, Leipzig, Berlin: B. G. Teubner.

Peters, B. (2001). 'Video Task' oder 'Daily Soap Szenario': Ein neues Verfahren zur kontrollierten Elizitation von Spontansprache. www.ipds.uni-kiel.de/pub_exx/bp2001_1/Linda21.html

(2006). Form und Funktion prosodischer Grenzen im Gespräch [Form and function of prosodic phrasing in conversation], PhD thesis, University of Kiel.

Pheby, J. (1975). *Intonation und Grammatik im Deutschen*, Berlin: Akademie-Verlag.

Pierrehumbert, J. (1980). *The phonology and phonetics of English intonation*, PhD thesis, MIT.

Pierrehumbert, J. and Hirschberg, J. (1990). The meaning pf intonational contours in the interpretation of discourse. In P. R. Cohen, J. Morgan and M. E. Pollack, eds., *Intentions in Communication*, Cambridge, Mass.: MIT Press, pp. 271–311.

Pierrehumbert, J. and Steele, S. A. (1987). How many rise-fall-rise contours? *Proceedings of the 11th International Congress of Phonetic Sciences (ICPhS)*, Tallinn, vol. III, pp. 145–8.

(1989). Categories of tonal alignment in English. *Phonetica*, 46, 181–96.

Pike, K. L. (1945). *The intonation of American English*. Ann Arbor: University of Michigan Press.

Rathcke, T. V.(2006). A perceptual study on Russian questions and statements. *Arbeitsberichte des Instituts für Phonetik der Universität Kiel (AIPUK)*, 37, 51–62. (English summary of Khromovskikh 2005.)

Repp, B. H. (1984). Categorical perception, issues, methods, findings. In N. J. Lass, ed., *Speech and language: Advances in basic research and practice*, vol. X, Academic Press: Orlando, pp. 244–335.

Rialland, A. (2007). Question prosody: An African perspective. In C. Gussenhoven and C. Riad, eds., *Tones and tunes: Studies in word and sentence prosody*, Berlin: De Gruyter, pp. 35–62.

Rousselot, l'Abbé P. J. (1892). *Les Modifications du langage, étudiées dans le patois d'une famille de Cellefrouin Charante*, Paris: H. Walter.

(1897–1901). *Principes de phonétique expérimentale*, Paris: H. Walter.

Saussure, F. de (1922). *Cours de linguistique générale*, ed. Ch. Bally and A. Sechehaye, Paris: Payot.

Schäfer-Vincent, K. (1982). Significant points: Pitch period detection as a problem of segmentation. *Phonetica*, 39, 241–53.

(1983). Pitch period detection and chaining: Method and evaluation. *Phonetica*, 40, 177–202.

Scheffers, M. and Rettstadt, T. (1997). xassp: User's manual (Advanced Speech Signal Processor under the X Window system). *Arbeitsberichte des Instituts für Phonetik der Universität Kiel (AIPUK)*, 32, 31–115. version 1.3.8 May 2000: www.ipds.uni-kiel.de/kjk/pub_exx/aipuk32/xassp_manual.pdf

Schegloff, E., Jefferson G. and Sacks, H. (1977). The preference for self-correction in the organization of repair in conversation. *Language*, 53, 361–82.

Schubiger, M. (1958). *English intonation*, Tübingen: Max Niemeyer.

Scripture, E. W. (1902). *The elements of experimental phonetics*, New York: Scribner's Sons/London: Arnold.

(1935). Bulletin of the International Society of Experimental Phonetics III. *Archives Néerlandaises de Phonétique Expérimentale*, 11, 133–47.

Searle, J. R. (1969). *Speech acts*, Cambridge University Press.

Selting, M. (1995). *Prosodie im Gespräch*, Tübingen: Niemeyer.

Sharp, A. L. (1958). Falling-rising intonation patterns in English. *Phonetica*, 2, 127–52.

't Hart, J. (1998). Intonation in Dutch. In D. Hirst and A. Di Cristo, eds., *Intonation systems: A survey of twenty languages*, Cambridge University Press, pp. 96–111.

't Hart, J., Collier, R. and Cohen, A. (1990). *A perceptual study of intonation: An experimental-phonetic approach to speech melody*, Cambridge University Press.

Trojan, F., Tembrock, G. and Schendl, H. (1975). *Biophonetik*, Mannheim, Vienna, Zürich: Bibliographisches Institut.

Trubetzkoy, N. S. (1939). *Grundzüge der Phonologie*, Göttingen: Vandenhoeck and Ruprecht (3rd edn 1962).

Truckenbrodt, H. (2002). Upstep and embedded register levels. *Phonology*, 19, 77–120.

Uldall, E. (1960). Attitudinal meanings conveyed by intonation contours. *Language and Speech*, 3, 223–4.

(1964). Dimensions of meaning in intonation. In D. Abercrombie, D. Fry, P. MacCarthy, N. Scott and J. L. Trim, eds., *In Honour of Daniel Jones*. London: Longman, pp. 271–9.

Vaihinger, H. (1920). *Die Philosophie des Als Ob*, Leipzig: Felix Meiner. English transl. by C. K. Ogden (1935). *The philosophy of 'as if'*, International Library of Psychology Philosophy and Scientific Method, London: Routledge and Kegan Paul.

Vaissière, J. (2006). *La Phonétique*, Paris: Presses Universitaires de France.

Voegelin, C. F. and Ellinghausen, M. E. (1943). Turkish structure. *Journal of the American Oriental Society*, 63, 34–65.

Wagner, P. (2002). Vorhersage und Wahrnehmung deutscher Betonungsmuster, PhD thesis, University of Bonn.

Ward, G. and Hirschberg, J. (1985). Implicating uncertainty. *Language*, 61, 747–76.

Waterson, N. (1956). Some aspects of the phonology of the nominal forms of the Turkish word. *In Honour of J. R. Firth, Bulletin of the School of Oriental and African Studies*, 18, 578–91.

Wegener, Ph. (1885). *Untersuchungen über die Grundfragen des Sprachlebens*, Halle: Max Niemeyer.

Wells, J. C. (2006). *English intonation: An introduction*, Cambridge University Press.

Wichmann, A. (2004). The intonation of please-requests: A corpus-based study. *Journal of Pragmatics*, 36, 1521–49.

Xu, Y. (1999). Effects of tone and focus on the formation and alignment of F0 contours. *Journal of Phonetics*, 27, 55–105.

Xu, Y. and Liu. F. (2012). Intrinsic coherence of prosodic and segmental aspects of speech. In Niebuhr, (2012), pp. 1–25.

Xu, Y. and Xu, C. X. (2005). Phonetic realization of focus in English declarative intonation. *Journal of Phonetics*, 33, 159–97.

Zwirner, E. and K. (1936, 2nd edn 1966). *Grundfragen der Phonometrie*. Basle: Karger.

Index